V-31-s

Geographisches Institut
der Universität Kiel
ausgesonderte Dublette

Geographisches Institut
der Universität Kiel
Neue Universität

Inv.-Nr. 3347

The Geography of Sweden

Geography is about people and nature. The aqueduct at Håverud, Dalsland.

The Geography of Sweden

SPECIAL EDITOR

Staffan Helmfrid

THEME MANAGER

National Atlas of Sweden, the Editorial Board

National Atlas of Sweden

SNA Publishing will publish between 1990 and 1996 a government-financed National Atlas of Sweden. The first national atlas, *Atlas över Sverige*, was published in 1953–71 by *Svenska Sällskapet för Antropologi och Geografi*, *SSAG* (the Swedish Society for Anthropology and Geography). The new national atlas describes Sweden in seventeen volumes, each of which deals with a separate theme. The organisations responsible for this new national atlas are *Lantmäteriverket, LMV* (the National Land Survey of Sweden), *SSAG* and *Statistiska centralbyrån, SCB* (Statistics Sweden). The whole project is under the supervision of a board consisting of the chairman, Sture Norberg and Thomas Mann (LMV), Staffan Helmfrid and Åke Sundborg (SSAG), Frithiof Billström and Gösta Guteland (SCB) and Leif Wastenson (SNA). To assist the board and the editors there is a scientific advisory group of three permanent members: Professor Staffan Helmfrid (Chairman), Professor Erik Bylund and Professor Anders Rapp. A theme manager is responsible for compiling the manuscript for each individual volume. The National Atlas of Sweden is published in book form both in Swedish and in English, and in a computer-based version for use in personal computers.

The English edition of the National Atlas of Sweden is published under the auspices of the *Royal Swedish Academy of Sciences* by the National Committee of Geography with financial support from *Knut och Alice Wallenbergs Stiftelse* and *Marcus och Amalia Wallenbergs Stiftelse*.

The whole work comprises the following volumes (in order of publication):
MAPS AND MAPPING
THE FORESTS
THE POPULATION
THE ENVIRONMENT
AGRICULTURE
THE INFRASTRUCTURE
SEA AND COAST
CULTURAL LIFE, RECREATION AND TOURISM
SWEDEN IN THE WORLD
WORK AND LEISURE
CULTURAL HERITAGE AND PRESERVATION
GEOLOGY
LANDSCAPE AND SETTLEMENTS
CLIMATE, LAKES AND RIVERS
MANUFACTURING AND SERVICES
GEOGRAPHY OF PLANTS AND ANIMALS
THE GEOGRAPHY OF SWEDEN

CHIEF EDITOR	Leif Wastenson
EDITORS	Staffan Helmfrid, Scientific Editor
	Märta Syrén, Editor of *The Geography of Sweden*
	Ulla Arnberg, Editor
	Margareta Elg, Editor
PRODUCTION	METRIA, Kiruna
SPECIAL EDITOR	Staffan Helmfrid
TRANSLATOR	Michael Knight
GRAPHIC DESIGN	Håkan Lindström
LAYOUT	Typoform/Gunnel Eriksson, Stockholm
REPRODUCTION	Media Repro, Luleå
COMPOSITION	Bokstaven Text & Bild AB, Göteborg
DISTRIBUTION	Almqvist & Wiksell International, Stockholm
COVER ILLUSTRATION	National Atlas of Sweden

First edition
© SNA
Printed in Italy 1996

ISBN 91-87760-04-5 (All volumes)

ISBN 91-87760-39-8 (The Geography of Sweden)

Contents

Geography 6
STAFFAN HELMFRID, PETER ÖSTMAN

A Changing Society 14
STAFFAN HELMFRID

The Land 16
CHRISTER JONASSON

Types of Terrain and Relief 16
Development of the Landscape 18
Quaternary Glaciation 22
Post-glacial Landscape Development 24
The Bedrock 26
Quaternary Deposits 28
Climate 34
Lakes and Watercourses 38
Plants and Animals 40

The Cultural Landscape 42
STAFFAN HELMFRID

Land Use 44
Regional Examples from the Atlas's Thematic Maps 46
The Cultivated Landscape 56
The Forest Landscape 60
Quarries and Mines 62
The Industrial Landscape 64
The Transport Landscape 66
Environmental Problems 68
The Urban Landscape 70
History in the Landscape 76
Recreational Centres 80
From Nature Conservation to Environmental Protection 82
Physical Planning 84

The Economy 86
ROGER ANDERSSON, JON HOGDAL, MATS LUNDMARK

From an Agrarian to an Industrial Economy 86
The Infrastructure 88
Urbanisation 90

The Industrial Structure of Urban Areas 92
Regional Specialisation 96
Work, Occupations and Industry 98
Agriculture and the Food Industry 100
Forestry and Forest Industries 104
Energy 108
Mining 112
Metal Industry 113
Engineering 114
Other Industries 116
Service Industries 118
Transport Flows and Gateways to the World 122
Foreign Trade 124
Internationalisation 126
Regional Division of Labour 128
Regional Change 130
Regional Development Policies 132

Living Conditions and Life Patterns 134
HANS ALDSKOGIUS

Population Development and Settlement Patterns 134
Health 140
Education 142
Households – Housing and Economy 144
Politics, Popular Movements and Associations 148
How we use Our Time 152
Cultural Life 156
Sports and Keep-fit Activities 160
Outdoor Recreation, Second Homes and Tourism 164

Sources and Methods 168
STAFFAN HELMFRID, PETER ÖSTMAN

The Contents of The National Atlas of Sweden 170

Index 175

Geography

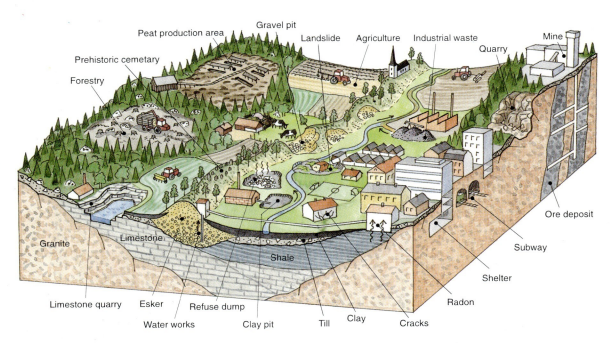

Geography looks for patterns and connections that describe the variations in the landscape. Geography uses maps to present reality, which means presenting selected information on a reduced scale.

The interaction between nature and human beings is one important aspect of geography, that of human ecology.

The landscape today, partly urbanized

The historical, rural landscape 1100–1800

The natural landscape

The landscape has been shaped over thousands of years. A historical perspective is important if we are to understand today's landscape.

A geographer on a journey likes to choose a window seat, so that he can observe the variations in the landscape: forests turn into fields, roads imply contact with other places, buildings mean human settlements. From a plane it is possible to observe variations in the earth's surface from a bird's eye point of view. The details are blurred, but the main features are clear. Areas where the land is used for the same purpose, agriculture, for example, form broad swathes. Rivers and roads are distinct lines that create a clear network.

Geography deals with the description of the earth's surface, but also with the interpretation of what is there. Geography lays the foundations of important general knowledge of the world we live in, and also, through research, provides information about changes. Geography is concrete knowledge, observable in our surroundings, but also theoretical knowledge which helps us to understand relationships and contexts.

When we describe various fields of knowledge, it is useful to ask questions. Historians deal with time perspectives, where relevant questions are: What happened? When did it happen? Why at that time? What were the consequences? Geographers deal with geographical (spatial) perspectives, where relevant questions are: What exists on the earth's surface? Where? Why there? Together with what? What are the consequences? Another way of formulating a central geographical question is: Why do natural phenomena and human activity vary from place to place?

A description of various fields of knowledge may also use current concepts as a starting point. Geography uses concepts such as position (location), distribution, spread, network, region and landscape. The focus of interest is on the relationships between mankind, the use of resources and impact on the environment. Thus geography gives us information about important environmental issues.

This geographical perspective is a way of saying that it deals with variations in the earth's surface. Analyses that describe and explain often lead to classification in the form of types of natural and cultural landscapes.

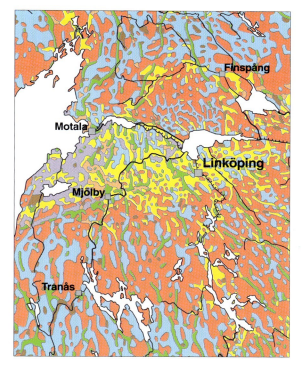 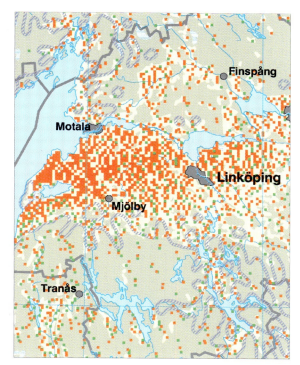

When comparing two different phenomena in one and the same region, it is possible to draw important conclusions about how physical conditions control future possibilities. The maps show Quaternary deposits and arable land and meadow. (T1, T2)

MAPS AND GEOGRAPHY

A knowledge of geography has always been necessary for the survival and prosperity of mankind. Both animals and human beings need to know their territory and its life-sustaining resources. The skill of setting down this knowledge on a map has been discovered in several cultures, thereby making it possible to transfer geographical information in time and space and build up new knowledge. The idea of representing "the whole world" in map form has existed for thousands of years. The oldest known "map of the world", 2,800 years old, is on a clay sherd from Babylon. China, too, has very old maps. But it was Europeans that completed the mapping of the earth with increasing precision, thanks to centuries of journeys of discovery on which the location of towns was determined and field measurements were made. The last large "white patches" in the interiors of the continents were filled in in the 19th and 20th centuries. In our own days the whole globe can be represented in a few seconds with the help of satellites.

Cartography has developed alongside geography and is today a science of its own, working closely with technology and art. One branch of cartography has become an invaluable tool of geographical research and teaching, thematic maps, exemplified by the maps in the National Atlas of Sweden. They are both information systems and professional tools for geographers.

The symbol language of thematic maps varies greatly. It shows in signs and colours the existence or quantity of a certain well-defined phenomenon at a certain point or within a certain area at a certain time. With this definition as a starting point we can learn how to use thematic maps to gain geographical knowledge. Here are three elementary examples. We can compare the occurrence of two different phenomena in the same area at the same time and — with some caution — draw conclusions about their inter-dependence or at least their co-variance. We can also compare the existence of one and the same phenomenon at different times and draw conclusions about changes. Finally, we can study the occurrence of a phenomenon at the same time in different areas and draw conclusions about general features of a geographical distribution pattern.

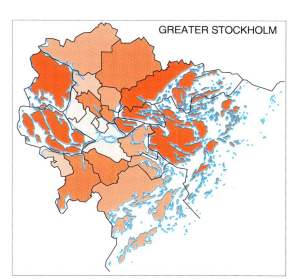 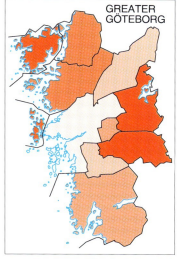

The maps show the number of children per woman; the more children, the darker the red. The features in common between two metropolitan regions are quite evident. (T3, T4)

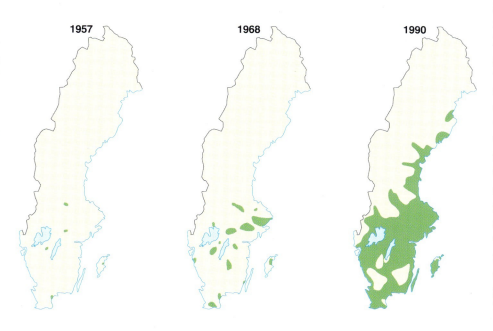

A series of maps of the same phenomenon at different points in time demonstrates a historical process. Here it is the distribution of the Grasshopper warbler in 1957, 1968 and 1990. (T5–7)

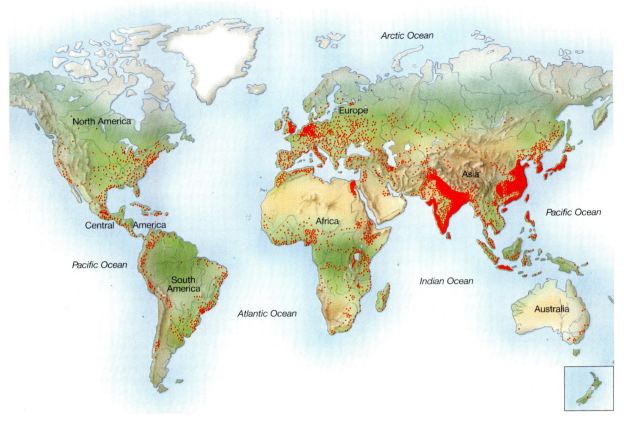

A geographer works with a range of scales. A map of the population of the world reveals the major urban areas on earth. One dot represents one million inhabitants. (T8)

REGION AND SCALE

Geographers deal with large or small sections of the earth's surface, with global questions concerning climate or local questions concerning the general planning of a town. The same geographical concepts, methods and theories are used for all these questions.

Geographers often try to mark off the boundaries of regions that do not coincide with states or other administrative areas or are characterised by uniformity of landscape, settlement and culture — homogeneous regions.

A homogeneous region is characterised by similarity in one or more respects within its boundaries. Bergslagen, Kurdistan, the Amazonas Basin and the Maize Belt (in the US) are examples of this type of region. But regions can also arise through the functional ties that exist between places. A functional region has a centre of intensity with diminishing intensity as one moves away from the centre. The sphere of influence (umland) of towns is an example of this type of region.

Maps help geographers to represent areas at the global, regional and local level on a reduced scale. This leads to varying degrees of generalisation of the information a map contains. A map's scale gives us information about the degree of generalisation and also makes it possible for us to compare quantities (for example distance) on the map with actual quantities. A map scale is given either as a ratio, 1:50,000, for example, or as a line, in kilometres or miles, for example. A map scale is always a distance scale. A scale of 1:50,000 means that one centimetre on the map is equal to 50,000 cm on the ground, that is, 500 metres.

A map at the scale of 1:500,000 covers a considerably larger area than a map of the same size at the scale of 1:50,000. Another way of expressing this is to use the terms large-scale and small-scale maps. Maps of the world and maps that cover large areas are small-scale maps. The larger the scale of a map, the smaller the area but with more details it can show. The scale of a map is chosen according to the amount of detail one wants the map to show and how large the area to be covered is.

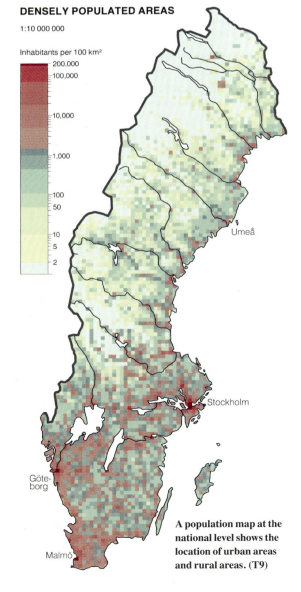

A population map at the national level shows the location of urban areas and rural areas. (T9)

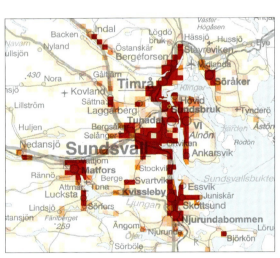

If a map of a limited area is enlarged, great differences in the density of population appear here, too. (T10)

A detailed map is able to show the location of individual houses and even how they are used, as second homes (red) or all-the-year-round homes (green), for example. (T11)

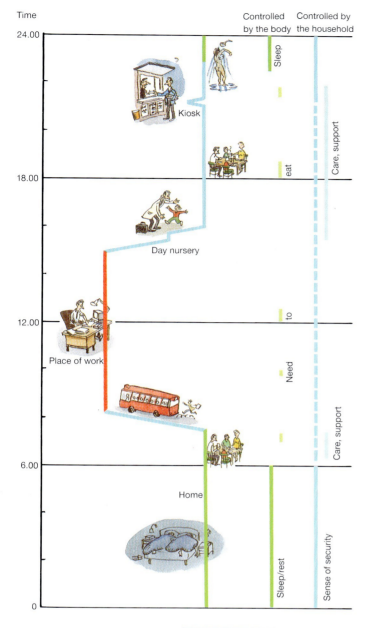

WHAT CONTROLS EVERYDAY LIFE?

Free activities

Programmes and times for television, cinemas, club activities etc. Personal contacts and recreation.

Kiosks: Regulations governing location, opening hours and goods for sale.

Day nurseries: Regulations for leaving and fetching children, fees etc.

Gainful employment

Working hours: Number, starting and finishing times, shifts, breaks, holidays, sick leave and parental leave.

Organisation of work: Assembly line, team work, dependence on machinery etc.

The working environment: Noise, air pollution, safety etc.

Pay: Monthly salary, hourly wages, piece rates, etc.

Transport: Road network, speed, parking, routes, regularity of service, bus stops etc.

Our everyday life is controlled by many factors, from those related to the person and the household to rules and regulations laid down by authorities and organisations. Every day and every hour we pass through "areas" controlled by other people.

THE TIME-GEOGRAPHICAL PERSPECTIVE

From a geographical point of view our lives consist of a large number of long or short periods spent at home or in various activities tied in time and place, and movements, daily, periodical or unique, between these places. The movements are made by various means of transport and the activities are governed by time limits such as opening hours and telephone hours.

Time geography studies the daily routines in time and place of individuals, families and groups in order to explain how society is structured and how it functions from a human point of view. The starting point is the inescapable fact that the amount of time is given — days, weeks, years and a lifetime are finite — and that we can only be at one place at a time and it takes time to move from one place to another. Our needs and wishes and our possibility to make choices and the choices open to us govern where we spend the hours of the day and night, the days of the week, the weeks of the year and the various phases of our lives.

Accessibility of places and what is available there, like water, food, work, services or recreation are not free but hedged in with restrictions.

Limiting factors are — capacity, connections and control. Together these restrictions illustrate the "rule system" that time and geographical place impose.

Restrictions on capacity mean, for example, that we have to eat and sleep and cannot at those times move freely between and make use of places. A lack of equipment, for example a car, is another instance of this type of restriction which prevents or restricts us from utilising the earth's surface. Restrictions of connections may lead to waiting, for example, if the time tables for different means of transport are not coordinated, or breakdowns in production if personnel, machinery, materials and other such factors in working life are not coordinated into functioning units. Restrictions of control limit our possibilities to utilise an area or take part in an activity, for example, if an "entrance ticket" is required in the form of membership or ownership.

Taken together these types of restrictions provide a model of our possibilities or lack of possibilities to utilise our surroundings for work, services, leisure and so on.

THE LIVES OF TWO PEOPLE

Here we show the movements of two people in time and space. Usually data for such complex processes are only dealt with by computers, but this dynamic map illustrates the constraints, connections and controls that affect our lives and the geography of society.

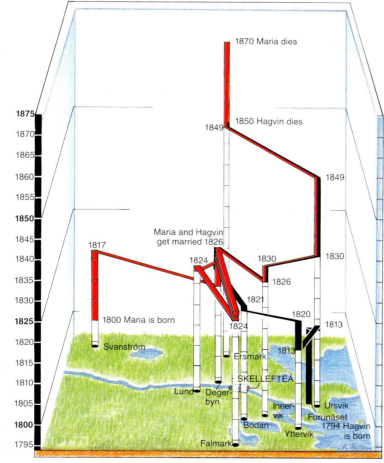

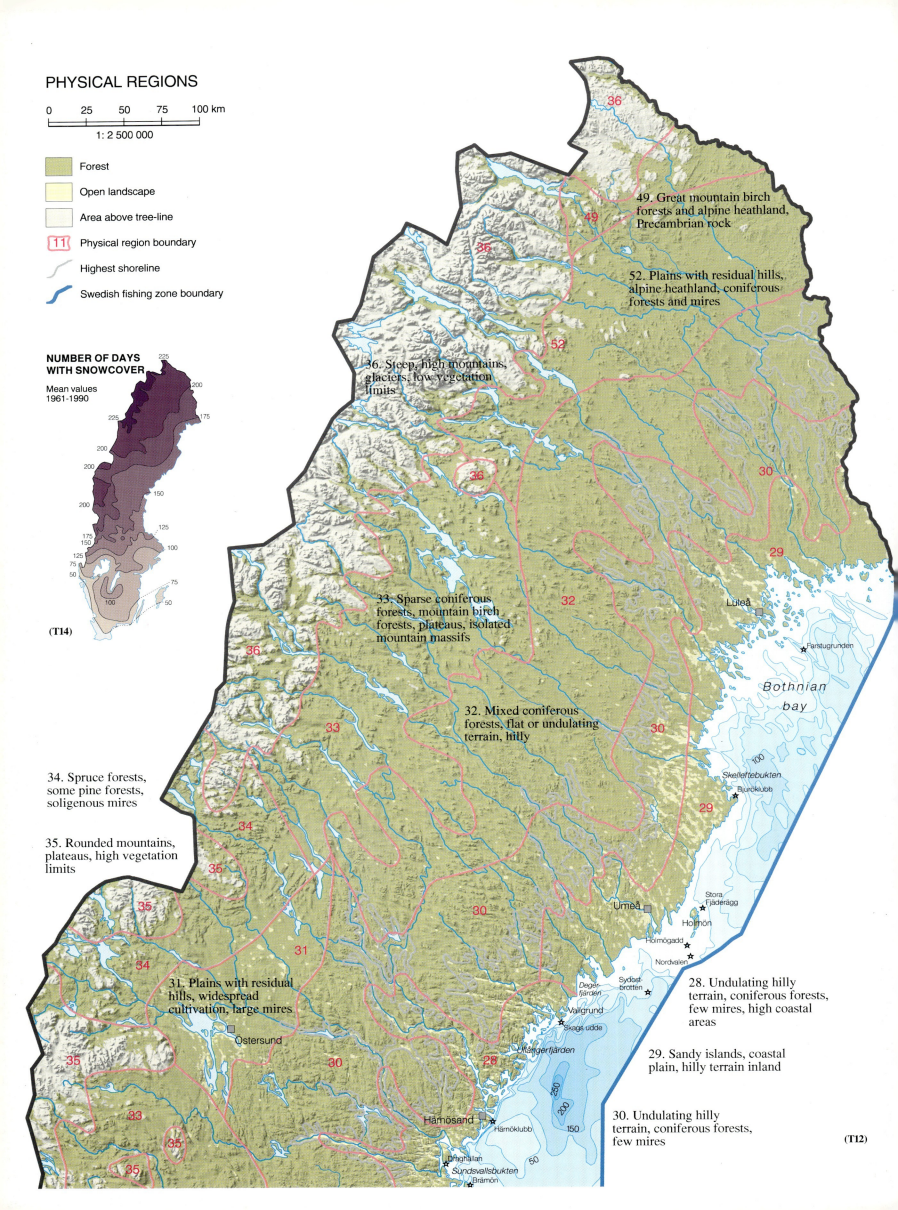

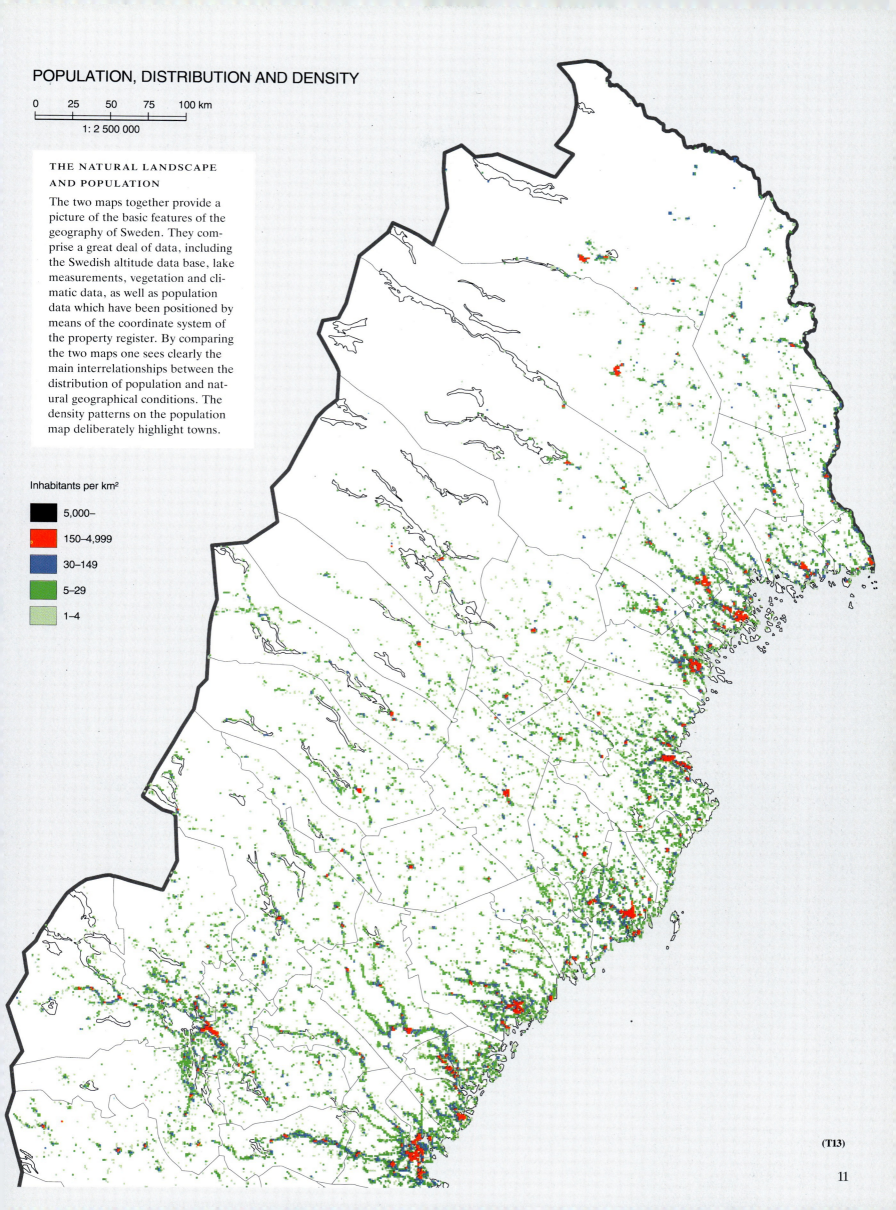

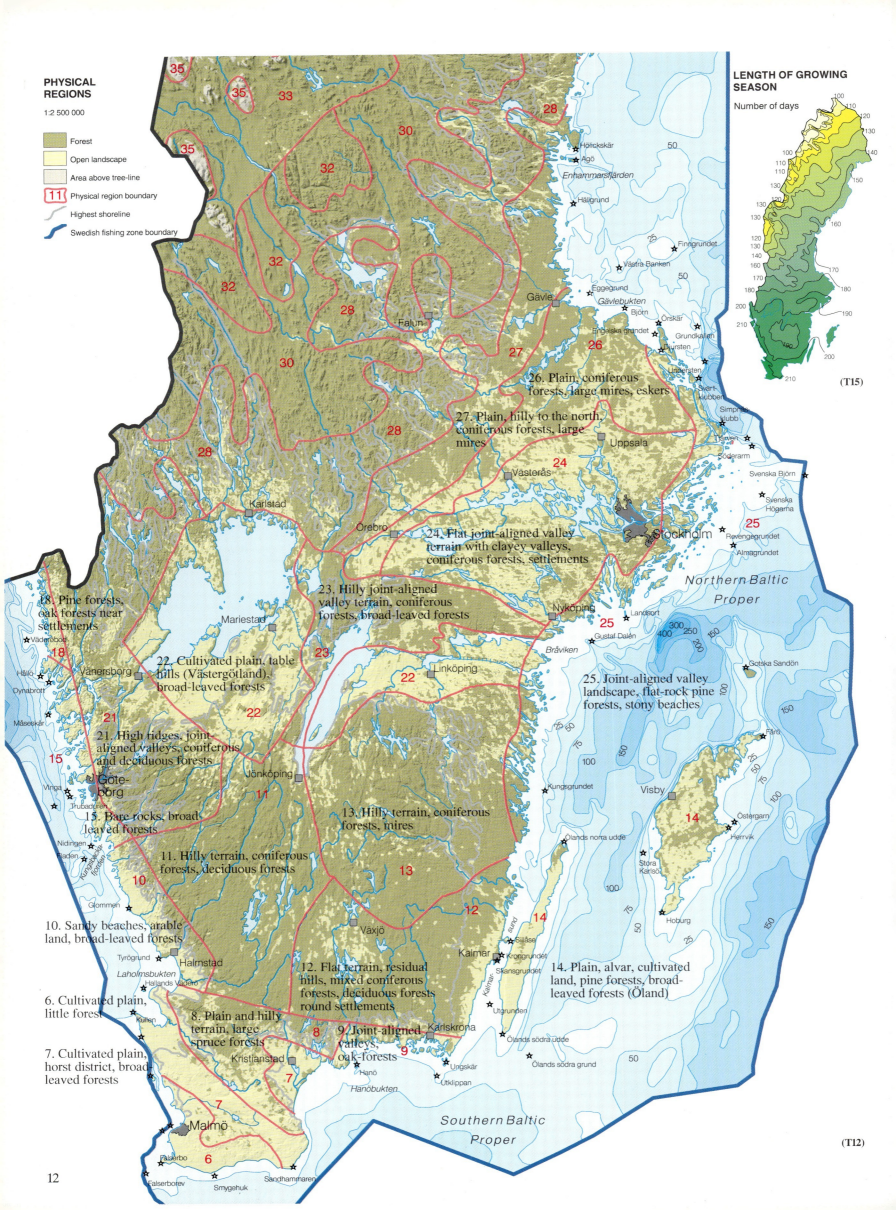

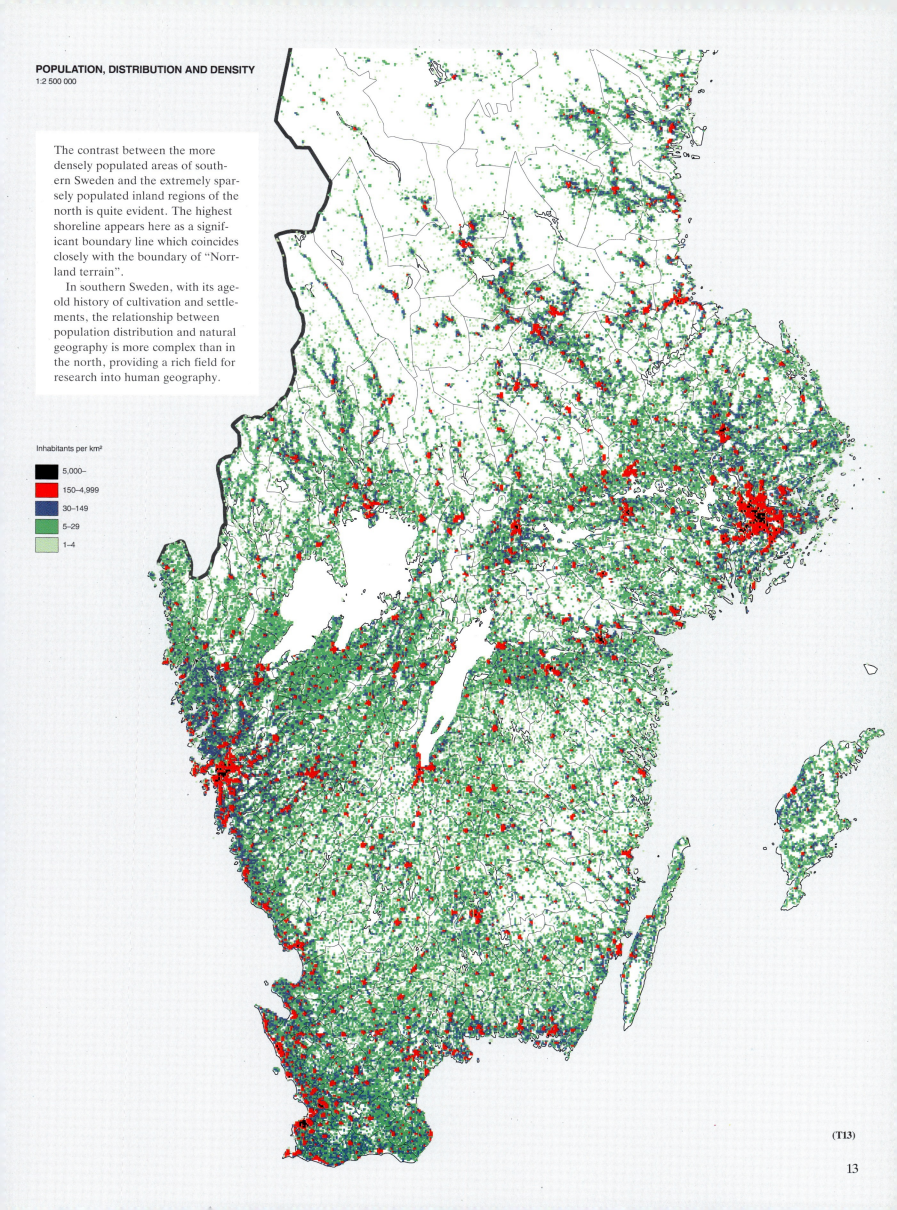

A Changing Society

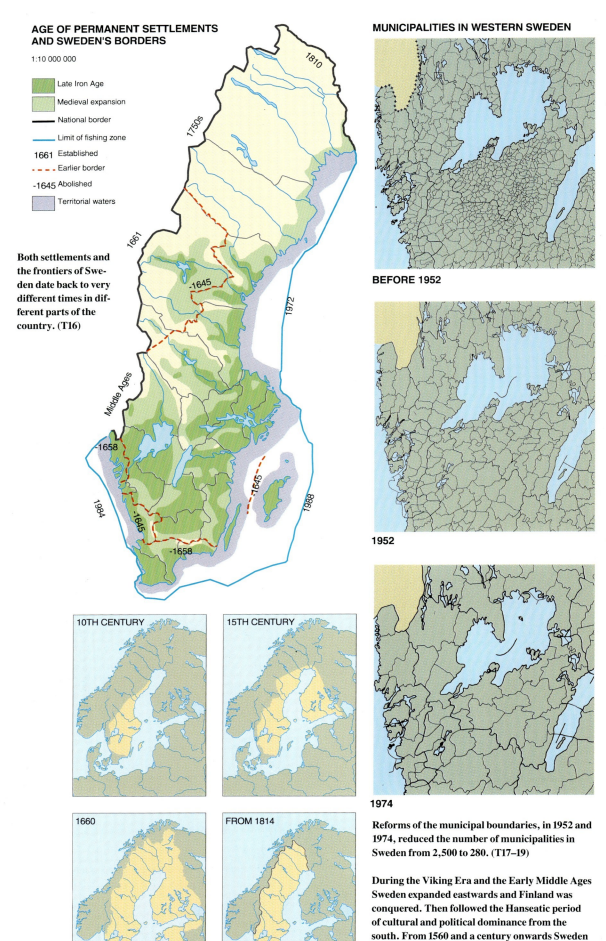

AGE OF PERMANENT SETTLEMENTS AND SWEDEN'S BORDERS
1:10 000 000

- Late Iron Age
- Medieval expansion
- National border
- Limit of fishing zone
- 1661 Established
- Earlier border
- -1645 Abolished
- Territorial waters

Both settlements and the frontiers of Sweden date back to very different times in different parts of the country. (T16)

MUNICIPALITIES IN WESTERN SWEDEN

BEFORE 1952

1952

1974

Reforms of the municipal boundaries, in 1952 and 1974, reduced the number of municipalities in Sweden from 2,500 to 280. (T17–19)

During the Viking Era and the Early Middle Ages Sweden expanded eastwards and Finland was conquered. Then followed the Hanseatic period of cultural and political dominance from the south. From 1560 and a century onwards Sweden conquered rich provinces round the Baltic, most of which were lost during 100 years of lost wars. Since losing Finland in 1814 Sweden has lived in peace within secure frontiers. (T20–23)

THE AGE OF THE CULTURAL LANDSCAPE AND ITS BOUNDARIES

As Sweden was gradually freed from the ice sheet 10,000 years ago, plants, animals and human beings who lived from fishing and hunting migrated into the country. In southern Sweden man has been shaping this landscape for as long as 6,000 years. The medieval colonisation settlements are some 600–1,000 years old, while large parts of northern Sweden were permanently settled by farmers only in the last 300 years.

The northern limit of Swedish settlement in the Viking Age was in Ångermanland. In the Middle Ages it expanded round the Bothnian Bay. The Swedish-Russian frontier was drawn in 1323 straight across the Finnish peninsula.

After the kingdom had been consolidated under Gustav Vasa, Swedish power was extended by a century of successful wars to comprise a multilingual and multi-cultural Baltic empire. It reached its greatest size in the late 17th century, when Sweden was one of the European superpowers.

After a hundred years of lost wars, from Poltava in 1709 to the Peace of Fredrikshamn in 1809, the Baltic Empire and Finland were lost. All that was left within Sweden's frontiers of conquered land were the former Danish provinces of Skåne, Blekinge and Halland and the former Norwegian provinces of Bohuslän, Jämtland and Härjedalen.

As late as the 13th century the national frontiers in Scandinavia were uncertain. The border between Dals-Ed and Sälen, however, has remained the same since the Middle Ages. The frontier to the north was marked out in the 1750s and the Finnish frontier in 1810. Not until our own days were the final limits of territorial waters settled.

ADMINISTRATIVE DIVISIONS

Sweden's administrative divisions have evolved as its society has changed. One example is the municipalities (*kommun*). The step from medieval parishes to modern municipalities was taken in the radical reforms of 1952–74. The division into parishes clearly reveals the contrast between the plain settlements with their small parishes and the vast, sparsely-populated parishes of the forest regions. This difference has to a large extent been obliterated in modern urbanised Sweden.

The Great Social Transformation

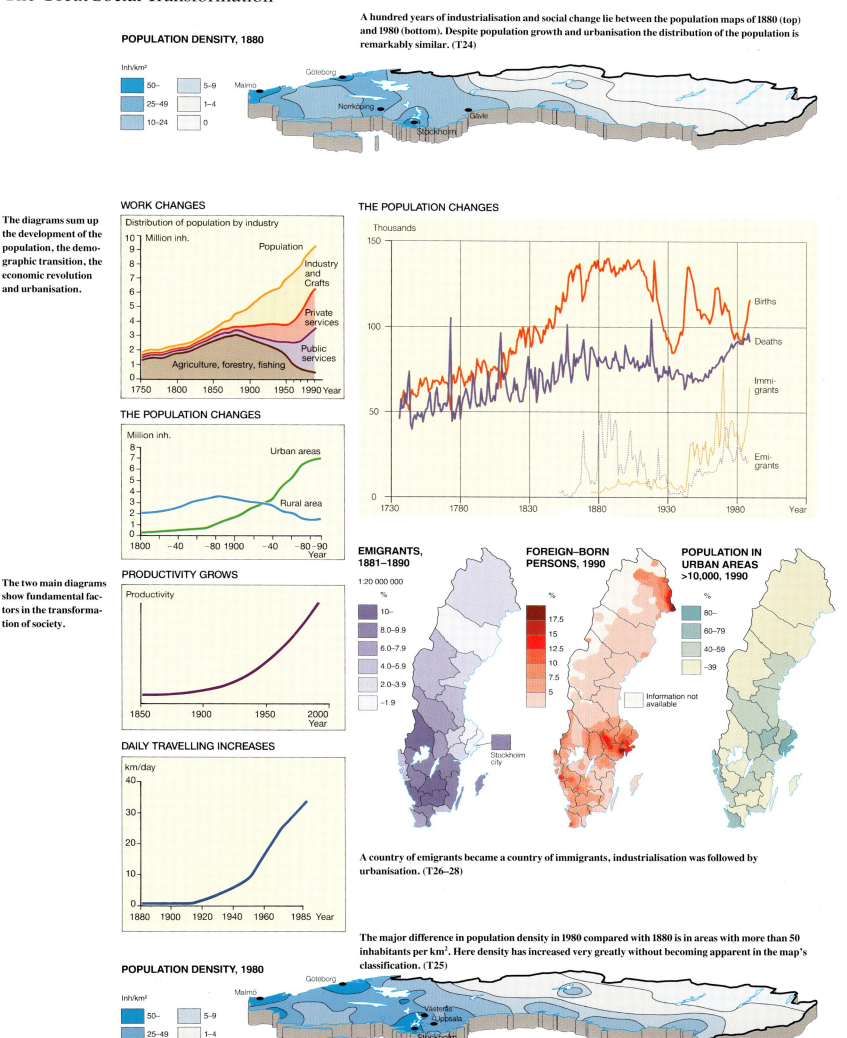

A hundred years of industrialisation and social change lie between the population maps of 1880 (top) and 1980 (bottom). Despite population growth and urbanisation the distribution of the population is remarkably similar. (T24)

The diagrams sum up the development of the population, the demographic transition, the economic revolution and urbanisation.

The two main diagrams show fundamental factors in the transformation of society.

A country of emigrants became a country of immigrants, industrialisation was followed by urbanisation. (T26–28)

The major difference in population density in 1980 compared with 1880 is in areas with more than 50 inhabitants per km². Here density has increased very greatly without becoming apparent in the map's classification. (T25)

The Land

TYPES OF TERRAIN

1:5 000 000

- Mountains and premontane region with well developed valleys
- Plains with residual hills
- Large scale joint valley landscape
- Undulating, hilly land with irregular valleys
- Joint valley landscape
- Sub-Cambrian peneplain
- Sub-Cambrian peneplain, uplifted and broken
- Horsts and grabens of the Tornquist Tectonic Zone
- South Småland peneplain
- Plain on sedimentary rocks
- Coastal plain
- The border of the Norrland Terrain
- Fault
- Lineament

These types of terrain represent the major characteristics of the landscape, which is mainly dependent on the appearance of the surface of the bedrock. These land forms have very varied origins, dating back to different eras. Mention may be made of the Precambrian peneplain, over 600 million years old, and the plains with residual hills, which are probably tertiary. (T29)

Types of Terrain and Relief

The forms of Sweden's terrain bear traces of a very long history. The external forms of the bedrock were mainly shaped long before the ice age of the Quaternary period. The morphology of the bedrock was mostly formed under different climatic conditions than those prevailing today. There has been a predominantly warm climate in Scandinavia for most of the past 600 million years. It was only during the past few million years that it had a climate in which glaciers could grow into inland ice sheets.

In contrast to Denmark and northern Germany, for example, the Swedish landscape is largely characterised by the terrains of its bedrock, for two reasons. One is that the soil in many parts of Sweden is relatively shallow, which means that the bedrock forms are more easily revealed. The other is that Sweden is in a totally different geological environment, with greater height differences in the bedrock than the flatter bedrock forms found in Denmark and northern Germany.

It is possible to distinguish a number of bedrock forms in Sweden. The term mountain refers to heights exceeding 800 metres above sea level. The mountains that dominate the north-west part of Sweden consist mainly of the Caledonide mountain chain. Most of the interior of Norrland and Svealand is dominated by what is called Norrland terrain. This type of terrain consists of scattered

The major slopes caused by faulting are often a striking feature of the landscape. The western edge of Omberg falls steeply down to the shores of Lake Vättern.

RELIEF

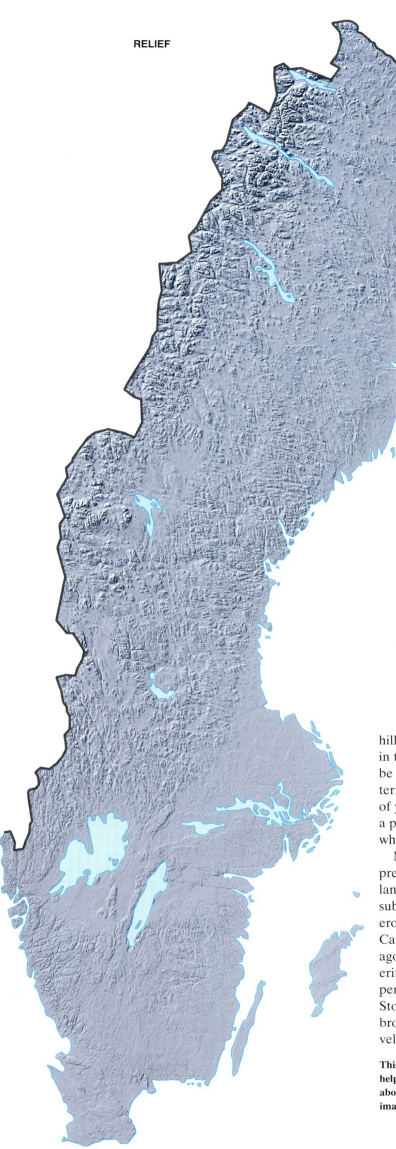

The interior of Norrland is characterised by a hilly terrain with height differences of some hundreds of metres. These hills are the remains of a previously comparatively even land surface whose valleys have disappeared. The photograph is from Moskosel in Lappland.

Along the High Coast, between Härnösand and Örnsköldsvik, the Norrland terrain runs out into the sea. This is a magnificent landscape of deep valleys and forest-clad mountains. Salsåker on Ullångerfjärden.

hills between 50 and 200 m high, but in the interior of Norrland they may be as high as 400 m. This Norrland terrain is the result of many millions of years of weathering and erosion of a previously flat ancient rock surface which was elevated.

Much of the central Swedish depression, eastern Götaland and Svealand, is characterised by the flat sub-Cambrian peneplain, which is an erosion surface formed before the Cambrian period, 570 million years ago. Tectonic movements and weathering and erosion have reshaped the peneplain in many places. In the Stockholm region the peneplain is broken up and the landscape has developed into a joint-valley landscape.

This relief map has been created digitally with the help of a height data base containing information about altitude above sea level. The map has an imagined illumination from the northwest. (T30)

SWEDEN'S COASTAL REGIONS

Sweden's 7,624 km-long coastline has a number of different coastal landscapes.

The coasts of the Bothnian Bay and the Bothnian Sea were mainly formed in the sub-Cambrian peneplain. The flat landscape is broken in many places by fluvial and glacial valleys, joint valleys and the like. It is this type of terrain we find in the coastal archipelagos. Along the High Coast the Norrland terrain with its distinct topography runs out into the sea. The Baltic coast south of Norrland is dominated by the peneplain and joint valleys, except for the hilly landscape of Blekinge, and the horsts, cliffs and coastal plains of Skåne. Along the west coast it is the coastal plain of the Kattegat and the hilly terrain and archipelago of the Skagerrak coast that are most outstanding.

GEOLOGICAL DEVELOPMENT OF BEDROCK IN CENTRAL SWEDEN

C. 2,000 MILLION YEARS AGO

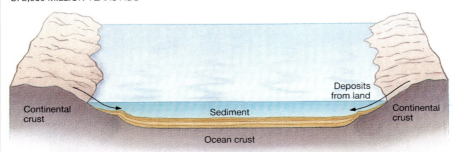

2,000 million years ago. At this time eastern Sweden is a sea basin where large amounts of sediment are deposited, including sand and clay from the surrounding land.

C. 1,900 MILLION YEARS AGO

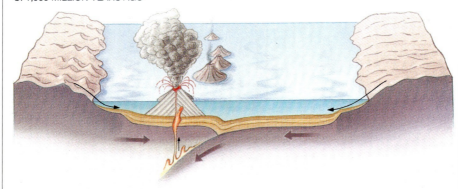

1,900 million years ago. The plates begin to move against each other. Many volcanic islands are formed and large quantities of lava, ashes and gases stream out. Continuous deposits of sediment become densely packed, creating sedimentary rocks such as slate, sandstone and greywacke.

C. 1,850 MILLION YEARS AGO

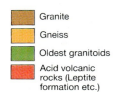

- Granite
- Gneiss
- Oldest granitoids
- Acid volcanic rocks (Leptite formation etc.)

1,850 million years ago. The plates collide, leading to metamorphism and mountain-building processes. The volcanic products become leptite while the packed layers of sediment form gneiss. Magma which is forced upwards is subjected to slight metamorphism, becoming gneissic granite.

C. 1,800 MILLION YEARS AGO

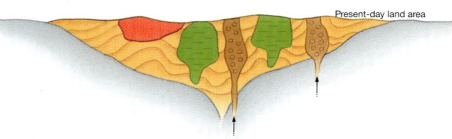

1,800 million years ago. After folding, the younger granites force their way into the earth's crust. After hundreds of millions of years of erosion the bedrock that was formed many kilometres down in the earth's crust has come to the surface.

Development of the Landscape

BILLIONS OF YEARS

The natural landscape we see today is in a constant state of change. There is not one single point on the earth's surface which does not change with time. Even the interior of the earth has been arranged in various layers with differing temperatures, materials and pressures.

Many of the changes which take place on the earth's surface are more or less cyclical. Even the largest land forms, the mountain chains, are in a long geological perspective only short-lived phenomena. The very flat areas that exist today in central Sweden, for example, were almost two billion years ago parts of a mighty mountain chain that stretched across much of Scandinavia. For many hundreds of millions of years this mountain chain was exposed to various weathering forces so that it is today almost obliterated. Instead of a mountain chain there is a peneplain.

The material that forms the surface of the earth, rocks and soils, is also liable to change. Sedimentary rocks that are exposed to heavy pressure or extreme heat are transformed into crystalline, metamorphic rocks which can melt down completely into magma and later form new mineral crystals in a magmatic rock.

Quaternary deposits, for example the material on a beach, also change. Material which is transported and deposited by waves is called littoral sediment. Certain particles of this sediment may be picked up by the wind and carried inland in the form of dunes. This deposit has now become a wind-transported sediment with its own special characteristics. If, because of movement in the earth's crust, the beach sinks and is covered by the sea and other sediments, the sand may become petrified in the form of sandstone. If this sandstone is then raised and exposed, exogenous processes can once more turn it into particles. This occurs, for example, when inland ice grinds and breaks off pieces of the bedrock which mix with older sediments, forming mixed till. This geological cycle is continuous. Many of the processes in the geological cycle are slow and continuous. Modern geology, however, has been able to reconstruct the way the landscapes of ancient times were formed.

It is not only the appearance of the earth's surface that changes. The level of the sea changes, too, in part owing to tectonic movements. The occurrence of sedimentary rocks in various parts of Sweden shows that the area has been submerged for long periods. Periods of submersion and sedimentation have been followed by land uplift and erosion. Changes in the sea level may also be due to the amount of water in the oceans. If much of the water is frozen in glaciers, the level falls. The temperature of the water is also a significant factor; as water temperature rises, its volume increases. In Scandinavia changes in the shoreline are a noticeable feature of the landscape which are due partly to the amount of water in the sea and partly to land uplift. Land uplift is mainly the result of the latest inland ice which compressed the earth's crust. Land uplift occurs in practically the whole of Sweden.

Apart from changes in the appearance of the earth's surface, the positions of its various parts also change. The land we call Scandinavia today has changed its latitude and orientation during a period of several billion years as a result of continental drift. These are the same forces that create mountain chains. It is presumed that convection currents in the mantle cause the lithosphere plates to move. The theory of continental drift was first put forward in the early 20th century by the German meteorologist Alfred Wegener, but it was not until the 1960s that it could be proved. His theory was more or less forgotten for several decades; thus a Swedish encyclopaedia dated 1947 says the following about the formation of mountains: "The causes of mountain formation were long considered to be the slow cooling of the earth's surface and its consequent shrinking. The often quoted example of the apple and its wrinkled skin was one expression of this theory. Nowadays it is presumed that mountain formation and the consequent volcanic and seismic disturbances are an expression of the earth's attempts to restore a loss of equilibrium caused by internal or external forces."

The oldest traces of changes in the landscape in Sweden are connected with Archaeic orogeny more than two billion years ago. These traces of mountain folding are found in the northernmost parts of the country. Much of Sweden's bedrock was formed in connection with the Svecokarelian orogeny.

The sedimentary bedrock on Gotland was formed when "Sweden" lay close to the equator. Holmhällar on southern Gotland.

EON	ERA	Million years	PERIOD
PHANEROZOIC	Cenozoic	2	Quaternary
			Tertiary
		65	
			Cretaceous
	Mesozoic	145	
			Jurassic
		210	
			Triassic
		245	
	Palaeozoic		Permian
		290	
			Carboniferous
		360	
			Devonian
		400	
			Silurian
		440	
			Ordovician
		510	
			Cambrian
		570	
PROTEROZOIC			Neoproterozoic
		1,000	
			Mesoproterozoic
		1,600	
			Palaeoproterozoic
		2,500	
ARCHAEOZOIC		4,600	BIRTH OF THE EARTH

The latitudinal positions and orientation of Fennoscandia during the past 2.7 billion years based on paleomagnetic studies. The area has not had the same appearance throughout the whole period. The most important events are shown in the diagram.

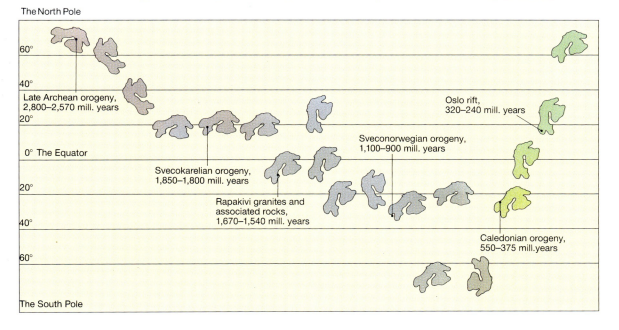

NAPPES IN THE SWEDISH MOUNTAIN CHAIN

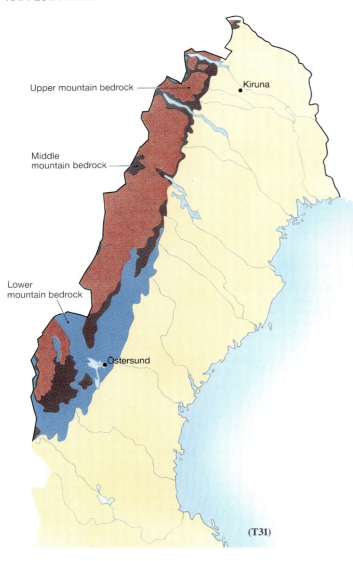

CROSS-SECTION OF EARTH CRUST AND MANTLE WHEN CALEDONIDES WERE FORMED

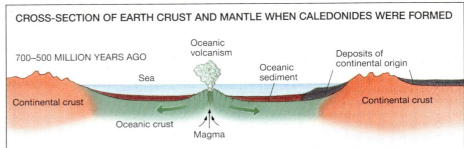

700–500 MILLION YEARS AGO

A super-continent breaks up and moves apart. The Iapetus Ocean expands. Between the continents, Baltica to the right and Laurentia to the left, diabase streams up to form the earth's crust in the Iapetus Ocean, which grows even larger.

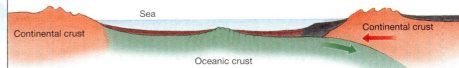

500 MILLION YEARS AGO

At the end of the Cambrian period the earth crust of the Iapetus Ocean bursts and becomes part of a separate plate. This is forced beneath the edge of the Baltica continent.

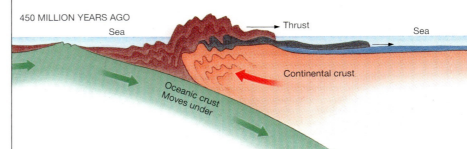

450 MILLION YEARS AGO

Oceanic sediment is forced together, tearing away parts of the edges of the continent. Parts of the earth's crust are forced over Baltica like enormous nappes.

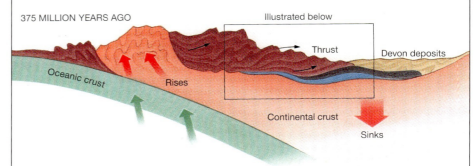

375 MILLION YEARS AGO

During the Devonian period the collision is completed and the oceanic earth crust is forced beneath the mountain chain. Enormous nappes slide down towards Baltica from the rising mountain chain.

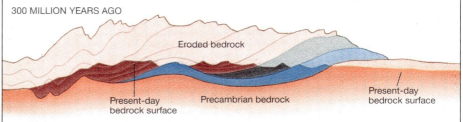

300 MILLION YEARS AGO

Towards the end of the Palaeozoic era the mountain chain has been eroded and the nappes are preserved only in the northwest. The formation of the Caledonides marks the beginning of the super-continent Pangaea.

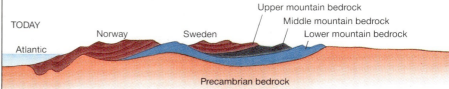

TODAY

Pangaea has broken up into the present continents. The western edge of the continent is lifted high up during the folding of the Alps and erosion creates the Scandinavian mountain chain.

The landforms of the mountain chain were in fact created by erosive, exogenous processes. During the course of millions of years these processes created a powerful landscape of valleys eroded into the previously fairly even surface. Rapaselet at Sarek, Lappland.

Many of the sedimentary deposits formed during the Cambrosilurian period consist of limestone. The lime works at Boda, Dalarna.

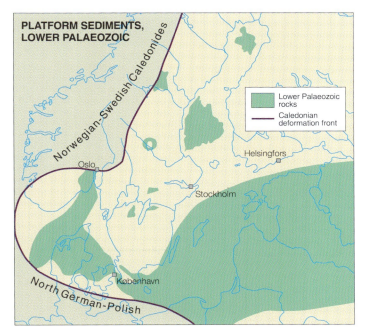

The scattered occurrences of mainly early Paleozoic layers in Swedish land areas suggest that practically the whole of Scandinavia was beneath the sea at this time. (T32)

The bands mark the probable extent of the now eroded marine layers. (T33)

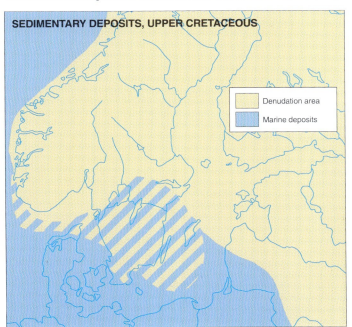

A TIME SPAN OF HUNDREDS OF MILLIONS OF YEARS

If we study geological phenomena and the changes in the landscape in Sweden that occurred after the Svecokarelian orogeny, we can once again claim that the landscape is in a constant state of change. From 570–245 million years ago, during the Palaeozoic era, there are primarily two geological phenomena that are still evident in the Swedish landscape: the Caledonian mountains and the occurrence of areas of sedimentary rock east of the Caledonides.

The Caledonides were formed 510–400 million years ago. Weathering and erosion of the mountain chain resulted in the Caledonides being almost completely eroded some 65 million years ago, forming a relatively flat area. During the Tertiary period, 65 million years ago, the western part of Scandinavia was lifted more or less along the present coast of Norway and a powerful fault created the 2,000-metre-high mountains. The erosion processes, mainly in the form of weathering and fluvial and glacial erosion, have since then created the land forms which characterise this mountain chain. Thus the land forms of the mountains are a result of geomorphological processes which in fact took place considerably later than the creation of the mountain chain itself.

During the period when the Caledonides were being formed, much of Sweden east of the mountain chain was covered with water. The sedimentary rocks that formed in this marine environment are presumed to have covered much of southern and central Sweden, but most of them have been eroded during the past few million years, so that only a few areas of sedimentary rock remain on the eroded Svecokarelian mountain chain. In Jämtland, Närke, Östergötland and Skåne it has been protected in sunken areas limited by faults. Some of the sedimentary rocks are found in the plateau mountains in Västergötland because they were covered by harder magmatic rock, diabase, which forced its way through cracks in the sedimentary rocks, settling on top of them like a protective lid.

Sedimentary rocks usually contain quite a lot of limestone, which makes these areas important for man in several respects. The till which forms from rocks rich in limestone, till clay, is very good agricultural soil. This is also true of the areas outside the limestone districts to which the inland ice transported the till. Concerning a present-day problem, these areas of limestone rock and calcareous soils will be much less affected by acid fallout from industry and traffic. Limestone has been and still is an important industrial resource.

During the period 570–245 million years ago there were, of course, also other types of landscape development in what we today call Sweden, but the two types described above are the most evident in the Swedish landscape today.

A spectacular event took place 360 million years ago. A giant meteor fell on Dalarna, creating a ring-shaped hollow in the bedrock, the Siljan ring, where remains of calcareous Cambro-Silurian bedrock are to be found. Thanks to its sunken position the easily eroded bedrock was protected from erosive processes. Instead the last inland ice crushed parts of the limestone bedrock, creating till clay, which is an excellent soil for cultivation. If a meteor had not fallen in the Siljan district, it would never have developed its present characteristic features.

The Västgöta table hills are capped with diabase which protected them from erosion. They are a characteristic landform in the otherwise flat landscape. Ålleberg south of Falköping.

Quaternary Glaciation

During the Quaternary, that is, during the past 2.5 million years, large parts of the earth's surface have been covered on several occasions with glaciers. Today 10 per cent of the land is covered with glaciers, while during the largest glaciation during the Quaternary 30 per cent was covered. The reason why glaciers grow and melt away is that the climate varies. About 10–15 million years ago there was a marked change in the climate. Temperatures fell at the same time as there were increasingly violent swings between periods of warmer and colder climate. During the Quaternary the temperature fell so much that the cold periods became glacial or ice ages, and the warmer periods interglacial periods. The interglacial periods had a climate reminiscent of our own. During the past million years the ice ages have lasted up to 100,000 years, while the interglacial periods have not lasted more than 1,000–20,000 years. During the cold periods the glaciers grew in the Scandinavian mountain chain until they finally created one large ice sheet, inland ice, across the whole mountain chain.

Glacial ice is plastic and due to its own weight flows from higher to lower levels. As it moves across the underlying surface the material can freeze to the ice and be transported. If the ice is frozen at its base, it will form an obstacle to the ice moving down from behind. This forces the frozen material upwards in the ice so that it can be transported over long distances. When the ice melts, stones, gravel, sand and the like will be deposited as till or re-sorted by the meltwater as glacio-fluvial deposits.

It is not entirely clear what the causes of climatic variations are. The fundamental cause of the regular, long variations which caused glaciations during the Quaternary, however, are considered to be connected with the fact that the distribution of solar radiation on the earth's surface has varied considerably. These variations are in turn considered to be the result of variations in the earth's orbit round the sun and regular changes in the orientation and inclination of the earth's axis.

GLACIATIONS IN SWEDEN

We do not know very much about the glaciations that affected Sweden during the early Quaternary period. The shapes of mountain valleys with their deep lake basins indicate that glaciations occurred several times, but traces in the form of deposits have been obliterated. During the past 250,000 years three glacial periods — the Elsterian, the Saalian and the Weichselian — have affected the Swedish landscape. These three glacials have consisted of several glacial phases. During the latest glacial period, the Weichselian, parts of central Sweden were covered with ice on perhaps ten occasions. In somewhat warmer periods during this glaciation the edge of the ice retreated towards the north, temporarily exposing parts of the land. When the Wechselian ice was at its full extent, 18,000 years ago, it reached as far south as where Berlin now lies. There was then a noticeable improvement in the climate and the ice began to melt. The deglaciation phase lasted about 10,000 years.

DEGLACIATION

The retreat of the ice has been reconstructed by studies of various glacio-geological phenomena which indicate its direction. End moraines, which are the most reliable evidence of an ice margin, occur in Sweden mainly in northern Norrland. De Geer moraines are mostly found in a zone running from the Stockholm area to

The early glaciations, the Elsterian and the Saalian, reached considerably farther south than the latest one, the Weichselian. The latest inland ice reached its maximum position 20,000 years ago. (T34)

EXTENSION OF THE ELSTER, SAALE AND WEICHSEL GLACIATION

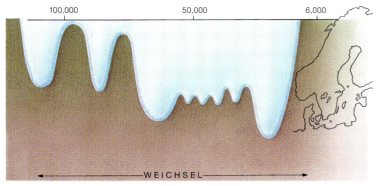

During the latest glaciation, the Weichselian, there were short periods when the climate improved, called interstadials. During the warmer interstadials the outer parts of the inland ice melted. The curve shows how far south the ice reached in comparison with the map to the right.

southern Värmland and in Norrland coastal districts. Ice ridges were formed at right angles to the ice margin. By studying successions of layers of the annual glacial clay varves it has been possible to follow the retreat of the ice margin in the areas which were covered by the early stages of the Baltic Sea as the ice melted. On the west coast the annual varves are poorly formed owing to the salinity of the water. Above the highest shoreline the main features of the melting ice have been reconstructed with the help of the shapes of the moraines and traces of the ice drainage. The age of the various ice-margin layers has been determined mainly by ^{14}C dating of organic material and studies of clay varves. A clay varve consists of two layers, one deposited in the summer and one in the autumn/winter. The clay-varve method is based on the fact that each varve in the clay deposited by the inland ice represents the sedimentation for one year.

NEW THEORIES IN GLACIAL RESEARCH

In recent years we have gained much new knowledge of glaciation, both with regard to the climatic mechanisms that govern glaciation and deglaciation and the effect of the inland ice sheet on the landscape. Changes in the North Atlantic currents are now considered to be of great importance for the comparatively rapid glaciations. As far as the landforms in the till and ice-river deposits that cover Sweden are concerned, these have hitherto been ascribed completely to the effects of the latest glaciation and meltwater. In recent years, however, more and more convincing evidence has shown that in much of northern Sweden till forms, but also "sensitive" forms like eskers, may be considerably older than the latest glaciation.

The map of deglaciation shows that the ice margin retreated considerably from the south towards a centre in the Lappland mountains. In Sweden, deglaciation took place between 14,000 and 8,500 years B.P. (T35)

Post-glacial Landscape Development

Since a relatively short period of time has elapsed since the last ice age, post-glacial landscape development has led to small changes. The last inland ice sheet in Sweden melted from 14,000 years ago to 8,500 years ago.

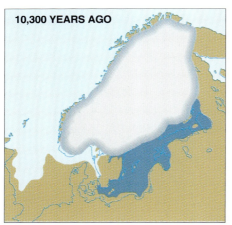

10,300 YEARS AGO

9,800 YEARS AGO

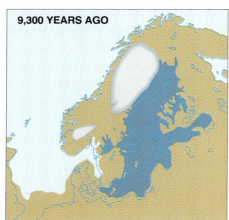

9,300 YEARS AGO

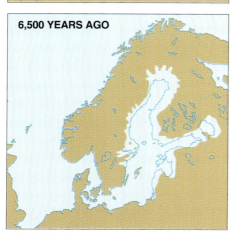

6,500 YEARS AGO

THE HIGHEST SHORELINE AND WAVE EROSION

An ice sheet compresses the underlying earth's crust by its weight. When the ice melts, the crust strives to return to its original position. This isostatic land uplift is a slow process which is still in progress in most of Sweden to this very day.

During the glaciations large amounts of water were bound up in the inland ice; probably the level of the oceans was about 100 m lower than today. When the inland ice sheet melted, this water returned to the sea, leading to a eustatic rise in its level. Eustatic changes in sea level take place considerably faster than isostatic land uplift. Changes in sea level can have both positive and negative effects. During warm periods, when the ice melts rapidly, the level will rise. During colder periods, when the glaciers grow again, the level will fall somewhat.

In areas which have been covered with ice the relationship between land and sea, shoreline displacements, will be the result of isostatic and eustatic changes. The highest level reached by the water in the North Sea or the Baltic Basin after glaciation is called *the highest shoreline*. The development of the highest shoreline in Sweden was complicated by the fact that the Baltic Basin was at times a lake isolated from the North Sea. Shoreline displacement diagrams show when the various parts of Sweden below the highest shoreline were no longer covered with water.

The highest shoreline in Sweden is not equally old everywhere. When it developed in southern Värmland 10,300 years ago, most of the country was still covered with ice. The highest shoreline is most recent in the far north of Norrland. In the parts of Sweden where the ice was thickest the highest shoreline is highest because the ice compressed the earth's crust most here.

At many places along the mountain chain and in areas in the southern Swedish highlands and in Skåne the meltwater formed temporary ice-marginal lakes in which the meltwater was dammed between the edge of the ice and local high terrain.

Each point in the Swedish landscape that lies below the highest shoreline was at some time during the post-glacial era a shore. If this shore was open to the sea, it would have been washed effectively by the waves, and the traces are still visible in the landscape. The large, almost bare areas along the west coast are the result of wave erosion; here high waves could be built up by west winds blowing across the open sea.

Plant remains in the form of fruits, seeds, needles and pollen grains are fossil groups that are used when explaining the history of vegetation. Pollen is spread by wind, water and/or insects and becomes embedded and preserved in peat and lacustrine deposits. This pollen diagram from southern Dalsland shows that broad-leaved trees were more common in the Stone Age when the climate was warmer than it is today. Spruce came to Dalsland about 4,000 years ago. At about the same time man's early influence on the landscape can be detected from the occurrence of cereals.

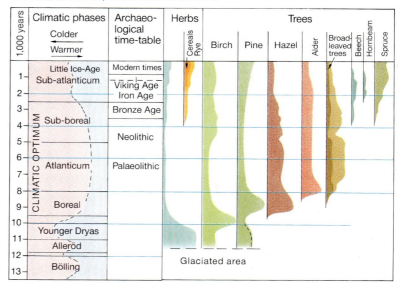

POLLEN DIAGRAM, SOUTHERN DALSLAND

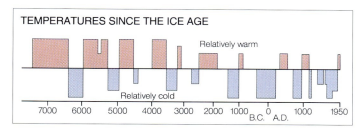

Studies of the Scandinavian mountains have shown that the size of the glaciers has varied since the last ice age. During cold periods the glaciers have grown larger. Finds of fossil pines at relatively high levels, where no pines grow today, indicate that the climate was at times warmer than it is today.

SHORELINE DISPLACEMENT AND RECENT LAND UPLIFT

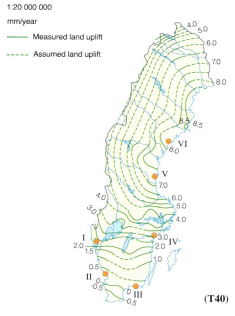

(T40)

Changes in the shoreline vary greatly in different parts of Sweden. In northern Bohuslän and north of Mälardalen land uplift has always been greater than the rise in sea level. The present rate of land uplift is greatest along the north coast of Norrland. In the far south land uplift is negative, that is, the land is sinking.

COLONISATION OF VEGETATION

After the last ice age plants rapidly colonised the areas freed from ice. In Skåne 14,000 years ago there was a tundra-like climate with vegetation consisting of hardy tundra plants. After the climate had improved the first trees, birch and pine, colonised the ice-free areas.

The history of vegetation during the post-glacial period varied from one part of the country to another. Climatic changes and human activities have changed its composition, as proved by studies of pollen in mires and in lake sediment.

In southern Sweden, following the tundra phase, initially forests of birch and then of pine and hazel grew up. During the warm period, which began 7,000 years ago, luxuriant deciduous forests were formed, but these changed in character due to changes in the climate and human activities such as slash-and-burn farming.

In central Sweden there was no tundra phase, and birch forests with pine and hazel began this stage in the development of the vegetation. During the warm period oak, elm and lime spread. Deciduous forests were predominant in central Sweden until the climate deteriorated 2,500 years ago.

In Norrland the history of vegetation also began with pine-dominated forests some 9,000 years ago. During the warm period the proportion of deciduous trees increased, mainly birch and alder but also hazel and oak.

Spruce is the species of tree that has most recently spread across Sweden. Some 4,000 years ago it immigrated from Finland and spread southwards. By the Bronze Age it had reached Svealand, and as a result of the deteriorating climate 2,500 years ago it continued its expansion into southern Sweden. Spruce does not grow naturally south of the mixed forest region.

GEOMORPHOLOGICAL DEVELOPMENTS

Geomorphological processes continued to reshape the Swedish landscape during the post-glacial period. In the mountains frost weathering resulted in rockfalls, creating rock-walls. In clay areas landslides are likely to occur and this is particularly true along the west coast, especially in the valley of the Göta älv, which has suffered several landslides in modern times, even in built-up areas. In areas where there is silt there is likely to be fluvial erosion which, combined with solifluxion, can create gullies. Gullies are a common feature of the landscape along the Norrland rivers. Every year the rivers of Sweden transport 9 million tonnes of dissolved material and mud from the surface of the earth to the surrounding seas. The coarsest material is deposited close to river mouths, forming deltas; the finer material is deposited over larger areas, forming thick layers of sea or lake sediment. In places the wind has played an important part in the geomorphological process in Sweden. There are often sand dunes on the large ice river deltas along the highest shoreline. These were formed when the glacial deltas rose from the sea as a result of land uplift. The wind was then easily able to move the sediment since no vegetation had yet got a foothold.

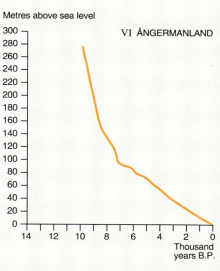
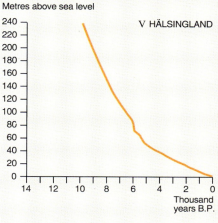
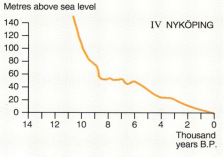
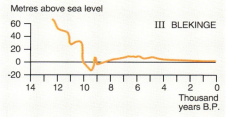
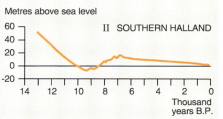
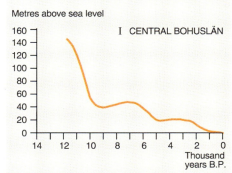

The Bedrock

Swedish bedrock consists of three main units: Precambrian bedrock, the Caledonides and sedimentary bedrock outside the Caledonides.

The Swedish Precambrian bedrock is more than 570 million years old; it is part of the Baltic Shield that extends from the Kola Peninsula in the north-east to south-western Norway. The Baltic Shield is one of many such bedrock shields on the earth, created by several orogeneses, when sedimentary and magmatic bedrock was folded and transformed at various depths in the earth's crust. Large quantities of magma, mainly of granitic composition, forced their way into the earth's crust during these orogeneses. The Baltic Shield is divided into a number of provinces according to their age and geological events: the Svecokarelian province, the Trans-Scandinavian granite-porphyry belt, the South-west Scandinavian province and the Blekinge region.

The Caledonides, which in Sweden correspond in principle to the mountain chain, are a 400-million-year-old mountain chain consisting of rocks from the Precambrian and Devonian periods. It extends along the Swedish-Norwegian mountain region and over into Scotland and Ireland. Previously this area was connected with Caledonian bedrock in eastern Greenland, Ireland, Great Britain and eastern North America, before the whole mountain chain was broken up when the present North Atlantic opened 65 million years ago.

Most of the sedimentary bedrock outside the Caledonides was formed during the Cambro-Silurian period and covers the Precambrian bedrock with a flat layer. This often contains fossils and is found principally on Gotland and Öland, and in Dalarna, Jämtland, Närke, Västergötland, Östergötland and Skåne. The Precambrian sedimentary bedrocks in Sweden comprise mainly the Visingsö group, 850–700 million years old, and Dalarna sandstone, 1,600–1,200 million years old.

BEDROCK PROVINCES

1. Svecofennian (incl. Kalevian) rocks
2. Transscandinavian Granite-Porphyry Belt
3. Blekinge region
4. SW Sweden, east of the Mylonite Zone
5. SW Sweden, west of the Mylonite Zone
6. Phanerozoic rocks
7. Caledonides
8. Archaean and Lapponian-Jatulian rocks

LIMESTONE BEDROCK AND CALCAREOUS DEPOSITS

1:20 000 000

- Limestone bedrock
- Calcareous deposits

The calcareous bedrock in Sweden is found mainly in the areas of sedimentary rocks. At the time of the glaciations the inland ice transported lime-rich till to other areas. As a result the effects of acidification are reduced and the lime-rich till clay is one of our finest soils for cultivation. (T43)

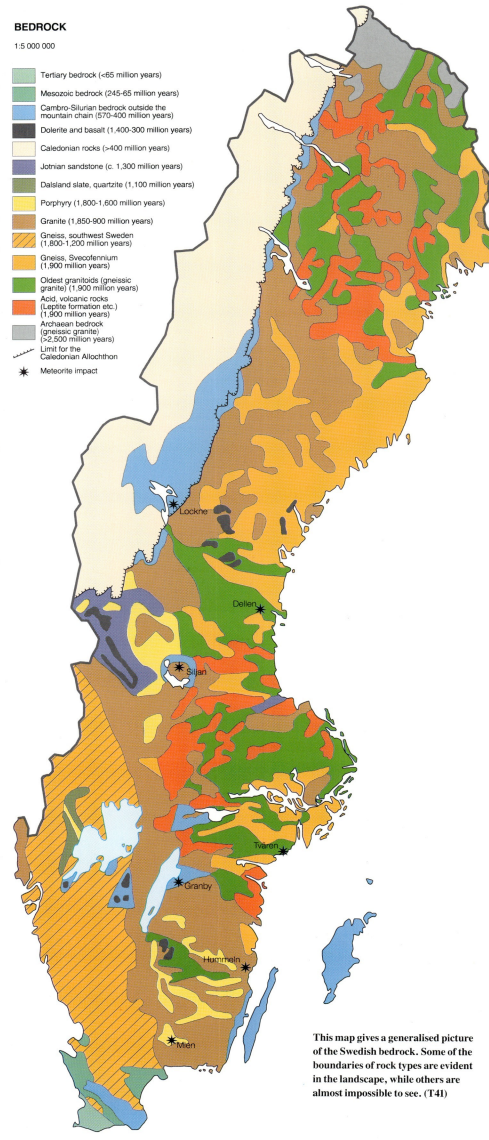

This map gives a generalised picture of the Swedish bedrock. Some of the boundaries of rock types are evident in the landscape, while others are almost impossible to see. (T41)

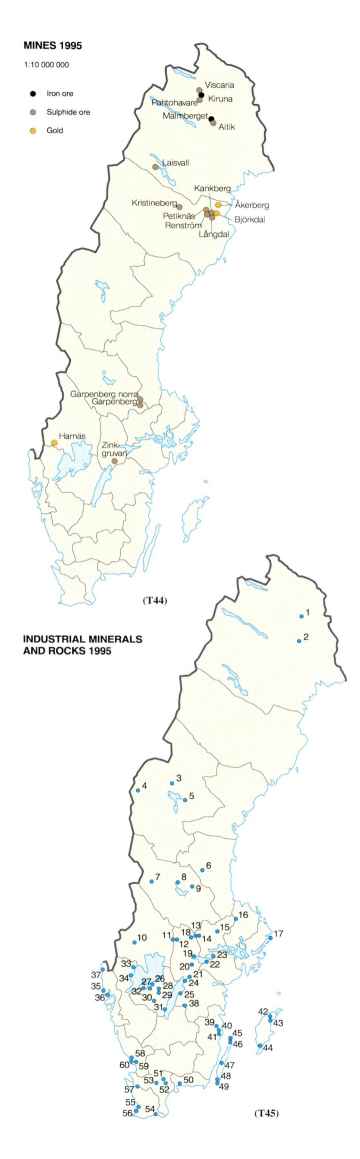

ORES AND MINERALISATION

An ore is a mineralisation, that is, a concentration of minerals from which metals or minerals can profitably be extracted. In Sweden metals were first extracted from ore more than two thousand years ago, when iron was obtained from bog and marsh ore. Mining of ore from rock began in Bergslagen: copper ore was extracted as early as 500 A.D. at Falun and iron ore was mined from the 12th century onwards. The copper mine at Falun, the silver mine at Sala and the iron mine at Dannemora are just a few of the mines which were of great importance for Sweden, especially during the period when Sweden was a major European power (1611–1718).

Apart from Bergslagen, which completely dominated mining up to the end of the 19th century, there are two important ore provinces in Sweden, at Kiruna and Malmberget, the only places where iron ore is mined today in Sweden, and the Skellefte field, where sulphide ores have been mined since the 1920s.

There are also many areas outside the three ore provinces which have mineralisation worth mining. In Sweden 420 ore deposits have led to commercial mining on a large scale; of these, 400 came into operation after 1890. In 1995 17 mines were in operation.

INDUSTRIAL MINERALS AND ROCKS

The term industrial minerals and rocks refers to those minerals and rocks which are extracted for purposes other than their metal content or fuel value. "Industrial minerals" is a very comprehensive term as far as range of uses, geological occurrence, mining technology and pricing are concerned. For example, quartz sand costs 50 S kr. a tonne while industrial diamonds cost 100 million S kr. a tonne.

Industrial minerals are used in almost all industries such as the chemical-technical and artificial fertiliser industries, the space and computer industries, the pharmaceutical industry and the paper and plastic industries. A few examples: apatite is used as a raw material for the production of artificial fertilisers; baryte is an important ingredient in the lubricant used when drilling for oil and gas; crushed dolomite is spread on fields and lakes to counteract acidification; feldspar is used extensively in the manufacture of sanitary ware; ground mica is used as a filler in roofing felt, asphalt, rubber and paint; quartz is the main component of glass.

Various rocks are used in the manufacture of paving stones, kerbstones, building stone and monument stone.

No	Mining site	Mineral/Rock	No	Mining site	Mineral/Rock
1	Masugnsbyn	Dolomite	31	Baskarp	Quartz sand
2	Hakkas	Olivine	32	Råda	Quartz sand
3	Offerdal	Mica schist	33	Ulered	Quartzite
4	Handöl	Soapstone, talc	34	Livarebo	Quartzite
5	Brunflo	Limestone	35	Hunnebostrand	Granite
6	Edsbyn	Graphite	36	Lysekil	Granite
7	Mångsbodarna	Sandstone	37	Strömstad	Granite
8	Hässbacken	Sandstone	38	Tranås	Granite
9	Jutjärn	Limestone	39	Tribbhult	Granite
10	Glava	Mica schist	40	Flivik	Granite
11	Gåsgruvan	Dolomite	41	Götebo	Granite
12	Grythyttan	Slate	42	Storugns	Limestone
13	Forshammar	Feldspar, quartz	43	Slite	Limestone
14	Höjderna	Feldspar	44	Burgsvik	Sandstone
15	Sala	Dolomite	45	Horn	Limestone
16	Gråmyren	Dolomite	46	Gillberga	Limestone
17	Vätö	Granite	47	Greby	Limestone
18	Larsbo	Dolomite	48	Degerhamn	Limestone
19	Glanshammar	Dolomite	49	Ventlinge	Limestone
20	Kvarntorp	Sandstone	50	Stärnö	Dolerite
21	Brännlyckan	Dolomite	51	Glimåkra	Hyperite dolerite
22	Forsby	Dolomite	52	Vånga	Granite
23	Näshulta	Dolerite	53	Ignaberga	Limestone
24	Lemunda	Sandstone	54	Fyledalen	Quartz sand
25	Borghamn	Limestone	55	Kvarnby	Limestone
26	Österplana	Limestone	56	Limhamn	Limestone
27	Brattefors	Limestone	57	Billesholm	Coal
28	Ryd	Dolerite	58	Getinge	Gneiss
29	Skövde	Limestone	59	Nannarp	Gneiss
30	Uddagården	Limestone	60	Tiarp	Gneiss

The Quarternary

The Earth's youngest period, the Quaternary, is characterised by alternating glacial and interglacial stages. The landscape is largely influenced by the latest glaciation (1–5) and its recession (6–16). Subsequently, the landscape has been reformed to a certain extent by isostatic uplift and wave-washing of shores at that time (17–22). The wind (23) and running water (24–29) erode the landscape and create new land-forms both above and below the highest shoreline (17), peatlands expand (30–31) and anthropological activities leave clear traces (32–33). The fictitious landscape in the illustration has been formed by a continental ice sheet that has moved from left to right; the retreat of the ice margin has taken place from right to left.

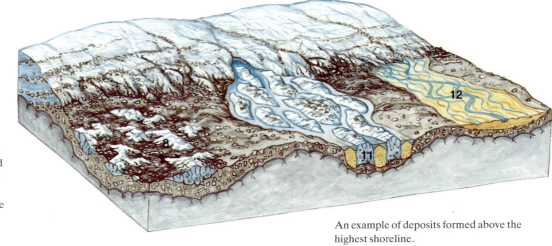

An example of deposits formed above the highest shoreline.

1. Roche moutonnée
2. Drumlin
3. Till
4. Cultivated till
5. End moraine
6. De Geer moraine
7. Ablation moraine
8. Humpback esker
9. Esker
10. Esker
11. Kame
12. Glaciofluvial out. wash plain, sandur
13. Glaciofluvial delta
14. Kettles
15. Erratic
16. Clay plain
17. Highest shoreline
18. Till-capped hill
19. Shingle field (klapper)
20. Raised beaches
21. Bare-washed bedrock
22. Sand beach
23. Dunes
24. Bluffs
25. Gullies
26. Meander
27. Oxbow lake
28. Recent delta
29. Slide scar
30. Bog
31. Soligenous mire
32. Ditched fen
33. Gravel pit

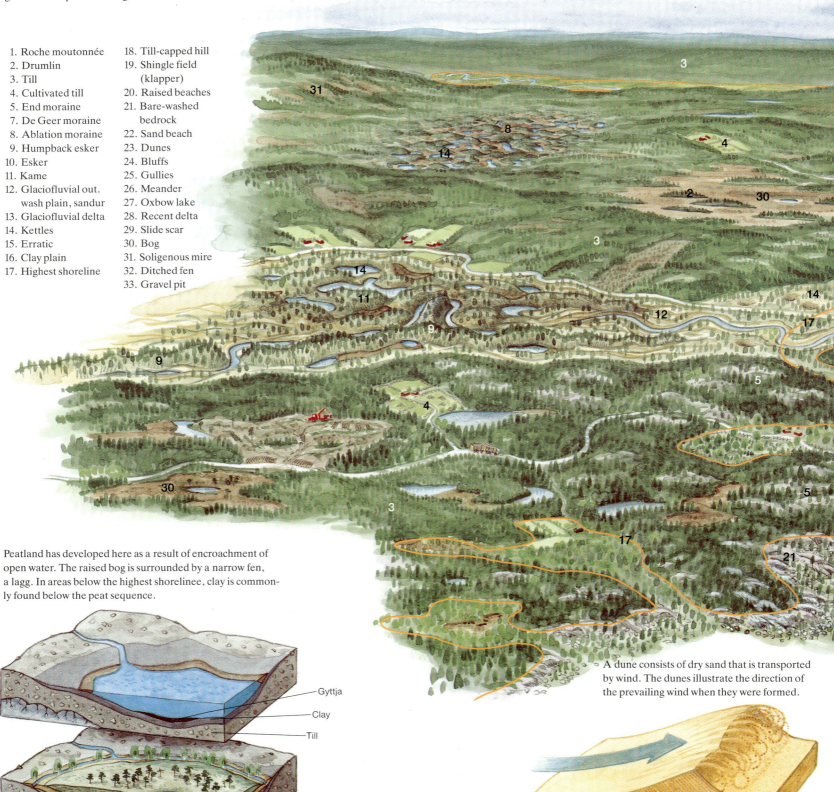

Peatland has developed here as a result of encroachment of open water. The raised bog is surrounded by a narrow fen, a lagg. In areas below the highest shorelinee, clay is commonly found below the peat sequence.

A dune consists of dry sand that is transported by wind. The dunes illustrate the direction of the prevailing wind when they were formed.

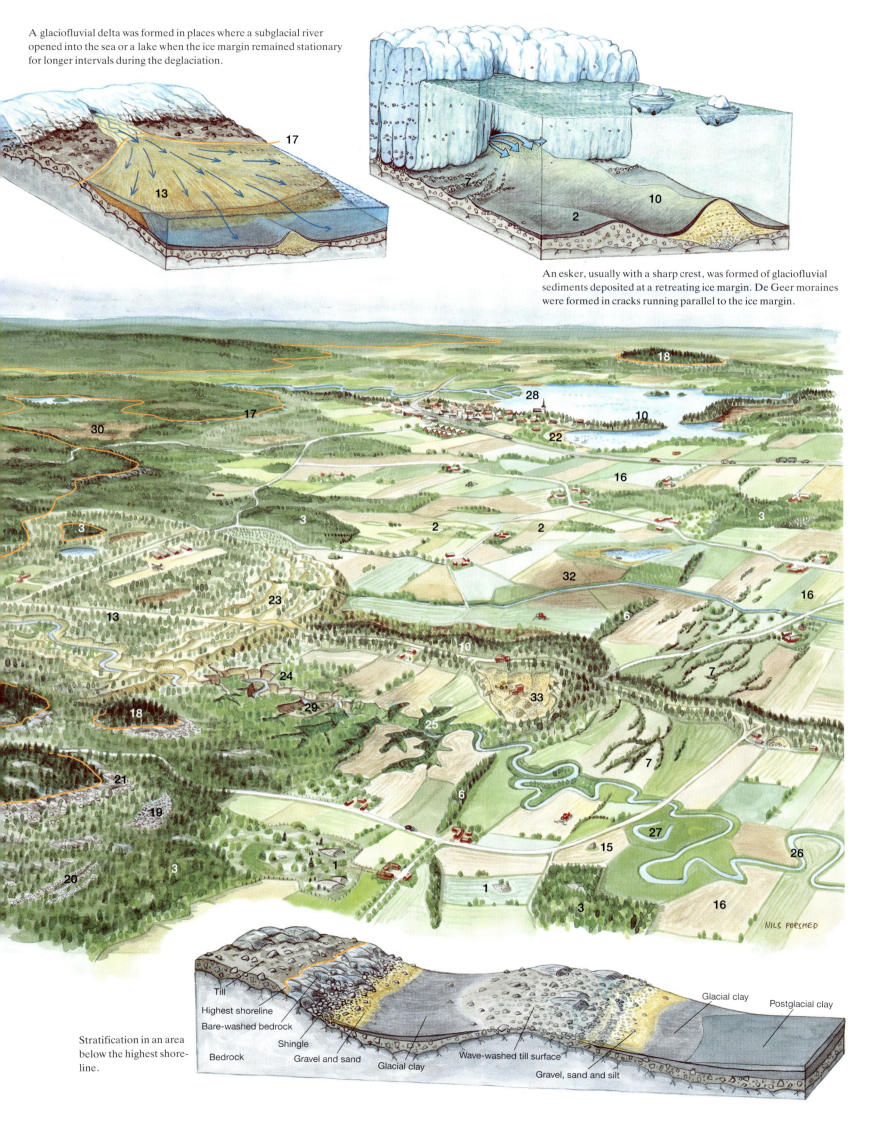

Quaternary Deposits

The term Quaternary deposit (as opposed to rock) refers to the loose material on the earth's surface. Most of Sweden's deposits were formed during the last ice age and the following period. This is true of other periods that were covered with ice during the Quaternary period. The deposits in areas not covered with ice differ noticeably from Sweden's. The most common type of deposit outside the glacial areas is weathering material, deposit that consists of weathered rock. Weathering material, in contrast to most Swedish Quaternary deposits, is not transported but is formed in situ. Sweden almost entirely lacks weathering material. It takes a long time to form and the period after the last ice age has been too short.

Swedish Quaternary deposits are classified according to the way in which they were formed, genesis, and the environment in which they were formed; for example, till is deposited by a glacier (genesis) and clay is deposited by stagnant water (environment).

This classification by genesis and environment falls into two main groups: glacial and post-glacial. Glacial deposits are formed by glaciers or meltwater from glaciers. Most of the Swedish glacial deposits were formed during the last glaciation, the Weichselian. Post-glacial deposits were formed after the ice had melted, without the influence of ice or its meltwater.

When they are formed, some deposits are sorted; this particularly applies to those deposited by ice rivers and rivers. At a certain velocity of water flow a certain size of particle will be deposited, while smaller particles will continue to be transported by the running water. This means that we find, for example, large deposits of sand (particles of 0.2–2 mm) close to places where rivers used to run. Quaternary deposit maps usually indicate both genesis and the environment in which the deposit was formed as well as particle size. It is important to know the size of the particles since this gives the deposit many of its physical properties such as capillarity, the ablity to absorb water, and permeability, the ability to retain and allow water to percolate through.

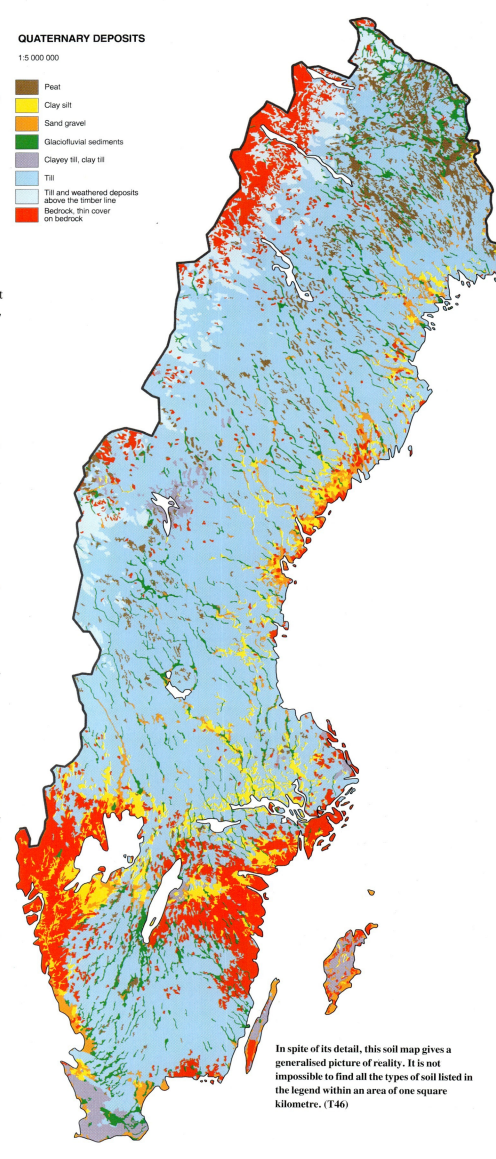

In spite of its detail, this soil map gives a generalised picture of reality. It is not impossible to find all the types of soil listed in the legend within an area of one square kilometre. (T46)

GLACIOFLUVIAL SEDIMENTS

1:10 000 000

- Glaciofluvial sediments
- Area above the highest shoreline
- Area below the highest shoreline
- Highest shoreline

Glaciofluvial deposits cover only a small part of Sweden but are of great importance as sources of sand and gravel and groundwater. Close to the highest shoreline the glacial delta broadens out. The alignment of eskers reflects the latest movements of the ice rivers. (T47)

Till soil sometimes has distinctive landforms. Rogen moraine in southern Härjedalen.

Eskers are a striking feature in the landscape and are an important natural resource in the form of sand and gravel and groundwater. The esker north of Uppsala.

GLACIAL DEPOSITS

Till is an unsorted type of deposit formed when the inland ice ground or broke off pieces of the bedrock, crushing and mixing the material with older deposits. The particle size in a moraine varies according to the kind of bedrock and the distance the ice transported the till. Usually till reflects the local rock composition since most of it has not been transported more than a kilometre or so. Till covers about 75 per cent of Sweden's land surface. It often lies directly on the bedrock, following its surface configuration, but it is also common for till to form its own configurations.

Glaciofluvial sediment consists of material that has been transported, sorted and deposited by meltwater from the inland ice. Three main landforms are connected with glaciofluvial sediment: eskers, clay plains and glaciofluvial deltas.

Eskers were formed when the coarse material — mainly stones, gravel and sand — was deposited in tunnels under the melting ice and at the mouth of these tunnels. As the edge of the ice melted, the material formed long, narrow ridges. These ridges have functioned as travel routes; sand and gravel are important natural resources and they are also vital groundwater reservoirs.

POST-GLACIAL SEDIMENTS

Marine and Lacustrine Sediment is mainly formed by wave-washing during land uplift. The particle size of this sediment varies considerably, from klapper, consisting of shingle and cobbles, to post-glacial clay.

Alluvial and Diluvial Deposits are deposited as banks in rivers or as deltas at the mouths of rivers, or alternatively along the sides of rivers.

Aeolian Deposits have usually been formed by old sediment such as glaciofluvial deposits or shore deposits which have been raised out of the sea by land uplift.

Peat is formed when dead and incompletely decomposed plant material accumulates at the place of growth, in overgrown lakes or where previously dry land becomes waterlogged, for example. Peat is the second most frequent deposit in Sweden, covering some 15 per cent of the land. Peat is used as fuel, as a soil conditioner and as litter in stables.

The various Quaternary deposits and their distribution in the Swedish landscape have affected the pattern of settlements and land use to a very high degree. Cultivatable deposits combined with a suitable climate and a supply of drinking water are, at least in a historical perspective, the three most important factors for human settlement.

Classification of Quaternary deposits and their names. The upper group is used by geologists, including the Geological Survey of Sweden, the lower group mainly by geotechnicians.

	0.002	0.006	0.02	0.06	0.2	0.6	2	6	20	60	200	600	2,000 mm
Clay	Silt			Sand			Gravel		Cobble		Boulder		
	Fine silt	Medium silt	Coarse silt	Fine sand	Medium sand	Coarse sand	Fine gravel	Coarse gravel	Pebbles	Cobbles	Fine boulders	Medium boulders	Coarse boulders

DISTRIBUTION AND DEPTH OF QUATERNARY DEPOSITS

A. Plain settlement dominated by clay till
Clay till is a type of soil transported by ice that is found in areas of lime-rich, sedimentary rocks. The lime-rich clay tills are among the best soils for cultivation in Sweden. Rönneberga hills, Skåne.

Legend:
- Peat
- Clay and silt
- Gravel and sand
- Glaciofluvial sediments
- Till
- Clay till
- Sedimentary rock
- Precambrian bedrock

The distribution of Quaternary deposits and their depth are greatly affected by factors like the local bedrock, its morphology and deglaciation. These variations are clearly visible in the landscape, sometimes by differences in land use.

B. Cultivated sandy area
The southern Swedish highlands are above the highest shoreline, so they lack large areas of fine-grained soil. Cultivation is often on sandy glaciofluvial deposits or small, irregular fields of till. Hallerum, Småland.

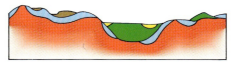

C. Joint-aligned valleys
The joint-aligned valley landscape of western Sweden lies mainly below the highest shoreline. As a result of land uplift, the exposed parts and clays were deposited in the ice hollows between the bare rocks. Kosteröarna, Bohuslän.

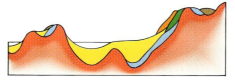

SOIL

A Quaternary deposit will change in the course of time, as a number of processes occur in the earth's surface, creating soil. Soil is characterised by horizons which often run parallel with the earth's surface. Usually the soil is 20–50 cm deep in Sweden. The horizons differ from one another in colour, particle size, consistency, porosity and measurable chemical, physical and biological properties.

The processes that affect the formation of soil vary according to:
- Climate — In areas where precipitation exceeds transpiration, the surplus of water will move downwards through the soil. If the surface water is acidic, metal ions will be leached from the upper parts of the earth profile and descend into its lower parts. In areas where precipitation is lower than transpiration, the water will instead move upwards. That is why there is often on the surface in dry areas a crust consisting of crystallized salts.
- Topography — There are often varying hydrological conditions at different levels along a slope. If parts of the overburden, owing to processes at work in the slope, slide downwards, soil formation will be affected.
- Type of soil — Depending on particle size the groundwater will move in various ways. In coarse, sorted soil such as sand permeability will be high. In soil containing a large proportion of clay drainage will be quite different.
- Vegetation — Soil which is formed in coniferous forests is affected by the naturally acidic litter which this type of vegetation creates. Soil formed on grass steppes is affected by the fact that the grass dries out every year, becoming part of the soil. Grass steppe soil is therefore rich in organic material.

D. Grazed eskers
In northern Götaland and in Svealand the exposed areas of till and eskers have been wavewashed. Areas lower down are covered with fine-grained soils deposited by water, where the postglacial clay covers the glacial clay. Vartofta, Västergötland.

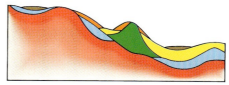

E. Cultivated river sediment
After deglaciation the Norrland river valleys were deep sea lochs where the sediment from the melting land ice was deposited. As a result of land uplift the rivers have cut through the sediment, a process that is still going on today. The river Ångermanälven at Forsmo, Ångermanland.

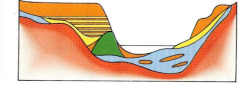

SOILS

1:10 000 000

- Weakly developed soils
- Haplic Podzols with a leached layer thicker than 6 cm
- Haplic Podzols with a leached layer thinner than 6 cm
- Dystric Cambisols
- Eutric Cambisols
- Leptosols

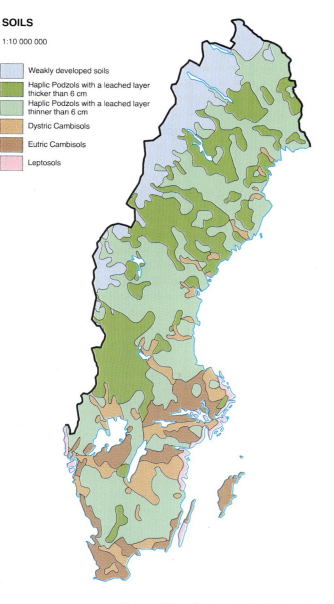

The map shows the types of soil which are most frequently found within each area. It is based on field studies, using a large number of sample pits. The distribution of soils in Sweden is not static. Changes in land use or changes in the climate also lead to changes in the soil. (T48)

In Sweden there are two main natural types of soil, podzol and cambisol, and transitional forms of these two types.

Podzol consists of a number of often clear horizons. It is formed mostly in coniferous forests, requiring a relatively cold climate with a surplus of precipitation. Beneath the litter and humus layers the acidic surface water will leach in particular iron and aluminium ions from the upper layers, creating a leached layer. Beneath the leached layer there is a rust-red, dark brown enriched horizon. Its colour comes mainly from complex compounds of humus, iron and aluminium. Beneath the enriched layer lies the unaffected mineral material.

Cambisols are formed mostly in clayey soils with a high level of biological activity of bacteria, worms and other digging organisms, which quickly mix the litter with the mineral material. This mixture is called mull. The natural vegetation on cambisols is deciduous forest. Because of the higher pH of cambisols compared with podzol, surface water is quickly neutralised and humus material, iron and aluminium are precipitated directly under the mull layer. For this reason there is no leaching layer. Cambisols may be stable or instable depending on their clay content, fertility and vegetation.

Soil formation is a dynamic process in which the distribution of the various soils changes with time. This change depends partly on time, but also on external factors caused by human activity. For example, podzol areas will grow as a result of acidification and planting trees on arable land.

The soil map is in the form of a frequency map, since the soil-forming factors vary from place to place, making it impossible for one particular type of soil to extend very far.

Alongside the two main types of soil in Sweden, and their transitional forms, there are also a number of areas consisting of:
- Azonal soils — Young soil formations such as dunes, fluvial sediments and talus material.
- Lithosols — Soils which form in very shallow layers directly on the bedrock.
- Wet soils — These comprise soil formations in wet environments and peatland.
- Rendzinas — A type of soil which forms in areas of limestone bedrock.

- Ground fauna — There are organisms in the soil that can transport material both upwards and downwards in the profile, thus preventing the formation of clear horizons.
- Age — The formation of soil is to a great extent a function of time. Young soils developed, for example, in recently exposed till or in recently deposited river sediment differ greatly from soils in the tropics where the processes started perhaps millions of years ago.
- Mankind — Of course human activities greatly affect soil formation. Wherever the land is cultivated, agricultural machinery and other tools will have altered the conditions for natural soil formation.

Cambisols. At the top is the dark earth, a mixture of humus and mineral elements. This earth becomes lighter the deeper one goes. There is a continuous transition towards the underlying, unaffected soil, with its own colour.

Podzols. Beneath the topmost dark layer consisting of organic debris and mor is the light, leached layer. Podzols are divided into various sub-groups according to the depth of the leached layer. Below the leached layer is the light red/dark brown illuvial layer.

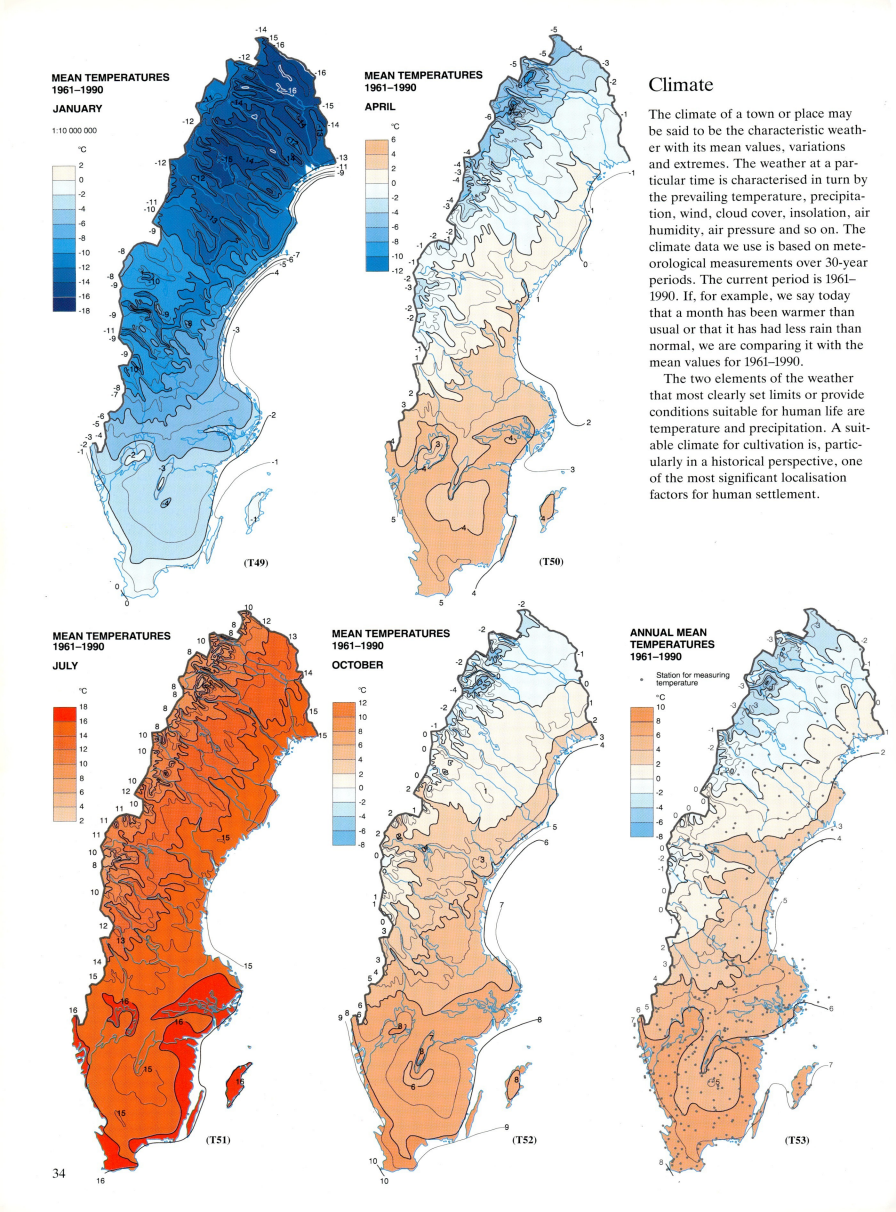

Climate

The climate of a town or place may be said to be the characteristic weather with its mean values, variations and extremes. The weather at a particular time is characterised in turn by the prevailing temperature, precipitation, wind, cloud cover, insolation, air humidity, air pressure and so on. The climate data we use is based on meteorological measurements over 30-year periods. The current period is 1961–1990. If, for example, we say today that a month has been warmer than usual or that it has had less rain than normal, we are comparing it with the mean values for 1961–1990.

The two elements of the weather that most clearly set limits or provide conditions suitable for human life are temperature and precipitation. A suitable climate for cultivation is, particularly in a historical perspective, one of the most significant localisation factors for human settlement.

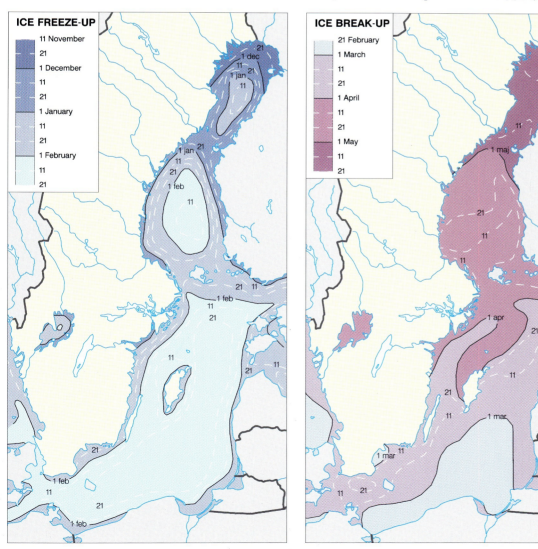

LENGTH OF GROWING SEASON

1:20 000 000
Average number of days with mean temperature above +5 °C 1961–1990

- 220
- 200
- 180
- 160
- 140
- 120
- 100

FROST FREQUENCY

Days
- 30
- 20
- 10
- 5

CONTINENTAL AND MARITIME AREAS

°C
- 45 ↑ Mostly continental
- 40
- 35
- 30
- 25 ↓ Mostly maritime
- 20

The vegetation period is defined as the time of the year when the mean temperature is above +5°C. The difference between southern and northern Sweden is more than 100 days. (T54)

It is mainly inland and in hollows which collect colder air that farmers run the risk of suffering frost damage to their crops during the vegetation period. (T55)

Much of Sweden has a maritime climate. Continentality is shown on the map as the sum of the difference in temperature between July and January and between night and day in June. (T56)

During a normal winter the Bothnian Bay, the northernmost part of the Baltic, the Baltic archipelagos, Kalmar Sound and the Bohus archipelago are covered with ice. It is very unusual for the whole of the Baltic to be covered with ice at the same time. (Mean values for the period 1963–1979.) (T57, T58)

ICE FREEZE-UP
- 11 November
- 21
- 1 December
- 11
- 21
- 1 January
- 11
- 21
- 1 February
- 11
- 21

ICE BREAK-UP
- 21 February
- 1 March
- 11
- 21
- 1 April
- 11
- 21
- 1 May
- 11
- 21

TEMPERATURE

Sweden's temperature is determined primarily by its northern position on earth and its location on the west side of a continent, close to a sea. Temperature decreases with latitude; the further north, the colder it gets. Temperature also decreases with altitude, by about 0.6 C, but at night and during the winter it is often colder on low-lying ground than on the surrounding higher terrain.

Despite their northern position Sweden, Norway and Finland have a unique density of population for their latitude.

A significant factor explaining these northern settlements in Sweden is their proximity to the Atlantic Ocean. The north-eastern branch of the Gulf Stream, the North Atlantic current, sweeps along the coast of Norway and, thanks to prevailing westerly winds, greatly affects the climate in Sweden as well. This relatively warm ocean current makes winter temperatures considerably higher than they otherwise would be, but summer temperatures are somewhat lower. All in all proximity to the sea and the westerly wind mean that Sweden has a positive temperature anomaly, that is, its mean temperature is higher than it would be if Sweden were not affected by the North Atlantic current. Our maritime climate has made it possible to farm in Sweden north of the Arctic Circle. Areas in corresponding latitudes in Canada, Alaska and Russia are for the most part covered with deep permafrost. Stockholm is actually at the same latitude as the southern tip of Greenland!

Yet it is the climate that sets the limits for human activity. Intense cold and deep frost have to be taken into account when building houses in northern Sweden, for example. Other outdoor work is also more difficult in the winter months. Long stretches of the road network have to be closed off or restricted to light traffic when the spring thaw sets in.

However, the cold climate does bring some benefits, for agriculture, for example. During the long period of frost insect pests and plant diseases cannot develop, which means that farmers do not need to use as much pesticide as farmers in warmer, moister climates. The frost is also important because it breaks up the clayey soils below the highest shoreline, making them easier to work. The moderate warmth also means that plants do not require so much water.

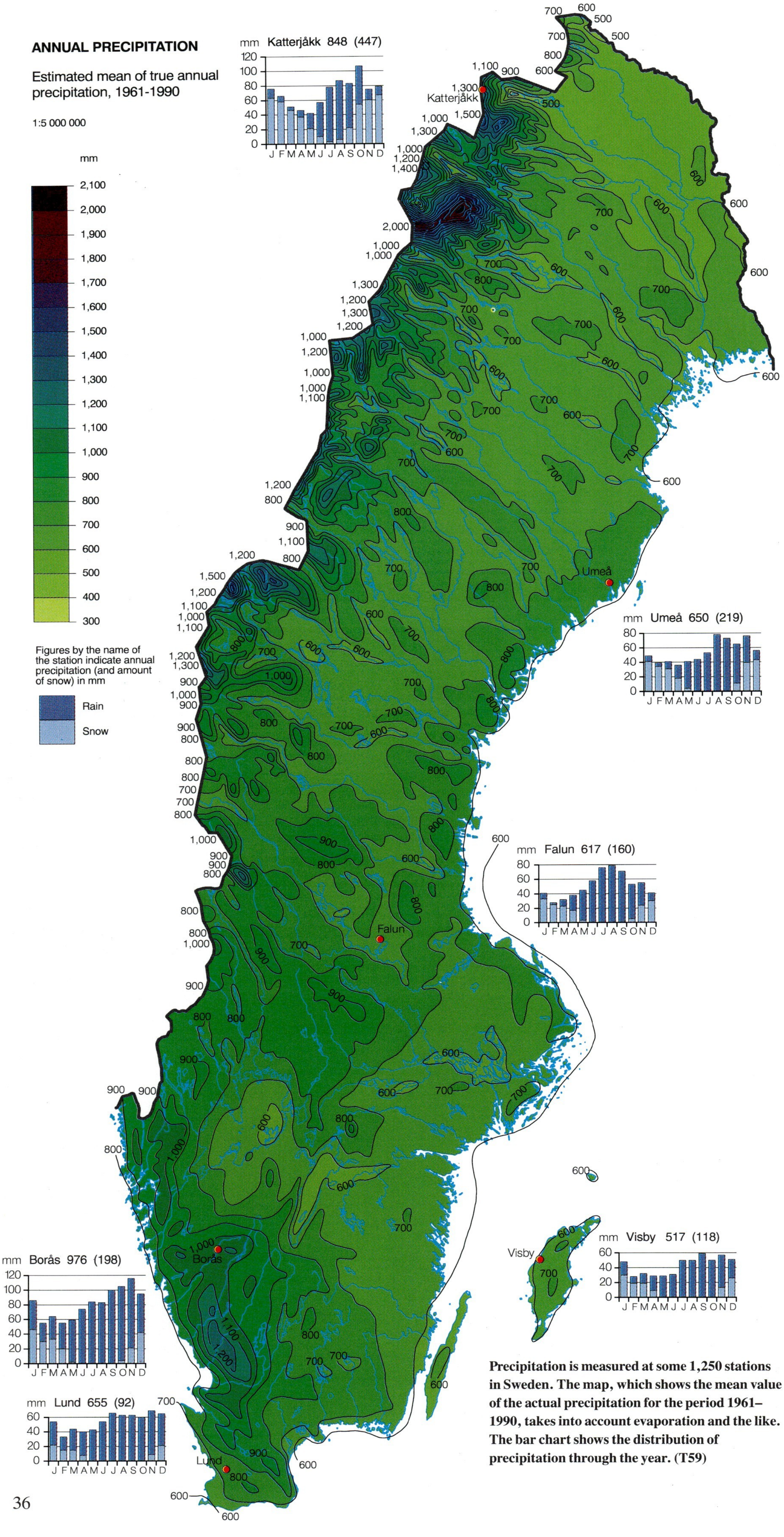

ANNUAL PRECIPITATION

Estimated mean of true annual precipitation, 1961–1990

1:5 000 000

Figures by the name of the station indicate annual precipitation (and amount of snow) in mm

- Rain
- Snow

Precipitation is measured at some 1,250 stations in Sweden. The map, which shows the mean value of the actual precipitation for the period 1961–1990, takes into account evaporation and the like. The bar chart shows the distribution of precipitation through the year. (T59)

PRECIPITATION

Swedish precipitation is determined mainly by weather systems that at our latitudes move mostly westwards. For most of the year there is a belt of westerly winds over the British Isles and Scandinavia. Within this belt temperature differences in the lower parts of the atmosphere create depressions and accompanying fronts with precipitation. Most of the depressions come from the west, so it is mainly western and south-western slopes that get a great deal of precipitation. Parts of the mountain range and the western side of the southern Swedish highlands receive especially heavy precipitation as a result of orographic reinforcement. Apart from these two areas there are also areas which receive relatively large amounts of precipitation along the east coast of Sweden. This is especially true of southern and central Norrland with its steep coastline. High forest areas like Tiveden, Tylöskog and Finnskogarna also receive a fair amount of precipitation, while large, wide valleys and lake basins do not receive as much as the surrounding terrain.

In general, the average amount of precipitation increases with altitude above sea level. Roughly speaking, annual precipitation increases by 30–40 mm per 100 m in the interior of northern Sweden. Further south the corresponding figure is 50–70 mm. In the western mountains and along the west coast the increase can be as high as 150–200 mm per 100 m. This increase is connected with proximity to the sea combined with orographic reinforcement.

The driest hollows of all are surrounded by high mountains and are found in the central mountain regions. The station with the least precipitation during the period 1961–1990 was at Abisko in Torneträsk, with a mean annual figure of 304 mm. The average annual precipitation for Sweden is 750 mm.

The annual sequence of precipitation is characterised by a minimum in the spring and a fairly low maximum from the height of summer through the autumn into the early winter in maritime areas close to the coast, while inland, especially in the north, there is a noticeable maximum in July and August. The fact that the summer is the season with the highest precipitation does not mean that it has the most frequent rainfall. It is rather October to December that is character-

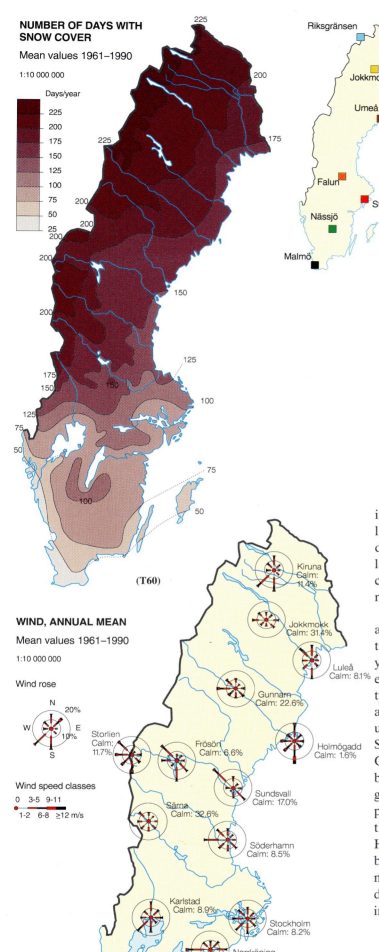

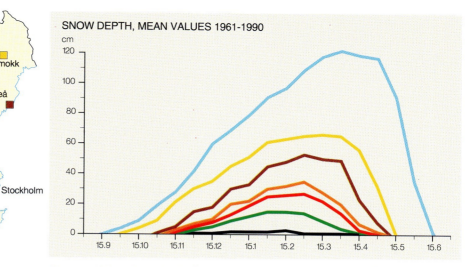

The ground in northern Sweden is almost always covered with snow from December to March, while in Skåne it is usually free of snow, even in mid-winter. The snow is deepest in February, except for the far north, where it is deepest in March or April.

ised by days of continuous rain. The large precipitation in the summer is due to its greater intensity, when large amounts of rain in short showers can account for a large part of the monthly precipitation.

The mean annual precipitation is an important climatic factor, but it tells us nothing about variations from year to year. The precipitation for each of the months varies during a typical ten-year period between 20 and 200 per cent of the normal figures. A very severe drought began in Sweden in mid-May, 1992. In parts of Götaland there was little or no rain between 13 May and 11 July. Plant growth was severely affected and parts of Götaland only harvested half the normal crop sown in the spring. Heavy rainfall for short periods has been measured mainly in the summer months. The Swedish record for one day is 237 mm, measured at Karleby in Skåne on 6 August, 1960.

The prevailing winds in Sweden are westerly, accompanied by depressions. These rotate anti-clockwise, which means that one and the same point on the ground can be affected by winds from all directions as a depression passes through. The topography also affects wind direction in the lower parts of the atmosphere. (T61)

WINDS

The air which surrounds us is in constant movement. The wind is an extremely important climatic element which greatly affects precipitation and temperature. The wind modifies, both at the micro and the macro level, the temperature contrasts that arise as a result of the uneven distribution of solar energy round the globe.

The winds in Sweden are primarily affected by the movement of depressions, yet they do not have a clear prevailing direction. There are two reasons for this. First, the terrain greatly influences wind direction close to the earth's surface; wind often moves along topographical lines such as valleys or coastlines. Second, winds connected with depressions blow anti-clockwise round the centre of a depression. This means that it is possible to observe every conceivable wind direction in the space of a day or so at any place through which a depression passes. In addition at certain times of the year there are weather situations which are not connected with depressions.

Average wind speeds in Sweden have been measured up to a maximum of 35–40 m/s at the coast and in the mountains. In the mountains gusts of winds up to 80 m/s have been measured.

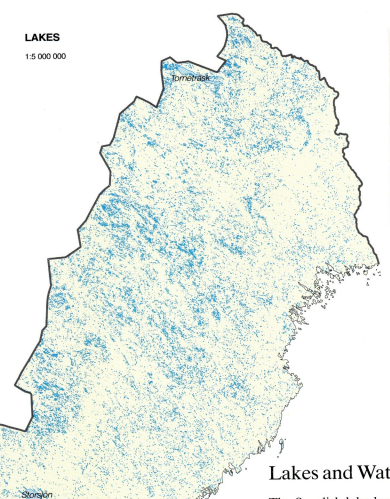

LAKES
1:5 000 000

AREA OF LAKES

Size (km²)	Number of lakes	Area (km²)	Area (%)
>1,000	3	8,662	21
100–1,000	21	4,594	11
10–100	371	9,317	22.5
1–10	3,533	9,735	23.5
0.1–1	20,227	6,854	16.5
0.01–0.1	68,256	2,301	5.5
Total	**92,409**	**41,463**	**100**

Lakes and Watercourses

The Swedish lake landscape is the result of a long geological evolution. Folds, faults and fissures in the bedrock millions of years ago created hollows that are filled with water today. The inland ice made hollows in the surface of the bedrock and spread till across most of Sweden. Many small lakes are in principle pools of water in the uneven till overburden. Almost 10 per cent of Sweden is covered with water; the corresponding figure for the parts of Europe that were not affected by glaciation in the Quaternary is less than 1 per cent.

The climate is, of course, an important reason for the large number of lakes in Sweden and the rest of Scandinavia. The mean annual precipitation in Sweden is on average more than twice as much as the evapotranspiration. If the relationship between precipitation and evapotranspiration were to change, the number and size of Swedish lakes would also change.

The number and size of Swedish lakes are changing all the time for other reasons than the climate. The lakes which receive sediment from rivers will sooner or later be filled with sediment. The delta of Lake Laitaure, into which the Rapaälven flows, is growing by about five metres a year. If this rate of sedimentation continues, the lake will be completely filled in 1,000 years. Many lakes on the plains, particularly the shallow ones, are becoming overgrown. By lowering the level of a great many lakes man has reduced their total area. This took place mainly at the end of the 19th century in an attempt to increase the area of arable land. But new lakes also appear. Along the coast of Norrland land uplift turns sea bays into lakes. Lakes are formed or enlarged also as a result of regulating water flow for hydro-electric power.

Lakes are a very important feature of the Swedish landscape as well as being a vital natural resource. Lake water is used to provide supplies of drinking water in many places. Lakes also receive less desirable substances such as fertilisers and pesticides from forests and fields, treated water from urban sewage plants and acid rain transported from afar. In the old days lakes made travel easier, by boat in the summer, by sledge in the winter.

Lake sediment is one of the most important archives for environmental history when scientists try to reconstruct the climate, vegetation and cultivation of earlier times. It has, for example, been possible to prove that lead was carried to Sweden 2,000 years ago by westerly winds.

Lakes cover almost 10 per cent of the area of Sweden. There are many small lakes in hilly country, whereas the plains have a few, large lakes. The lake landscape is in a state of change: some lakes become overgrown, while new ones are formed as a result of land uplift. (T62)

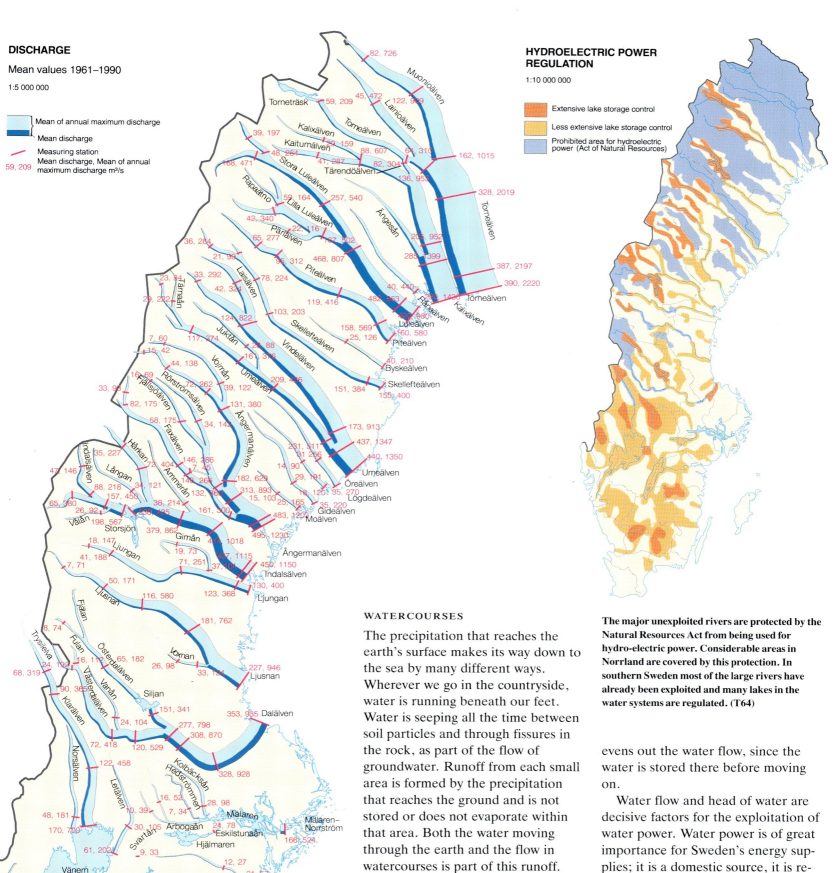

DISCHARGE
Mean values 1961–1990
1:5 000 000

- Mean of annual maximum discharge
- Mean discharge
- Measuring station
- 59, 209 Mean discharge, Mean of annual maximum discharge m³/s

HYDROELECTRIC POWER REGULATION
1:10 000 000

- Extensive lake storage control
- Less extensive lake storage control
- Prohibited area for hydroelectric power (Act of Natural Resources)

WATERCOURSES

The precipitation that reaches the earth's surface makes its way down to the sea by many different ways. Wherever we go in the countryside, water is running beneath our feet. Water is seeping all the time between soil particles and through fissures in the rock, as part of the flow of groundwater. Runoff from each small area is formed by the precipitation that reaches the ground and is not stored or does not evaporate within that area. Both the water moving through the earth and the flow in watercourses is part of this runoff.

The water that runs off forms a network of small streams that combine to make larger watercourses. Along these watercourses, from their sources to the sea, the drainage areas increase in size and the tributaries in number. The large number of lakes evens out the water flow, since the water is stored there before moving on.

Water flow and head of water are decisive factors for the exploitation of water power. Water power is of great importance for Sweden's energy supplies; it is a domestic source, it is renewable and it does not pollute much. Approximately 16 per cent of the energy production is provided by this source of energy, and almost 50 per cent of Sweden's electricity is produced by water power. One disadvantage is its serious effects on the landscape and ecosystems. Some 70 per cent of Sweden's watercourses have been exploited and only four of the large mountain rivers, the Torneälven, the Kalixälven, the Piteälven and the Vindelälven, and a few forest rivers like the Byskeälven and the Råneälven, are protected by law.

Discharge is a function of precipitation, evaporation and storage in snow, lakes, surface water and groundwater. Because of their enormous drainage areas, the rivers in northern Sweden have a considerably larger discharge than those in southern Sweden. The large differences in height along the Norrland rivers make them suitable for hydro-electric power. (T63)

The major unexploited rivers are protected by the Natural Resources Act from being used for hydro-electric power. Considerable areas in Norrland are covered by this protection. In southern Sweden most of the large rivers have already been exploited and many lakes in the water systems are regulated. (T64)

VEGETATION ZONES

1:10 000 000

- Alpine Zone
- Northern Boreal Zone
- Middle Boreal Zone
- Southern Boreal Zone
- Boreonemoral Zone
- Nemoral Zone

The classification of vegetation zones is based mainly on the dominant types of trees. (T65)

Plants and Animals

VEGETATION ZONES

Sweden is a well-forested country — almost 70 per cent of the land is covered with forests. Most of the country, from the biological Norrland boundary, *limes norrlandicus*, to the mountain chain in the north, lies within the vast coniferous forest belt, the taiga, which covers the northern polar regions. In the far south Sweden lies within the central European deciduous forest zone. Between the northern coniferous forests and the nemoral forests in the south lies a belt of mixed forest consisting of coniferous forest containing a good deal of birch and aspen on till soil and groves of nemoral trees in the cultivated landscape.

Variations in the natural vegetation generally reflect climatic differences in different parts of the country. Within one and the same climate zone topography, soil conditions and hydrography create rich local variations with many types of vegetation close to each other.

Changes in natural conditions lead to changes in the distribution of plants. The most radical change has been in cultivated and grazed land over the past centuries, in some districts over the past millennia. This has permanently altered the vegetation on at least 10–15 per cent of the land, especially in the southern vegetation zones. Even vegetation types that today seem "natural" and are not used for agriculture or forestry, such as heaths and sand dunes, are in many cases the direct result of human land use. In olden days slash-and-burn farming and gathering wood for fuel for mining and iron-manufacturing, for example, impoverished the forests of southern and central Sweden. In our own times almost all forestland is affected by modern methods of felling and reforestation. Large areas of forest are plantations, some of them containing species of foreign origin.

In principle both agriculture and forestry lead to an intentional reduction of the natural diversity of species and a desire to create uniform crops for rational harvesting. In order to preserve our biological diversity, which is an important natural asset, and to preserve understanding and enjoyment of natural vegetation, national parks and nature reserves have been set aside in various parts of the country.

The vegetation of Sweden is divided into four main zones. The **alpine zone** is divided from the north downwards into a upper-alpine zone of boulder fields and snow patches with very sparse vegetation, a middle-alpine zone of grass and dwarf-shrub heathland and a lower-alpine zone of dwarf-shrub heathland, meadows and willow thickets. Lower down the mountains are surrounded by sub-alpine dwarf birch forest which, with more pine and spruce, becomes the **boreal zone** (Boreas, Gr.= north wind), the vast coniferous forestland of the taiga with its huge mires. In a southern boreal zone towards central Sweden there are also some nemoral trees. South of *limes norrlandicus*, which in general marks the northern limit of the oak, most of central and southern Sweden is covered by the **boreonemoral zone** (nemus, Latin = grove) of mixed forests. Nemoral trees are found mainly in cultivated districts, while birch and aspen are the commonest deciduous trees in the coniferous forests. Only the far south of Sweden and the west coast lie in the **nemoral zone** of the nemoral forests. Beech is the most characteristic of the nemoral trees (elm, ash, beech, maple, lime and oak). Forest plantations have meant that the more profitable spruce has taken over consider-

Alpine Zone

Boreal Zone

Boreonemoral Zone

Nemoral Zone

CANADA GOOSE
1:20 000 000
- 1965
- 1980
- Introduction

Canada geese were introduced into Sweden (at Kalmar Sound) about 1930, but as late as 1965 this species was still sparsely distributed. But in the 1970s the population increased rapidly and by 1980 Canada geese could be found practically all over Sweden. (T66)

able areas within this otherwise mainly cultivated vegetation zone. Since 1984 nemoral forests have been protected by law to prevent them decreasing in area.

ANIMAL LIFE

The immigration of animals to Sweden after the last ice age mostly followed two routes, a southern one and a northern one. From the south land animals were able to make their way to Sweden during the period when Skåne was connected to Denmark. Animal immigration and colonisation of new areas is still going on today. In fact there are today more animals entering the country than disappearing from it. As in the plant world, there is greatest diversity of animal life in the southernmost parts of Sweden. However, many species of animals such as field vole, squirrel and fox can be seen almost all over the country.

Animals cannot as easily as plants be divided into regions, but in the 1920s Sweden was divided into three zoogeographical provinces. In the **arctic province** species such as mountain fox, mountain lemming, snow bunting and charr are typical. In the northern Scandinavian forests, the **upper boreal province**, we find species like bean goose, willow grouse and grayling, while the **southern Scandinavian province** is characterised by hedgehog, coot and sand lizard.

Two phenomena which, owing to Sweden's northern position, characterise the animal world are the seasonal migration of many bird species across the climate zones and the hibernation of many land animals.

For thousands of years the trapping and hunting culture enjoyed rich supplies of wild animals, fish and fowl, providing a livelihood for the inhabitants of our country. If in the past it was hunting that intentionally decimated the populations of predators in particular, in modern times it is environmental changes that are threatening many species. Clear-cutting old forests, draining wetlands, large-scale and highly effective agricultural methods, toxic substances and air pollution—all these have decimated and endangered several animal species.

Considerable efforts to conserve nature, stricter environmental legislation and the reintroduction of species have begun to give results. For example, today the white-tailed eagle and the peregrine falcon are increasing in numbers after having been under severe pressure, mainly because of pesticides. It is difficult to control the situation in the water and the air, so international cooperation is required in the Baltic Sea. Global thinking is necessary to counteract threats like air pollution and the greenhouse effect.

One example of a species that has benefited from human activities is the moose. The moose population has grown greatly in the 20th century as a result of the good supply of bushes and undergrowth in the many clear-cut forests, combined with the absence of natural enemies. However, in recent years the moose population has been reduced by hunting.

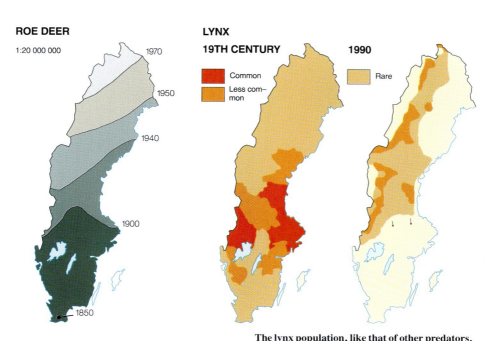

In the mid-19th century the Swedish population of roe deer was almost extinct; only a few hundred animals had survived in Skåne. Improved hunting regulations and a better understanding of game preservation resulted in roe deer spreading northwards in the early 20th century. (T67)

The lynx population, like that of other predators, has been decimated by hunting. In recent years lynx have also been attacked by mange and feline distemper, which has even further reduced the population. In the early 1990s the Swedish population was estimated to be 700 animals. (T68, T69)

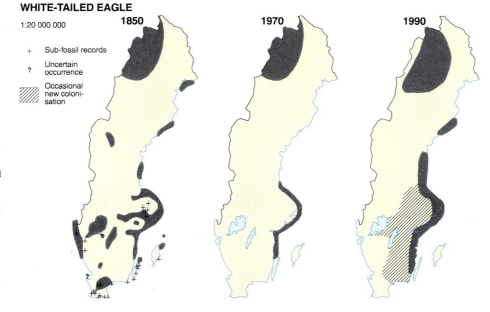

In the mid-19th century the population of white-tailed eagles had been decimated by hunting. After a slight recovery in the early 1950s they were hit by toxic substances, in particular DDT. During the past ten years this species has begun to recover. (T70–72)

This satellite map has been created by processing data from Landsat 5, SPOT 1 and SPOT 2. Land use is recorded in 500 x 500 m squares. This grid is too large for roads to be visible.

When analysing the map it is important to note that open land is not only or even mostly arable land. It also consists of rocky outcrops, clear-cut forests, heaths and bogs. The large, continuous stretch of open land along the Norwegian border is bare mountain. The open land in the forests in the north is mostly bogs.

The deciduous forests in the north are mainly of birch, while further south they are a mixture of birch and other deciduous trees and in the far south they are mainly broad-leaved forests.

What the satellite map primarily gives is a detailed picture of the forest landscape; but the towns also appear in a somewhat generalised form with their densely built-up areas.

The Cultural Landscape

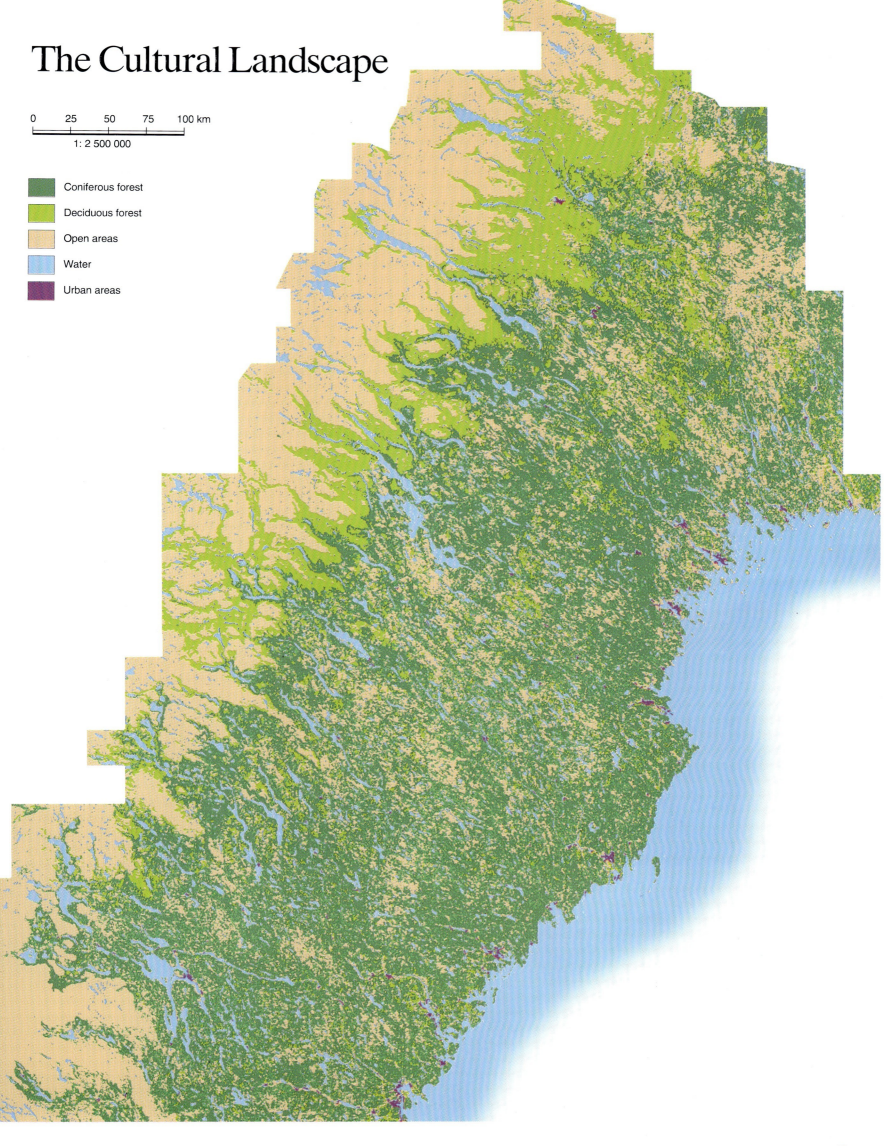

Land Use

THE GÖTEBORG REGION

Founded in 1621 at a strategic position close to the mouth of the Göta älv, Göteborg developed rapidly into the second largest town in Sweden after Bohuslän and Halland had become part of Sweden in 1658.

The harbour, which to begin with was a canal in the middle of the heavily fortified old town, moved out into the Göta älv in the 19th century, with a number of large shipyards on the north bank of the river, Hisingen. Like other ports in the world Göteborg has begun to develop the old docklands for commercial and residential use since the shipyards closed down, cargo shipping needed less space for quays thanks to roll-on roll-off traffic and the trans-oceanic passenger lines were superseded by airlines. Göteborg is still a large industrial city, even though the traditional dominant industries no longer employ so many people. The islands and the coast are densely built-up with second homes.

Torslanda Airport on Hisingen has been replaced by Landvetter Airport inland to the east.

Göteborg has very heavy through traffic, demanding a large road network using tunnels to the east and a new bridge to the west of the city centre to cross the river.

THE MALMÖ REGION

In Sweden's south-west corner the country's third largest urban region, with several town centres dating back to the Middle Ages, is expanding across the arable fields of Sweden's best agricultural land. This urban expansion is taking the form of a dense network of communities held together by a common local labour market.

The coastline facing the Sound has been affected by fill-ins, including the whole of Malmö's harbour. The vast chalk quarries at Limhamn and Klagshamn are very conspicuous. The hilly landscape east of Malmö, with its lakes and beech forests, is important for recreation in the region, which lacks "countryside". The broad highways run like arcs round the inner city; soon they will be connected to the Öresund Bridge.

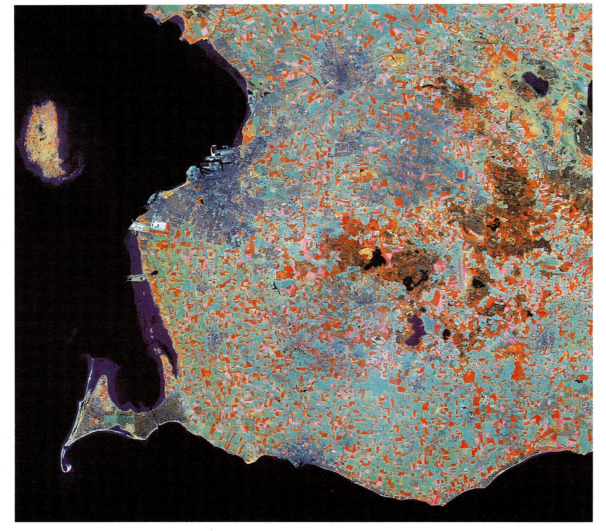

The illustrations on this page have been recorded by Landsat Thematic Mapper. A computerised image-analysis system is responsible for classification and colouring.

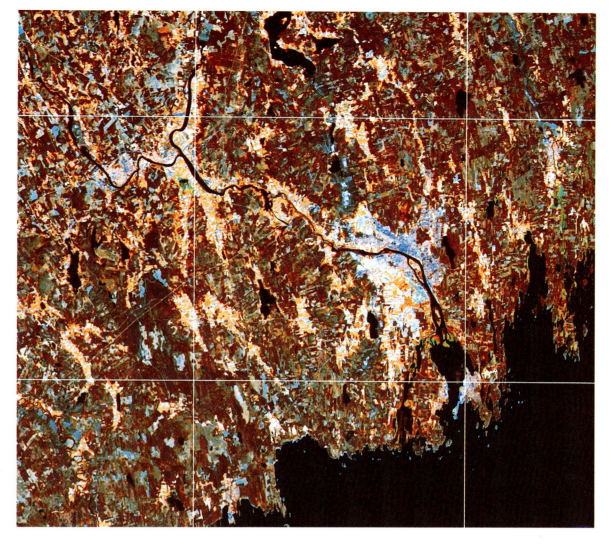

THE UMEÅ REGION

Umeå was founded in the 1620s on the river Umeälven as far up from its mouth as large ships were able to go. As late as the Viking Age a broad sea bay stretched all the way up to here. Land uplift and the formation of a delta have created new, broad, flat land, where, for example, Umeå Airport is located. Land uplift and the increasing draught of modern ships has moved the centre of shipping towards the river mouth at Holmsund.

There is agriculture in sediment-filled hollows and valleys, while the till on the higher terrain is used for forestry. This area is below the highest shoreline. Where the Vindelälven meets the Umeälven there is a broad, cultivated sedimentary plain, protected from flooding by embankments. The buildings traditionally stand in rows on natural banks on the once flood-threatened plain.

The lines of drumlins running from north to south are a characteristic feature of the coastal districts.

THE STOCKHOLM REGION

Stockholm was founded in the 13th century on a small, strategically placed island at the entrance to Lake Mälaren, from which it had to expand into an archipelago. From being a means of communication in early times the various stretches of water have now become a serious traffic problem in this metropolitan region. Stockholm has been governed by its topography. The southern shore of Lake Mälaren is rocky cliffs, its northern shore rather flat. To the south lay large areas of sparsely populated land, to the north the town met farming settlements and villages.

As late as the mid-19th century the Old Town was the town, the home of central government, the head offices of industries, the main shopping streets. Towards the end of the 19th century, owing to a shortage of space, the town centre began to move to lower Norrmalm, which became the commercial, administrative and political heart of Sweden, the focal point of local, national and international transport systems. Since the early 20th century the built-up areas have expanded radially along the main roads and railways within a radius of 25–30 km. Between these built-up areas green "segments" reach deep into the centre, while second homes have spread farther and farther along the coast and into the islands.

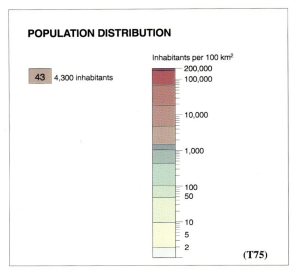

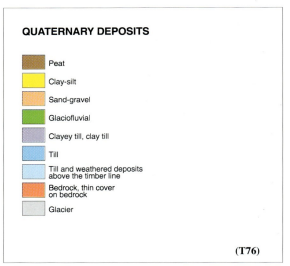

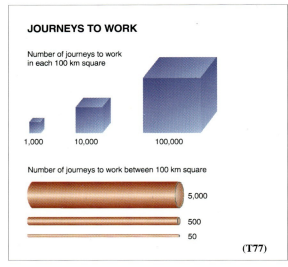

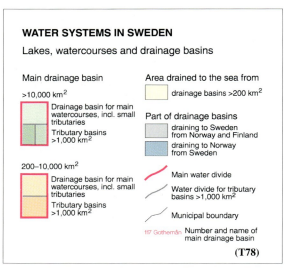

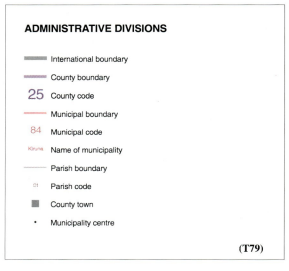

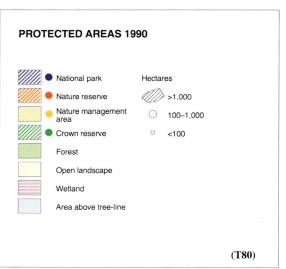

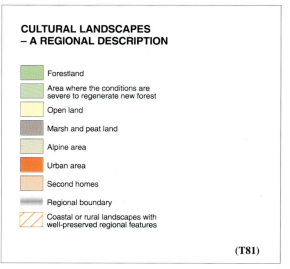

Regional Examples from the Atlas's Thematic Maps

The largest scale for the maps of the National Atlas is 1:1,250,000. Each map at this scale requires eight pages of the atlas, so it has been used fairly sparingly. The following 15 maps at this scale occur in the thematic volumes of the atlas: Bedrock, Quaternary Deposits, Groundwater in Bedrock and Quaternary Deposits, Magnetic Field of the Earth Crust (Geology), Disturbed and Undisturbed Waters, Protected Areas (The Environment), Water Systems in Sweden (Climate, Lakes and Rivers), Places of Biological Interest (Geography of Plants and Animals), Land Classes and Land Use (The Forests), Arable Land and Meadow (Agriculture), Cultural Landscapes — a Regional Description (Landscape and Settlements) Places of Tourist Interest in Sweden (Cultural Life, Recreation and Tourism), Population Distribution (Population), Journeys to Work (Work and Leisure) and Administrative Divisions (The Infrastructure).

In the following pages, for nine regions in Sweden extracts from eight of these maps have been compiled to allow comparative studies to be made, both between thematic maps within one and the same area and between different parts of Sweden.

Regional descriptions become fragmentary in such a small sample of thematic maps, but this study can raise methodical questions concerning regional analysis, relationships and "explanations", and factors of importance for geographical understanding which are not presented in the sample. Topography, which is a fundamental factor in many geographical divisions, is one of these. It can be studied in the large Map of Sweden 1:700,000 in the National Atlas, Maps and Mapping. Similarly, industry and employment are not presented, nor are the road and railway networks. However, these and a broad range of other factors can be studied in maps, admittedly at smaller scales, in other volumes of the National Atlas. Those interested will no doubt also search in other sources.

What is most lacking for a geographical description of the regions, based on the Atlas's maps at 1:1,250,000, is economic geography. It has not been possible to produce and include in the Atlas an integrated economic-geographical map on a large scale.

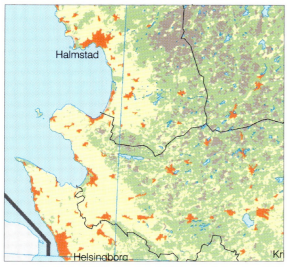
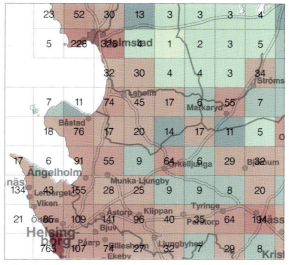
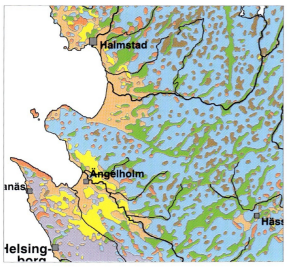
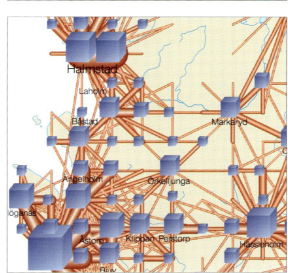

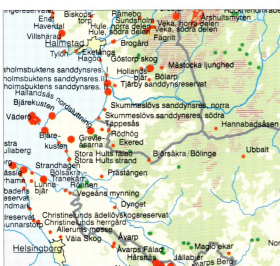
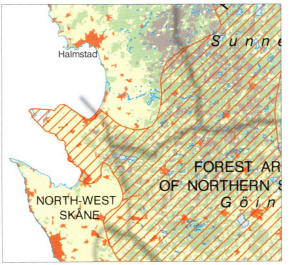

Helsingborg–Halmstad

This map extract comprises all or parts of the following municipalities: Helsingborg, Bjuv, Klippan, Perstorp, Hässleholm, Örkelljunga, Ängelholm, Höganäs and Båstad in the county of Kristianstad, Laholm and Halmstad in the county of Halland and Markaryd and Ljungby in the county of Kronoberg.

The bedrock horst of Hallandsåsen divides the rich, well-wooded settlements of the plains of southern Halland and north-west Skåne from each other. The old national border between Denmark and Sweden passes through sparsely populated forest districts between Markaryd–Ljungby and the other municipalities.

Coastal towns like Helsingborg and Halmstad were important centres even in medieval times, strongly fortified against attacks by the Swedes. Various stretches of the coastline have a very large summer population in second homes.

Söderåsen and Kullaberg are among the most valuable parts of Sweden's natural landscape.

North-west Skåne has a wide range of industries, including the food industry, spread over a dense network of townships. This area enjoys the most favourable climate in Sweden for early crops of price-sensitive vegetables such as potatoes. There are evident traces of earlier mining (coal) in the form of great piles of waste rock alongside the old mines.

The estates of north-west Skåne include magnificent palaces from the Danish period.

The ferry port of Helsingborg attracts much goods and passenger traffic from both Sweden and Norway. The main roads between Copenhagen–Oslo and Copenhagen–Stockholm split at a large, three-level cloverleaf junction outside Helsingborg.

In contrast to the coastal towns, Hässleholm is a young town, a product of the railways. Tracks from five directions meet at the station that was built on the Hässleholm estate in the 1860s.

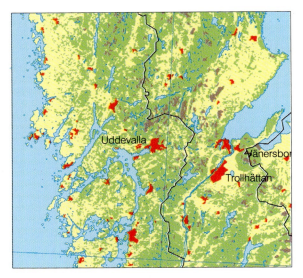
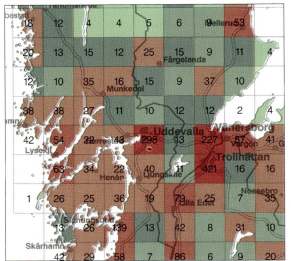
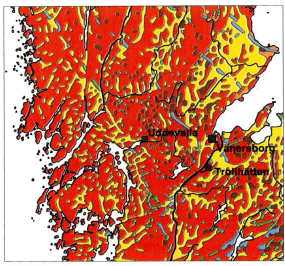
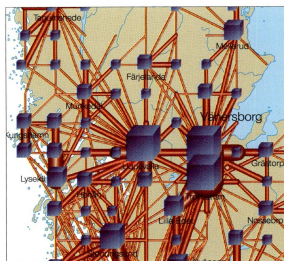

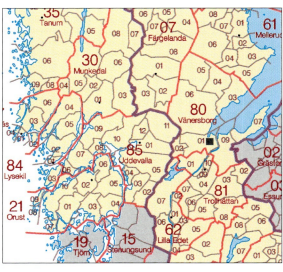
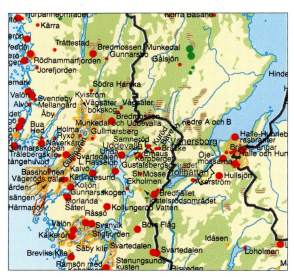
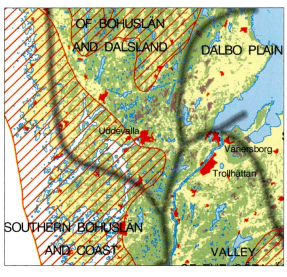

Vänersborg–Uddevalla

This map extract comprises all or parts of the following municipalities: Kungälv, Stenungsund, Tjörn, Orust, Uddevalla, Lysekil, Sotenäs, Munkedal and Tanum in the county of Göteborgs and Bohus, Färgelanda, Mellerud, Vänersborg, Trollhättan, Lilla Edet, Ale and Alingsås, in the county of Älvsborg and Essunga and Grästorp in the county of Skaraborg.

Until 1658 Bohuslän north of Kungälv was Norwegian territory. Kongahälla (Kungälv) was an important town in Viking Norway and Bohus was the Norwegian border fortress. Apart from large industrial centres like Uddevalla and Stenungsund (petrochemicals), it is the archipelago with its fishing villages, bare rocks and cliffs with traces of stone quarrying, and summer visitors that give this district its modern profile. Tanum is a rich storehouse of remarkable Bronze Age art treasures, rock carvings, which are on UNESCO's world heritage list.

The West Coast railway and Highway E6 are both busy transport links between Norway and Denmark.

The valley of the Göta älv was always of strategic importance for Sweden, which has controlled the river mouth since medieval times, while the land to the north and the south belonged to Norway and Denmark. Not until 1658 did the young city of Göteborg secure its future; its many forerunners had always been destroyed by war.

The completion of the Trollhätte Canal in 1916 (1844) opened Lake Vänern for shipping, and the exploitation of water power using Vänern as a reservoir made it possible to industrialise Trollhättan, Vargön and Lilla Edet. It also destroyed the mightiest waterfall in northern Europe.

The Canal deprived Vänersborg of much of its economic power, the shipping on Lake Vänern.

North of Vänersborg the Dalsbo plain extends to Mellerud and the great Vara plain begins east of Halleberg and Hunneberg.

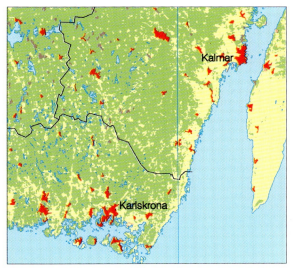
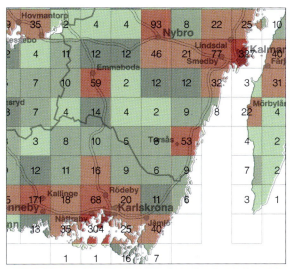
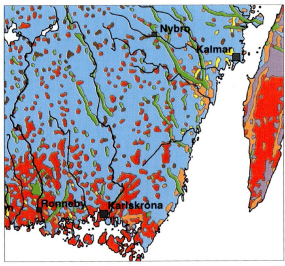
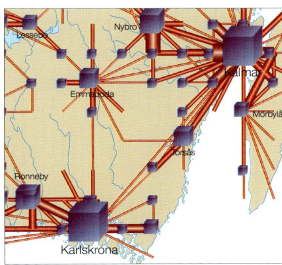
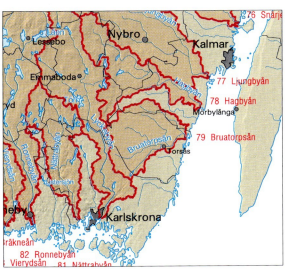

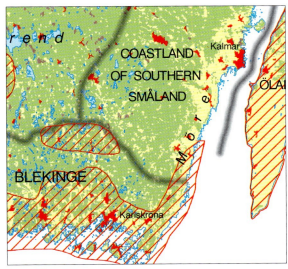

Kalmar–Karlskrona

This map extract comprises all or parts of the following municipalities: Ronneby and Karlskrona in the county of Blekinge, Emmaboda, Torsås, Nybro, Kalmar, Mörbylånga and Borgholm in the county of Kalmar and Tingsryd and Lessebo in the county of Kronoberg.

Until 1658 the southern tip of Öland was the southernmost point in Sweden and Kalmar was an important border fortress. Medieval Kalmar round the castle which was destroyed during the Kalmar War, 1611–1613, was to have been rebuilt with modern defences but was moved instead to Kvarnholmen, which became a powerful fortress. The Öland Bridge has helped tourism greatly, as well as allowing Öland to retain it population through commuting.

In the 1680s Karlskrona was built up as the forward Swedish naval base, while medieval Ronneby was stripped of its town charter, which was not restored until 1882. By then Ronneby Spa was an important source of income; today it is an important high-tech centre. The islands and coastline with their sparse vegetation, a belt of fertile farmland and forests to the north characterise Blekinge, whose climate encourages rich deciduous forest vegetation.

The coast south of Kalmar is a narrow plain of fertile till clay. On the other side of Kalmar Sound the coast of Öland is also well cultivated, but the centre of the island is a treeless limestone plateau of steppe vegetation, the Great Alvar, which is also bordered on the east by farmland and large linear villages.

In the forestland west of Kalmar the studio glass industry has made this district "the kingdom of glass", famous far beyond Sweden's borders. Some 20 glassworks and studios are still in operation, the oldest, Kosta, since 1742. Originally an ironworks district, a number of different manufacturing industries grew up here after the 1860s when the Iron Era had ended.

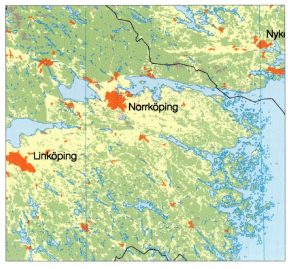
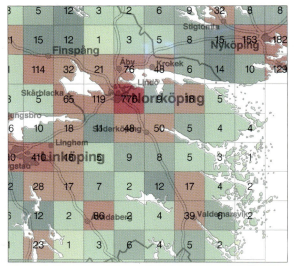
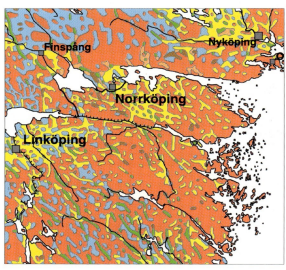
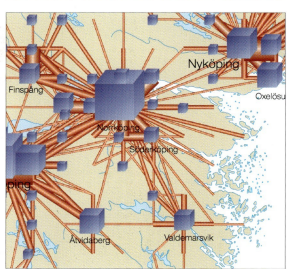

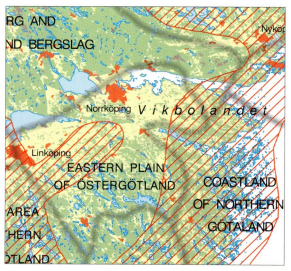

Linköping–Nyköping

This map extract comprises all or parts of the following municipalities: Linköping, Kinda, Finspång, Åtvidaberg, Valdemarsvik, Söderköping and Norrköping in the county of Östergötland and Katrineholm, Nyköping and Oxelösund in the county of Södermanland.

Linköping on the Stångån in the middle of the Östgöta Plain is the province's ancient centre, one of Sweden's medieval bishoprics and today a university town with important industries. East of Linköping the plain is more like a transitional district in a landscape of fissure valleys and a large archipelago. Norrköping, which stands on the Motala ström where it falls rapidly, was one of Sweden's most important industrial centres as early as the 17th century. Today its centre is a monument to the textile industry of the 19th century. In olden times Söderköping was the leading port and market town of eastern Östergötland, connected with the German Hansaeatic League but with roots going back to the Viking era. The town was protected by Stegeborg Castle at Slätbaken, one of Sweden's most powerful fortresses in the Middle Ages.

The forest districts to the north and south were dotted with old mill towns.

While the plain rises almost unnoticeably towards the forests in the south, there is a sharp boundary to the north. The towering fault scarps of Kolmården are particularly striking along the shore of Bråviken. At Vånga between Lakes Roxen and Glan two scarps meet at a sharp angle.

North of Kolmården stands the Södermanland lake plateau with its small villages and valleys. Nyköping is the province capital with a castle dating back to the Middle Ages. Its sister town Oxelösund has a very different character. Here, at the iron-ore terminal, at the terminus of the Grängesberg–Oxelösund railway, was built one of Sweden's largest ironworks. It was founded in 1913 but was greatly extended by the Gränges Group, using the money that the state paid in 1957 as compensation for the mining rights at Kiruna. The sheltered, ice-free harbour is expanding by opening ferry lines, for example.

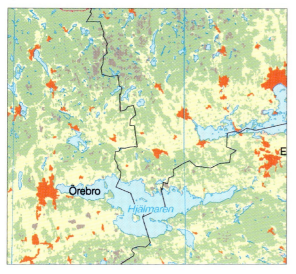
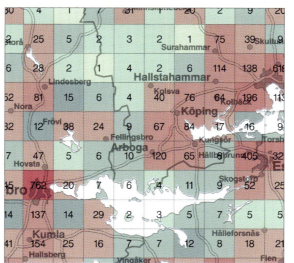

Västerås–Örebro

This map extract comprises all or parts of the following municipalities: Hallsberg, Kumla, Örebro, Nora, Lindesberg and Ljusnarsberg in the county of Örebro, Eskilstuna, Flen, Katrineholm and Vingåker in the county of Södermanland and Västerås, Sala, Fagersta, Surahammar, Hallstahammar, Kungsör, Arboga, Köping and Skinnskatteberg in the county of Västmanland.

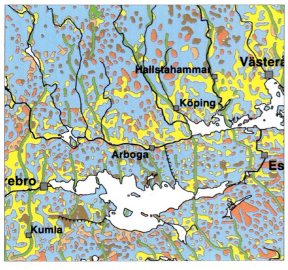
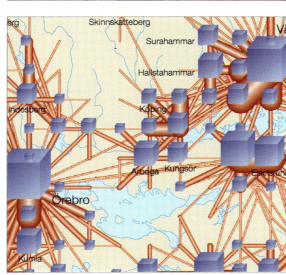

The map goes deep into the hills of Bergslagen with its mines and mill towns, its countless mine shafts and ruined mine buildings from the centuries of iron manufacturing which has now come to an end. It also contains some of Sweden's most important industrial towns today. A string of medieval towns round Lake Mälaren, Västerås, Köping, Arboga, like Torshälla, bear witness to the lake's ancient role as a transport route between Bergslagen, the farming districts and Stockholm. The Crown located vital iron and arms factories at Eskilstuna in the 17th century, which in the 19th century developed into various large industries.

In the Middle Ages Örebro grew to be the centre of the fertile Närke Plain and in the 17th and 18th centuries it became an important commercial centre for Bergslagen, at the same time as Nora and Lindesberg were flourishing. Its castle marks the town's historical importance. From 1830 onwards the Hjälmare Canal, dating back to 1640, provided an important shipping route to Stockholm until the railways were built.

Västerås was one of Sweden's most important towns and a bishopric even in the Middle Ages. ASEA, which moved there from Stockholm, has made Västerås world famous.

The water system of the Kolbäcksån, which penetrates the heart of Bergslagen, is lined with a large number of old mills and industrial towns, one of which is Ängelsberg, now on UNESCO's world heritage list as a complete, well-preserved ironworks.

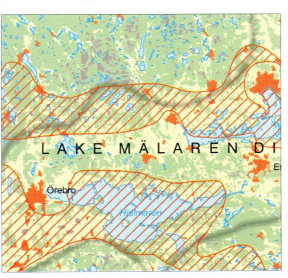

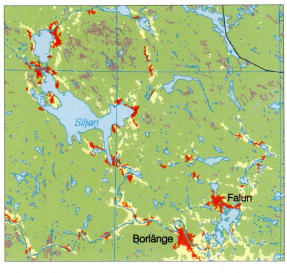
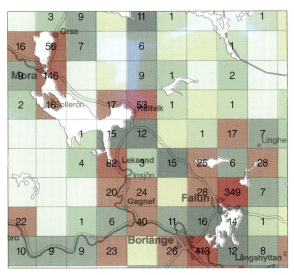
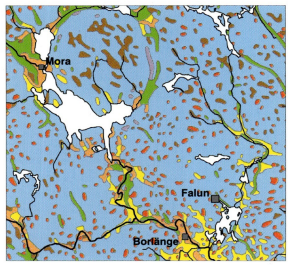
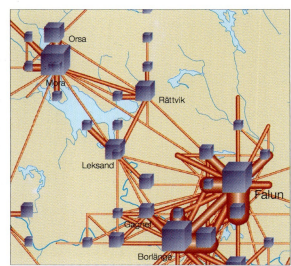

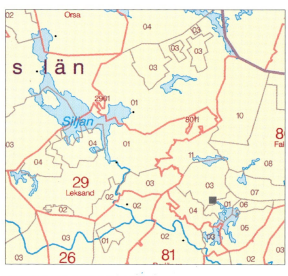

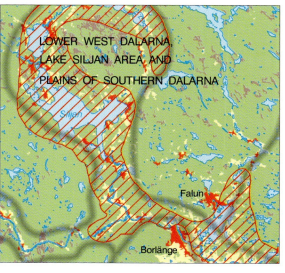

Borlänge–Mora

This map extract comprises all or parts of the following municipalities: Borlänge, Gagnef, Vansbro, Falun, Leksand, Mora, Orsa and Rättvik in the county of Kopparberg and Ovanåker in the county of Gävleborg.

This area includes one of Sweden's most distinctive cultural regions, the Siljan district and its perhaps most remarkable industrial monument, Kopparberget (the Copper Mine) at Falun.

The district round Lake Siljan, favoured by a lime-rich soil, is surrounded by forested high land about 300–600 m above sea level. The lake is one part of the Siljan Ring, which was formed by one of the greatest meteorites known to have struck the earth.

The large clustered villages round Siljan and on fluvial sediment, several of which have become modern towns with small industries and tourism as their sources of income, were formed from smaller settlements which were the result of dividing farm properties over several generations.

The livelihood of the small farms was maintained by migrant workers, local handicrafts and other part-time industries. Today the main sources of income are forestry and tourism. One special feature of farming was the shealing system. Every possible spot in the forests round the villages was utilised as a summer pasture with a croft. Some of these crofts still function, but most of them are now second homes.

At Stora Tuna the river valley broadens out into a wide plain. After the railways had come and Domnarvet Ironworks and Kvarnsveden Papermill had been built in the late 19th century, urban areas grew up which were united in 1944 to form the town of Borlänge.

Falun, too, has an industrial origin — but it is 700 years older. Copper may have been mined there as early as the Viking era, but during the Middle Ages a mining company developed there. The oldest known share certificate for the mine is dated 1288. This was the evidence when STORA celebrated its 700th anniversary as the oldest existing company in the world. The mine had its heyday in the 17th century, when it was the backbone of Sweden's economy. Mining ceased for good in 1992. Falun is a county town, a garrison town, and a centre for skiing and tourism.

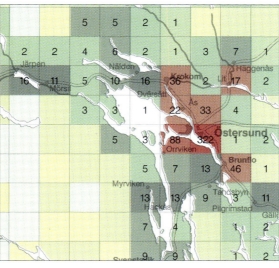
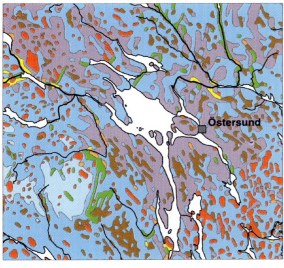
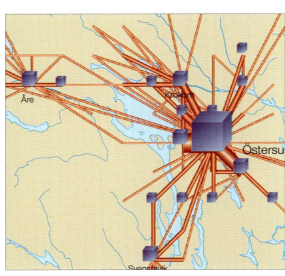
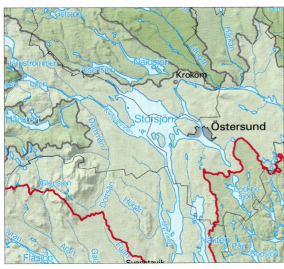
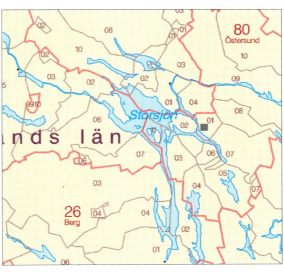

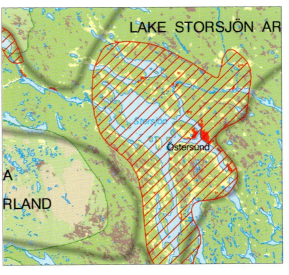

Östersund–Järpen

This map extract comprises all or parts of the following municipalities: Berg, Bräcke, Åre, Östersund and Krokom in the county of Jämtland.

Calcareous soil from underlying cambrosilurian bedrock is the basis of a rich farming district dating back to prehistoric and medieval times. The centre of this district was Frösön in Lake Storsjön. Round this district there is a sparsely populated forest region and to the west the mountain chain, visible from Frösön.

The main county town, Östersund, is a young town, founded in the late 18th century. It developed more rapidly after the railway arrived in 1879. With its population of about 50,000 it is the central place for an area as large as Switzerland. People needing special services such as a hospital may have to travel up to 200 km to get there. In winter many people's journeys are shortened by driving across the frozen Lake Storsjön.

Svenstavik is the centre of the municipality of Berg that stretches all the way up to the Norwegian border at Sylarna. West of Svenstavik there are a number of shealings still in use. This is also the beginning of the reindeer grazing grounds belonging to the Lapp villages further west.

The railway running along the valley of the Indalsälv to Storlien opened up the mountains in the 1880s for large-scale recreation and tourism. This river valley is the ancient route between the former Norwegian Jämtland and Trondheim; old forts still standing at Järpen and Mörsil are a reminder of its importance.

A large number of ancient remains including trapping pit systems and rock paintings, well-preserved old farming settlements on high ground, many areas of natural beauty value and rich animal life are all found in the Krokom district north of Storsjön.

The water power of the Indalsälven has been exploited in a series of hydro-electric power stations.

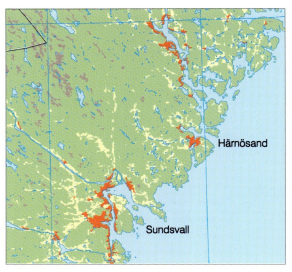
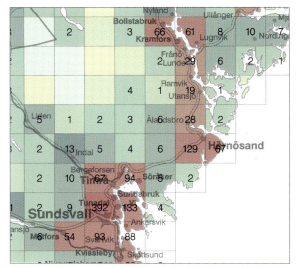
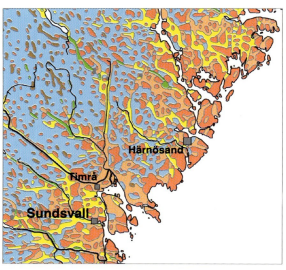
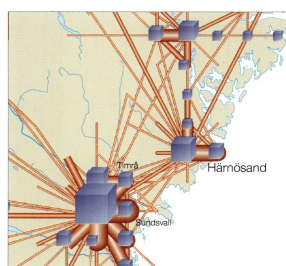

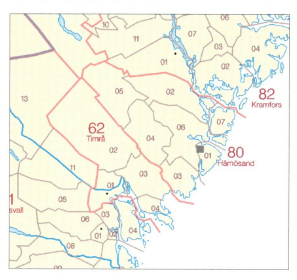

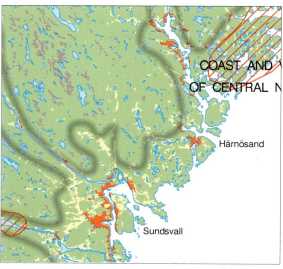

Sundsvall–Kramfors

This map extract comprises all or parts of the following municipalities: Sundsvall, Timrå, Härnösand, Kramfors and Sollefteå in the county of Västernorrland and Ragunda in the county of Jämtland.

In the coastal strip below the highest shoreline there are scattered farming communities of great age, but it is industry that has set its mark on this region. Two of Sweden's largest and most traditional forest industry regions, the Sundsvall district and Ådalen, lie within the area, but it also has one of the country's most beautiful landscapes, the Nordingrå district, often called the High Coast.

Sundsvall has been a commercial centre since the 17th century.

From the mid–19th century onwards the world's largest forest industry district grew up round Alnösundet, with steam-powered sawmills as its distinctive feature. Its location between the mouths of two great rivers running down from the forests provided the best possible conditions for success. After 1900 paper and pulp processing industries gradually began to develop. Rationalisation in the sawmills resulted in many small mills having to close down. Today Tunadal is the only sawmill still in operation.

Härnösand dates back to the Middle Ages and was in the 17th century the administrative and cultural centre of upper Norrland, with a high school founded in 1648.

The first sawmill at Kramfors on the Ångermanälven was built as early as the middle of the 18th century, but after 1852 steam-powered sawmills were the basis of a large forest industry district along the river, just as they were at Alnösundet. Sandslån, upstream from Kramfors, had until 1982 the largest timber sorting terminal in the world. A large new suspension bridge, closer to the mouth of the river, is to be built as a complement to the Sandö Bridge, with the longest span in Sweden, downstream from Kramfors.

Along the coast a number of small fishing villages with cottages from the 17th century are a reminder of the time when the citizens of Gävle to the south used to fish off the coast of Norrland.

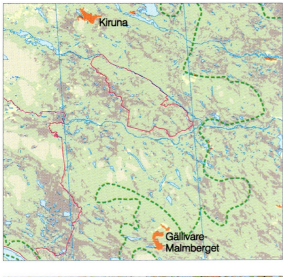
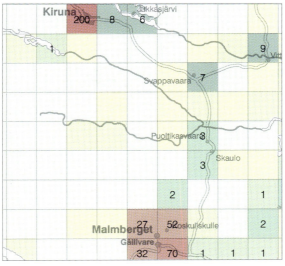

Gällivare–Kiruna

This map extract comprises parts of the municipalities of Gällivare and Kiruna.

This area lies at the foot of the Lappland mountains, and is ancient reindeer grazing ground. The mining industry here has created sizeable urban areas in the wilderness, surrounded on all sides by vast, almost uninhabited expanses of sparse forest, mires and mountains. Sjaunja, west of Gällivare, is reckoned to be the largest mire system in Europe.

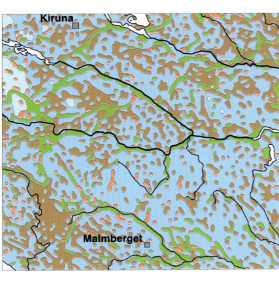
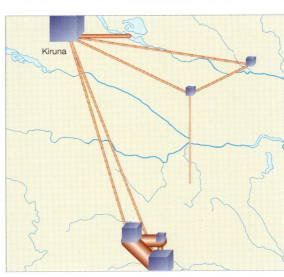

Gällivare has had a law court and a church since the mid-18th century. Deposits of iron ore were known to exist there in the 17th century but could not be exploited until the railway from Luleå was completed in 1888. Malmberget grew up alongside the mine, initially as a shanty town and then, since the beginning of the 20th century, as a planned urban district. Much of central Malmberget, including the school and the church, had to be demolished in the 1970s owing to the risk of subsidence when it was decided to continue to mine the Captain's seam of ore, which runs below the town centre. To the east of Malmberget lies the mining village of Koskullskulle.

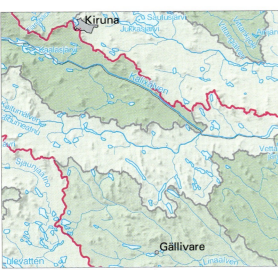
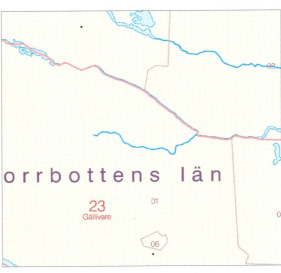

Kiruna, 140 km north of the Arctic Circle, is the child of the mining industry at Kirunavaara and Luossavaara, the site of one of the world's largest deposits of ore with a very rich content of iron. Mining and the township came into being when the railway arrived in 1902. Kiruna was planned and built as a model community with its own special character.

Iron ore has been mined at Svappavaara at various times, but today the main industry is a pellet works.

Rationalisation in the mining industry as well as international competition is a threat to employment here. Large investments have been made to give Kiruna a new future. The establishment of the space rocket base at Esrange north of Kiruna led to a number of high-tech industries in the Space House there, including METRIA, which produces the maps for the National Atlas.

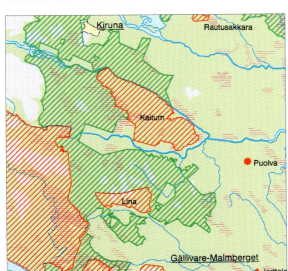
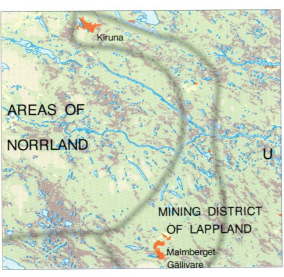

The church village of Jukkasjärvi, with its early 17th-century church, local arts-and-crafts museum and inn, has become a centre for tourism.

The rivers have not been exploited for hydro-electric power.

DISTRIBUTION OF CULTIVATION
1:10 000 000

- More than 2/3 of the land is cultivated
- 1/3–2/3 of the land is cultivated
- Less than 1/3 of the land is cultivated
- No arable land
- Alpine areas

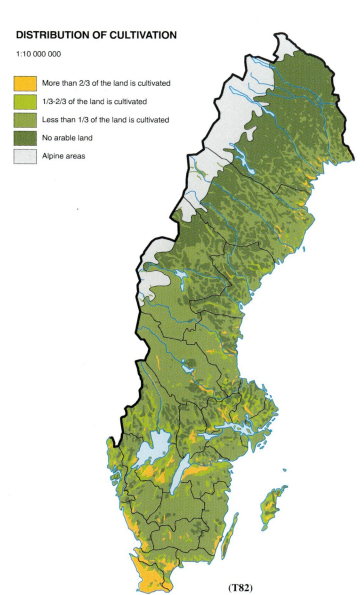

(T82)

The Cultivated Landscape

Ever since C-J Anrick carried out a detailed survey of Sweden's arable land in 1918–1921, the degree of cultivation has been used as a means of classifying the cultivated landscape. The map, taken from "Atlas of Sweden", shows four classes of cultivation. Extracts from the economic map illustrate different types of agricultural districts.

The most distinctive agricultural districts appear as scattered "islands" in a sea of forests. Large areas of uninhabited land, "wilderness", cover a third of Sweden. The uninhabited districts in Dalarna lie only 200–300 km from the urban areas of Mälardalen.

TRANSFORMATION OF THE AGRICULTURAL LANDSCAPE

— Meadows + Fields
– – Total area of fields
- - - Pasture

Changes in land use in agriculture in the 20th century have greatly affected the cultural landscape.

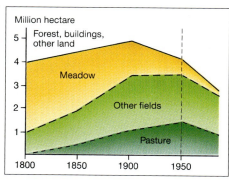

In southern and central Swedish forest districts the cultivated land is in the form of scattered clearings in the forest; there are few large fields here. Åtvidaberg in southern Östergötland.

There is often a high level of cultivation, about 50 per cent, with fields lying close together, in the clay-filled fissured landscape of central Sweden. Vikbolandet in eastern Östergötland.

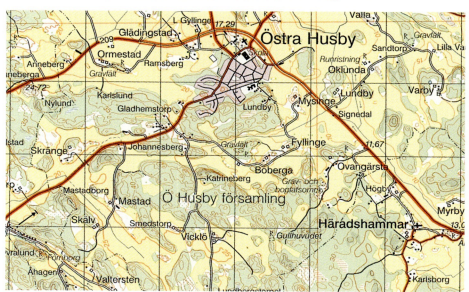

In the farming districts on the plains, characterised by their large fields, all land except that used for roads and housing has been ploughed up. All obstacles to cultivation in the fields have been cleared and all drainage is piped. An extract from *The Green Map* showing Österlen.

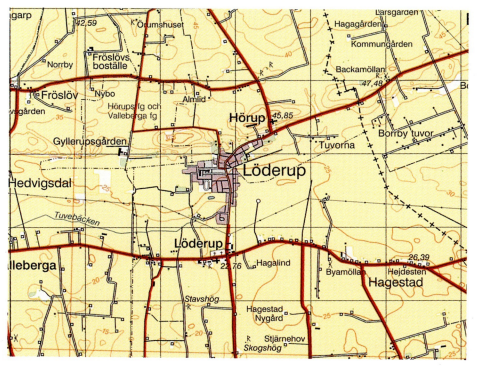

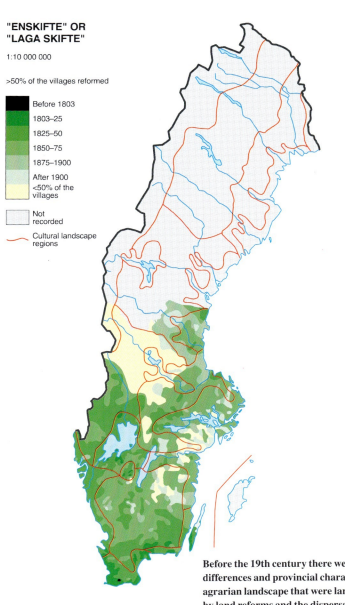

"ENSKIFTE" OR "LAGA SKIFTE"
1:10 000 000

>50% of the villages reformed
- Before 1803
- 1803–25
- 1825–50
- 1850–75
- 1875–1900
- After 1900
- <50% of the villages
- Not recorded
- Cultural landscape regions

Before the 19th century there were clear regional differences and provincial characteristics in the agrarian landscape that were largely obliterated by land reforms and the dispersal of villages. Some 20 regions could be distinguished. (T83)

In central Sweden the old settlements stand in small clusters on dry slopes, built on the clay sediment or at the edge of a forest facing south. Lids-Örsta in Södermanland.

The southern Swedish plains are scattered with isolated farms and the remains of villages, some of which have become urban areas. The plain at Hammenhög, Österlen.

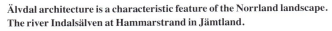

Älvdal architecture is a characteristic feature of the Norrland landscape. The river Indalsälven at Hammarstrand in Jämtland.

THE OLD AGRARIAN LANDSCAPE AND LAND REFORM

The traditional village landscape which was broken up by the land reforms of the 18th and 19th centuries had regional differences which had evolved during a thousand years of social development. The most uniform region was eastern Sweden, with its *solskifte* (solar) system, its geometrically arranged linear villages dating back to the Middle Ages and its farms with their two-field rotation system. The largest villages were in the three-field districts of Skåne and Västergötland and on Öland. The forest districts had the most scattered settlements. The villages in the north, round Lakes Siljan and Storsjön and in the river valleys, were less closely related and often the result of the division of isolated farms. Regional differences were also evident in building techniques and materials as well as in the arrangement of the farm buildings.

Inspired by Denmark, Rutger Maclean, the owner of the Svaneholm Estate in Skåne, carried out a radical land reform in the 1780s, which led to a major transformation of the Swedish rural landscape. The mixed ownership and closely-knit communities of the villages were broken up by legislation in 1803 and 1827. Countless farms were moved to amalgamated land; meadow and pasture land was cultivated, and the forestland was divided up so that all that was left in the villages were a few farms, the church and the school, where it was not possible to use the "pie" system of division. These reforms were carried out in stages over a period of one hundred years.

LOWERED AND RECLAIMED LAKES

drained to gain or improve arable land

1:10 000 000

- Lowered
- Reclaimed

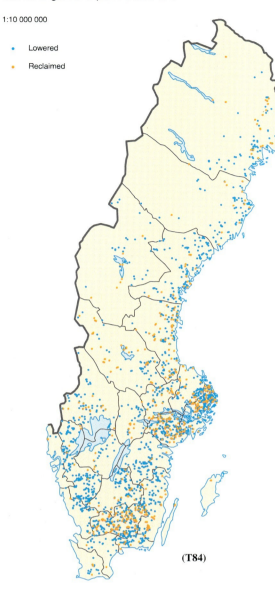

(T84)

DRAINAGE AND IRRIGATION

During the 19th century in particular lakes and rivers were greatly altered in order to increase the area of productive land. In settlements on and round the plains of southern and central Sweden innumerable lakes were drained, often with little effect because of the state of the lake bottoms and the groundwater level. The largest single operation was the complete draining of Lake Kvismaren in Närke. The drainage of Hornborgasjön, Tåkern and Angarnsjön was successful, as new bird lakes were created. The draining of wetlands in southern Sweden led to the disappearance of the stork.

There are still traces in the interior of Norrland of the intricate network of canals built to flood meadows that could thereby treble their harvest.

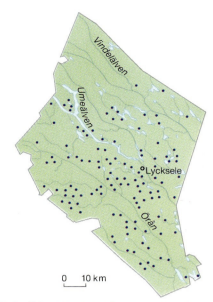

In the 19th century more flooding systems for sedge cultivation were built in Lycksele than in any other parish. (T85)

Irrigation system on part of Hemnäset on the Öreälven in Ångermanland. The flow of water from the river Fehusvallsbäcken to channels was regulated by sluice gates.

Since cultivation ceased in the forest districts in the 1960s–1980s some of the old farmhouses have been used as second homes, while other people still live there permanently if there is work within commuting distance. This example is from southern Närke in 1948 and 1981.

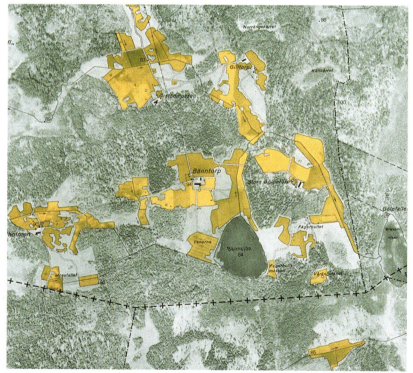
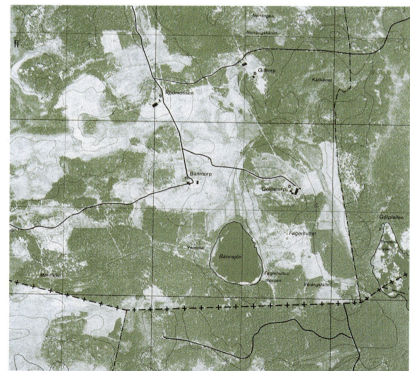

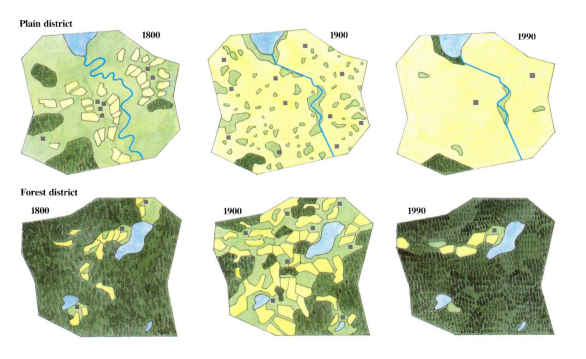

Plain district 1800 1900 1990

Forest district 1800 1900 1990

The cultivated landscape expanded as new areas came under cultivation during the centuries. In the 19th century the amount of arable land increased at the expense of meadowland. During the late 20th century more intensive farming methods were introduced on the plains, where all obstacles to large-scale cultivation were removed. In contrast the scattered fields of the forest districts have been abandoned, becoming forest once again.

EFFECTS OF MODERN AGRICULTURE

If the growth of population in the 19th century resulted in the expansion of cultivated land into poorer soils, drainage and irrigation, the effects of modern agriculture are connected with intensifying production in a shrinking acreage. On the one hand the size of fields on the farms in the plains has increased, and obstacles such as ditches, boulders, wooded "islands" and marl pits have been removed to allow the full use of agricultural machinery. On the other hand increased use of artificial fertilisers, herbicides and pesticides has affected nature's metabolism.

Increased farm productivity on the plains combined with a national surplus in agriculture is forcing farms in districts with poorer conditions to close down. Overgrown fields are a characteristic sight in both forest and transitional districts.

The requirements of agricultural machinery have created modern, effectively worked areas in the form of large, open fields. Krageholm in Skåne.

Nitrogen circulation in modern agriculture, and its implications for the environment. The figures show kilos of nitrogen per hectare for one year.

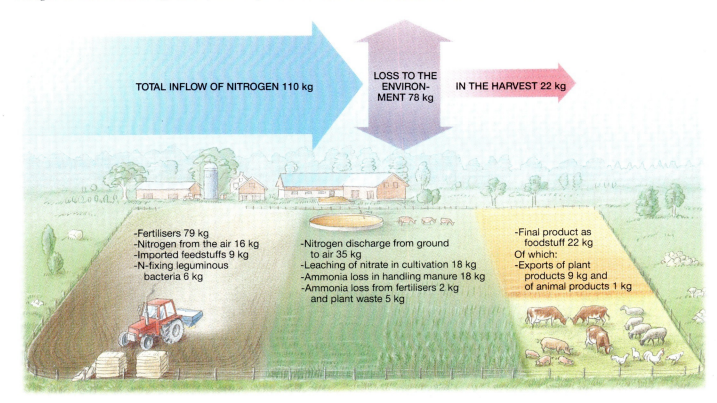

TOTAL INFLOW OF NITROGEN 110 kg — LOSS TO THE ENVIRONMENT 78 kg — IN THE HARVEST 22 kg

- Fertilisers 79 kg
- Nitrogen from the air 16 kg
- Imported feedstuffs 9 kg
- N-fixing leguminous bacteria 6 kg

- Nitrogen discharge from ground to air 35 kg
- Leaching of nitrate in cultivation 18 kg
- Ammonia loss in handling manure 18 kg
- Ammonia loss from fertilisers 2 kg and plant waste 5 kg

- Final product as foodstuff 22 kg
Of which:
- Exports of plant products 9 kg and of animal products 1 kg

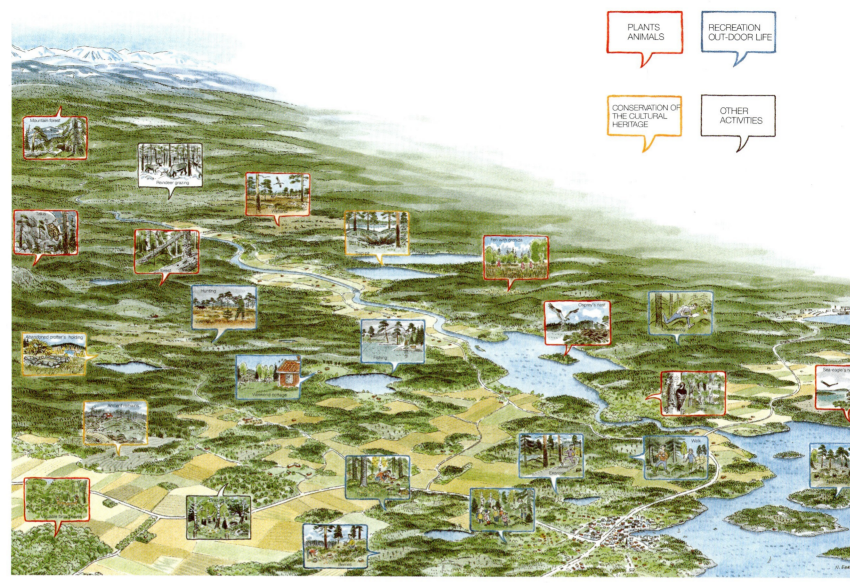

Forests are not just trees...

The Forest Landscape

Most of Sweden lies within the coniferous forest belt round the polar region; 65 per cent of its area is reckoned to be forestland, although there are open stretches of peatbogs, mires and bare rock. Only a small part of the forestland is still natural forest, most of it close to the mountains and in wetlands. The rest is plantations or self-sown secondary forests characterised by silviculture and uniform stands of even-age class. During the period 1950–1980 large-scale, mechanised forestry methods were developed, involving clear-cutting, soil scarification, drainage and the use of artificial fertilisers. These methods have considerably increased productivity. Of all the forestland in Sweden only 32 per cent lies less than 500 m from a forest road.

At the same time the forests are

CLEAR-FELLED AREAS IN JÄMTLAND AND VÄSTER-NORRLAND

1:200 000

- Clear-felled areas
- Young forest
- Medium-aged and old forest
- Other areas

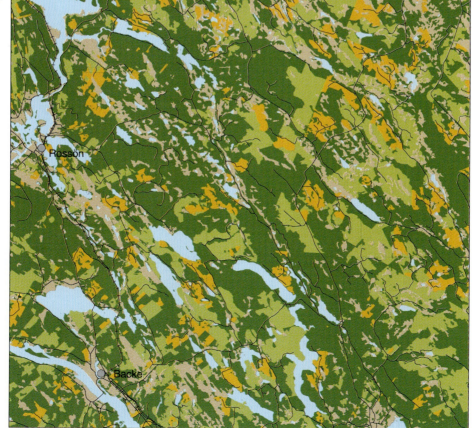

Extract from the Vegetation Map of Fjällsjö 20G NO, on the border between Jämtland and Västernorrland County; 10 per cent of the area is clear-cut and young forest (2–10 m tall trees), 23 per cent of the total area of coniferous forest (1993). (T86)

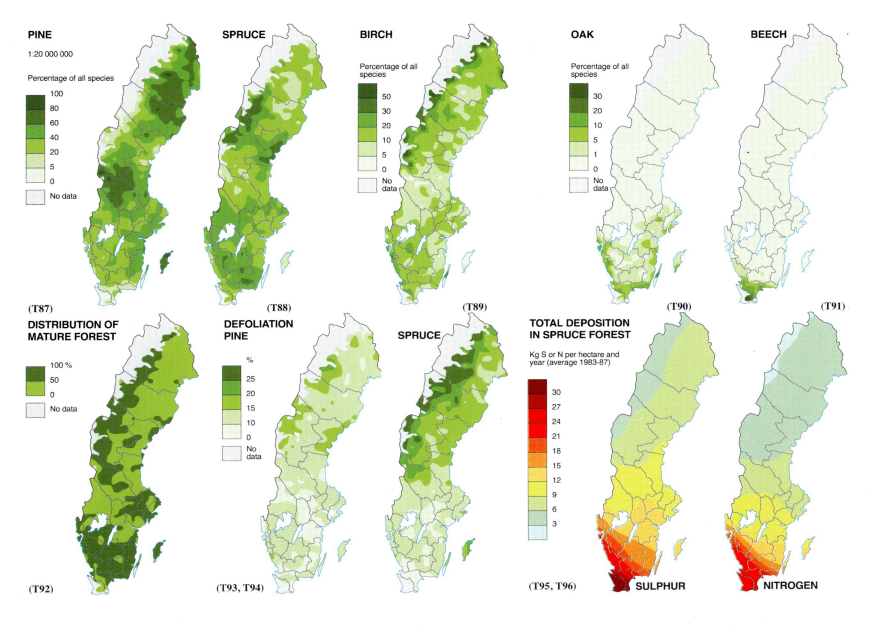

our main recreational environment, as well as producing plenty of wild berries and edible fungi. So it was quite natural that modern forestry techniques aroused many protests, which led to less harmful methods being used in the 1990s.

In olden times the forests of southern and central Sweden were seriously affected by slash-and-burn farming, wood-cutting for ironworks, the production of charcoal and tar, and cattle grazing. The first sawmills cut deep into the forests of northern Sweden until silviculture and reforestation were introduced.

Nature conservation takes care of the biologically most valuable forest areas, which are often unproductive from a forestry point of view. National parks, nature reserves and other legal protection provide long-term protection for about 6 per cent of Sweden's land.

VARIATIONS IN THE FOREST LANDSCAPE

Swedish forests are comparatively poor in species, and modern forestry methods are reducing the variety of species and biotopes.

Spruce, one of the most widespread tree species on earth, flourishes on bedrock till and in snowy climates. It stands shade and requires moist conditions. Generally speaking pine grows on drier soil, sandy ridges and heaths. It requires plenty of light. Sweden's third most common forest tree, birch, is the first tree to establish itself on clear-felled areas and after forest fires. It forms forests above all in a zone above the coniferous forest line.

Forest environments can also be changed locally and regionally by the introduction of foreign tree species. Contorta pine in southern Norrland is an example of this.

The vegetation of the forest ecosystem has a rich variety of fungi and berries which anyone is free to pick.

Nemoral forests of beech, oak, ash, elm and the like are found only in southern Sweden and offer the biologically richest forest environments. Without forming forests deciduous trees also play an important role in the landscape of all the agricultural districts of southern Sweden.

FOREST DAMAGE

The effects of acid rain on lakes and the land were discovered in Sweden in the 1960s. The most serious effects on the forest ecosystem come from the sulphur fallout in rain and snow, which increases the natural acidification process in the most common types of Swedish forestland. Sulphur fallout has so far functioned as a fertiliser, but can reach a critical level which hastens acidification. Calcareous soils are affected least.

Most of the pollution is carried into Sweden on southerly winds. Since the early 1980s studies have been made of its effect on the crowns of spruce and pine, the most evident sign of a serious disturbance in the ecosystem. The same phenomenon had been observed in Central Europe, where whole mountain forests had been destroyed. So far we have no clear explanation of the mechanisms that damage tree crowns and destroy forests.

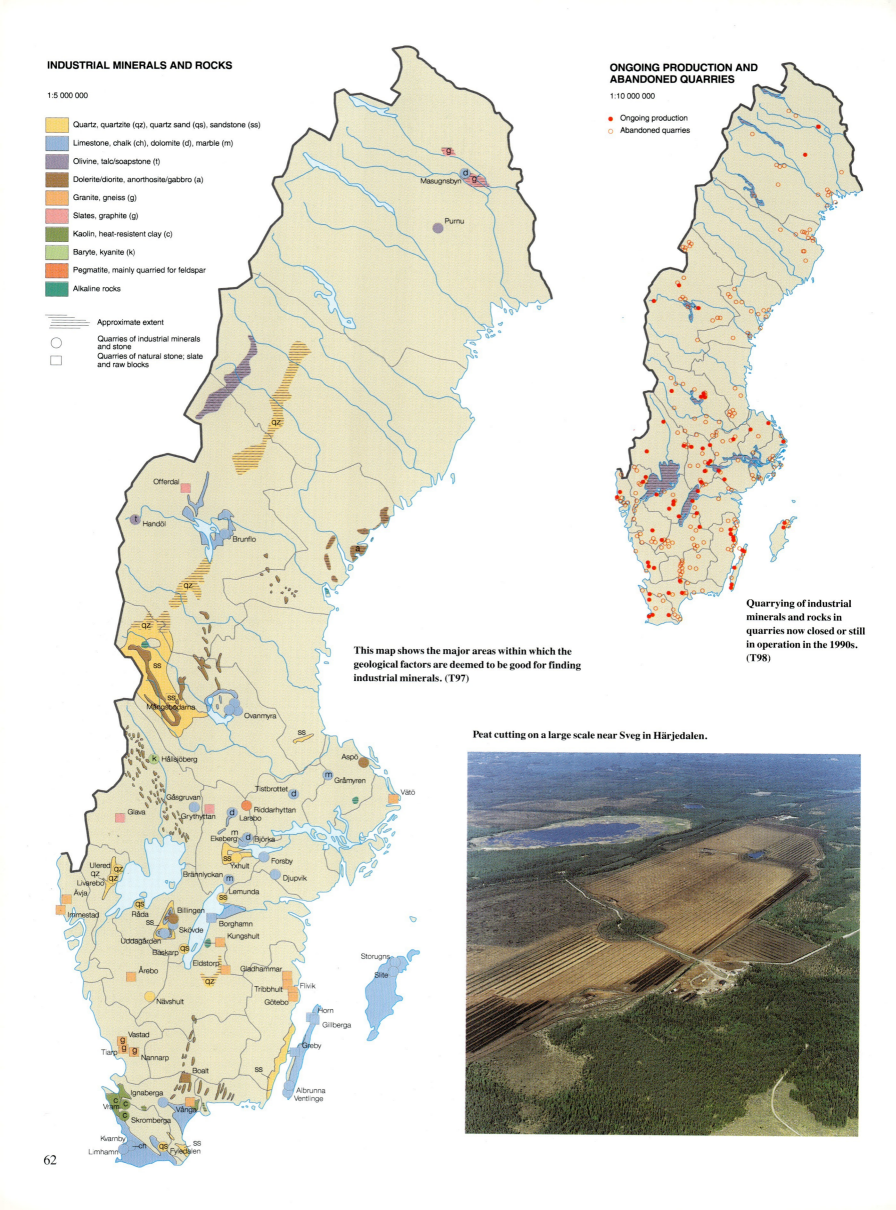

ENERGY PEAT

1:10 000 000

Area of production, hectares

- 250–
- 100–250
- –100

Fifteen per cent of the land is covered by layers of peat at least 0.5 m thick. (T99)

Mines and quarries are dramatic features in the landscape. Stone quarry at Åstorp in Skåne.

Iron ore was mined at Dannemora in Uppland until 1992.

Quarries and Mines

The extraction of ore and minerals, as well as of peat, gravel and soil, has considerable local effects on the landscape and the environment. In regions where there are rich deposits of useful material the cultural landscape may be characterised by these activities, which used to be carried on in numerous places throughout Sweden. Competition from other countries and other materials, however, has limited production to a few places today. Only three of Bergslagen's hundreds of mines are in operation; countless quarries for various kinds of stone are today nothing but open wounds in the landscape. Protection of the eskers has reduced the number of gravel pits and peat is extracted when it is difficult to import fossil fuels.

Ore has been mined in Bergslagen since the early Middle Ages; copper may have been mined at Falun even in the Iron Age. But the last mine closed down in 1992, the same year as the closure of the mine at Dannemora, after operating for 500 years. Like the silver mine at Sala which was closed down in 1962, both are internationally important historical attractions. Since 1890 400 ore mines have been in operation, leaving ineradicable marks in the landscape: mine shafts, slag heaps and ponds, as well as numerous historical buildings. Långban in Värmland has become a mecca for mineral collectors from many countries. The active mine landscapes are now restricted to Lappland and the Skellefteå district.

The extraction of industrial minerals and stone leaves holes and precipices in the terrain as well as piles of broken rock. A small part of Sweden's deposits have been exploited.

Clay is usually extracted at shallow depths over large areas, which are later covered by vegetation. It is equally easy to conceal the marks left by extracting soil from land close to large towns.

Peat is extracted by machines over large areas in various parts of Sweden, often in places out of sight of habitation or roads. The very extensive gravel pits in eskers and other sand deposits from the glacial period have serious effects on the landscape. Strong demand has led to increased production of macadam, particularly round large towns. Annual production of gravel and macadam amounts to some 11 tonnes per capita in Sweden.

Any mining or quarrying involves responsibility for restoring the landscape when extraction is completed.

INDUSTRIAL AREAS, 1960
1:10 000 000

- Mining, metals
- Wood, pulp, paper
- Joinery
- Textiles
- Leather
- Small-scale industry
- Glassware
- Fishery
- Other

(T100)

INDUSTRIAL REGIONS ACCORDING TO WILLIAM-OLSSON

Some of the characteristic industrial regions that William William-Olsson was able to survey in the 1940s and 1950s have been completely wiped out and others have lost their character or been transformed. The shoe, textile and steel industries and mining are examples of this. But the observant traveller will see everywhere traces of the old industrial regions in buildings and plant, either dilapidated or put to new uses.

A heavy concentration of high-tech industry looks more or less like an office district. Kista just north of Stockholm.

Old industry was dependent on a nearby source of energy. Trollhättan before 1900.

The Industrial Landscape

The transformation of the countryside when villages were dissolved and new production systems introduced, obliterating much of the old cultural landscape, was still in progress when industrialisation accelerated with the building of the railways in the second half of the 19th century. New industrial regions grew up on the basis of old craft traditions and proto-industrial activities, leaving their mark on various parts of Sweden. The old mill communities were important sites for the growth of the new industries in southern and central Sweden.

Rapids and waterfalls, river estuaries, ports and railway junctions were attractive places for all kinds of industrial activities. The buildings and plants were organised according to the needs of the industries, often acquiring a typical appearance. Where there was a specially good potential for a particular industry, large groups of uniformly designed industrial buildings grew up.

As late as the mid-20th century these industrial regions stood out as characteristic features of Sweden's economic geography and landscape. The "Second Industrial Revolution" that got going in the latter half of the 20th century has in the space of a few decades wiped out much of this cultural landscape. Motor transport and motorways, effective energy-distribution systems, computerisation, large-scale warehousing and processing, the closing down of service points and railway stations, the total mechanisation and robotisation of work processes — these are but a few of the factors of change. Modern high-tech industry and services are hardly noticeable. They operate to a large extent in buildings that might just as well be office or apartment blocks.

But out in the landscape the old industrial buildings and plants are still standing with their characteristic silhouettes, as ruins or historical monuments, or rebuilt for new functions, if they have not been demolished to make rooms for new developments.

Unlike the coal-mining countries, where the coalfields became the centres of industrial regions, Sweden developed industries scattered among a large number of small towns. It was common for towns to be dominated by one large factory. The reconstruction of industry for large-scale production has devastated many of these

small, one-sided industrial towns. The redistribution of employment from old, stagnant industries in small towns to modern, research-oriented, growth industries typically located close to large towns has led to stagnation and depopulation in the traditional industrial regions. Rationalisation of the railway system, with fewer stations outside the large towns, has led to the decline of many railway towns.

RURAL AREAS DEVELOP INTO INDUSTRIAL LANDSCAPE

From Skellefteå to Skelleftehamn/Rönnskär the countryside along the lower reaches of the River Skellefteälven is characterised by intensive industrial activity. For northern Sweden there is an unusual conglomeration here of medium-large and large industries, mainly in the metal and engineering branches. It started with timber, when in 1860 steam-powered saws were built at the mouth of the river, and when the 15-year-old town of Skellefteå still only had 347 inhabitants. The pulp and paper industry came later. Large-scale industry started with mining at Boliden in 1926, and Boliden smelter was built at Rönnskär. Metal processing led to a wider range of industries being established during several decades of rapid population increase up to about 1970. This industrial development is illustrated by the two editions of the Economic map from 1958 and 1984. (The original scale of 1:10,000 has been reduced by 50%.)

The Transport Landscape

THE ROAD NETWORK

The road network is 415,000 km long and consists of state roads, municipal roads and private roads. There are more than 15,000 bridges and 49 ferries in this network. More than 70 per cent of the state roads are tarmacked. The road network has spread across the densely-populated parts of the country and has been improved and differentiated for local and long-distance traffic and light and heavy traffic. In recent decades extensive road networks have been built to provide access to natural resources. Apart from the public roads there is today a private forest-road network of about 200,000 km.

These roads coincide with most of the road network that existed at the end of the 17th century and had by then been well adapted to horse-drawn traffic. Since then routes have been adjusted in countless places to eliminate bends, hillcrests and other obstacles to high speed and accessibility. That is why there are innumerable old stretches of road preserved round the present network. Just south of Stockholm, for example, it is possible to see the remains of half a dozen stretches of the old road to the south, ranging from medieval bridle paths to cleared 17th-century coach roads and later A-class roads right up to the latest stretch of the E4 European highway.

The old road network ran directly into the town streets, but since twenty years or so ago the main roads have bypassed towns or been rerouted to avoid towns, with cloverleaf junctions to facilitate long-distance traffic. At the same time a new road landscape has been created, with service stations for long-distance drivers, goods terminals for lorries and central warehouses alongside main roads.

THE RAILWAY NETWORK

When the 1853–1854 Riksdag voted to allow the state to build a network of main railway lines in Sweden, a transport revolution began that made a permanent impression on the country's geography. The main lines were intentionally placed inland where the population was sparse and there were no waterways. The superiority of the railways for transportation quickly attracted industries and people to the railway stations, especially the junctions. Railway communities with

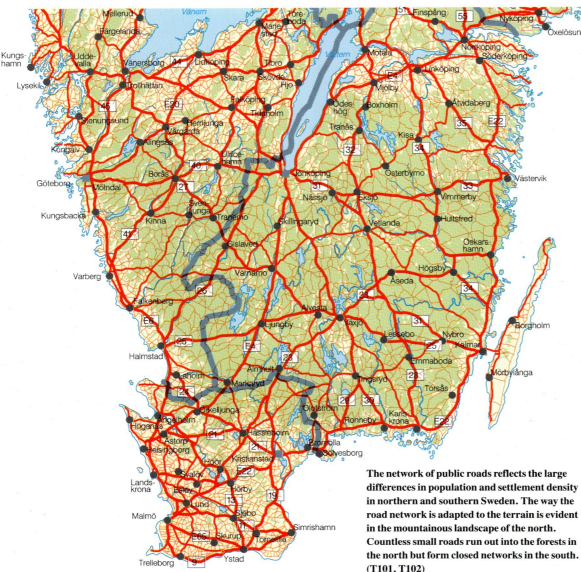

The network of public roads reflects the large differences in population and settlement density in northern and southern Sweden. The way the road network is adapted to the terrain is evident in the mountainous landscape of the north. Countless small roads run out into the forests in the north but form closed networks in the south. (T101, T102)

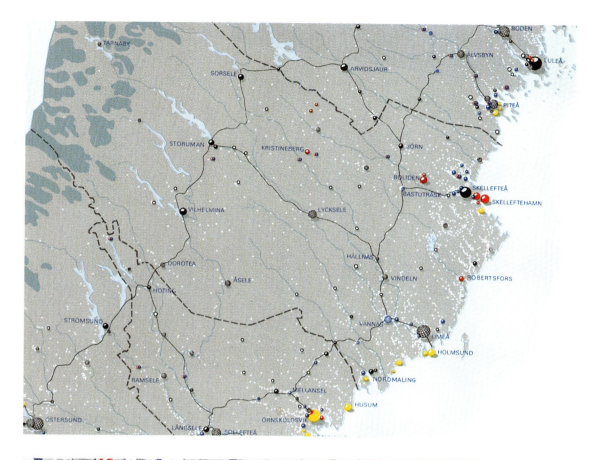

stations and shunting yards that corresponded to the importance of the place — many became towns — were the contribution the railway epoch made to Sweden's place system.

In less than 50 years southern and central Sweden had a dense railway network, while in the north construction continued for another 50 years.

In contrast to the state railways private railways were built where there was already a need for transport. In 1938 the total network reached its peak length of 16,900 km. In 1939 it was decided to nationalise all important private railways.

After the Second World War competition from cars and aeroplanes forced the closure of stretch after stretch of the railway network, but above all there was a great reduction in the number of halts. What remained were countless small railway towns whose raison d'etre had disappeared and 9,700 km of railway track in operation.

INLAND WATERWAYS

At the beginning of the 19th century, after heroic efforts, a dream was realised, a dream that Gustav Vasa had also had, to build a canal across Sweden — the Göta Canal. Its purpose was originally to avoid the Sound, which was then under Danish control. Other canals were built to meet the growing need for transport between Bergslagen and the Baltic. But the canal era was a short one. Before they had covered their costs they were driven out of business by the railways.

PORTS AND AIRPORTS

Shipping and airport terminals are locally dominant features of the landscape. During industrialisation ports grew in both size and number, some with equipment for various types of goods, others very specialised. The rationalisation of shipping by using ro-ro vessels has reduced the need for quayside space and concentrated operations in fewer ports.

In contrast airports have continued to grow in the 1990s, both in size and number. The role airports are expected to play in local economic growth explains the municipalities' inability to agree on co-operative solutions.

Like the road network, the railway network differs from north to south. In southern Sweden the railways created chains of urban communities. In the north important railway junctions became new towns. From the Economic Map of Sweden by William William-Olsson, 1960. (T103, T104)

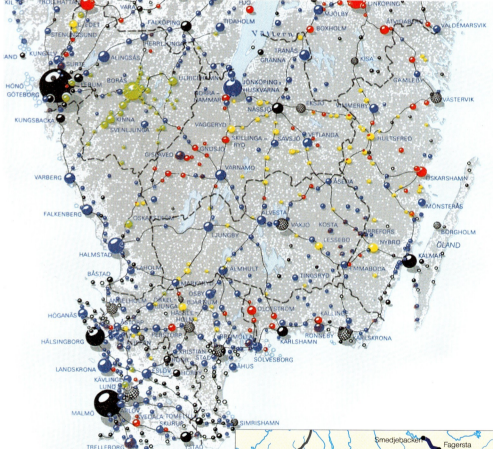

In the forest and iron-mining communities of central Sweden canals were the transport routes of the 19th century. Today only Trollhätte Canal and Södertälje Canal operate commercial traffic, while tourism keeps the other canals alive. (T105)

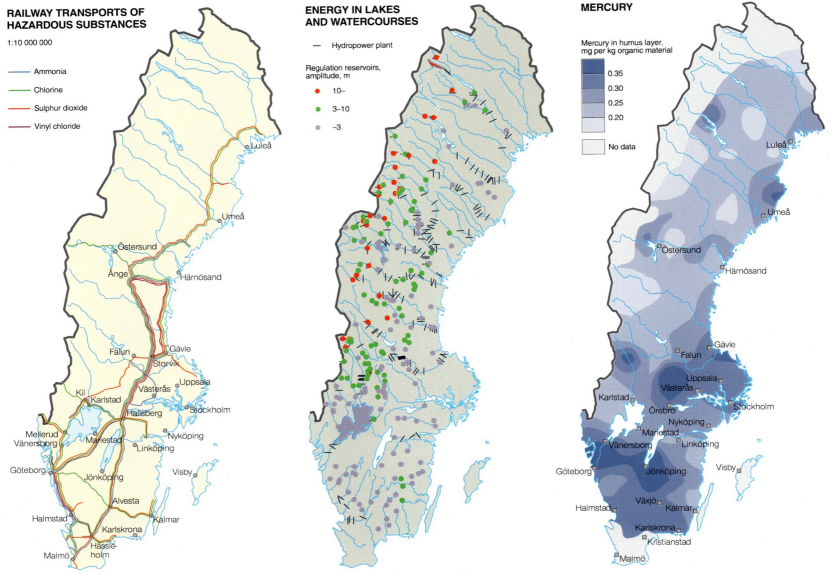

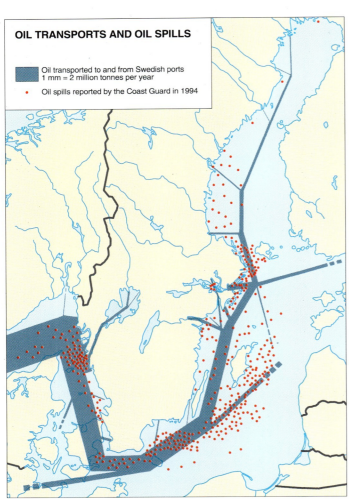

Condensed gases like ammonia, chlorine, sulphur dioxide and vinyl chloride are mostly transported by rail. (T106)

Exploiting rivers for hydro-electric power transforms the landscape, creating reservoirs and destroying rapids and waterfalls. (T107)

Every year millions of tons of oil are shipped in Swedish coastal waters. Oil discharges during 1994 were calculated by the Coast Guards to be 400m³, from 415 identified sources. (T109)

It is usually possible to trace the sources of mercury effluents. The levels today are mainly the aftermath of old emissions. (T108)

Environmental Problems

The attitude early industrialism had towards natural resources and systems was often naive. The interplay and balance between life-sustaining systems were often poorly understood and to begin with mankind's intrusion on them was very limited. Growing exploitation of raw materials and energy, increasing disruptions of the natural systems and more and more pollution of land, air and water with solid, gaseous or liquid waste made the dangers evident. After about 1955 a debate arose in the US which, by the end of the century, had placed environmental issues at the centre of social debate in many parts of the world. Sweden is one of the countries that identified the problems at an early stage.

Water power is Sweden's most valuable domestic energy resource. It is renewable and clean in production, distribution and consumption. But to exploit it involves serious disruptions of nature's hydrological system and the landscape. Regulating lakes damages shore zones, damming often destroys cultivated and grazing land.

There may be direct risks of disasters when transporting dangerous substances by land or sea. Shipping results in countless minor oil slicks and when tankers run aground they can cause enormous oil disasters.

It was more difficult to identify the slow-working but in the long term most dangerous environmental effects of our industrial society — the pollution of nature by solid, liquid and

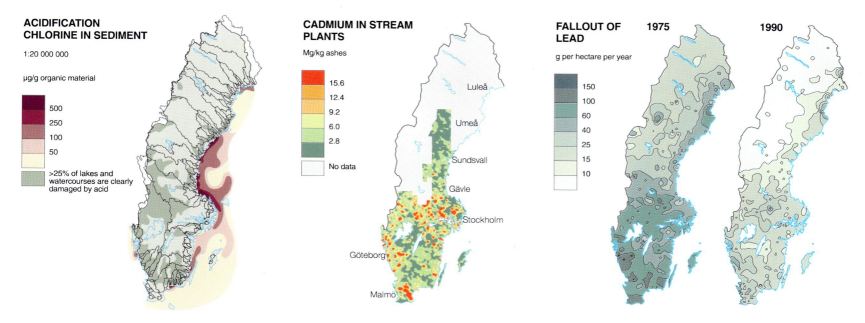

ACIDIFICATION CHLORINE IN SEDIMENT

Environmental problems on land and at sea. Acidification from sulphur fallout, concentrations of chlorine from industries along the coast which collect in the bottom sediment. (T110)

CADMIUM IN STREAM PLANTS

Cadmium is poisonous and is found in certain minerals. In acidified areas it is leached out and spreads, but calcareous rocks bind cadmium in the ground. (T111)

FALLOUT OF LEAD

The total fallout of lead in Sweden was halved between 1975 and 1990, a success for environmental conservation. (T112, T113)

gaseous waste products. Swedish scientists drew attention to he insidious chemical pollution of soil and water by mercury, PCB and acid rain, for example, which caused damage to plant and animal life. After the problems had been identified and measures adopted to reduce pollution, improvements in the environment have been noted, for example with respect to lead pollution.

Acid rain comes mainly from sulphur in fossil fuels like coal and oil. Most of it is carried to Sweden by southerly winds. The closure of some power stations in East Germany fired by brown coal has improved the situation. On the other hand nitrogen oxide exhaust effluents from traffic have continued to increase in Western Europe.

As a result of burning fuels and processing all kinds of metals the air, land and water receive various metal particles, often after being carried long distances by winds. Several of these metals are harmful to all living organisms, among them lead, cadmium, copper, mercury and zinc. As a result of measures taken within and outside Sweden the total fallout of lead and cadmium in Sweden has been halved since the mid-1970s. Iron, chromium and zinc fallout has also been halved in the past 25 years, but the metal content in the soil remains high although industrial discharges have almost ceased.

The sea is the final resting place for the pollution that mankind discharges. The Baltic catchment area has a population of 70 million, mostly without sewage treatment. The largest sewer is the Vistula which carries untreated sewage from most of Poland out into the Baltic. An anti-clockwise current in the Baltic carries water from the Vistula round Gotland and down the east coast of Sweden.

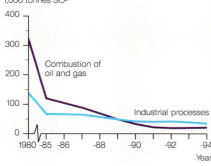

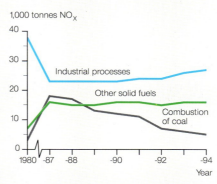

Between 1980 and 1987 the total discharge of sulphur dioxide decreased by over 50 per cent.

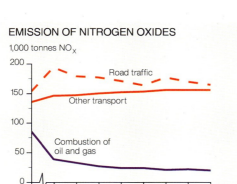

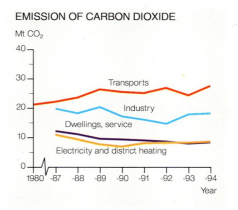

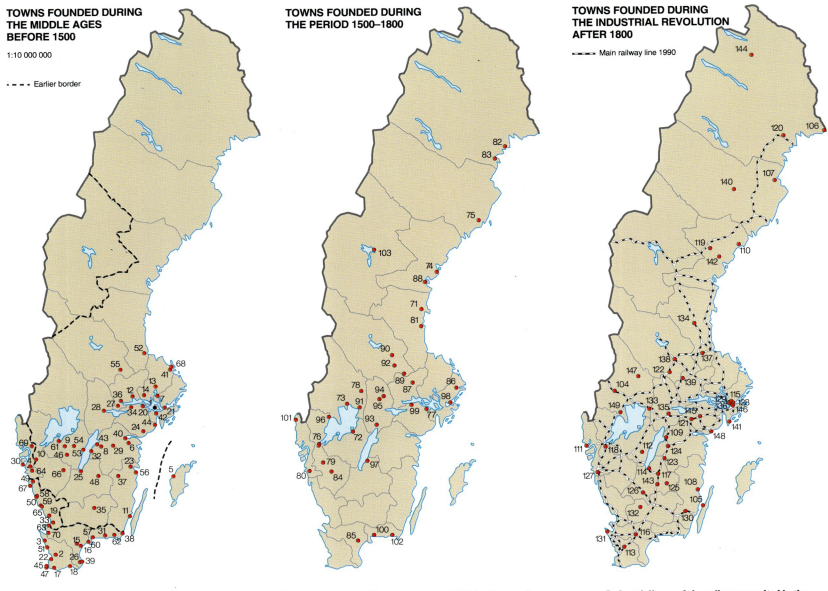

TOWNS FOUNDED DURING THE MIDDLE AGES BEFORE 1500

1:10 000 000

- - - - Earlier border

TOWNS FOUNDED DURING THE PERIOD 1500–1800

TOWNS FOUNDED DURING THE INDUSTRIAL REVOLUTION AFTER 1800

━━━ Main railway line 1990

The medieval market towns lie in the oldest farming districts or on the coast for fishing, shipping and trade. (T114)

New towns were established by royal decree during the 17th century for economic or strategic purposes. (T115)

Industrialism and the railways resulted in the creation of a large number of new settlements, many of which grew into towns in the 19th and 20th centuries. (T116)

TOWNS FOUNDED DURING THE MIDDLE AGES

1 Birka (prehistoric township)
2 Lund
3 Helsingborg
4 Kungahälla/Kungälv
5 Visby
6 Söderköping
7 Sigtuna
8 Skänninge
9 Skara
10 (Gamla) Lödöse
11 Kalmar
12 Västerås
13 Uppsala
14 Enköping
15 Vä
16 Åhus
17 Trelleborg
18 Ystad
19 Halmstad (Övraby, Broktorp)
20 Strängnäs
21 Stockholm
22 Malmö
23 Västervik (Gamleby)
24 Nyköping
25 Jönköping
26 Tommarp
27 Arboga
28 Örebro
29 Linköping
30 Marstrand
31 Ronneby
32 Hästholmen
33 Laholm
34 Torshälla
35 Växjö
36 Köping
37 Vimmerby
38 Avaskär/Kristianopel
39 Simrishamn
40 Norrköping
41 Östhammar
42 Södertälje
43 Vadstena
44 Trosa
45 Skanör
46 Falköping
47 Falsterbo
48 Eksjö
49 Kungsbacka
50 Varberg/Getakärr
51 Landskrona
52 Gävle
53 Hjo
54 Skövde
55 Hedemora
56 Västervik
57 Elleholm
58 Ny Varberg
59 (Gamla) Falkenberg
60 Sölvesborg
61 Lidköping
62 Lyckå
63 Båstad
64 Nya Lödöse
65 Nya Falkenberg
66 Bogesund/Ulricehamn
67 Gåsekil
68 Öregrund
69 Uddevalla
70 Luntertun/Ängelholm

TOWNS FOUNDED DURING THE PERIOD 1500–1800

71 Hudiksvall
72 Mariestad
73 Karlstad
74 Härnösand
75 Umeå
76 Brätte/Vänersborg
77 Mariefred
78 Filipstad
79 Alingsås
80 Göteborg
81 Söderhamn
82 Luleå
83 Piteå
84 Borås
85 Kristianstad
86 Norrtälje
87 Sala
88 Sundsvall
89 Avesta
90 Falun
91 Kristinehamn
92 Säter
93 Askersund
94 Lindesberg
95 Nora
96 Åmål
97 Gränna
98 Vaxholm
99 Eskilstuna
100 Karlshamn
101 Strömstad
102 Karlskrona
103 Östersund

TOWNS FOUNDED DURING THE INDUSTRIAL REVOLUTION

104 Oskarsstad/Arvika
105 Borgholm
106 Haparanda
107 Skellefteå
108 Oskarshamn
109 Motala
110 Örnsköldsvik
111 Lysekil
112 Tidaholm
113 Eslöv
114 Huskvarna
115 Djursholm
116 Hässleholm
117 Nässjö
118 Trollhättan
119 Sollefteå
120 Boden
121 Katrineholm
122 Ludvika
123 Tranås
124 Mjölby
125 Vetlanda
126 Värnamo
127 Mölndal
128 Lidingö
129 Sundbyberg
130 Nybro
131 Höganäs
132 Ljungby
133 Karlskoga
134 Bollnäs
135 Kumla
136 Solna
137 Sandviken
138 Borlänge
139 Fagersta
140 Lycksele
141 Nynäshamn
142 Kramfors
143 Sävsjö
144 Kiruna
145 Flen
146 Nacka
147 Hagfors
148 Oxelösund
149 Säffle

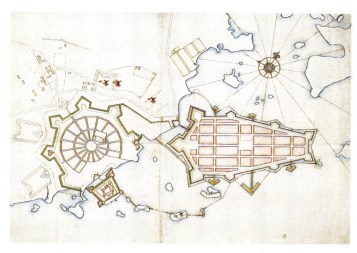

Until the 17th century Kalmar was the most important fortified town in the south of Sweden. After the 1611–13 war the town was rebuilt with radial streets and bastions, but these soon became obsolete and the town was moved in the mid–17th century to Kvarnholmen, which was fortified. In 1822 these fortifications were found to be useless and were replaced by parks and public buildings.

Ystad dates back to the 13th century and has preserved its medieval street plan and old buildings. Air photo from the west. There is a clear boundary between the medieval and later districts.

There was a radical adjustment of the street plan in Uppsala in 1643. What was left of the medieval town were a few streets and buildings and the pattern of house plots in certain districts.

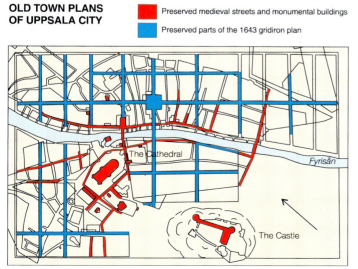

The Urban Landscape

HISTORY AND PLANNING

In present-day Sweden there are about 150 known places which have had town status. The legal concept of a town was introduced on the German pattern in the 13th century. Trade and with few exceptions crafts could only be practised in towns until liberalism ended the system in the 19th century. Later the differences remained mostly in the way local government functioned and in the application of special town regulations such as fire regulations. All legal differences between towns and municipalities were revoked in 1970.

Isolated townships had existed since Viking times; two of them, Lund and Sigtuna, became towns and still are today. Others like Birka were deserted or like Vä were abandoned for a new town founded later for military reasons, Kristianstad.

Some 70 towns can trace their roots back to the Middle Ages, six of them to before 1100: Sigtuna, Skara, Lund and Helsingborg, Visby, the now-vanished Lödöse and Kongahälla (Kungälv). During the 13th century the number of towns grew rapidly under strong German influence. The Swedish town system was concentrated along the west-east axis running from Lödöse on the river Göta älv to Viborg on the Gulf of Finland, the central belt of the kingdom. Denmark and Norway built the towns along the west and south coasts. Some of the medieval towns still have street plans, building plots and buildings which recall the original terrain and roads which had been adapted to the townships. The centre of a medieval town is its market place.

The 17th century, when Sweden was a great power, saw the creation of many new towns, usually built on a gridiron plan. A few important fortress towns were planned on Renaissance and Baroque models: Göteborg with its Dutch style, Kalmar fortress town and Karlskrona with a Baroque pattern. Only Östersund was founded in the 18th century.

Tree-lined boulevards came into fashion in the early 19th century. Industrialisation and the railways in the latter part of the 19th century led to a great expansion of towns and the creation of railway towns. The 1874 fire regulations encouraged the building of boulevards as fire-breaks in the towns, which up to then had mostly had wooden buildings. The 20th century brought ideas from the continent and England of garden cities, town plans adapted to the terrain and the elimination of social segregation. The Stockholm Exhibition of 1930 encouraged functionalism and the opening up of the enclosed barrack-like apartment blocks to light and air.

After the Second World War urbanisation accelerated at an unbelievable rate. High-rise buildings were the characteristic feature of this period. The ideas behind more carefully planned suburbs were based on integrated satellite suburbs with zoned residential areas and industrial areas and services provided at the block, district and group district levels. These were called ABC suburbs. Vällingby, a suburb of Stockholm, became an internationally famous model. When a serious housing shortage arose, areas built in the 1960s and 1970s became more and more stereotype, using industrial building techniques, in order to reach the political goal of one million new housing units in 10 years.

The 1864 town plan for Umeå shows broad avenues and narrower crossing streets. Boulevards were built in 1879 for fire protection, and in 1898 a star-shaped open place was built at the railway station. After 1922 the street plan was adapted to the terrain.

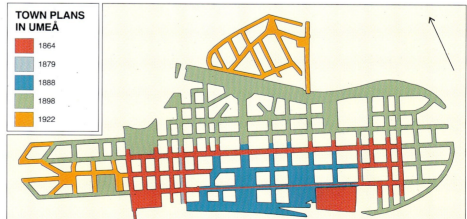

Vänersborg in 1985. The Yellow Map, Vänersborg 8B:48, scale 1:20,000.

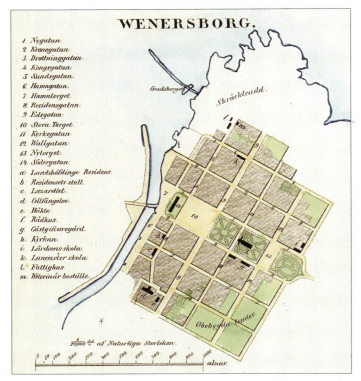

Vänersborg around 1860. From Gustaf Ljunggren's Atlas of Swedish Towns. The "sloppy" coastline is part of the hand-coloured original.

VÄNERSBORG — A 17TH-CENTURY PLANNED TOWN

At the southern end of Lake Vassbotten, close to where the Göta älv runs out of Lake Vänern, lay the market town of Brätte, which was mentioned as a town in 1583. In 1620 it was granted town privileges by Gustaf II Adolf (Gustavus Adolphus). But this small town on the border of Norwegian–Danish Bohuslän was in an exposed position in the constant warfare at that time, so in 1624 the government ordered the citizens of Brätte to move to a newly-established town 5 km to the north, on a headland between Vassbotten and Vänern. Brätte was abandoned. The only remains are a few excavations and a monument commemorating the town.

The new town, called Vänersborg, was granted town privileges in 1644. As early as 1679 it became the county town of the newly-established Älvsborg County, created from Dalsland and southern Västergötland. The new town was given the characteristic gridiron plan of the time, which has survived to the present day. The width of the streets and the size of the blocks were standardised and strictly enforced by prominent Swedish surveyor-engineers of the time. Toll gates were built at Edsvägen, Rånnumsvägen and Dalbovägen. A church was built on the very spot where the church stands today, and an impressive two-storied residence for the county governor. As in most other towns in the country, the rest of the buildings were low, timbered houses, with street facades of vertical boarding.

Like practically every other "wooden" town Vänersborg suffered from fires. The most devastating one broke out on 4 October 1834. After burning for 14 hours, only 14 of the town's 316 buildings were left standing, apart from the 18th-century church and the new residence, designed by Carl Hårleman and built in 1754. When the town was rebuilt, following the old rectilinear street plan, one row of plots was left unbuilt at the suggestion of Nils Ericsson and Carl Andersson, to be planted with trees as a firebreak right through the centre of the town. It started at the residence and had the church in the middle. Round the "plantation" between the church and the residence the museum and other stone buildings were erected. This boulevard plan set the style for Swedish town planning throughout the 19th century and was stipulated in the 1874 building regulations.

For many years Vänersborg was a strategically-placed shipping and trading centre. After 1752 Lake Vänern was connected by a canal (Karlsgraven) via Vassbotten to the Göta älv. When the Trollhätte Canal was enlarged for through traffic using heavy coastal and lake tonnage, the town lost its importance. Industrialisation following the arrival of the railways and the expansion of the Göta älv power stations only slightly affected the town, while not far away heavy industry grew up at the waterfalls on the Göta älv at Vargön and Trollhättan. With its 20,000 inhabitants Vänersborg is one of the few county towns which is not the largest town in its county. But in return it was able to preserve its idyllic atmosphere celebrated by the poet Birger Sjöberg.

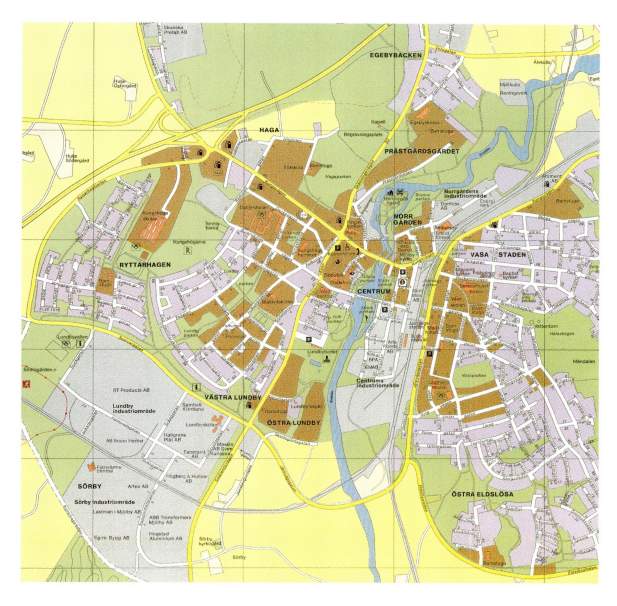

Mjölby in 1991. Tourist and Information Map of Mjölby; original scale 1:10,000 reduced here to 1:20,000.

Mjölby in 1770. Land reform map. In the mill village there was the parish church, six farms, an inn and several mills and mill cottages.

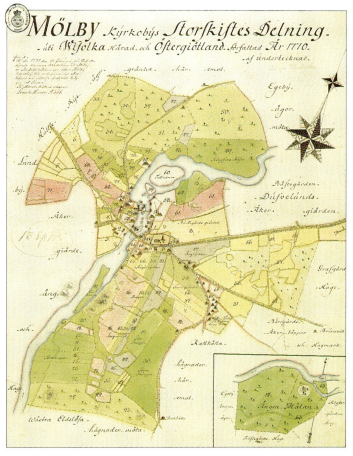

MJÖLBY — A DYNAMIC YOUNG TOWN

Mjölby lies where the southern Swedish highlands meet the Östgöta plain, creating a short stretch of waterfalls on the Svartån with a total drop of 12 m. These waterfalls were already exploited in the Middle Ages to drive mills, both flour mills and industrial mills. The oldest written record of mills is dated around 1200. The name Mjölby, which can be traced back to medieval times, is not surprisingly connected with the word "mill". The old parish church, named after the village down by the river, is at Kungsvägen, the old "Highway One", just east of where it crosses the Svartån.

In 1771 this village was destroyed by a fire, which also burnt down the church, apart from its 12th-century tower, onto which the church had been built in the 1770s. Mjölby was an important road junction where roads from Tranås and Skänninge met the highway west of the Svartån. From the 18th century onwards Mjölby was the court town in the Vifolka Hundred. In the mid-19th century there were along this short stretch of the river 10 mills and a number of small factories.

When the railway was built in the 1870s Mjölby became an important junction on the state railway network. The Stockholm-Malmö line ran from Linköping via Mjölby on the east side of the Svartån and south along the river valley. A branch line from Hallsberg in the north joined the main line here, providing connections via Krylbo with towns further north. There were also connections with the private railway network on the Östgöta plain, to Hästholmen and Ödeshög, for example. This is when the economy took off with a series of new industries; a community grew up round the railway station which moved the centre and expansion of Mjölby east of the river. Here a square was built with administrative buildings, a post office and telegraph station and a courthouse for the court which was now called Folkungabygdens Domsaga. A number of manufacturing industries settled in Mjölby. A new mechanised mill was also built close to the railway after the many old watermills had been amalgamated in 1874. A municipal power station was built on the Svartån to exploit the nine-metre head of water there. After 1900 Mjölby was a municipal township and in 1920 it became a town proper.

The square was rebuilt in urban style around 1940, with a modern town hall, for example. When the town grew however, its centre was again moved to the west of the river, where a large new town hall, library and People's House were located as a result of the amalgamation of municipalities in 1971. Even though the railway that runs through Mjölby is still one of the busiest in Sweden, it is road traffic that has governed the town's development since the Second World War. Right up to 1963 the ever-increasing traffic ran along "Highway One" right through Mjölby, under the railway bridge and across the river. Since 1963, however, the heavy traffic has taken the motorway north of Mjölby, connected to the town by the junction at Kungshögarna to the west, which has also now become the fastest-growing part of the town.

VÄSTERÅS — A TOWN WITH A LONG HISTORY

Västerås is one of the towns in Mälardalen which had important national functions from early medieval times. Västerås developed into one of the major cities of Sweden with a fortified castle, a cathedral, a bishopric since 1120, and a monastery. A few ruins remind us of its site where the Lillån ran into the Svartån. The street which runs over the now underground Lillån was later called Munkgatan (Monk Street). The town prospered because it was the port for the mining districts of Dalarna with copper and iron, as well as the silver from Sala. In 1623 Bishop Johannes Rudbeckius founded the first grammar school in Sweden at Västerås. When the streets were reorganised in 1644, parts of the southern town were built on a gridiron plan round a main street running from east to west, Stora gatan. The present streets named Smedjegatan and Kungsgatan through Stortorget (the Square) correspond to the original Eriksgatan that ran through the town. Towards the end of the 19th century new changes were made to complement the 1644 plan.

The arrival of the railway led to rapid industrialisation, most importantly ASEA's move from Stockholm in 1891. ASEA's growth and development into a multi-national group, ABB, has left its mark on the history of the town in the 20th century. Industrial sites expanded alongside the railways and port. As was usual in ports, the railway had been laid on unoccupied land close to the lake shore, creating what for us seems an awkward barrier between the town and the lake.

The growth of heavy industry led to a rapid increase in population and consequent housing construction. In the district round Karlsgatan and Utanbygatan large two and three-storeyed apartment blocks for workers were erected in the early 20th century. After extensive rebuilding of the town centre in the 1970s and 1980s to create a modern shopping and conference centre, all that remains of the old pre-industrial church, school, market and county town are the wooden houses along the Svartån, the area round the cathedral and the culturally protected area of Kyrkbacken to the north. Since the Second World War new housing estates have been built in ever-widening circles round the medieval town.

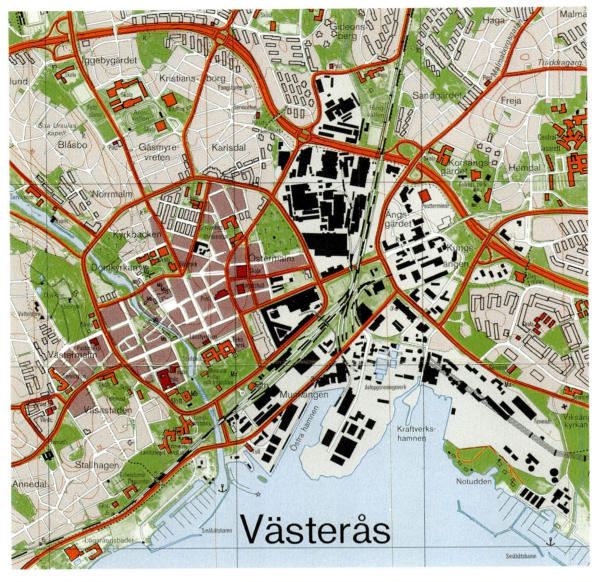

Västerås in 1991. The Yellow Map, Västerås 11G:17, scale 1:20,000.

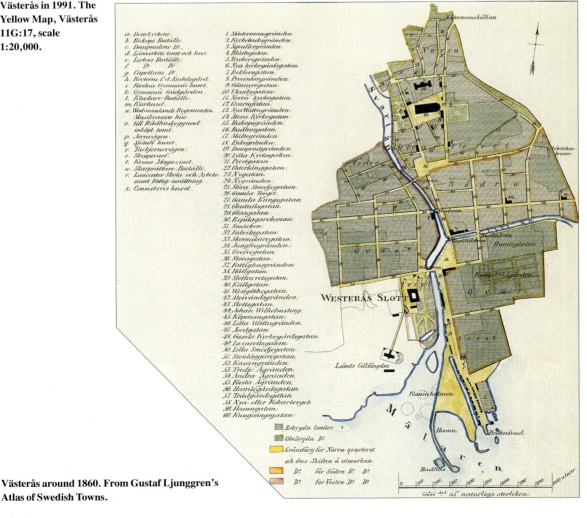

Västerås around 1860. From Gustaf Ljunggren's Atlas of Swedish Towns.

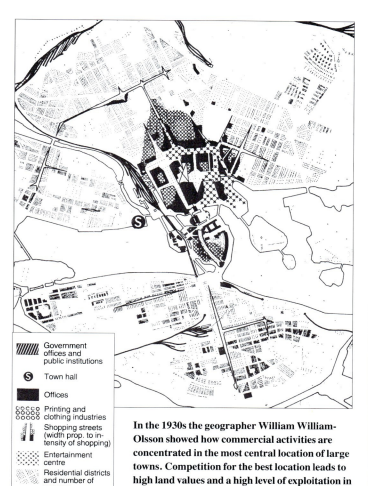

In the 1930s the geographer William William-Olsson showed how commercial activities are concentrated in the most central location of large towns. Competition for the best location leads to high land values and a high level of exploitation in town centres.

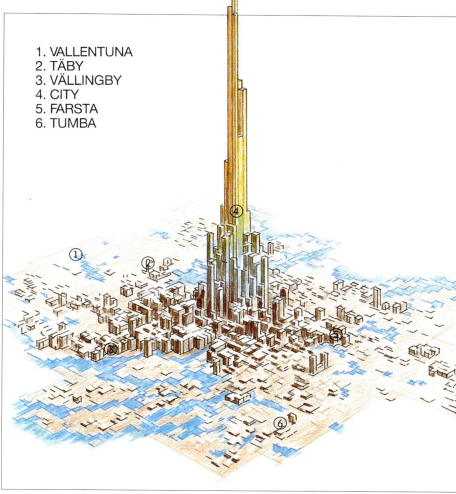

A diagram of the rateable values in Greater Stockholm resembles that of a large American city. The high land values in the centre correspond to a very high level of exploitation and office skyscrapers.

With Stockholm Palace as its historic centre the organs of government with the Riksdag and the government offices are concentrated round Norrström. Commercial offices, banks and the largest retail stores form the city centre proper in Nedre Norrmalm.

CHANGES IN TOWN CENTRES

A town is characterised by its diversified economic activities which are dependent on good communications. The nature of this need varies according to the activities and has changed continually over the years. Old towns have seen their inner structure altered by economic and technical advances. In extreme cases towns have had to move in order to keep their good communications. This is the case along the coast of the Bothnian Bay, which has been seriously affected by land uplift.

Competition for the best locations leads to internal differentiation in the use of land and buildings. Industry competes for access to harbours, railways and motorways. Central locations are occupied by offices, central services and specialised retail shops. Housing areas, which occupy the largest area in a town, are historically differentiated according to social group. The communication network lies at the centre. The strength of the economic field which governs the choice of location is revealed by great variations in land value. A town centre has a land value far exceeding that of the surrounding neighbourhood.

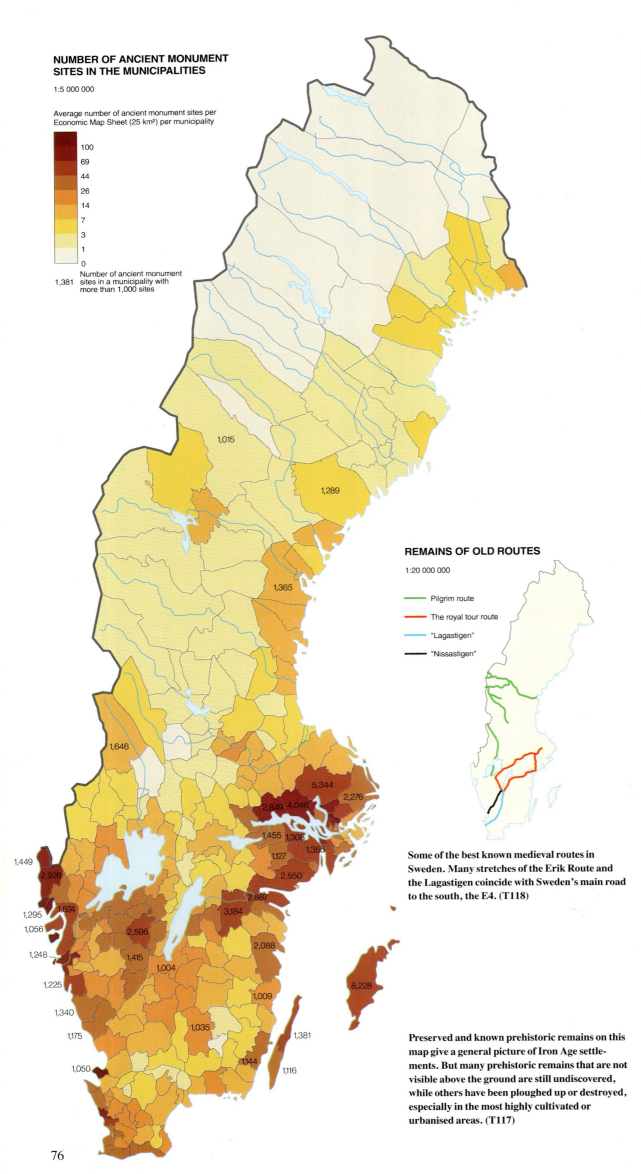

History in the Landscape

There are historical remains from every era in the landscape, which makes it an important archive for research. Much of its contents can only be interpreted by experts, but it also contains countless clearly visible signs of the work, life — and death — of previous generations.

Thanks to their great number and wide distribution, certain kinds of historical monuments can throw light on early periods in our history. For prehistory these are principally graves and cemeteries. The graves of the Viking Era (800–1050 AD) are usually clearly visible mounds; the rune stones that have been preserved also throw light on the main settlement areas of the Viking period. The regional differences are due not only to the distribution of the population but also to varying customs. The ancient hunting and trapping culture of northern Sweden has left many trapping pits which were built over many centuries and belong to different historical eras.

Regional differences in the ages of settlements but also in language and place names are revealed by special types of place names, some of them prehistoric, other medieval or from later periods. The commonest of the prehistoric place names in Sweden are those that end in -sta(d) or -by. Among medieval names in southern Sweden -torp occurs most frequently. All these places names have a wide geographical distribution.

Medieval settlements are revealed by the presence of monasteries and medieval churches. The monasteries represent those orders that settled in towns (the begging orders) and those on the outskirts of settlements that tried to colonise the surrounding forestland. The most important of them in medieval Sweden was Vadstena Monastery, founded as a centre for the Birgitta Order by Birgitta Birgersdotter, who was canonised in 1391 and is buried in the abbey.

It is still possible to see, in many parts of Sweden, the remains of old paths and roads in their original form. The old royal Eriksgata or royal route is still marked here and there by rune stones and sunken roads. Other well-known routes from the Middle Ages are the pilgrims' routes to Nidaros (Trondheim) Cathedral, the most important shrine in Scandinavia in Catholic times. Lagastigen and Nissastigen were ancient routes to the south.

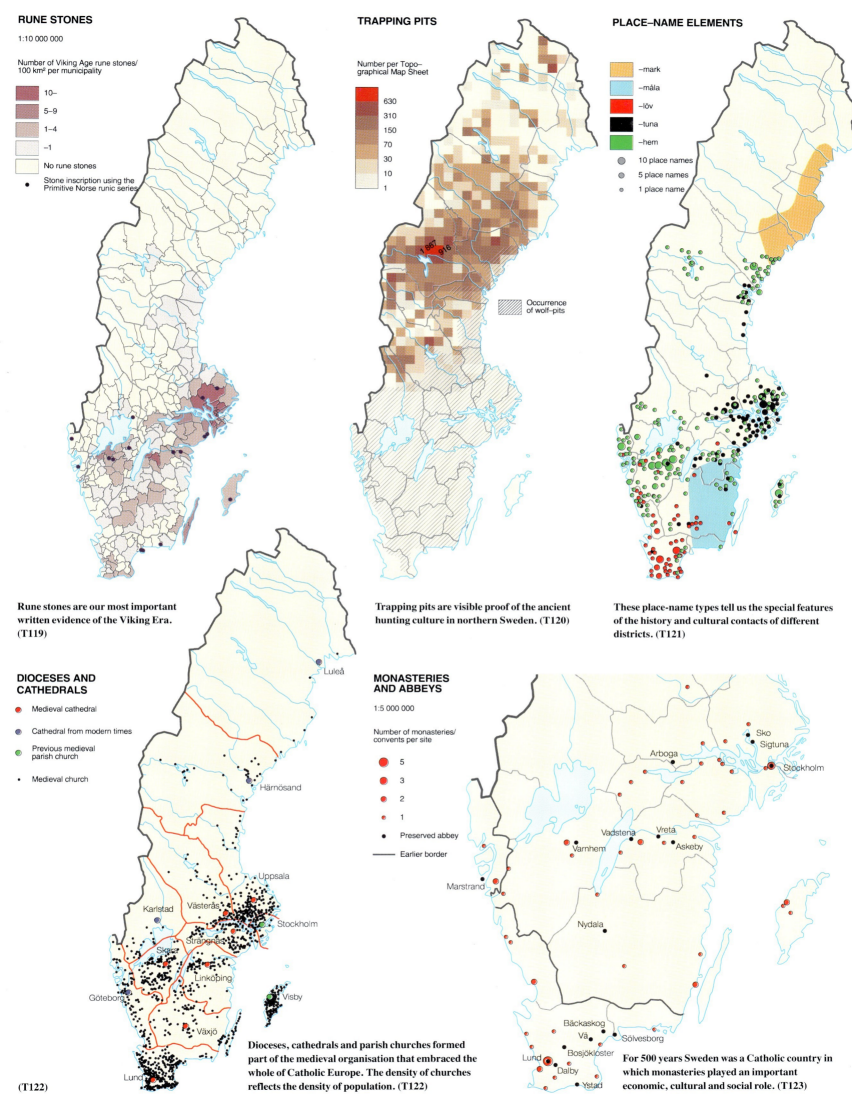

SELECTED URBAN AREAS

1:5 000 000

- ✝ Church "town" (overnight accommodation for churchgoers)
- ● Fishing village
- ■ Spa
- ⚓ Seaside resort
- ● Old market town
- ● Railway town or village
- — Railway

A sample of six different categories of villages that are usually included in the list of places of national interest for cultural preservation. Other villages may have been destroyed or spoiled and their documentation is incomplete. (T124)

ANCIENT MONUMENTS OF WORKING LIFE

Ancient monuments remind us of the daily life and conditions of our forefathers. Small towns which have been marked by a local industry but have stood still in time often have a special period atmosphere. Small towns often live dangerously as living cultural monuments. Depending on their location and character they may be threatened by total depopulation and

The distribution of the shealing system and its variants round 1900 covered a considerably larger area than the surviving shealing system today. Many crofts are used today as second homes, but cattle are still pastured at a few of them. (T125)

Medieval palaces and castles were either the fortified private homes of the nobility or royal residences or formed part of Sweden's national defence. (T126)

CASTLES AND MANOR-HOUSES

SHEALING SYSTEM AROUND 1900 AND TODAY

1:20 000 000

- Half-site system
- One-site system with enclosed hay field
- Several-site system
- One-site system without enclosure
- Boundary of the shealing system
- Shealing site, in use in 1990

Castles legend:
- ■ From before 1530
- ■ From 1530–1630
- ■ From 1630–1730
- — Earlier border

Place names (north to south)

Sandskär, Ammarnäs, Gillesnuole, Älvbyn, Malören, Nederluleå, Småskären, Arvidsjaur, Norrfjärden, Pite landsförs., Hortlax, Rödkallen, Fatmomakke, Storuman, Byske, Ankarede, Vilhelmina, Skellefte landsförs., Bjurön-Fällan, Vindeln, Lövånger, Snöan, Trysunda, Ulvöhamn, Marviksgrunnan, Ragunda, Norrfällsviken, Bönhamn, Lörudden, Brämön, Kuggören, Kråkö, Agö, Alfta, Skärså, Freluga, Prästgrundet, Ockelbo, Jädraås, Fågelsundet, Vansbro, Krylbo, Grisslehamn, Sätra, Furusund, Loka, Saltsjöbaden, Sandhamn, Malmköping, Dalarö, Porla, Gnesta, Huvudskär, Laxå, Katrineholm, Trosa, Utö, Spiken, Medevi, Gustavsberg, Hjo, Himmelstalund, Lysekil, Mössebergs Kurort, Harstena, Käringön, Björkskär, Tranås, Väderskär, Lickershamn, Häftings, Agbod, Gnisvärd, Hammars, Kovik, Grynge, Kapellet, Vitvär, Hörte, Varberg, Hus, Tomtbod, Träslövsläge, Landeryd, Runnö, Holm, Tylösand, Hamneda, Värlebo, Mönsterås, Båstad, Älmhult, Pataholm, Arild, Mölle, Ronneby, Bergkvara, Gamla Viken, Kristianopel, Ramlösa, Utlängan, Teckomatorp, Eslöv, Vitemölla, Falsterbo, Smedstorp, Kivik, Vik, Baskemölla, Brantevik, Skillinge, Kåseberga

Castles area: Ornäs, Salsta, Mörby, Grönenborg, Vik, Skokloster, Tidö, Venngarn, Steninge, Penningby, Örebro, Fiholm, Anhammar, Ericsberg, Läckö, Finspång, Nyköpingshus, Mariedal, Vadstena, Ekenäs, Rotenberg, Linköping, Sturefors, Torpa, Hovdala, Trolle-Ljungby, Svenstorp, Vittskövle, Borgeby, Torup, Glimmingehus, Dybäck, Marsvinsholm

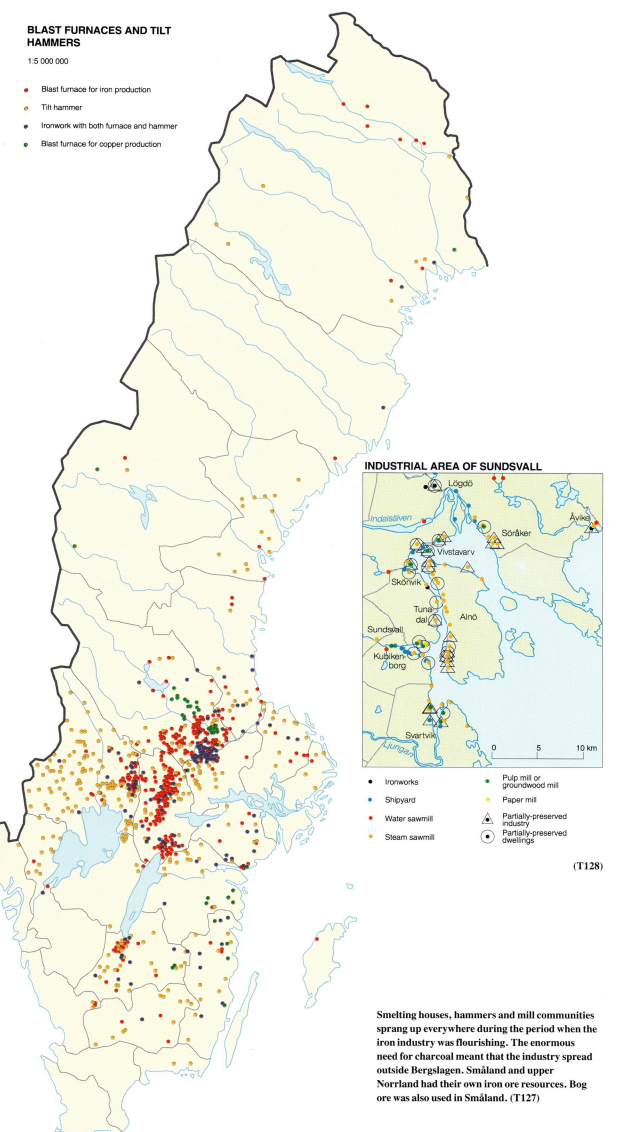

BLAST FURNACES AND TILT HAMMERS
1:5 000 000

- Blast furnace for iron production
- Tilt hammer
- Ironwork with both furnace and hammer
- Blast furnace for copper production

INDUSTRIAL AREA OF SUNDSVALL

- Ironworks
- Shipyard
- Water sawmill
- Steam sawmill
- Pulp mill or groundwood mill
- Paper mill
- Partially-preserved industry
- Partially-preserved dwellings

(T128)

Smelting houses, hammers and mill communities sprang up everywhere during the period when the iron industry was flourishing. The enormous need for charcoal meant that the industry spread outside Bergslagen. Småland and upper Norrland had their own iron ore resources. Bog ore was also used in Småland. (T127)

decline, or, as attractive holiday resorts, by the desire of rich summer visitors, to "beautify" or modernise them.

Castles, palaces and country houses reflect the development of the class society and architecture from the fortified manor houses of the Middle Ages to Renaissance and Baroque palaces and mansions and 18th-century Rococo country houses, Gustavian classicism and the Empire style of the early 19th century. The royal castles were part of the administration and the defence system. Most of the many 17th-century country houses built for the military and administrative nobility stand round Lake Mälaren. Flourishing mill towns in the mid-18th century resulted in the building of many mansions. In the 19th century the boom in agriculture led to palace-like country houses being built on the plains.

The shealing system is a dying cultural form, but it has contributed significantly to the architecture of the northern forest districts. With their traditional timbered cottages high up in the hills, providing spectacular views, many shealings now have a new function as second homes. But countless cottages that lie off the beaten track have fallen into rack and ruin.

No part of Sweden has a larger concentration of industrial monuments than Bergslagen after centuries of mining and iron manufacture. The closure of both mines and ironworks in the 20th century has created great preservation problems. Ängelsberg is a well-preserved mill town with an ironworks. The Walloon mill towns in Uppland that used the ore from the Dannemora mine are some of the finest industrial environments that can be seen in Europe. Among them are Leufsta, Österby and Forsmark.

The largest and most concentrated forest industry district in Europe developed towards the end of the 19th century round Alnösundet, near the mouths of two rivers used for timber floating. The good supply of wood fuel initially attracted iron and glassworks. Later 22 shipyards, 43 steam sawmills and 8 pulp mills were established here. The Tunadal steam sawmill was founded in 1849 as the first of its kind in Sweden and is today the only sawmill in operation in the district. In the 20th century the paper and pulp industry expanded and sawing was concentrated at fewer and more effective mils.

MARINAS

1:10 000 000

Number of berths
- 6,401–
- 3,201–6,400
- 1,601–3,200
- 801–1,600
- 401–800
- 201–400
- 101–200
- 1–100

INDOOR ICE-HOCKEY ARENAS

Year built
- 1958–1973
- 1974–1995
- District boundary

Spectator capacity
- 7,001–
- 4,001–7,000
- 1,001–4,000
- –1,000

DOWNHILL SKIING FACILITIES

1:10 000 000

Number of ski lifts: 100, 75, 50, 25, 10, 5, 1

Maximum drop in metres
- 601–
- 401–600
- 251–400
- 151–250
- 101–150
- –100

The number of moorings in marinas, including guest moorings, by municipality in 1990. As might be expected most of them are in the metropolitan regions and along the coast. (T129)

Indoor ice-hockey stadiums. These are now also found in quite small places. (T130)

The most accessible alpine districts for southern Sweden are those most heavily exploited for downhill skiing with ski-lifts. (T131)

Recreational Centres

Higher incomes, more leisure time and greater mobility have made it possible for people to enjoy the recreational resources of the landscape. Second homes are found all over the country, mainly along the coasts close to the big cities. Quite a few farmhouses and fisherman's cottages have been converted into holiday homes, but more and more of these second homes are located in planned areas.

For nature lovers the Swedish Touring Club began to mark the first trails and build cottages for overnight stays in the mountains in the early 1880s. The present-day state-managed network of mountain trails covers 5,500 km, the longest of which is the King's Trail (*Kungsleden*) from Abisko to Hemavan. The whole country is also criss-crossed today by a network of well-marked walking and cycle tracks, some of which are part of the European network. Outside the mountain districts walking and cycle tracks make use of existing lanes, paths, shores and old railway lines.

Some of the more important commercial investments in Swedish outdoor life are the numerous marinas and service stations along the coasts and on the islands, ice stadiums in towns and skiing resorts in the mountains and other districts where there are high enough hills and enough snow. Ski-lifts and accompanying service facilities have set their mark on the landscape round the mountain resorts. Åre has the longest ski slope, 5.8 km, dropping 860 m. The great popularity of ice-hockey has meant that municipalities have invested very large sums of money in ice stadiums.

Golf courses and riding schools have also considerably affected the landscape in the last twenty years or so, often providing an alternative use for abandoned farmland.

Golf is a sport that requires plenty of space and creates its own landscape.

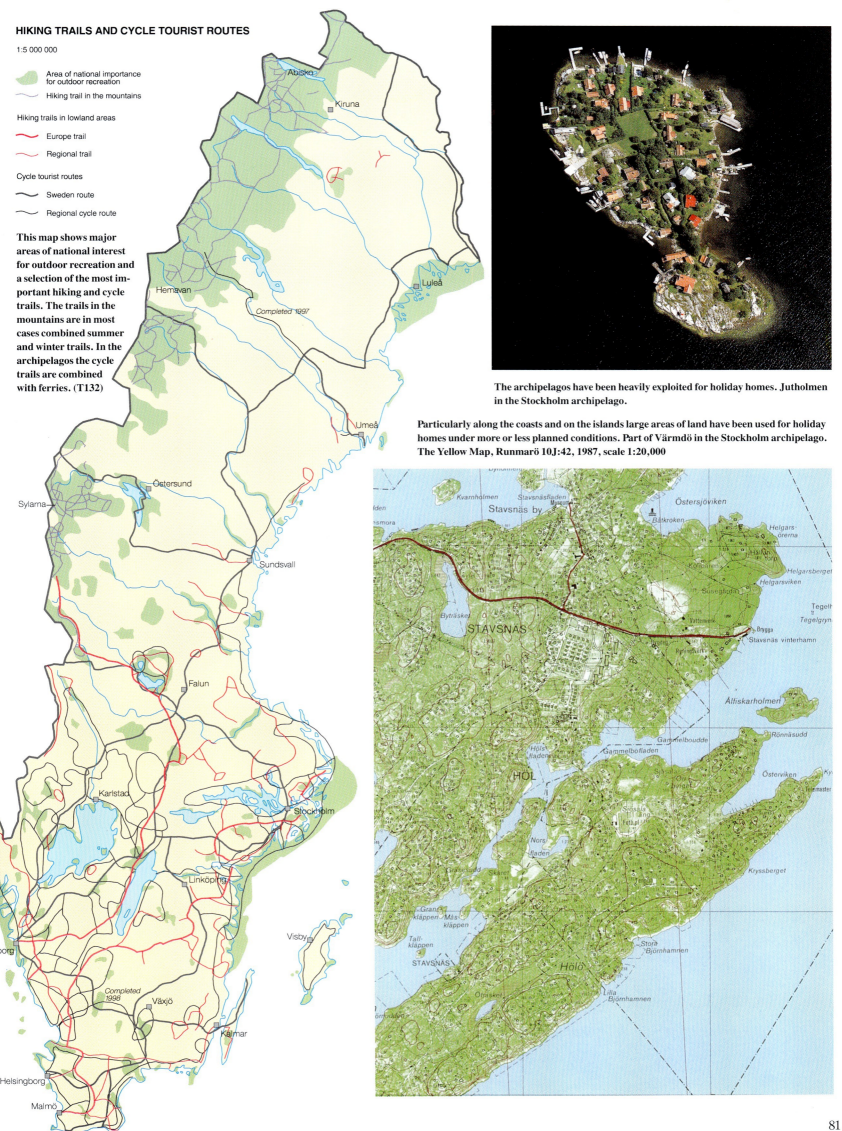

HIKING TRAILS AND CYCLE TOURIST ROUTES
1:5 000 000

- Area of national importance for outdoor recreation
- Hiking trail in the mountains

Hiking trails in lowland areas
- Europe trail
- Regional trail

Cycle tourist routes
- Sweden route
- Regional cycle route

This map shows major areas of national interest for outdoor recreation and a selection of the most important hiking and cycle trails. The trails in the mountains are in most cases combined summer and winter trails. In the archipelagos the cycle trails are combined with ferries. (T132)

The archipelagos have been heavily exploited for holiday homes. Jutholmen in the Stockholm archipelago.

Particularly along the coasts and on the islands large areas of land have been used for holiday homes under more or less planned conditions. Part of Värmdö in the Stockholm archipelago. The Yellow Map, Runmarö 10J:42, 1987, scale 1:20,000

LANDSCAPES PROTECTED BY LAW

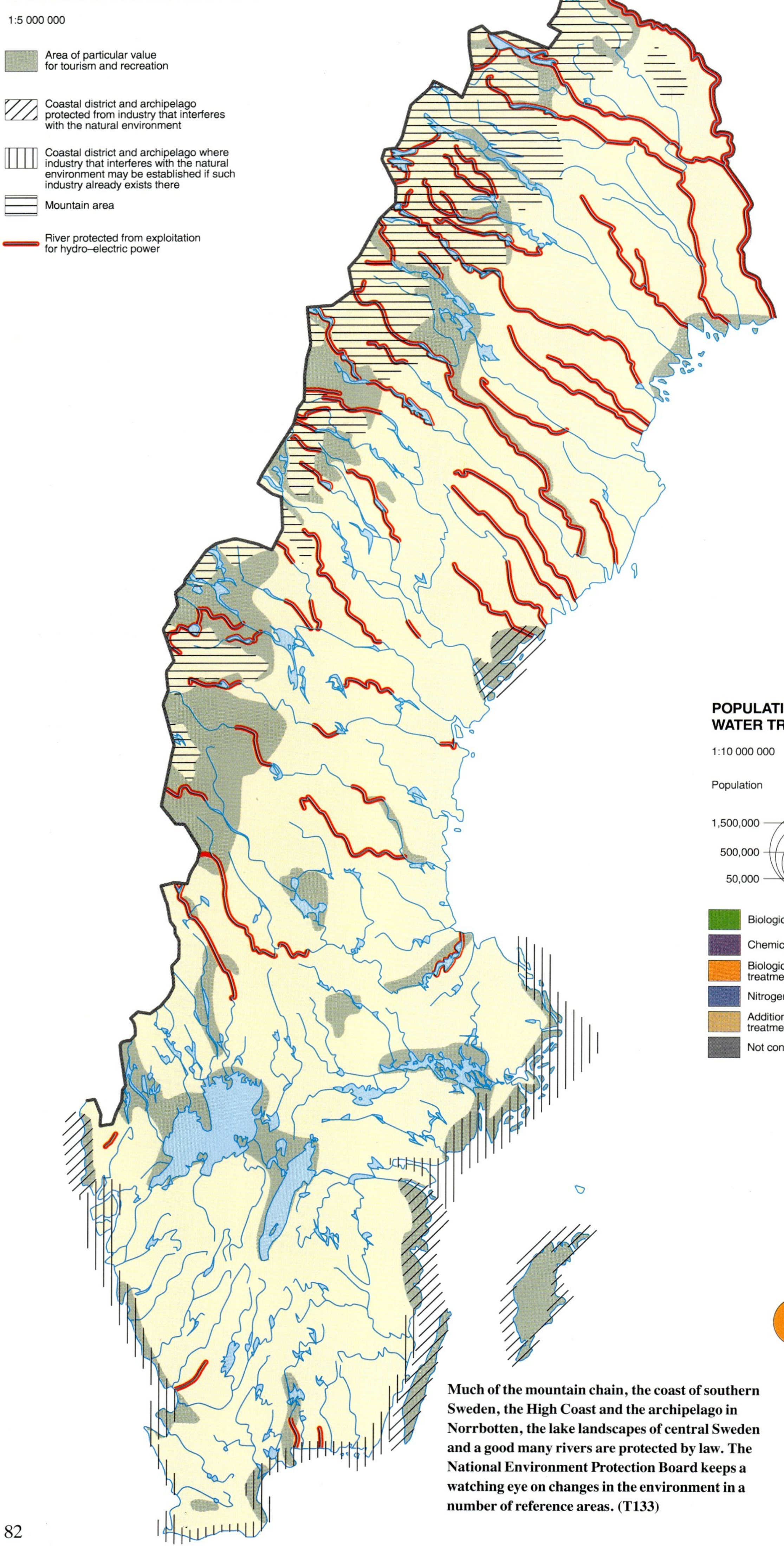

1:5 000 000

- Area of particular value for tourism and recreation
- Coastal district and archipelago protected from industry that interferes with the natural environment
- Coastal district and archipelago where industry that interferes with the natural environment may be established if such industry already exists there
- Mountain area
- River protected from exploitation for hydro-electric power

From Nature Conservation to Environmental Protection

The need for nature conservation was debated in the early 20th century, a time of rapid industrialisation, exploitation of natural forests, lake draining schemes, hydro-electric power plants and railway construction. The first national parks were created in 1909. During the second half of the 20th century legislation has developed various forms of protection but also active conservation projects. More attention is being paid to the pollution of the air, land and water as a direct threat to our ecological system.

The use of land and water is controlled today by several laws. The Natural Resources Act (NRL) mainly provides a framework for a number of other laws, principally the Planning and Building Act (PBL). Both these laws were passed in 1987. The opening section of the NRL states: "Land, water and other physical environments are to be used so that good

POPULATION CONNECTED TO WASTE-WATER TREATMENT PLANT, 1990

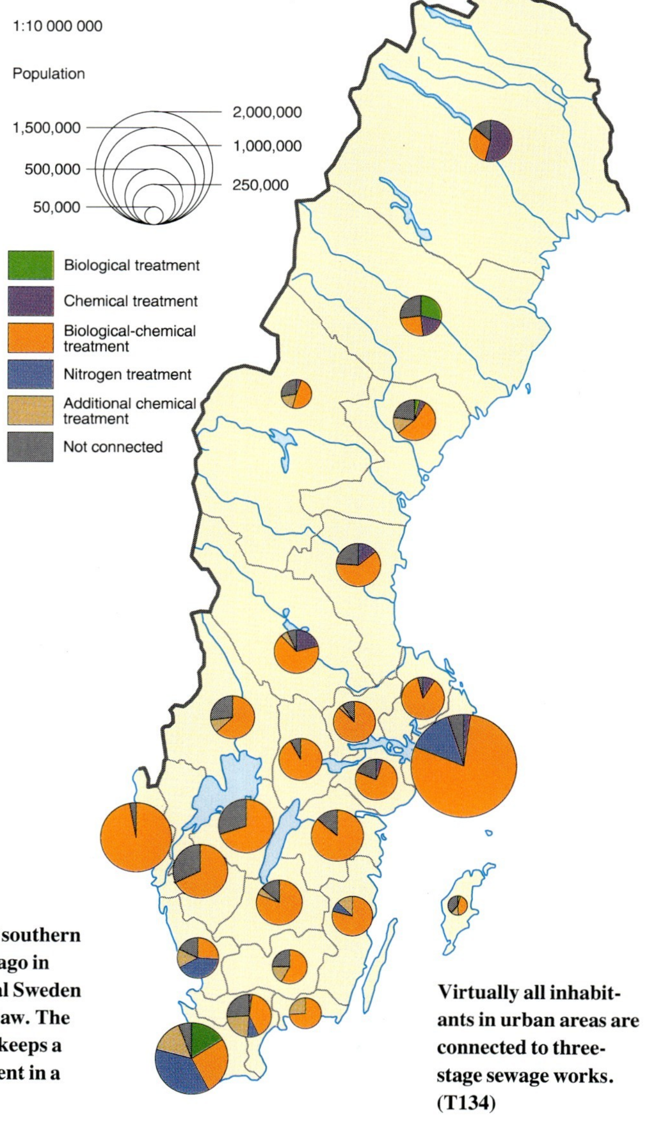

1:10 000 000

Population: 2,000,000 / 1,500,000 / 1,000,000 / 500,000 / 250,000 / 50,000

- Biological treatment
- Chemical treatment
- Biological-chemical treatment
- Nitrogen treatment
- Additional chemical treatment
- Not connected

Much of the mountain chain, the coast of southern Sweden, the High Coast and the archipelago in Norrbotten, the lake landscapes of central Sweden and a good many rivers are protected by law. The National Environment Protection Board keeps a watching eye on changes in the environment in a number of reference areas. (T133)

Virtually all inhabitants in urban areas are connected to three-stage sewage works. (T134)

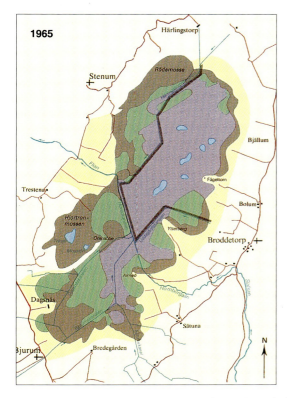
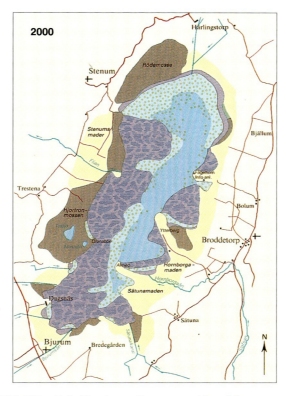

Before the fourth drainage scheme in 1905 bird life at Lake Hornborgasjön was very rich and there were large areas of open water. By 1965 almost the whole lake was overgrown with reed and bushes and the bird life had suffered. The lake is now being restored in one of the largest projects that nature conservation has ever embarked on. The water level is to be raised 85 cm and reed and bushes are to be cleared. Around the year 2000 it is expected that the lake will have regained its former importance as a breeding and resting ground. (T135, T136)

- Mainly open water
- Rushes
- Reed
- Quagmire
- Bog, wet forest
- Arable land, meadow
- Bushes, sedge, reed
- Dike

long-term management is promoted from ecological, social and economic points of view." Areas that as a whole are of outstanding national interest with regard to their natural and cultural values are specially mentioned in the NRL. It is the duty of the municipalities to follow the guidelines of the NRL in their physical planning, which is checked by the county administrative boards.

Since 1978 the National Environment Protection Board has been running a country-wide programme to observe environmental quality (PIK). Some of the measurements involved were begun earlier and are amongst the longest series in the world. Data is collected from more than 1,000 stations. In certain national parks and nature reserves observations are made of plant and animal life as well as the chemical composition of the precipitation, soil, groundwater and runoff.

An expensive investment for the environment was the upgrading of municipal sewage works, making Sweden one of the leading countries in this field.

In special cases no efforts have been spared to repair damaged environments. The largest project of this kind was the restoration of Lake Hornborgasjön in 1965.

Vallentuna is a municipality on the outskirts of Greater Stockholm, where metropolitan expansion meets an agricultural district. In its town planning both its proximity to the capital and its rich store of prehistoric remains and of valuable country environments play an important role. (T137)

VALLENTUNA – APPROVED PLANS AND REGULATIONS

- Approved detailed plan
- Planning regulations according to Sections 7 and 19, NVL (Preservation of the Environment Act)
- Protected area for groundwater, water supply
- Planning regulations according to Section 15, NVL

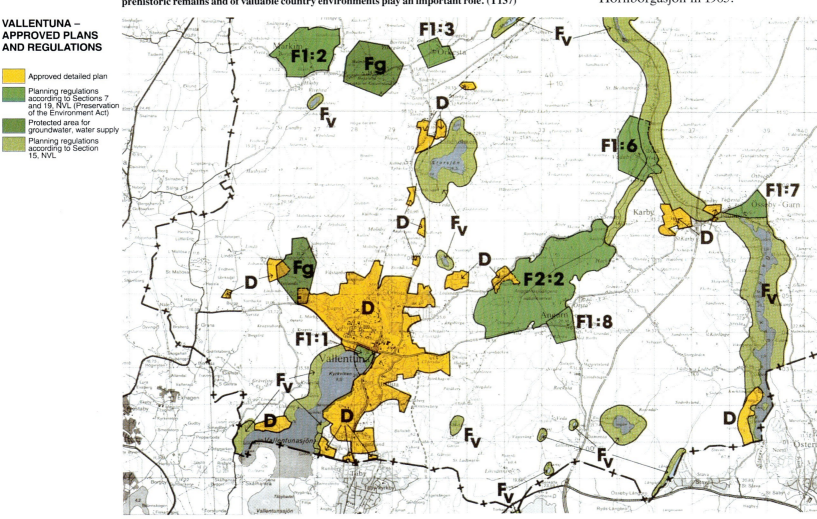

Physical Planning

The future of the cultural landscape and its architecture is controlled by the general laws that apply to physical planning. They concern the use of land, water and other natural resources and the location of buildings and plant of various kinds and they are in the first place the responsibility of the municipalities. The forms and contents of planning are regulated by the Planning and Building Act (PBL)

A *Comprehensive Plan* (Öpl) for the whole of a municipality must show the main guidelines for the use of land and water, changes to and preservation of buildings, and the way in which the municipality intends to meet the national interest expressed in the Natural Resources Act (NRL), such as main transport routes, areas important for natural and cultural conservation, recreational areas and so on. The Öpl is a statement of political policy but is not binding on future decisions.

District Regulations are binding and are used to ensure that the aims of Öpl are attained for limited areas.

Detailed Plans contain binding regulations for land use and construction within an area that is to be exploited. In general *Planning Permission* is required from the municipality to build, extend or make major changes in the use of a building.

Plans approved before 1987 remain in force until they are replaced by a new plan. Most detailed plans refer to very small areas. Between 1,000 and 3,000 detailed plans are approved every year.

In certain parts of Sweden it is necessary to have a physical planning policy that covers more than one municipality, not least for traffic planning. Water and sewage, refuse collection, housing and employment are other areas covered by regional plans. The Stockholm area has had regional planning since 1935; nowadays the county council is responsible for regional planning. In south-west Skåne and the Göteborg region regional planning is managed by the Association of Local Authorities. It is the individual municipalities that decide what is to be covered by the regional plan.

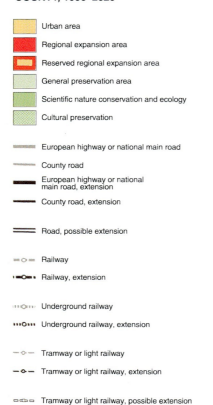

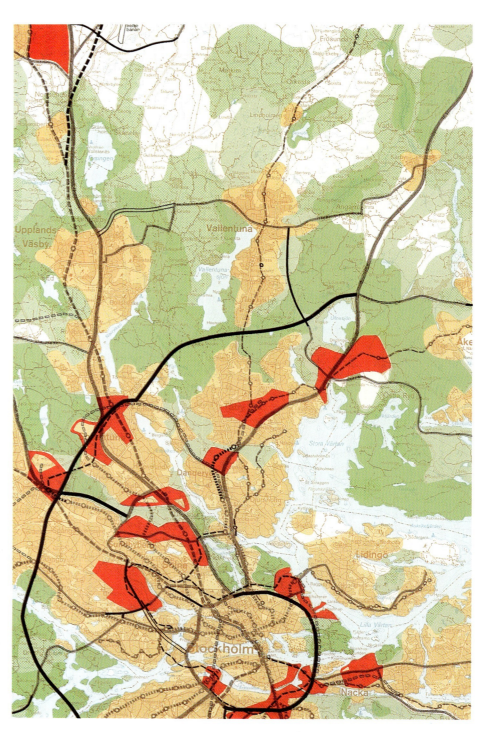

The expanding capital was the first city in Sweden to apply regional planning, starting with a general traffic plan in 1935. Extensive regional planning proposals have been put forward since the 1960s, reflecting changing forecasts and planning ideals. A decisive factor is whether growth or stagnation has been expected in the region. A critical debate which was triggered off by a regional planning proposal in 1966 has led to more cautious regional planning, which is now the responsibility of the county council. The 1966 proposal included a satellite town with 25,000 inhabitants and an underground line to Lake Angarnsjön, which today is a nature reserve and the finest bird lake in the county. (T138)

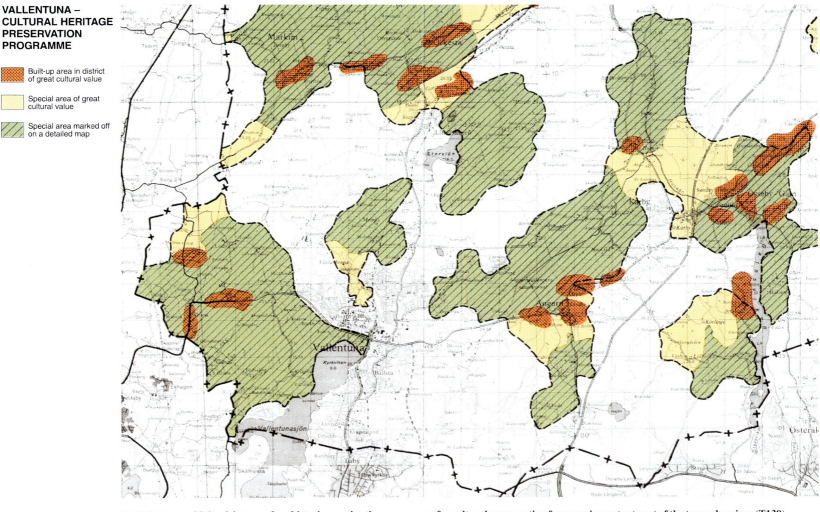

In Vallentuna with its rich store of prehistoric remains the programme for cultural preservation forms an important part of the town planning. (T139)

Unlike general plans, detailed plans are legally binding and include all the necessary regulations. They must be formulated with great care, so that they live up to environmental demands and their future role. (T140)

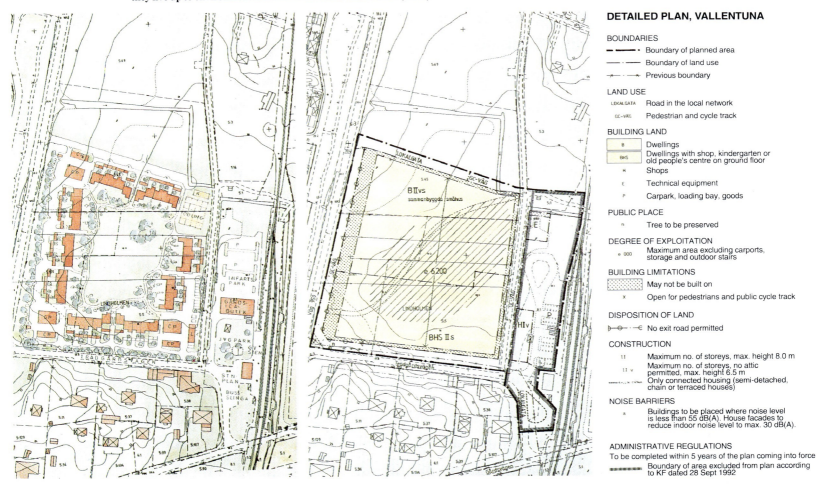

The Economy

From an Agrarian to an Industrial Economy

Sweden's basic natural resources in the form of water, energy sources, forests, agricultural land and minerals together with its geographical location in Europe and the world influence its economic geography even today. But most of these influences are indirect, the heritage of earlier forms of production, settlement patterns, knowledge and traditions.

The transformation of industrial life is leaving its mark on cities, towns and rural districts. This is visible in the landscape in the form of abandoned artefacts, dilapidated enclosures, deserted farms, abandoned mine shafts, smithies and hammers, fishing huts and sawmills. These structural changes are not, however, limited to primary industries and occupations. Closed village stores, cooperative shops, railwaymen's cottages, schools or military barracks bear witness to the transformation of service industries in both content and location.

Until the latter part of the 19th century Sweden was an agricultural country. After 1820 there was a rapid increase in the population, partly due to declining death rates. The population had doubled by 1900 in spite of emigration. The economic base for this increase in population, despite industrialisation in the late 19th century, was agriculture and its associated industries. The cultivation of meadowland and other new cultivation resulted in an increase in the area of arable land from just over 1 million ha to 3.5 million ha. During the same period agriculture underwent a radical change as a result of various land reforms. Farms were moved away from the villages and had their land strips amalgamated. Agriculture was also gradually integrated with the expanding market economy.

When sowing and harvesting, ploughing and carting were mechanised in the 20th century, agricultural yields increased dramatically, at the same time as fewer and fewer people were employed. In 1870 just over 70 per cent of the labour force was engaged in agriculture and associated industries, compared with 4 per cent in 1990. Agriculture's share of the GNP fell from 38 per cent to 1.5 per cent. The past close relationship between agricultural yields and changes in the population has not existed in recent decades.

The spread of the market economy across Sweden did not follow a uniform pattern in the regions. The towns played an important role, the

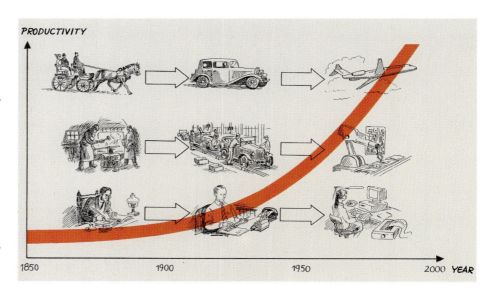

The most revolutionary factor in economic conditions is the increase in productivity, production per hour of work, which has been made possible by new technology and a growing stock of capital and human resources.

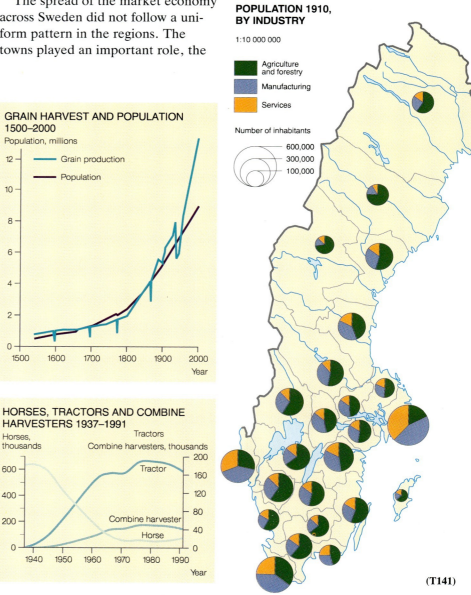

(T141)

POPULATION BY INDUSTRY
1870, 1940 OCH 1990

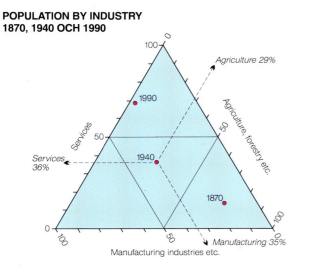

The triangular diagram shows the distribution of the population of Sweden by industrial sector in 1870, 1940 and 1990. The sum of the sectors is always 100%. The values for 1940 are given outside the triangle, alongside the arrows showing how the diagram should be read along each axis.

EMPLOYMENT BY INDUSTRY, PER COUNTY, 1990

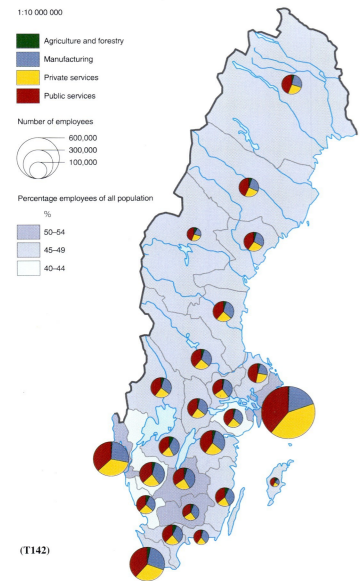

(T142)

EMPLOYMENT, 1990, %

	Women	Men	Total
Agriculture, forestry, etc	2	5	4
Manufacturing and other production of goods	14	42	28
Services	84	53	68

population close to large towns being drawn into a money economy and a life of paid employment at an earlier date than in other parts of Sweden. The composition of industry in Stockholm County in the early 20th century illustrates this pattern. The agrarian society was being replaced by an industrial and service society, a process which was already far advanced in the metropolitan regions by 1900.

Swedish society has become more and more closely knit during the past two centuries. Both physical links like roads, railways and other infrastructure and the flow of goods, people and information have expanded greatly. But the strengthening of less visible links, like the dependence of regions on each other, has also helped to bring various parts of the country closer together in a new way. This integration has resulted from, but also been a necessary factor for the dynamics of the market economy and increased social division of labour, whereby new industries and occupations have been created. The diminishing role of agriculture is one aspect of this industrial differentiation.

The population of Sweden now gets its livelihood to a large extent through paid employment in industries that did not exist before the Industrial Revolution, or that existed in the form of unpaid work in the home. Many of today's important industries were unknown at that time. Jobs in health care, child care, education, the media, commercial services and the banking, insurance and finance sector were few and far between in the agrarian society of the early 19th century. The forces that bring about these structural changes may be found both in factors influencing the market and in production technology. Competition increases when barriers to mobility fall, so that more producers can operate within the same geographical area. Technological innovations that raise productivity have the same effect. Less efficient producers are forced to rationalise or produce other goods which are more competitive.

Productivity has risen particularly rapidly in the transport sector, agriculture, industry and parts of the service sector. It has, however, proved considerably easier to rationalise — fewer employees doing the same or more work usually thanks to new technology and/or greater investments — in direct material production, especially in agriculture and forestry and in mining and manufacturing than in, for example, education, health care and child care. In particular since women entered the labour market in the 1970s, leading to the decline of unpaid domestic work, the need for labour in the above-mentioned sectors has increased greatly. This growth in the production of services has to a large extent occurred in the public sector in Sweden.

Present-day Sweden has a dual employment system: both men and women are gainfully employed. The return of women to the labour market after a short period of relatively large numbers of "housewives" is one of the major changes in the post-war employment pattern.

Against the background of these fundamental changes in employment the large-scale geographical changes in the Swedish population appear relatively small. The geographical changes are, however, dramatic in a small-scale perspective. The urbanisation process and the increased flow of goods and people in the extended physical networks are the most evident cultural-geographical expressions of the expansion of the market economy and industrialisation. Even though urbanisation is changing the settlement pattern throughout Sweden, the process is to a large extent an intra-regional one, in which the depopulation of rural areas and the growth of cities and towns has been the most typical phenomenon.

PASSENGER TRANSPORT
1900, 1950 AND 1990

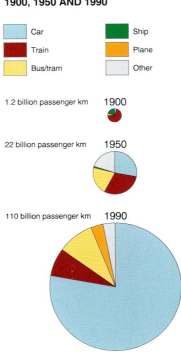

18TH-CENTURY ROAD NETWORK
1:5 000 000

- Province boundary
- Road
- ● Town
- ✳ Fortress

A quarter of a millennium, ten generations, separates these maps. Anyone used to today's road standards might hesitate about including the 18th century's five-six ell-wide (two-three metre) country roads under the heading roads. Not even the most important roads could be fully used by horse-drawn carriages, and the winter roads, not shown here, were vital for local transportation. By comparing the two maps, however, it is possible to see both the continuity and the changes in the road network. The most obvious difference is the absence of roads in the interior of northern Sweden on the 18th-century map.

MAIN ROAD NETWORK 1990
1:5 000 000

- European highway
- National main road
- Primary county road

The map from the 1990s shows the 25 per cent or so of the road network that the state is responsible for. (T144)

(T143)

THE RAILWAY NETWORK
1:10 000 000

— State railway
— Private railway
— Remaining net 1996
■ Junction
● Provincial capital

1916 (T145)

1956/1996 (T146)

THE STEAMBOAT ERA IN SWEDEN
in the mid-19th century

The infrastructure for transportation aims to reduce the friction that all spatial movement has to overcome. The reduction in friction offered by investment in networks causes a time-space compression – to use a concept that is becoming more and more common in human geography. (T147)

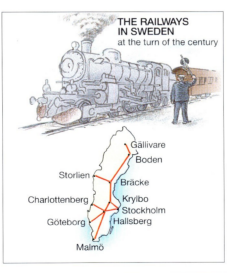

THE RAILWAYS IN SWEDEN
at the turn of the century

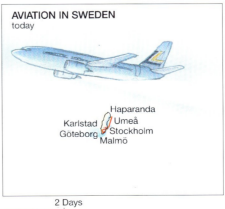

AVIATION IN SWEDEN
today

The Infrastructure

The linking of Sweden's regions and places by various kinds of infrastructure has been particularly intensive since the Industrial Revolution in the late 19th century. It is true that the monarchy tried to standardise road maintenance and the road network as early as the Middle Ages and with greater success in the 17th and 18th centuries; but it was not until 1841 that the state took more active responsibility for planning and financing road and bridge building. The 1853–54 Riksdag decided that the state should construct and operate a network of main railway lines.

The state railways committee decided in the 1850s that the railways should not run parallel with other traffic systems. Instead they should run inland away from the coast and the inland waterways which totally dominated all long-distance goods and passenger transport before the railway age. The railways were to give new life to "slumbering" areas. This meant that the railways had great significance for regional development. With the additional condition that the new transport technology should link up the industrial and economic centres of the country, the railways helped to strengthen the position of the most important towns as well as offering new opportunities for the less well-developed parts of Sweden.

The differences between the road and railway networks are also quantitative. At its peak in 1938 the railway network had 16,999 km of track. Even then, before motor traffic had become widespread, the state road network was more than five times longer. Since then the railway network has diminished while the road network has continued to expand. If one adds to the state road network the roads which are maintained by municipalities and private persons, the Swedish road network, with a total length of 415,000 km, would run more than ten times round the world.

The rapid expansion of the domestic airline network over the past 25 years has shrunk Sweden even more. This relative shortening of distances is, however, like the effects of new investments in express trains, unequally distributed over the country. Access to the largest towns is increasing, while it may even be decreasing to small towns.

Industrial development in the Skellefteå district has transformed the old agricultural area on the north bank of the river downstream from the town. Remains of the old buildings can be seen down by the river.

Urbanisation

NORTHERN VÄSTERBOTTEN — A REGIONAL EXAMPLE

The urbanisation process in the area consisting today of the municipalities of Skellefteå, Norsjö and Malå both resembles and differs from urbanisation in other Swedish regions. Urbanisation often leads to both increases and decreases in the density of population: towns and urban districts increase their populations, while sparsely inhabited areas lose even more of their populations. The urbanisation of the Skellefteå region is the result, as elsewhere, of the spread of industrialism and the market economy, but compared to many parts of southern Sweden industrialisation has come fairly late and the post-war growth of the public sector has meant a great deal for urban communities in northern Västerbotten.

An important difference from the process in southern Sweden is also that the rural parishes have not only retained their populations for a long time, but even increased them. The reason is that this early urbanisation is taking place to a certain extent alongside a colonisation of the sparsely populated inland districts, which the government has long been encouraging.

The history of settlement in the Norrland river valleys is a very long one. In the eastern parts of northern Västerbotten the population lived mainly along the coast and in the lower Skellefteå valley in the Middle Ages. There was also a more isolated concentration round Lakes Bjurträsket and Bygdeträsket. The population were for the most yeomen farmers, who could only to a limited extent get their livelihood from their rather small farms. Cattle farming was by far the most dominant activity and meadows for hay harvests and grazing occupied a major part of the arable land. As in other parts of northern Sweden hunting and fishing also played an important role.

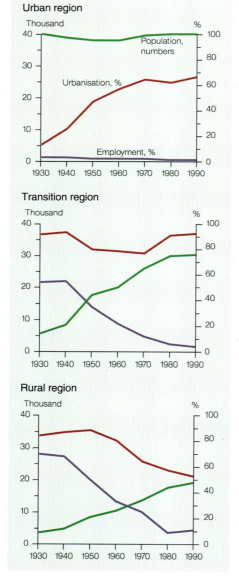

POPULATION, URBANISATION AND EMPLOYMENT IN FORESTRY AND AGRICULTURE 1930–1990

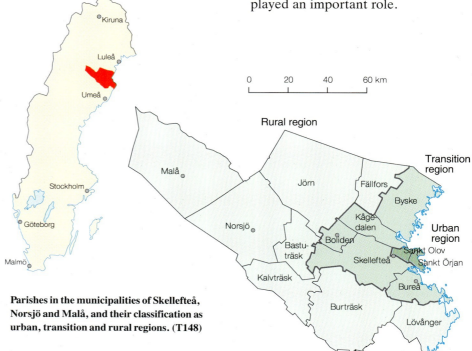

Parishes in the municipalities of Skellefteå, Norsjö and Malå, and their classification as urban, transition and rural regions. (T148)

GROWTH OF POPULATION, 1860–1990, IN NORTHERN VÄSTERBOTTEN

District/Parish	1860	%	1930	%	1990	%	Degree of density 1990, %
Urban region	,347	1.2	5,203	6.9	26,668	31.5	99.8
Transition region	14,724	48.9	36,665	48.5	37,006	43.6	75.8
Rural region:	15,058	50.0	33,755	44.6	21,109	24.9	47.8
Malå	,784	2.6	3,782	5.0	4,154	4.9	65.1
Norsjö-Bastuträsk	2,117	7.0	6,846	9.1	5,371	6.3	52.9
Burträsk-Kalvträsk	5,766	19.1	9,923	13.1	5,332	6.3	40.6
Lövånger	3,713	12.3	4,655	6.2	2,696	3.2	32.9
Fällfors	1,174	3.9	2,700	3.6	1,098	1.3	22.3
Jörn	1,504	5.0	5,849	7.7	2,458	2.9	51.1
Whole area	**30,129**	**100**	**75,623**	**100**	**84,783**	**100**	**76.4**

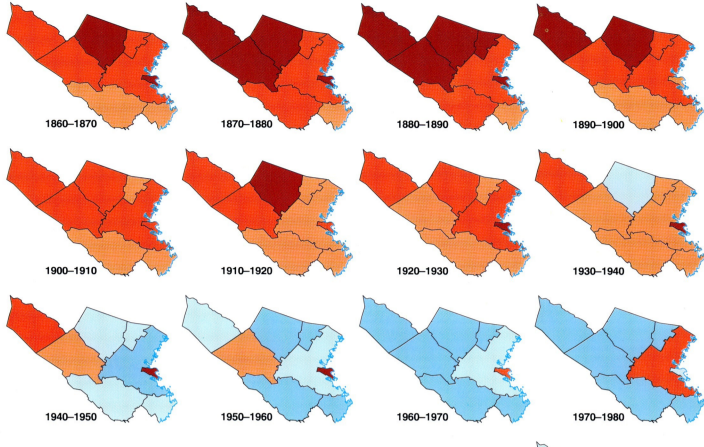

CHANGE IN POPULATION 1860–1990

0 30 60 km

Index
- 120–
- 110–119
- 100–109
- 95–99
- –94

Index with a moving base-year. Index 1860, 1870 etc = 100

This series of maps show schematically relative changes in the population of northern Västerbotten between 1860 and 1990 in ten-year periods with a variable base year. Index = 100 at each even period of ten years. (T149)

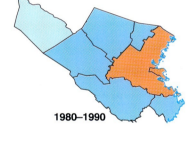

Even though sawmills were in operation at an early date here, it was not until the steam-driven sawmills were established in the Skellefteå district around 1860 that the wood industry became an important driving force in the industrialisation process and the expansion of the market in northern Västerbotten. Some of the small farms surviving on limited resources were now able to supplement their income with lumberjacking, timber floating and sawing. A more detailed analysis of the urbanisation process in this region might well use the year 1860 as its starting point. At that time, 15 years after it had been granted town status, Skellefteå had only 347 inhabitants; only one per cent of the total population of 30,000 in the area lived in the town. Despite its small size the town was the region's contact point with the outer world, and no other place in the district could match its leading mercantile position.

Not until the 20th century was well under way was the growth of Skellefteå matched by a corresponding decrease in the populations of the inland parishes. Several factors combined to break the previously positive population trends inland. Among the most important ones were greater industrialisation resulting from the creation of the Boliden Mining Company in the 1920s, the lack of competitiveness of the small farms and a continually falling birth rate. After this there was also a local urbanisation process in several of the inland parishes, above all in the present municipal centres of Norsjö and Malå. The share of the urban population in the rural parts of the area rose from 9 per cent in 1930 to 48 per cent in 1990.

From the 1950s onwards the areas outside the Skellefteå urban district did not manage to retain their populations in spite of continuing local urbanisation. The result was depopulation, deserted farms, a rising average age in the remaining population and an even greater dependence on state and municipal grants and allowances to maintain employment and services. Increasing mechanisation in forestry and mining reduced the demand for labour in sectors that were traditional in the region. The population of the rural areas decreased from 35,000 in 1950 to 21,100 in 1990.

The urban region of Skellefteå, which had been growing for many years as a result of people moving in from the inland districts, has not been able to maintain the same rapid rate of expansion as before 1970. Like other medium-sized towns Skellefteå is expanding and the rise in population is mainly in the western parts of the town, but this is a growth in population that cannot balance the serious decreases inland. The consequence is that there are now somewhat fewer people living in the whole of the area under investigation in northern Västerbotten than there were in 1960. Its share of Sweden's population fell from 1.15 per cent in 1960 to 0.99 per cent in 1990. Nevertheless there is reason to claim that the colonisation effects of the late 19th and early 20th centuries on the region as a whole have not yet totally disappeared. In 1870 only 0.78 per cent of Sweden's population lived there.

The increase in population is found today mainly in the urban Skellefteå region, about 40 per cent of whose population in the late 1970s consisted of people whose birth place was in the rural region (13%) and in the intermediate region (26%). Only 30 per cent of Skellefteå's population consists of people born in the town, a figure somewhat below the average for Swedish towns.

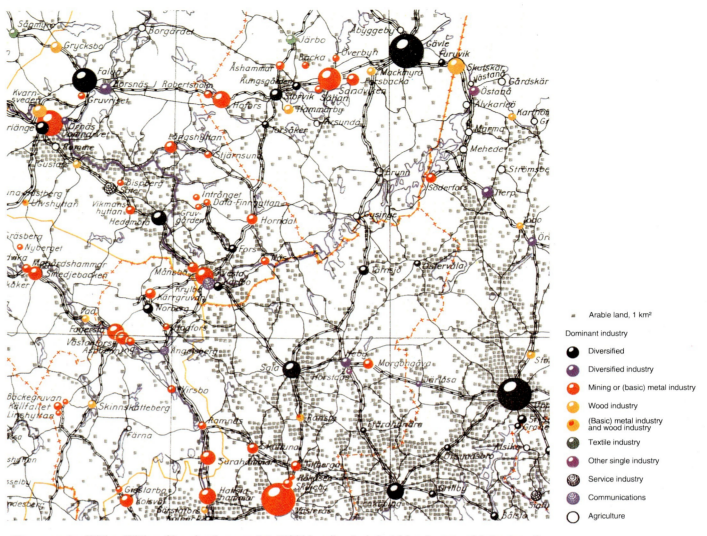

The geographer William William-Olsson's urban map dated 1946 describes the industrial and commercial structure of Swedish urban areas in 1940. Industrial towns were in the majority at that time. There were especially many mining and metal-industry towns in Bergslagen. The structural changes in Swedish industry in the 1970s and 1980s created great problems in many of these places. (T150)

The Industrial Structure of Urban Areas

After exhaustive studies William William-Olsson (1902–1990) published in 1946 an economic map of Sweden which presented a comprehensive picture of the industrial life of Sweden's urban areas in 1940. Apart from this description of the industrial character of Sweden's 1,210 or so independent urban areas, as they are called, an accompanying commentary also describes the industrial life of rural areas. William-Olsson's original map at the scale of 1:1 million showing part of central Sweden is reproduced here.

William-Olsson's description of the industrial character of urban areas is based on data concerning the distribution of occupations in the various industries. Usually a criterion is applied whereby if more than half those working in a particular urban area work in manufacturing, the place is called an industrial urban area. Furthermore if half of those working in manufacturing work in one particular industry, that industrial urban area is termed one-sided—for example, 175 wood-industry urban areas, 144 mining and metal-industry urban areas. Diversified industrial urban areas (113) do not have this one-sided character, just as a diversified urban area (377) is not dominated by one sector.

During the 50 years that have passed since William-Olsson surveyed the industrial character of urban areas, most of them have undergone a considerable transformation. This transformation has been so complete that William-Olsson's criteria for classifying urban areas can no longer be fully applied when describing today's industrial life and its new variations. This is particularly true of the service sector, whose growth at the expense of primary industries and manufacturing is one of the most remarkable features of the post-war period. The term "clerical urban area" was given by William-Olsson to those urban areas (26) that had less than half its workers employed in manufacturing but more than 25 per cent employed in the production of services. In addition he classified on a similar basis 34 urban areas as communication urban areas. Using this 25% criterion in 1990 would mean that almost 90 per cent of all urban areas with more than 50 employees would be classified as clerical urban areas.

Employing the 50% criterion for the production of services and also making a distinction between the public and private service sectors gives a better picture of the variations in the urban-area system in the 1990s.

Generally speaking large urban areas have a more diversified structure than small urban areas. For this reason large urban areas will have a relatively uniform balance between the production of goods (manufacturing, electricity, gas, district heating and construction work), the production of public services and the production of private services. In contrast small urban areas will have greater specialisation in one of these three sectors. This relationship may

INDUSTRIAL STRUCTURE OF URBAN AREAS BY NUMBER OF PEOPLE EMPLOYED

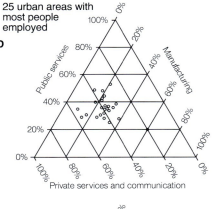
25 urban areas with most people employed

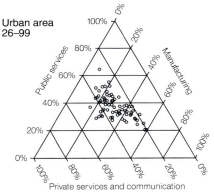
Urban area 26–99

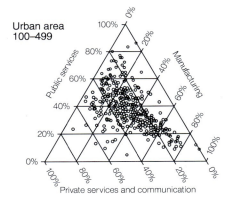
Urban area 100–499

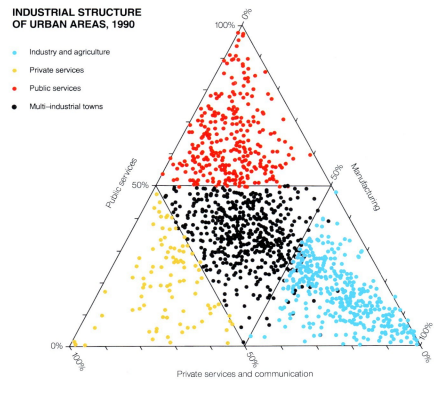
INDUSTRIAL STRUCTURE OF URBAN AREAS, 1990

- Industry and agriculture
- Private services
- Public services
- Multi-industrial towns

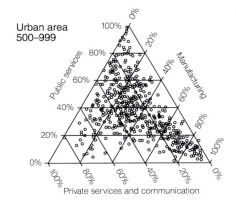
Urban area 500–999

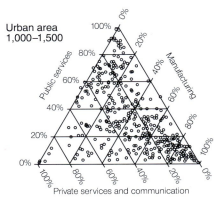
Urban area 1,000–1,500

Statistics Sweden's statistics for the work places of the population do not have the same precision and coverage as the statistics for dwelling. About 15 per cent of those gainfully employed in 1990 were registered as "work place unknown", although it was possible to specify for almost all of them the municipality in which they worked and their particular branch of industry. By means of a proportionalising method persons with an unknown work place have been allocated for each municipality to urban and rural areas.

be observed by first ranking the urban areas according to the number of people employed and then describing them according to their industrial structure.

The 25 largest urban areas usually have less than 40 per cent of employment in goods production and more than 25 per cent in private and in public service production respectively. The next 75 urban areas often have less private service production but more goods production. The smaller the place we examine, the greater the likelihood that we will find strong specialisation in one of the three sectors.

Using a triangular diagram the diversified urban areas appear in the centre while the specialised ones are in or near the corners. Those employed in each urban area (the day population) have been allocated to the three main sectors: the production of goods, public services and private services. These sectors always add up to 100%, which is also a pre-requisite for using the triangular diagram.

INDUSTRIAL CHARACTER OF SWEDISH TOWNS, 1990

Type of town, >50 % employed in one industrial sector	No of towns	Inhabitants '000	Inhabitants %	Nos. employed '000	% of all employees
Agriculture, forestry	12	7	0.1	3	0.1
Industry:	394	632	8.9	367	9.0
>50 % employed in:					
Mining and metal manufacturing	24	103	1.4	59	1.4
Engineering	125	203	2.8	132	3.2
Forest industries	106	149	2.1	85	2.1
Other places with one dominant industry	100	95	1.3	49	1.2
Places with many different industries	39	83	1.2	43	1.0
Private services	116	1,264	17.7	793	19.4
Public services	345	649	9.1	264	6.4
Multi-industrial towns	633	4,454	62.5	2,266	65.0
Places with <50 employees	341	122	1.7	7	0.2
Total, all towns	**1,841**	**7,128**	**100**	**4,100**	**100**

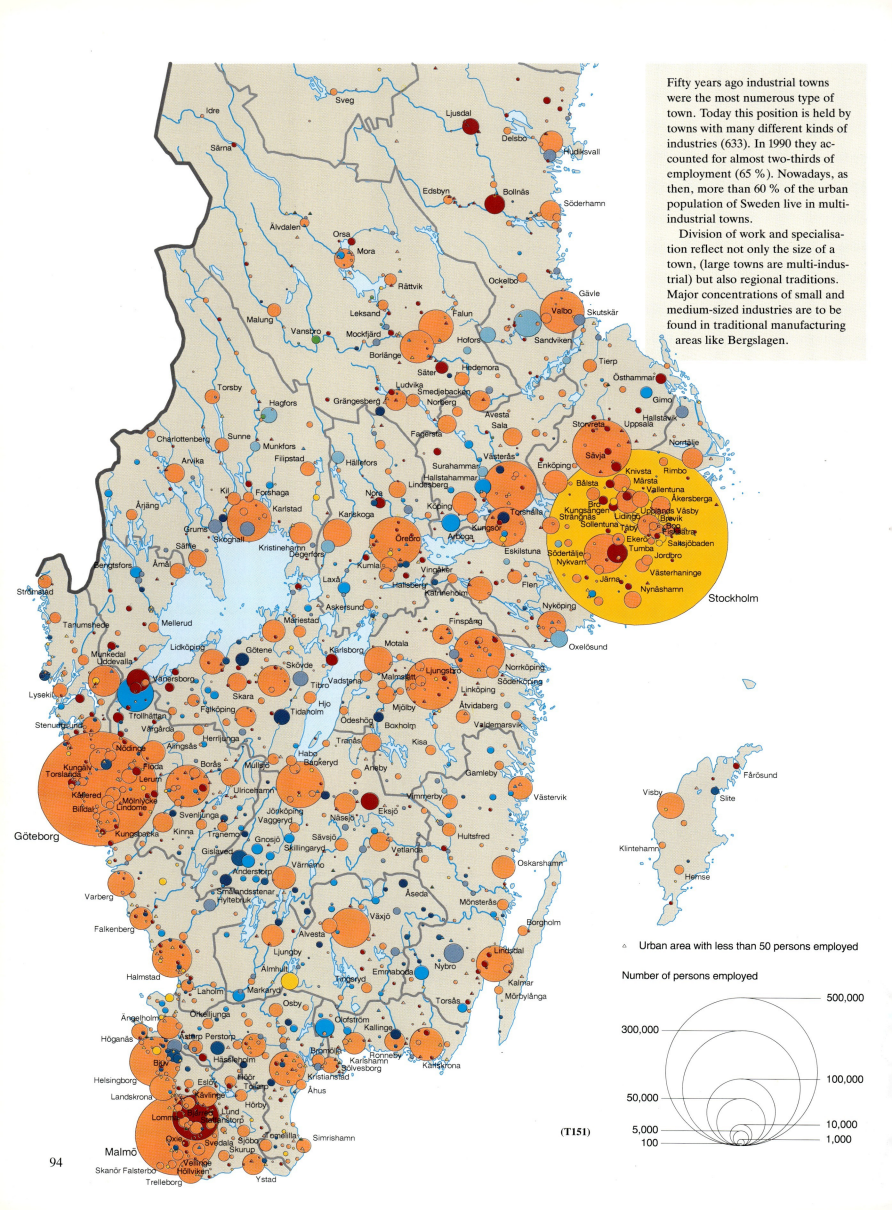

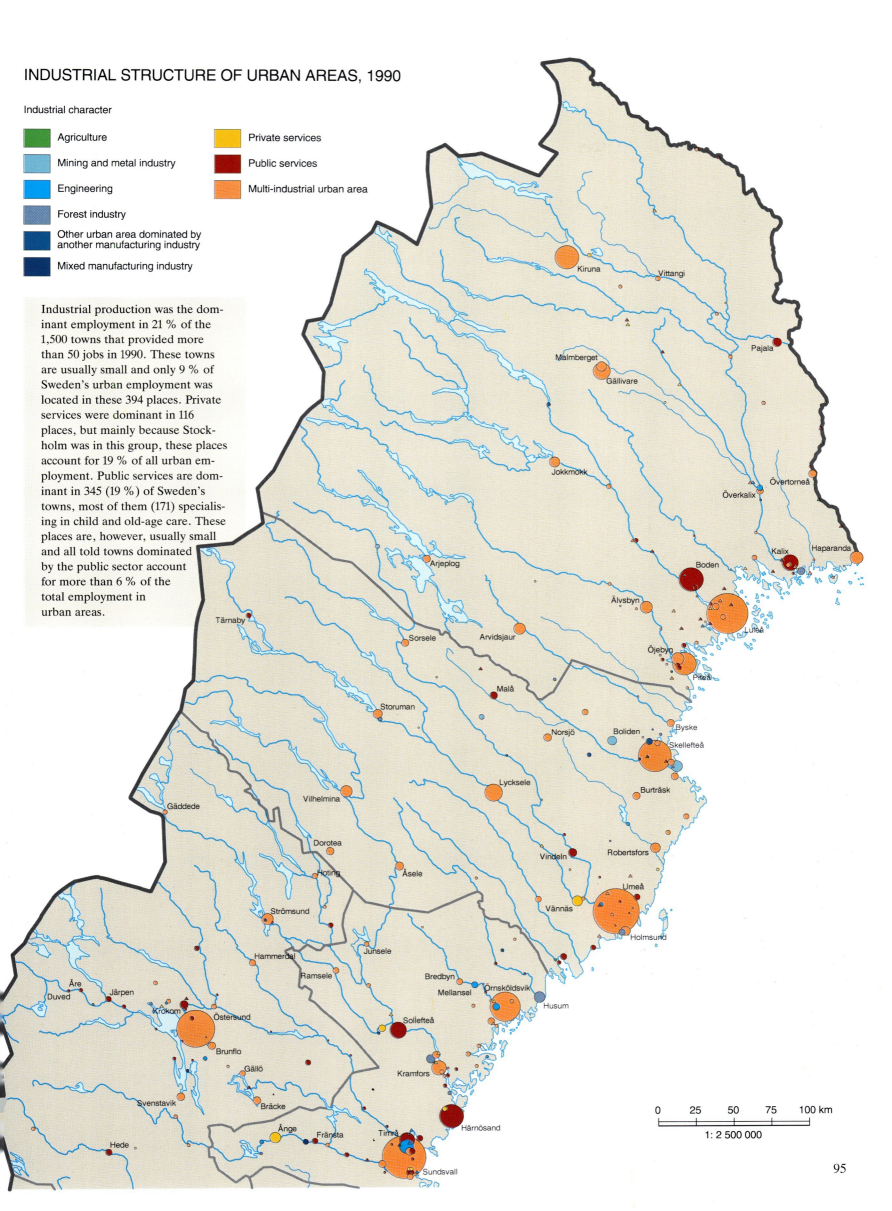

Regional Specialisation

The industrial specialisation that developed in Sweden as a result of industrialisation to a large extent followed a sectoral pattern. Certain regions manufactured iron and steel products, others forest products or cloth and clothing, etc. The basis for this was often the regional distribution of raw materials and natural resources, but also the traditions of handicraft production. Many of the communities that grew up in such regions remained strongly dominated by the original industry. The Bergslagen region, for example, became at an early date a generally speaking continuous area of mill towns manufacturing iron and steel products. Similarly the expanding forest industry developed at a later date a large number of industrial communities along the coast of Norrland. The textile industry in Borås and the glass and furniture industries in Småland are further examples of early regional specialisation.

These locational patterns are still evident today. At a more general industrial level it is evident, for example, that capital-intensive industries are still relatively important for the Bergslagen and Norrland counties. Knowledge-intensive industries, including the important car industry, have a strong position in south-west Sweden, whereas labour-intensive industries are over-represented in the interior of southern Sweden. The research and development-intensive industries are mostly concentrated in the Stockholm area and in Östergötland.

It is only natural that regions dominated by large companies fit into the locational pattern of the capital-intensive process industries. Bergslagen, the area round Lake Vänern, the coast of southern Norrland and the mining district of the far north stand out on the map.

In contrast small firms are a characteristic feature of industry in areas like the interior of Norrland, western Dalarna and northern Värmland. Parts of Småland and neighbouring regions are also dominated by small firms. Gnosjö is a well-known example of a municipality with many small firms engaged in small-scale manufacturing.

In recent years great attention has been paid to a number of successful regional economies in North America and Western Europe. These "industrial districts" are characterised by a rich diversity of small and medium-sized companies within the same or connected sectors, with intensive internal flows of goods, services, information and personnel. These regions also

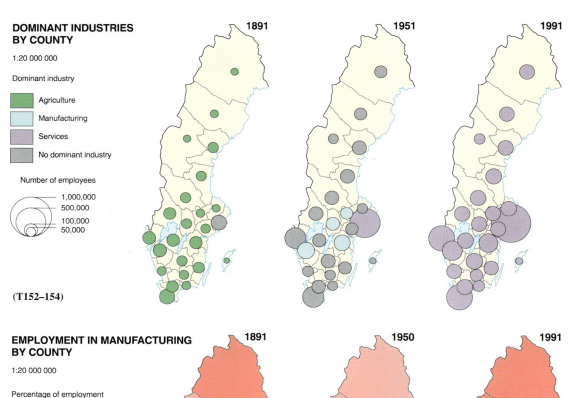

THE CHANGING CHARACTER OF INDUSTRY

The maps show Sweden's transformation from a country primarily engaged in agriculture, via industrialisation to a situation in which most people are employed in service industries. The circles show employment in absolute figures within each of the main sectors of industry, according to county, for various years. In the late 19th century agriculture dominated all the counties, but 100 years later the service sector is predominant.

INDUSTRIAL EMPLOYMENT

The regional concentration of industry may be measured by comparing the share of industrial employment of the total employment figure at the county level with industrial employment in the country as a whole. In the late 19th century a high percentage of industrial employment in a county was due to the fact that the primary sector played a relatively minor role. A hundred years later the relative level of industrial employment is highest in those counties that have a lower level of employment in the service sector.

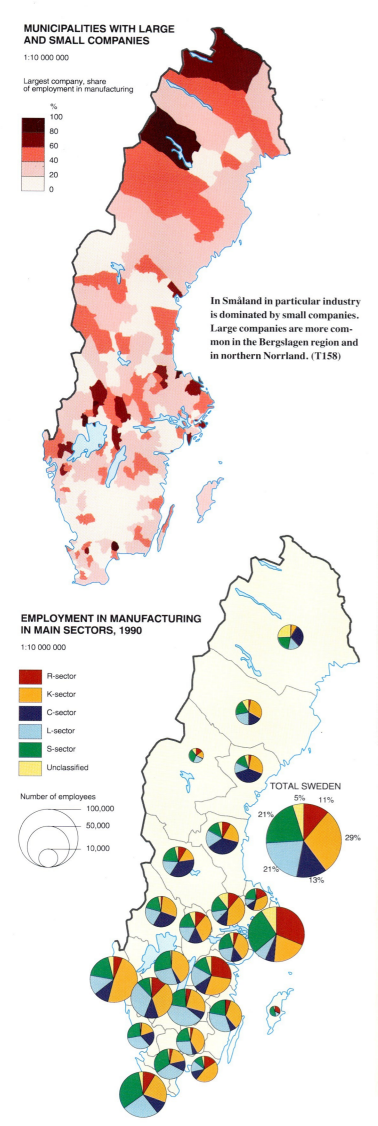

MUNICIPALITIES WITH LARGE AND SMALL COMPANIES
1:10 000 000

Largest company, share of employment in manufacturing
%
100
80
60
40
20
0

In Småland in particular industry is dominated by small companies. Large companies are more common in the Bergslagen region and in northern Norrland. (T158)

EMPLOYMENT IN MANUFACTURING IN MAIN SECTORS, 1990
1:10 000 000

- R-sector
- K-sector
- C-sector
- L-sector
- S-sector
- Unclassified

Number of employees: 100,000 / 50,000 / 10,000

boast considerable social, cultural and institutional networks which contribute to the favourable working climate and well-developed forms for co-operation between companies and local and regional institutions and actors. A well-known international example of a region like this is the Third Italy (central and north-east Italy), with its small-scale firms mainly in textiles and clothing. Apart from the small-scale engineering and wooden goods industries in Småland there are similar agglomerations of energetic small firms in the areas round Mora and Skellefteå and elsewhere.

Since the mid-1960s manufacturing has lost much of its share of employment in Sweden. Instead, the expansion of the service industries has made most regions very dependent on various parts of the service sector. In particular the strong growth of the public sector during the post-war period has helped to make the structure of working life, both locally and regionally, more homogenous.

The regions' natural and raw-material resources may be expected to diminish in importance for future regional specialisation. High-tech companies in electronics and the computer industry, pharmaceuticals or advanced business services are dependent in the first place on information and knowledge-rich environments with good communications, both in their own region and with more remote centres. Many of these high-tech and knowledge-intensive activities are also influenced by strong agglomerative forces, that is, the benefits of being located in the same area as similar companies and important clients and suppliers. Apart from the big cities, some of the university towns in Sweden also provide these advantages.

MAIN SECTORS IN INDUSTRY

R-sector (R & D-intensive): Consists of industries which devote large resources to research and development, such as the electronics, the computer and the pharmaceutical industries.
K-sector (Knowledge-intensive): Industries with a high level of technology, such as the car industry and engineering.
C-sector (Capital-intensive): Raw-material industries requiring large capital investments in relation to the processed value, such as the paper and pulp industries and the chemical industry.
L-sector (Labour-intensive): Industries with large numbers of employees in relation to the processed value, such as the textile industry.
S-sector (Sheltered sector): Industries oriented towards the home market, such as parts of the food industry and parts of the mineral goods industry.

Research-intensive industry plays an important role in Stockholm and Östergötland, whereas labour-intensive activities are over-represented in Jönköping County and Älvsborg County. Capital-intensive industry is important in the two northernmost counties and in parts of central Sweden. (T159)

Research and knowledge-intensive work is increasing in importance, while labour-intensive and sheltered industry are declining.

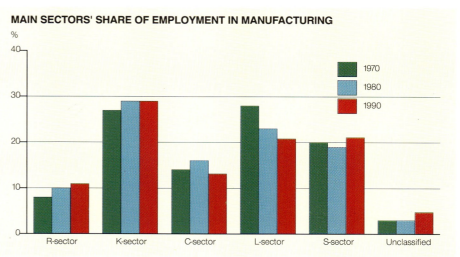

MAIN SECTORS' SHARE OF EMPLOYMENT IN MANUFACTURING

(1970, 1980, 1990 across R-sector, K-sector, C-sector, L-sector, S-sector, Unclassified)

INDUSTRIAL CONTRIBUTION TO EMPLOYMENT, GNP AND EXPORTS, 1993

Industry	Number employed	% of women	% of GNP	Exports, Tkr	Exports, net value Tkr
Agriculture, forestry, fisheries	101,966	25.1	2.5	1,360,699	−9,172,246
Mining and quarrying	9,960	11.6	0.3	5,151,773	−15,230,891
Manufacturing industries	758,266	27.7	21.1	373,515,239	75,229,466
Food industry	74,587	38.9	2.4	7,420,883	−11,863,028
Textiles, clothing, footwear	21,853	57.3	0.4	7,474,733	−18,602,590
Sawmills and wooden goods	59,083	20.9	1.3	23,154,315	16,992,936
Pulp, paper and graphics	110,858	32.5	3.3	50,163,806	40,536,215
Chemicals, plastic, oil	66,198	35.9	2.9	60,697,305	−1,519,891
Stone and clay goods	20,926	20.4	0.4	4,325,032	−1,726,009
Metal manufacturing	35,403	16.3	1.0	26,135,073	11,525,944
Engineering	363,201	23.0	9.2	194,144,092	39,885,889
Electricity, gas, heating, water	31,740	20.1	3.3	948,109	461,320
Construction	255,503	8.6	6.4	–	–
Commerce, hotels and catering	548,313	49.5	10.9	–	–
Transport, post, telephones	290,772	31.4	6.3	–	–
Banking, insurance, estate management, consultancy	373,919	45.4	26.1	–	–
Public sector	1 619,040	71.3	23.1	7 314,414	2 745,699
Total	**3,119,287**	**48.9**	**100**	**388,290,249**	**54,033,318**

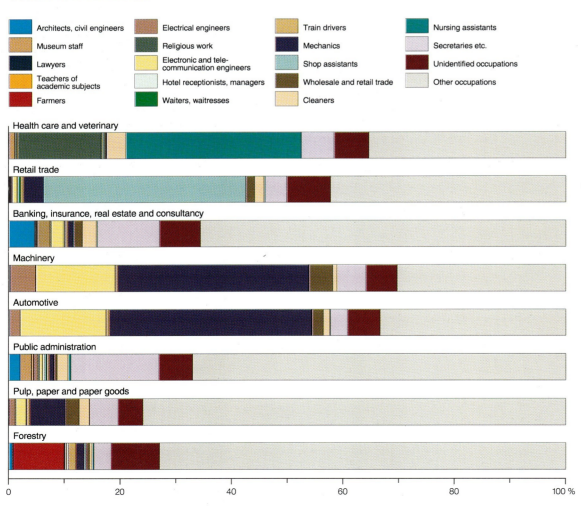

Work, Occupation and Industry

Sweden's industries are presented in the following section with a traditional division into branches. The concept of industrial branch is established on the labour market; both employers' federations and trade unions make use of this division. In traditional basic industries like agriculture, forestry and the iron and steel industry a division into branches of industry also ties in with chains in the production process from raw material to finished product.

While there are good reasons for studying Swedish industry from the point of view of its branches it is important to realise that these branches contribute to very different extents to the total production and the national economy. The forest industry, for example, accounts for only 4 per cent of the GNP and 5 per cent of employment. Yet this industry has a large net export value, which is due to the small amount of imported components. Thus the forest industry contributes more to the balance of payments than the whole manufacturing industry, which uses a great deal of imported components.

If one divides the GNP up regionally, that is, the value of the goods and services produced in Sweden in a year, another pattern appears. Regions dominated by capital-intensive work such as energy production or process industries usually have a high gross regional product (GRP). The same is true of regions with a large percentage of knowledge-intensive services industries. In contrast sparsely populated areas, dominated by agriculture and forestry, have a low GRP.

Another connection that cuts right across industrial branch divisions is the relationship between branch and occupation. This means that people with a specific occupation may only be employed in one or a few industrial branches, while a different specific

In this diagram the eight sectors that had the largest number of employees in 1990 are matched with the 20 occupations held by the largest number of people. All in all every fifth employee is covered by this combination. Certain occupations are highly concentrated in one sector, for example teachers, farmers, shop assistants and nursing orderlies, while secretaries, for example, can work in almost any sector. Conversely certain sectors employ a small range of occupations while others may employ people with very different occupations.

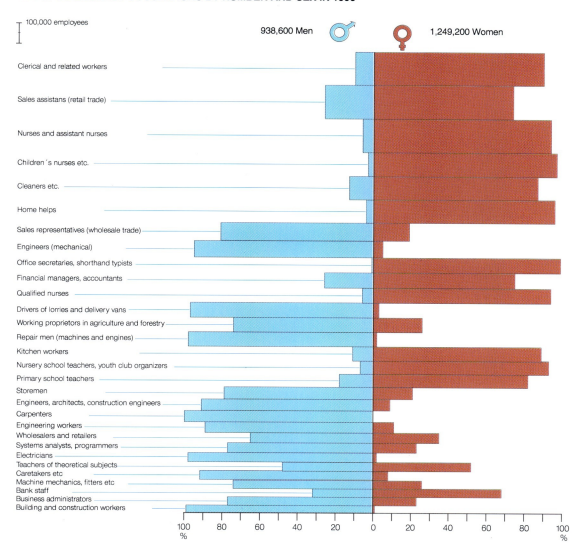

THE 30 COMMONEST OCCUPATIONS BY NUMBER AND SEX IN 1990

938,600 Men 1,249,200 Women

Clerical and related workers
Sales assistans (retail trade)
Nurses and assistant nurses
Children´s nurses etc.
Cleaners etc.
Home helps
Sales representatives (wholesale trade)
Engineers (mechanical)
Office secretaries, shorthand typists
Financial managers, accountants
Qualified nurses
Drivers of lorries and delivery vans
Working proprietors in agriculture and forestry
Repair men (machines and engines)
Kitchen workers
Nursery school teachers, youth club organizers
Primary school teachers
Storemen
Engineers, architects, construction engineers
Carpenters
Engineering workers
Wholesalers and retailers
Systems analysts, programmers
Electricians
Teachers of theoretical subjects
Caretakers etc
Machine mechanics, fitters etc
Bank staff
Business administrators
Building and construction workers

GROSS REGIONAL PRODUCT

1:10 000 000

100–130
90–99
85–89
75–84

Index, total Sweden = 100

set of skills may be useful in a number of branches.

This unilateral dependence on both branch and occupation is particularly evident among women, because the care functions of the public sector and the private service sector, especially in administration and the retail trade, employ a large number of women in just a few occupations.

The traditional picture of industry divided up into branches has up to now been reflected in the regional distribution of unemployment. Recessions or structural crises in certain branches have hit certain parts of the country more harshly than others. The problems facing the forest industry were clearly reflected in increased unemployment in the Norrland counties. The structural crisis in the steel industry in the 1970s resulted in a higher level of unemployment in Bergslagen.

During the recession of the early 1990s, however, the geographical distribution of unemployment presented new patterns. Instead of striking the traditionally hard-hit branches and regions, unemployment showed a more even geographical distribution, embracing a larger percentage of office workers than previously. There are several reasons. When goods-producing companies disappeared because of bankruptcy and closures, one result was a high level of unemployment among office workers because of the increasing amount of service work involved in the production of goods. Nor has the public sector been utilised, as it was previously, to even out the business cycles.

In three counties – Stockholm, Göteborg and Bohus, and Västernorrland – the production value per inhabitant was greater than the national average in 1990. The counties of Älvsborg, Skaraborg, Halland, Kristianstad and Blekinge also have a low regional product. (T160)

When unemployment was still comparatively low among white-collar workers in 1990, Norrbotten and Västerbotten were the hardest hit. When unemployment reached very much higher levels in 1995, it was more equally spread and affected the whole country. (T161–163)

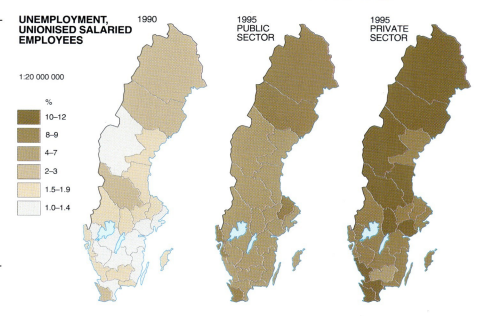

UNEMPLOYMENT, UNIONISED SALARIED EMPLOYEES

1990 | 1995 PUBLIC SECTOR | 1995 PRIVATE SECTOR

1:20 000 000

%
10–12
8–9
4–7
2–3
1.5–1.9
1.0–1.4

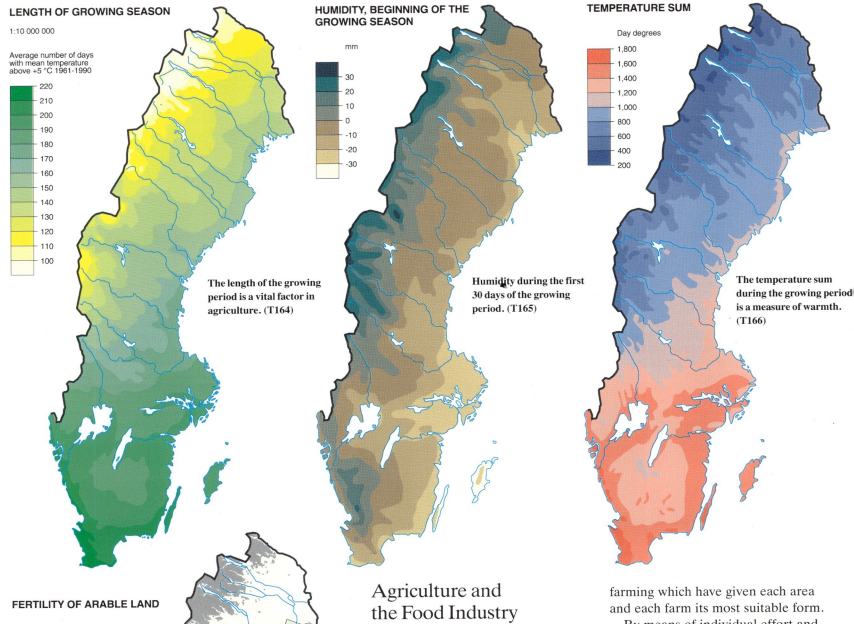

LENGTH OF GROWING SEASON
1:10 000 000

Average number of days with mean temperature above +5 °C 1961-1990
- 220
- 210
- 200
- 190
- 180
- 170
- 160
- 150
- 140
- 130
- 120
- 110
- 100

The length of the growing period is a vital factor in agriculture. (T164)

HUMIDITY, BEGINNING OF THE GROWING SEASON

mm
- 30
- 20
- 10
- 0
- -10
- -20
- -30

Humidity during the first 30 days of the growing period. (T165)

TEMPERATURE SUM

Day degrees
- 1,800
- 1,600
- 1,400
- 1,200
- 1,000
- 800
- 600
- 400
- 200

The temperature sum during the growing period is a measure of warmth. (T166)

FERTILITY OF ARABLE LAND
1:10 000 000

High
Low
Area above tree-line

Rough classification of the productivity of arable land – the higher the class, the better the land. (T167)

Agriculture and the Food Industry

Situated in the intermediate zone between the cultivatable part of the earth and the wilderness of the polar regions, Sweden is divided by the limit for many of the cultivated plants of the cold-temperate zone. That is why the conditions of Swedish agriculture vary so greatly, depending on soil, precipitation and temperature. The vegetative period is almost twice as long in the south as in the north of the country. The important water-retaining qualities of the ground at the beginning of the vegetative period vary mainly in an east-west direction and there is greatest warmth in the central and southern plains and coastal areas, where the glacial rivers and seas deposited the richest soils.

Under these conditions Swedish agriculture has developed between two poles for the most favourable use of land — arable farming and horticulture in the south and cattle farming in the north. Regional and local variations have then changed the combinations of arable farming and cattle farming which have given each area and each farm its most suitable form.

By means of individual effort and state projects for drainage, new cultivation and colonisation the area under cultivation was increased to cope with the rapidly growing population of the 19th century. The area under cultivation more than doubled between 1800 and 1930, when it was at its peak. Since then it has decreased, while productivity has increased.

Historically, agriculture developed from cattle farming, but at the same time as arable farming improved its productivity greatly after the 1850s, thanks to land reform and new technology, food processing concentrated more and more on animal products. The restructuring of agriculture over the past few decades, which has aimed at reducing the grain surplus, is reinforcing this trend. Arable land provides more productive grazing than the pastures that were traditionally grazed. These changes in production and land use mean that the districts on the plains account for an increasing share of production.

The fact that agriculture has statis-

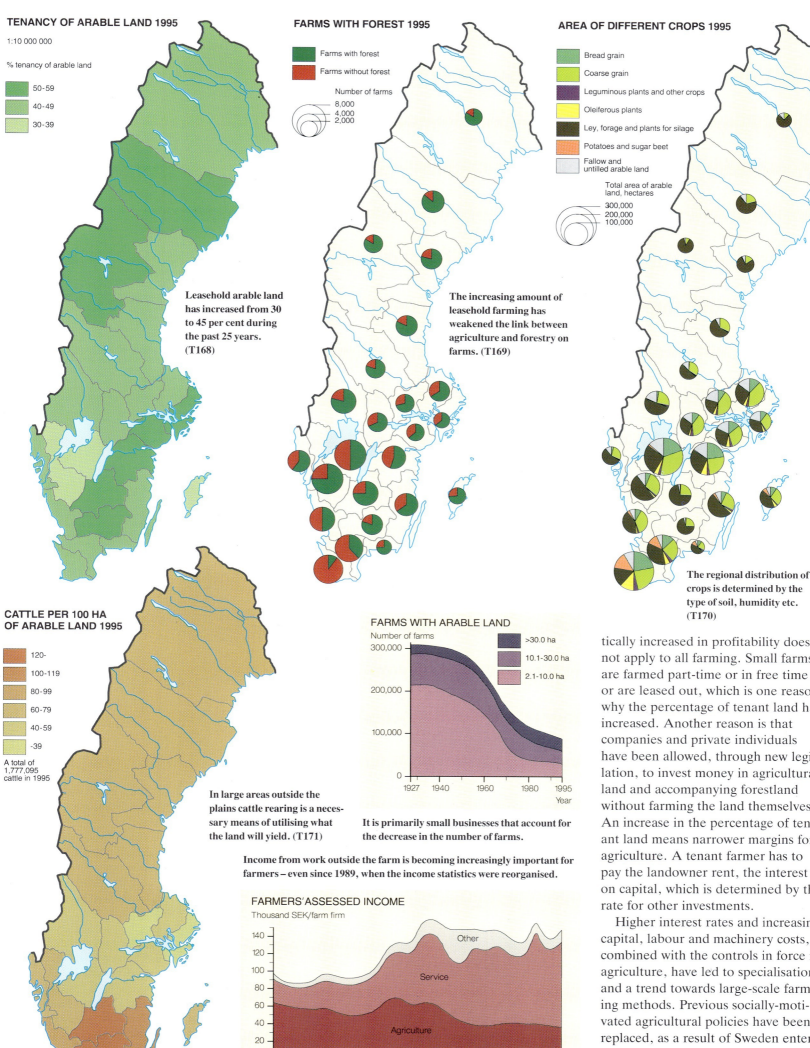

TENANCY OF ARABLE LAND 1995

1:10 000 000

% tenancy of arable land
- 50–59
- 40–49
- 30–39

Leasehold arable land has increased from 30 to 45 per cent during the past 25 years. (T168)

FARMS WITH FOREST 1995

- Farms with forest
- Farms without forest

Number of farms: 8,000 / 4,000 / 2,000

The increasing amount of leasehold farming has weakened the link between agriculture and forestry on farms. (T169)

AREA OF DIFFERENT CROPS 1995

- Bread grain
- Coarse grain
- Leguminous plants and other crops
- Oleiferous plants
- Ley, forage and plants for silage
- Potatoes and sugar beet
- Fallow and untilled arable land

Total area of arable land, hectares: 300,000 / 200,000 / 100,000

The regional distribution of crops is determined by the type of soil, humidity etc. (T170)

CATTLE PER 100 HA OF ARABLE LAND 1995

- 120–
- 100–119
- 80–99
- 60–79
- 40–59
- –39

A total of 1,777,095 cattle in 1995

In large areas outside the plains cattle rearing is a necessary means of utilising what the land will yield. (T171)

FARMS WITH ARABLE LAND

Number of farms
- >30.0 ha
- 10.1–30.0 ha
- 2.1–10.0 ha

It is primarily small businesses that account for the decrease in the number of farms.

Income from work outside the farm is becoming increasingly important for farmers – even since 1989, when the income statistics were reorganised.

FARMERS' ASSESSED INCOME

Thousand SEK/farm firm

Other / Service / Agriculture

---

tically increased in profitability does not apply to all farming. Small farms are farmed part-time or in free time or are leased out, which is one reason why the percentage of tenant land has increased. Another reason is that companies and private individuals have been allowed, through new legislation, to invest money in agricultural land and accompanying forestland without farming the land themselves. An increase in the percentage of tenant land means narrower margins for agriculture. A tenant farmer has to pay the landowner rent, the interest on capital, which is determined by the rate for other investments.

Higher interest rates and increasing capital, labour and machinery costs, combined with the controls in force in agriculture, have led to specialisation and a trend towards large-scale farming methods. Previous socially-motivated agricultural policies have been replaced, as a result of Sweden entering the EU, by a product-regulating policy within a broad European framework.

SWEDISH AGRICULTURE IN TERMS OF ENERGY

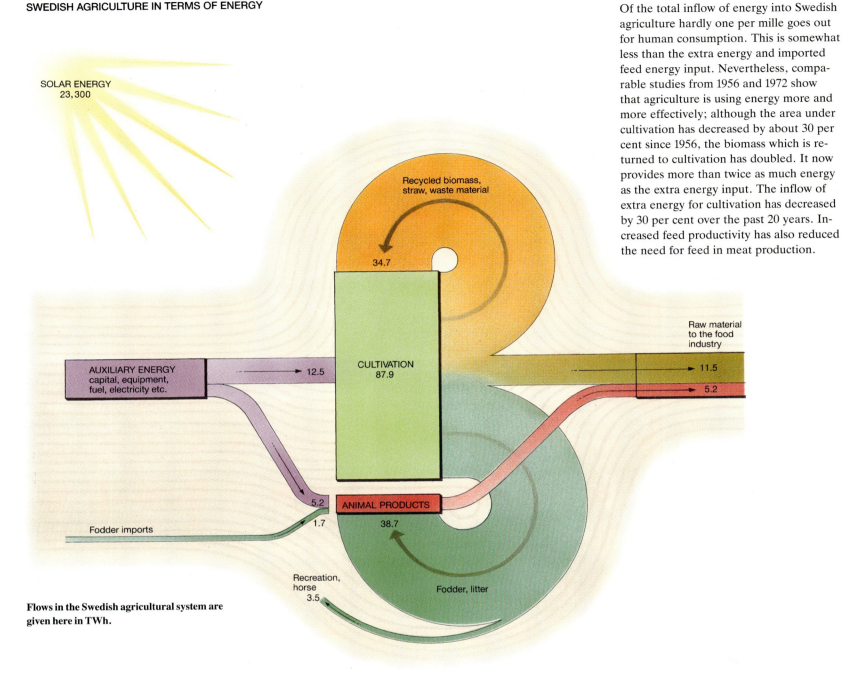

Flows in the Swedish agricultural system are given here in TWh.

Of the total inflow of energy into Swedish agriculture hardly one per mille goes out for human consumption. This is somewhat less than the extra energy and imported feed energy input. Nevertheless, comparable studies from 1956 and 1972 show that agriculture is using energy more and more effectively; although the area under cultivation has decreased by about 30 per cent since 1956, the biomass which is returned to cultivation has doubled. It now provides more than twice as much energy as the extra energy input. The inflow of extra energy for cultivation has decreased by 30 per cent over the past 20 years. Increased feed productivity has also reduced the need for feed in meat production.

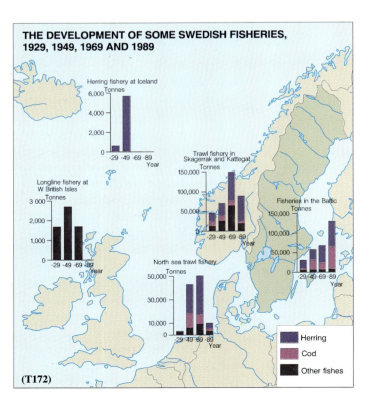

(T172)

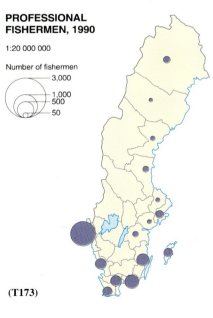

(T173)

THE FISHING INDUSTRY

The post-war period has meant a decline from just over 15,000 professional fishermen to fewer than 3,000 in the fishing industry. Regionally, in southern Sweden and on the west coast, however, fishing is still important. In the 1990s the catch value per kilo of fish has fallen to the lowest level this century. But thanks to technical developments in boats, equipment and navigational aids the productivity of the remaining fishermen has increased tenfold in the past 20 years. The fishing areas off Iceland and the Shetlands have been abandoned, North-Sea fishing has decreased in importance and the fish are now caught in the Skagerrak, the Kattegat and the Baltic Sea. The fish-processing industry is concentrated in Bohuslän, Skåne and Blekinge.

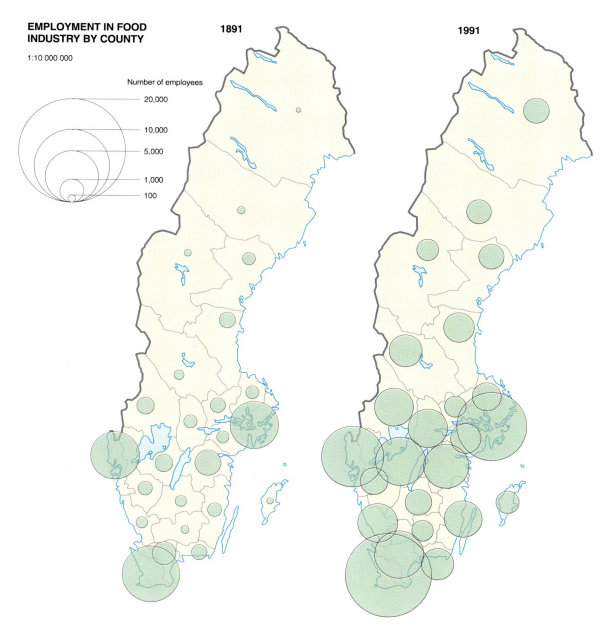

EMPLOYMENT IN FOOD INDUSTRY BY COUNTY
1:10 000 000

Number of employees: 20,000 / 10,000 / 5,000 / 1,000 / 100

1891   1991

ESTABLISHMENTS AND EMPLOYEES IN FOOD INDUSTRY

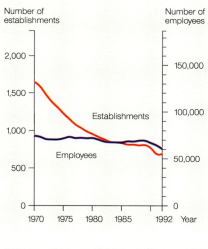

EMPLOYMENT IN FOOD INDUSTRY BY OWNER, 1992

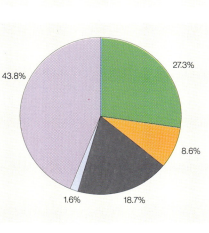

- Farmers cooperatives — 27.3%
- Consumer cooperatives — 8.6%
- Foreign ownership — 18.7%
- State-owned — 1.6%
- Other privately owned — 43.8%

The growth of the foodstuff industry in the past 100 years reflects the markets created by urban concentration. (T174, T175)

THE FOOD INDUSTRY

The food industry in Sweden evolved from specialisation in the agrarian society at the same time as industrialisation and urbanisation created markets. As a result of price agreements and import tariffs it has developed into a domestic-market industry.

The units were small to begin with — local flour mills, slaughterhouses, dairies and breweries. The problem of transporting fresh goods limited their scope. Thus, when food production began to appear in industrial statistics, the localisation picture corresponded closely with the distribution of the population.

As packaging technology developed, thanks to canning, vacuum-drying and deep-freezing, improved keeping qualities and more rapid transport allowed longer transportation and the markets expanded. As small units were gradually amalgamated to make a few large ones, the food industry became more and more clearly market-located. This was also facilitated by the long-distance transport of refrigerated raw materials. Thus, even though the conditions governing localisation have changed radically and companies have increased their level of production and employment, the localisation picture is in general still the same. The most densely populated counties in southern Sweden also have the largest share of the food industry.

Behind the apparently natural expansion and geographical concentration of the food industry lie great changes in ownership. The farmers' cooperative movement has integrated its production with the production of convenience food in cooperatively owned companies like Scan, Arla and Cerelia. From the opposite direction cooperative consumer societies, through the Cooperative Wholesale Society, have created an integrated chain from retailers to their own food manufacturers like Juvel Bakeries, Winner and Foodia. As a result of a number of rescue operations the state has also become the owner of food companies.

Altogether the state and producer/consumer cooperatives owned 37.5 per cent of the food industry in 1992. Another large group of owners are the foreign groups that have been able to get a foothold on the protected Swedish home market by buying up Swedish companies. An extreme example is Marabou, which was first taken over by Norwegian Freia and is now, together with Swiss Suchard, part of the global Philip Morris group with 170,000 employees and an annual turnover of S kr. 75 billion.

Take-overs like these also change the market orientation. For example, about one third of Marabou's production is now exported. Sweden's entry into the EU is in all probability going to lead to a new period of restructuring in the Swedish food industry. Some will turn to exports to survive, others will be driven off the market by competition from imports. The need for fresh capital will open the door to foreign investments. Swedish companies, which up to now have concentrated on the home market, will then be drawn into increasingly large production systems in which production will be divided up within Europe or even globally.

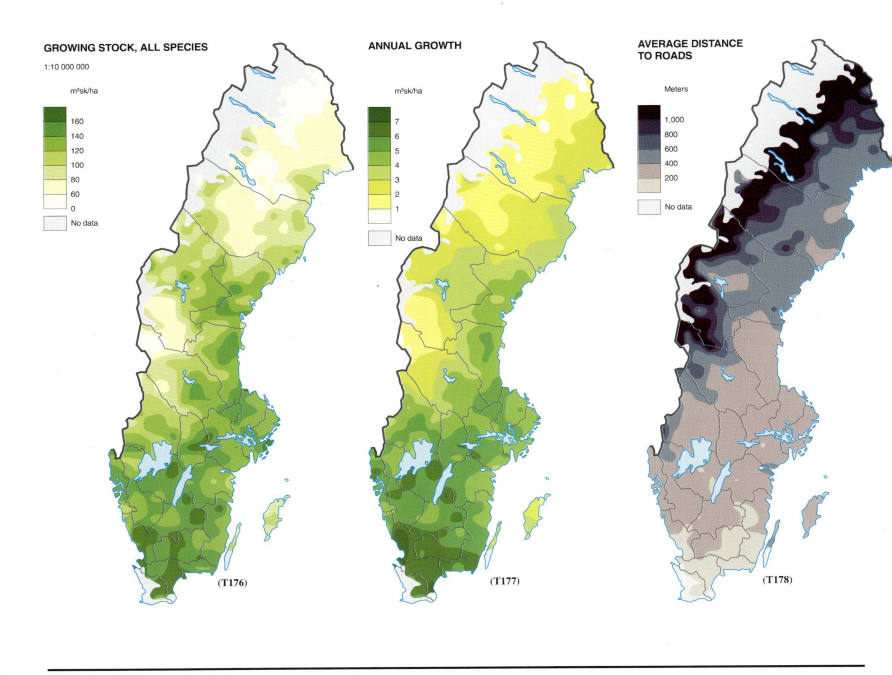

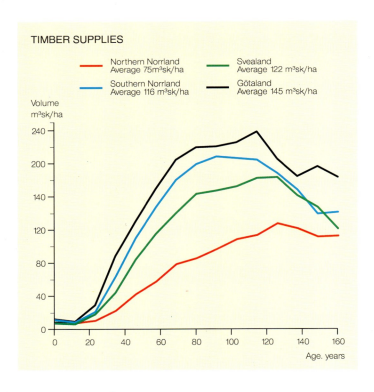

Forestry and the Forest Industries

The Swedish forest industries, which export 80 per cent of their production and account for 20 per cent of Sweden's total exports, are 90-percent based on Swedish raw materials. Thus a study of the Swedish forest industries should start with the source of the domestic raw materials.

The annual rate of growth of the Swedish forests is estimated at present to be 100 million m³, of which the industry extracts between 60 and 70 million m³. The rate of growth and the amount of timber extracted depend on the productivity of the forestland, the climate and environmental factors such as acidification. Sweden's cold climate and long winters slow down the flow of nutrients in the ground, which affects growth.

It is possible, by analysing the age distribution of the volume, to estimate the supply of timber. Age is significant for the supply of timber to the various forest industries and to be able to forecast future declines in the availability of timber.

The transport of timber, which is almost entirely by rail or road today, reinforces the picture of southern and central Sweden and the inland and coast of southern Norrland as being the most important raw-material areas, since they have a larger share of the volume and faster growth.

Which timber and how much of it is extracted each year is also dependent on felling conditions, ownership, price and tax regulations. Three-quarters of all forests are privately owned

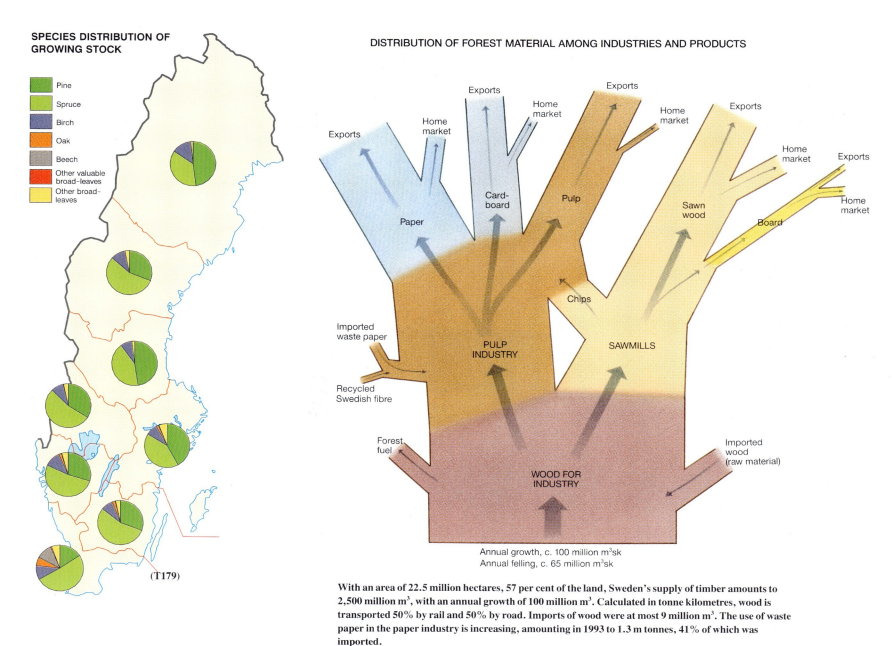

With an area of 22.5 million hectares, 57 per cent of the land, Sweden's supply of timber amounts to 2,500 million m³, with an annual growth of 100 million m³. Calculated in tonne kilometres, wood is transported 50% by rail and 50% by road. Imports of wood were at most 9 million m³. The use of waste paper in the paper industry is increasing, amounting in 1993 to 1.3 m tonnes, 41% of which was imported.

---

and the private forest owners are in the majority in southern and central Sweden, even though there are large areas of company-owned forests in the old milltown forests. Even the forest companies in central and northern Sweden which have large forests of their own are dependent on supplies from private forest owners. The regulations that govern felling affect the whole of the forest industry.

Swedish silviculture has for centuries been a regulated part of the national economy. The forest management plans that every forest owner is obliged to draw up provide the basis for the timber balance in each area. If forestry is to survive, the rate of felling has to be less than the rate of growth, which it is at present.

The Swedish forest industries' raw material requirements could be met within Sweden, but in fact timber is imported to meet the demand for special qualities, kinds and dimensions of wood which are not available or because the prices of imported wood are lower.

The various forest industries, for example the pulp mills and the sawmills, compete to some extent for raw materials and have different opinions about the way timber should be extracted. However, there are synergy effects in the supply of raw materials; sawmills, for example, supply wood chips to the pulp mills and shavings to the board factories.

Up to 90 per cent of Swedish forest exports go to Western Europe. The largest Swedish forest companies — STORA, SCA, MoDo, Korsnäs, AssiDomän and Munksjö — have all merged with other large compa-

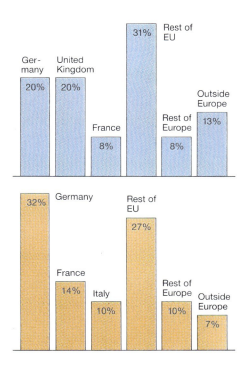

Exports in 1995 of paper and cardboard (top) and pulp (bottom) by recipient country.

SAWMILLS

1:10 000 000

Sawmill for conifers, m³
- • <100,000
- ● 100,000–200,000
- ● >200,000

Sawmill for broad-leaved trees, m³
- • 1,000–10,000
- ● >10,000

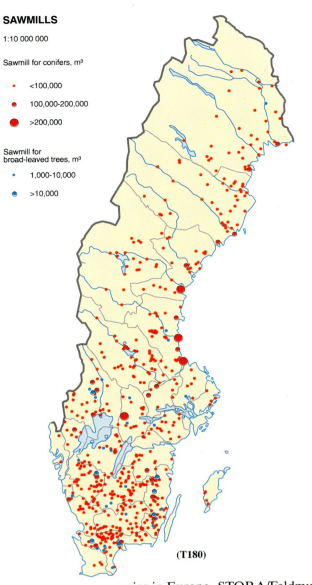

(T180)

PULP INDUSTRY, 1995

1:5 000 000

- Sulphite pulp
- Sulphate pulp
- Semi-chemical and semi-mechanical pulp
- Mechanical pulp
- CTMP

tonnes: 400,000 / 200,000 / 50,000

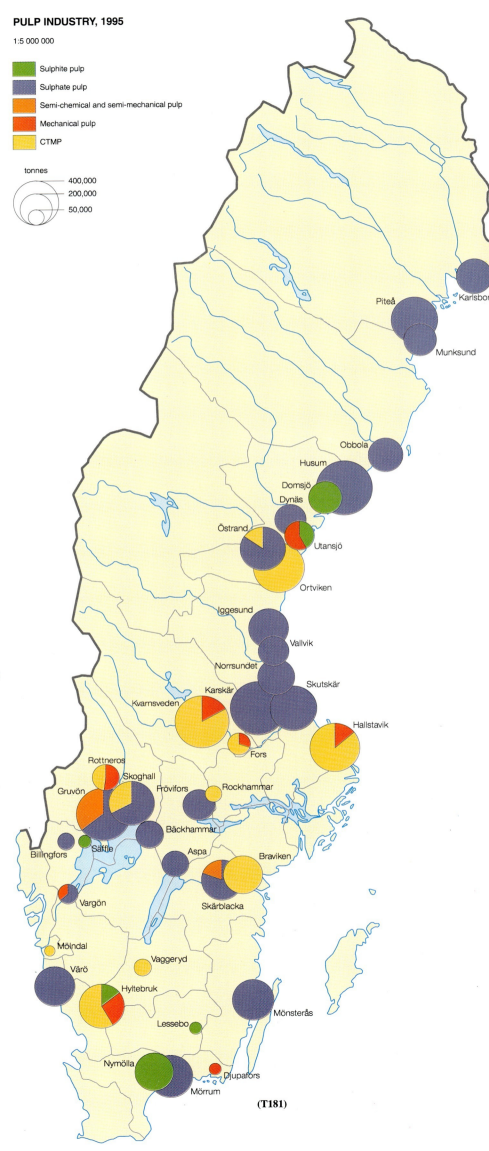

(T181)

nies in Europe. STORA/Feldmuhle is the fifth largest forest company in the world.

Sawmills are spread throughout the country, whereas paper and pulp mills are in the main located along the coasts. It is the power technology of the sawmills that has governed their locations in two stages.

In the first stage, after the 1850s, steam power freed the previously water-driven inland sawmills so that they could move down to better positions for export along the coast. Later many of the early paper and pulp mills were established close to these coastal sawmills. Being located close to each other meant that the companies could coordinate their raw material supplies and transportation to the sawmills and pulp mills. Since the mid-1960s there has also been increasing integration between the pulp and paper industries.

Electrification in the 20th century gave the sawmills a new freedom to relocate. The coastal sawmills grew in size, while smaller and medium-sized sawmills were established inland for local and regional markets.

The twenty largest, and approxi-

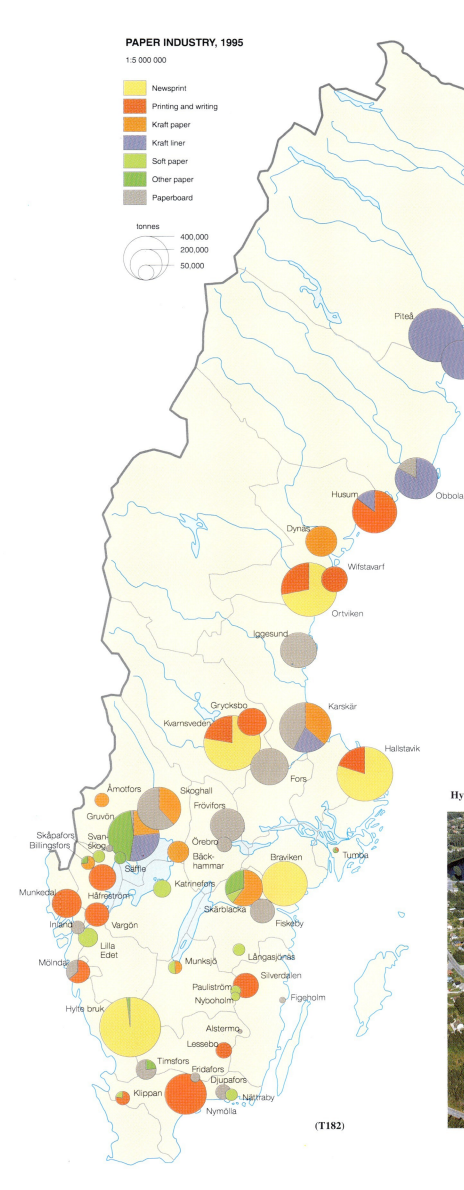

mately equally-sized, pulp mills are relatively evenly distributed along the coast from Norrland to southern Sweden. This is the result of both increasing take-overs and closures and newly established mills like those at Värö, Hylte and Mörrum in the south of Sweden.

There are historical links with the pulp industry and the sawmills in the localisation pattern of the paper industry. As a result of specialisation and market sharing, with consequent variations in export market shares, there is no simple connection between location and market. The newsprint and magazine papermill at Hallstavik, which was originally established by Holmens in Norrköping to be closer to the Stockholm graphic industry, now exports 75 per cent of its production.

The board industry (plywood, chipboard and fibreboard) was forced to reduce its production between 1985 and 1995. Its sales are dependent on the building industry and the furniture industry.

With no more than 100,000 employees the forest industries' contribution to the Swedish economy is considerable. Exports are high, 70 per cent for sawn wood and 80 per cent for paper and pulp, while imports of goods for the industries are relatively small. Thus the forest industries contribute S kr. 50 billion, corresponding to 20 per cent of the net exports of Swedish industry. Even though Swedish forest products are sensitive to market and price changes, the long-term forecast is still continuing growth.

Hylte papermill, founded in 1908, on the river Nissan in Halland.

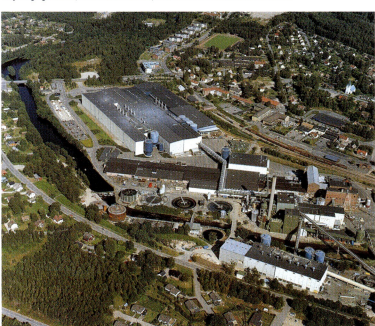

NUMBER OF HEATING DEGREE DAYS
Annual means 1961/62–1978/79

- 6,800
- 6,000
- 5,200
- 4,400
- 3,600
- 2,800

The number of degree days corresponds to the energy requirements for heating, which are approximately twice as large in Norrbotten as in Skåne. (T183)

TOTAL ENERGY CONSUMPTION, 1994

GWh per county
- 50,000
- 20,000
- 10,000
- 5,000

Domestic heating and vehicles account for a great deal of energy consumption in the metropolitan areas, while energy-demanding industry characterises some of the Norrland counties. (T184)

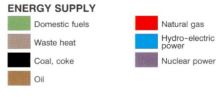

ENERGY SUPPLY
- Domestic fuels
- Waste heat
- Coal, coke
- Oil
- Natural gas
- Hydro-electric power
- Nuclear power

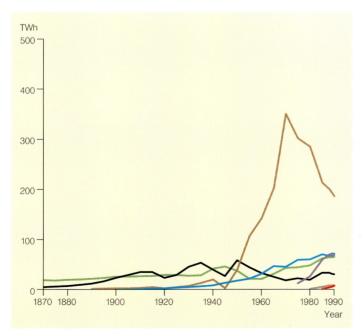

Before 1900 domestic fuels consisted of wood and peat, supplemented by imported coal and coke. Water power increased its share during the following period, while oil dominated the scene after the Second World War. Nuclear power and natural gas are relatively new sources of energy, and nuclear power alone accounts for a considerable share. Solar energy and wind power do not show up on the diagram at this scale.

Energy

Sweden's energy needs are determined in the first place by its climate, housing standards and general standard of living, its production and its need of communications and choice of transport. Thus the geographical distribution of energy consumption reflects the distribution of the population and the location of energy-demanding industries, as well as regional differences in the climate.

A corresponding geographical distribution of the production of heat and electricity shows that the levels of energy consumption and production agree fairly well. The nuclear power plants in southern Sweden, which account for over 40 per cent of Sweden's production of electricity, balance the hydro-electric power stations in Norrland.

The combined power and heating plants and the district heating plants are naturally enough situated where the population is most concentrated. However, the fact that the maps showing energy consumption and production are basically similar does not mean that Sweden does not suffer heavy power transmission losses in its sparsely and unevenly populated countryside. To get the full picture, the transportation of people and goods, which accounts for approximately a quarter of all energy consumed, should also be taken into consideration.

Behind this apparently close correspondence between energy production and consumption there is, however, historically speaking, uneven regional development. Until the mid–19th century the distribution of consumption and production was mainly determined locally, since it was based on wood, charcoal and water power. From then on the picture changed, initially through coal imports, which weakened the inland location of the iron and steel industry, for example.

At the next stage the regional distribution of energy production was changed by the major national and large-scale electrification projects centred on Trollhättan, Älvkarleby and Porjus.

In recent decades energy production has shown a more even geographical distribution because of the nuclear power plants in southern Sweden.

Half of Sweden's energy supplies

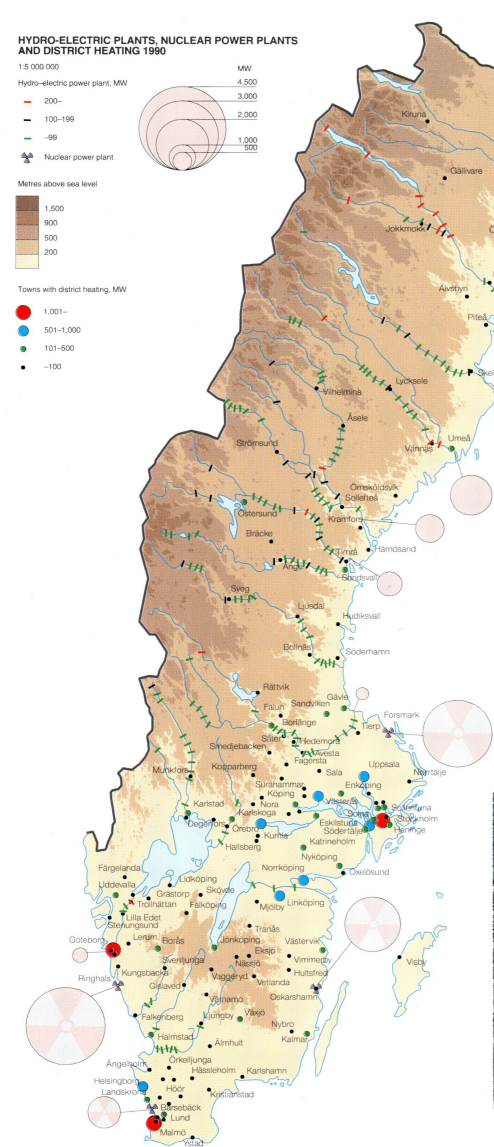

HYDRO-ELECTRIC PLANTS, NUCLEAR POWER PLANTS AND DISTRICT HEATING 1990

1:5 000 000

Hydro-electric power plant, MW
- 200–
- 100–199
- –99

△ Nuclear power plant

Metres above sea level
- 1,500
- 900
- 500
- 200

Towns with district heating, MW
- 1,001–
- 501–1,000
- 101–500
- –100

MW
- 4,500
- 3,000
- 2,000
- 1,000
- 500

Only hydro-electric power stations generating more than 10 MW are shown on the map. Most district heating plants provide less than 100 MW. (T185)

are based on imports, of oil and coal in particular. Nuclear power also depends on the importation of raw materials, since it was decided not to exploit the large uranium deposits at Billingen. The distribution picture for the supply and final consumption of energy shows how oil, coal and natural gas reach their consumers in transportation, industry and domestic heating. Generally speaking, this distribution pattern will probably continue for the foreseeable future, unless the systems and technology for domestic heating and transportation are radically changed, or the supply from one of the sources of energy is greatly limited.

Sweden's electric power requirements are normally completely met by its own power stations, mainly nuclear and hydro-electric and to some extent combined oil or coal-fired power and heating plants. Only hydro-electric power is based on native sources of energy.

When assessments are made of the ways in which energy production may change in the future, it is consumption that must first be considered. Lowering indoor temperatures by one degree would lead to a reduction in consumption of 5 TWh. Reducing private car traffic by one tenth would give the same result. If the pulp and paper industry, which is the single largest industrial consumer of energy, were able to cut its consumption by 10

The combined heating and power plant at Västerås. Burning fossil fuels requires a location close to a quay with large storage facilities.

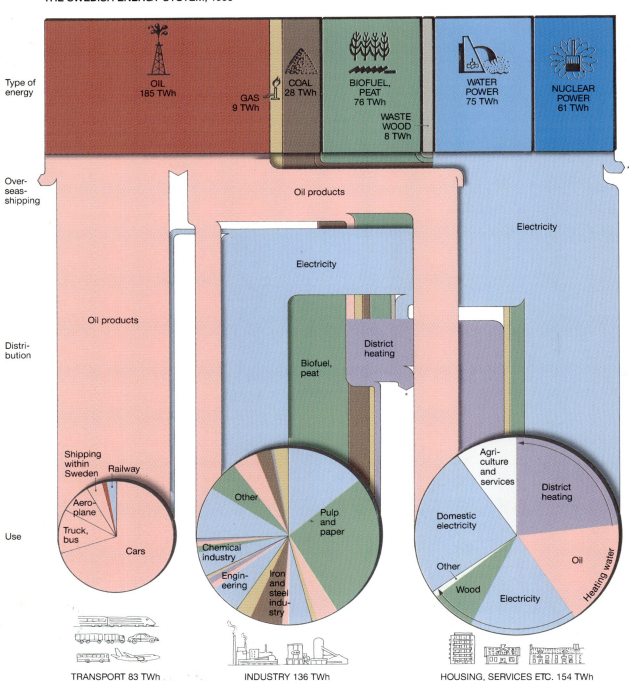

THE SWEDISH ENERGY SYSTEM, 1993

*Losses, own use and use for non-energy purposes, total c 40 TWh

During the past 25 years energy supplies have remained constant at a level around 450 TWh. Beneath this stable surface, however, there have been major changes in the Swedish energy system. The percentage contributed by oil fell from 77 per cent in 1970 to 42 per cent in 1993. The percentage of electric energy in the same period increased from 10 per cent to 31 per cent. Electricity generated by hydro-electric stations doubled and nuclear power entered the scene. Biofuels and peat also increased their share from 9 per cent to 17 per cent.

The diagram showing energy supplied and consumed can be utilised to assess possible changes in the energy system. It is evident that dependence on oil is connected primarily with the transport sector and domestic heating; in contrast oil is used relatively little for district heating. There would have to be radical changes in the transport system to reduce dependence on oil. Any further reduction in the use of oil would also affect industry and domestic heating.

The diagram shows that the largest percentage of biofuels is used in the forest industries, the pulp industry in particular. This is fuel that is available within the forest industries' own processes. Just over 40 per cent of electricity is produced by nuclear power. When alternatives to nuclear power are discussed, it is important to bear in mind that electricity production is a complex system, in which nuclear power meets basic energy requirements and hydro-electric power has been exploited to meet peak needs.

per cent by means of improved technology, this would mean a saving of 6 TWh.

It may be presumed that the future deregulation of the electricity market and the internationalisation of electricity prices will also change both supply and consumption patterns.

Regardless of how nuclear power is utilised in the future, changing prices may make other sources of energy competitive, which in turn may change the picture of regional energy production.

Bioenergy has the greatest potential of the renewable sources of energy that are proposed as alternatives for future energy production — wind power, solar energy and bioenergy. Assessments of how great it is differ widely. The use of raw materials in the forest industry, the conditions for cultivating biofuel, the economic size of electricity and heat-generating plants based on biofuel and the development of transport systems are some of the most vital factors affecting the role of bioenergy in the overall production of energy in Sweden.

Water power has during the past few decades been expanded by making

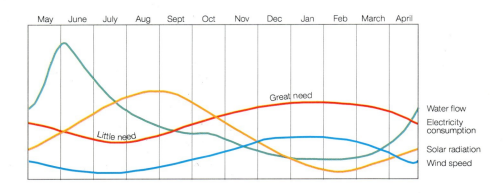

VARIATION IN ELECTRICITY CONSUMPTION, WIND, WATER AND SUN

Among the natural sources of energy, water, sun and wind, wind power matches annual variations in power consumption best. Both water power and solar energy require seasonal storage.

existing plants more effective. This development is the result of nuclear power taking over as the primary source of energy, which means that water power now has to be used to regulate peak demand at short notice. The remaining commercially exploitable rivers are estimated to be able to provide another 30 TWh.

Wind power has been estimated to be able to provide 2 per cent of Sweden's electricity by 2010, but so far only provides 0.05 per cent. Although wind power, compared with water power and solar heating, has the most suitable seasonal variations, since it is windier in the winter when energy requirements are high, economic and technological obstacles as well as competition for land have restricted its exploitation.

Solar energy can be converted into electricity by means of solar cells and used for heating by means of solar heating systems. The efficiency of solar cells is so far too low for solar energy to have any general commercial application, but in geographically isolated places it has been put to use. For example, the National Administration of Shipping and Navigation had by 1995 equipped 400 lighthouses with solar panels to provide a supply of electricity.

Solar heating systems require seasonal storage of heat. On a large scale it is commercially viable to store heat in the form of hot water in large underground tanks. In an international perspective Sweden is well prepared for this solution thanks to its large-scale municipal district heating systems.

The high-tension grid in Scandinavia with its connections to Europe via Denmark and Germany makes it possible to even out variations during the day and the seasons. When the electricity market is deregulated, this exchange will increase. (T186)

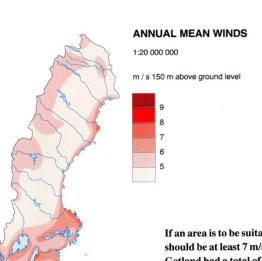

(T187)

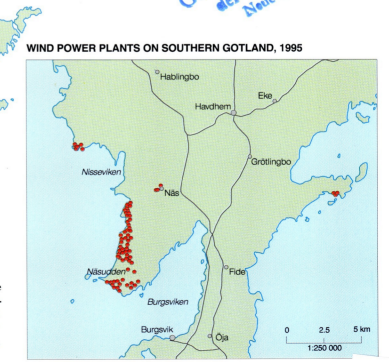

If an area is to be suitable for a wind-power plant the winds should be at least 7 m/s for six months of the year. In 1996 Gotland had a total of 86 wind-power plants connected to the grid which generated between 55 and 3,000 kW, corresponding to half of the wind-power energy installed in Sweden and 8% of the energy needs on Gotland. Most of the wind-power plants on Gotland are located on the south part of the island, 64 at Näsudden. (T188)

EMPLOYMENT IN MINING AND QUARRYING BY COUNTY
1:20 000 000

Number of employees: 10,000 / 5,000 / 1,000 / 100

1891 · 1911 · 1991

Mining was concentrated in Bergslagen and central Sweden up until 1900, but when the Kiruna mine was opened the main focus moved to the north. Nowadays iron ore is mined only in the Norrbotten fields and the Skellefte field dominates the mining of sulphide ores. (T189–191)

Mining

In the 1950s Sweden accounted for 10 per cent of the world's production of iron ore but as much as half of the world's trade. Swedish iron-ore production then trebled up to the mid-1970s, but in world trading its position was weakened by new mines in Canada, South America, West Africa, India and Australia. At present Sweden accounts for 2 per cent of world production and 5 per cent of world trading.

The Swedish mining industry, which has been of decisive importance for the Swedish economy for 800 years in spite of a cyclical market, now has only 6,000 employees engaged in iron-ore extraction, and is no longer one of the major industries. In two areas, iron ore in Norrbotten and sulphide ores in Västerbotten, mining is still of great regional importance. The industry is dominated by two large companies: LKAB in Norrbotten and Boliden in Västerbotten.

Nowadays iron ore is mined only in the Kiruna-Malmberget field in Norrbotten. The ore is processed to a high level of iron content. Four fifths is exported and one fifth is divided among the Swedish steel companies in Luleå and Oxelösund.

The sulphide ores in the Skellefte field contain principally copper, zinc, lead, silver and gold. These ores, which have a low metal content, are processed at Boliden to reduce transport costs. Lead and copper can then be melted and refined at the Rönnskär plant. Zinc and copper are exported as ore concentrate from the Skellefteå field, as well as from Dalarna and Närke.

Mineral prospecting is vital for the mining industry's future. At the same time as prospecting costs have been rising continuously, state grants have decreased, and ceased altogether in 1993. As a result prospecting has declined although Norrbotten and Västerbotten form one of the four most geologically interesting areas in Europe.

Reduced prospecting means shorter time plans, and the known sulphide reserves in Sweden are now estimated to last for only another 5–10 years, and iron ore for 20 years. Alongside the mining of the basic ores, foreign companies in particular are prospecting on a small scale for industrial minerals, diamonds and precious metals.

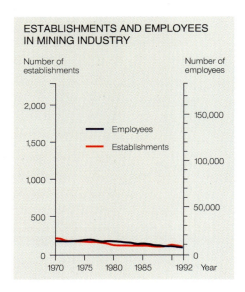

ESTABLISHMENTS AND EMPLOYEES IN MINING INDUSTRY

Most of the iron ore from Norrbotten is exported, but it also supplies Sweden's two remaining blast furnaces at Luleå and Oxelösund. (T192)

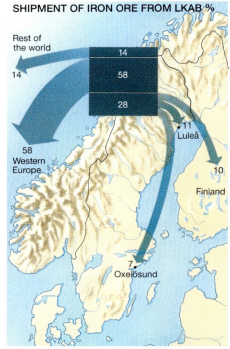

SHIPMENT OF IRON ORE FROM LKAB %

Rest of the world 14 · Western Europe 58 · Finland 10 · Oxelösund 7 · Luleå 11 · 14 / 58 / 28

ORE DEPOSITS AND MINERALISATIONS IN THE SKELLEFTE FIELD

The Skellefte field contains sulphide ores containing copper, gold, silver, lead and zinc. These ores are mined within an area of 150×50 km at eight different places, while 21 mines have been closed and 15 are not in operation at present. (T193)

Dominating metal: Copper · Zinc · Nickel, cobalt · Gold, silver · Sulphur

Operating 1993 / Closed / Prospect — Ore, mill. tonnes: >10, 1–10, 0.1–1, <0.1

BASIC METAL INDUSTRIES, EMPLOYMENT BY LOCATION, 1993

1:5 000 000

Dominant field
- Iron and steel
- Ferro–alloys, non-ferrous metals
- Iron and steel casting
- Semi-finished non-ferrous metal products
- No dominant field

Number of employees
- 2,000–4,999
- 1,000–1,999
- 500–999
- 100–499
- 50–99
- 10–49

The historically identified location picture for most of the metal industry, and the steel industry in particular, should also include a few plants at ports, like the aluminium plant in Sundsvall, the copper plant in Helsingborg and the steelworks at Oxelösund. (T194)

Metal Industry

Sweden's production of steel, copper and aluminium corresponds more or less to the demands of the domestic market, almost 4 million tonnes a year. Behind this apparently simple equation, however, lie considerable imports and exports, varying from metal to metal and with regard to quality; this can be explained by increased specialisation and divided markets.

The companies in the Swedish iron and steel industry developed from initially fairly standardised production to a wide variety of production methods and products during the period 1850–1950. In the past 30 years international competition has forced the companies to abandon their varied production programmes and concentrate on extreme specialisation. In several cases this has been done by merging with foreign companies.

The concentration of the steel industry in Bergslagen reflects historical links with the mines in central Sweden. Now, however, there is no longer a simple connection between mining and metal processing. This is because world demand for metals stagnated during the 1970s and 1980s and because the production of basic metals like steel, copper, zinc and aluminium is based more and more on recycling the metal that is already in circulation. The advantage of scrap metal is that it requires less energy for processing.

As far as the needs for raw steel of Swedish steel production are concerned, about half comes from domestic ore mined in Norrbotten. Svenskt Stål AB has the two remaining blast furnaces in Sweden — in Luleå and Oxelösund. They primarily provide their own steelworks with raw steel for conversion into thick and thin sheet iron. The steelworks that produce special steel use only scrap metal as raw material. The division into general steel (unalloyed steel for plate, beams and rails) and special steel (alloyed steel for tools and stainless steel) is somewhat misleading since the production of general steel is also being developed and adapted to suit the customers' needs.

Copper and aluminium scrap accounts for about one third of the requirements of these metals. While the raw material for Swedish copper production is taken from the Skellefteå mines, raw aluminium is imported from the Caribbean and Australia.

Engineering

Since the 1950s Swedish industry has been transformed, with the basic industries playing a less important role and engineering growing in importance. Today almost half of the industrial activity can be classified as engineering. Its share of total export value has increased from 25 per cent in the late 1940s to about 50 per cent today. In contrast to the forest industry, however, engineering is rather dependent on imports. In particular the large engineering companies in Sweden are also highly internationalised in the sense that much of their production is abroad. Another typical feature of the engineering sector is the high level of technical know-how and in some cases of intensive research and development. The locational pattern is one of wide regional distribution, but the most densely-populated areas and the regions with a long tradition of metal processing are somewhat over-represented.

The engineering industry comprises the production of a wide range of goods. Usually engineering is divided into five branches: metal goods, machinery, electrical, automotive and instruments.

THE METAL MANUFACTURING INDUSTRY

Metal manufacturing first developed as a natural extension of iron and steel production, above all in the ironworks of central Sweden. Later metal manufacturing also gained a foothold in the towns, often thanks to inventors or entrepreneurs who started a business there. Eskilstuna is an early metal-manufacturing town that provided a favourable industrial climate for many Swedish inventors. Similarly the Småland metal-manufacturing industry developed from an earlier craft and cottage industry tradition. Even though metal manufacturing is the

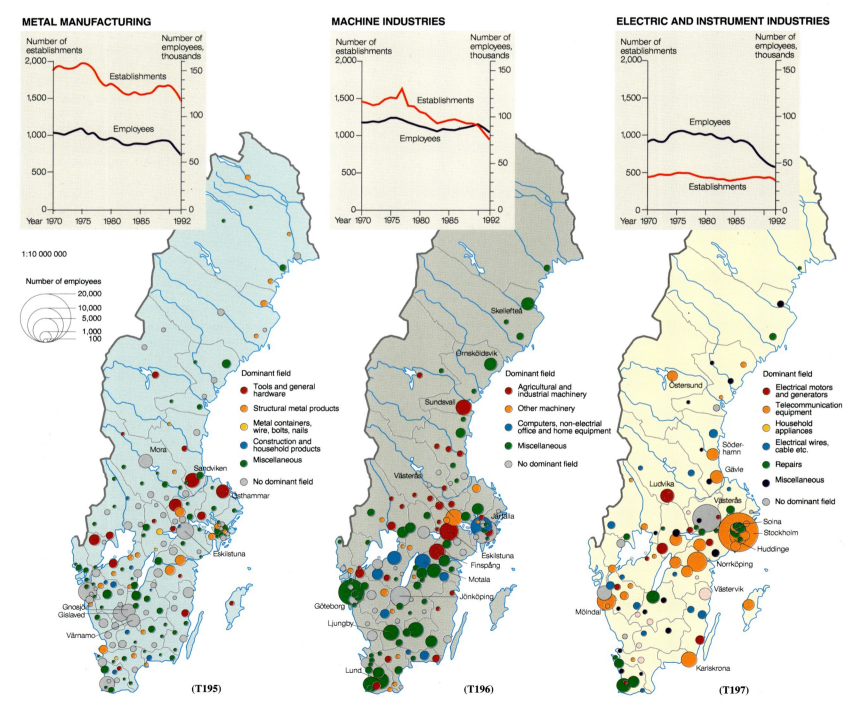

most widely scattered branch of manufacturing, a certain concentration may still be found in Mälardalen, Bergslagen and Småland. This scattered pattern may be attributed partly to the dominance of many small firms and workshops. The metal goods industry has lost ground among the manufacturing industries in the past few decades, a development that may partly be explained by the replacement of metal by other materials, in particular plastics.

THE MACHINE INDUSTRY

In many cases the machine industry grew up as a natural extension of products previously manufactured by metal-manufacturing companies. Its development is also closely connected with inventors and entrepreneurs; two of the most successful companies in this respect are SKF, manufacturing ball-bearings in Göteborg and Alfa-Laval, manufacturing milk separators in Stockholm. A typical feature of the location of the machine industry is its early concentration in Stockholm, Göteborg and Malmö. Because of shortage of space many big-city companies have now moved their production to the suburbs. Otherwise the machine industry is relatively widely distributed, with large towns in eastern Sweden like Norrköping, Linköping and Finspång somewhat over-represented.

Like the metal goods industry this sector is characterised by many small firms, but a number of large companies account for the major part of the employment and production. Among them are SKF, Tetra Laval, Electrolux (white goods), Atlas Copco (compressors) and ESAB (welding equipment). The machine industry is highly internationalised (75 % of production is exported), above all the companies that specialise in machinery for the pulp and paper industries, tool-making and hydraulic pumps.

THE ELECTRIC AND INSTRUMENT INDUSTRY

The most rapidly expanding sector of the engineering industry since the 1960s is the electric and electronic industry. This comprises the manufacture of products such as electric motors and generators, telecommunication equipment, electronic components, television and radio sets, electric wire and cable, batteries, lamps and electronic measuring instruments. It is dominated by a few large companies, among which Ericsson and Asea Brown Boveri (ABB) are the largest Swedish ones, but multinational foreign-owned companies like IBM, Siemens, Philips and Landis & Gyr are also very active in Sweden. Swedish-owned Gambro, which produces medical equipment, is the leading world company in this field.

The regional distribution of the electric industry follows the locational pattern of the large companies. Not least Ericsson's and ABB's home bases in Stockholm and Västerås respectively influence the map. Much of the electric and instrument industry is characterised by a high level of research and development, R&D, which usually means a preference for large cities or university towns, where there is a good supply of skilled labour and opportunities for applied research projects.

Like other parts of the engineering industry, this sector is highly internationalised. A limited home market combined with gradual deregulation of the international telecommunications markets has resulted in Ericsson exporting most of its production of telephone exchanges (AXE exchanges) and mobile telephone systems. Expansion during the 1980s was mainly by direct investment overseas.

THE VEHICLE INDUSTRY

Developments in the automotive sector have been an important force behind economic growth since the Second World War. World trade increased rapidly and geographical mobility improved with innovations in the field of transport. Apart from the car industry, this led to the rapid growth of the shipbuilding industry. However, shipbuilding, mostly in the form of tankers, suffered greatly from the oil crisis in the early 1970s and increasing international competition. What remains of the shipbuilding industry today concentrates on repairs and naval production in a few shipyards.

The Swedish automotive industry is dominated today by the production of motor vehicles (cars, trucks and buses). Sweden has one of the largest car industries in the world in relation to the size of its domestic market and a very large part of its production is exported. The industry is dominated by Volvo and Saab Automobil, which sub-contract to a large network of Swedish and foreign manufacturers. For this reason the pattern of location is relatively scattered, even though Saab's and Volvo's factories in Göteborg and Trollhättan dominate the picture. The need to be close to sub-contractors and assembly plants is clearly shown by the concentration of the Swedish car industry in western Sweden.

Apart from vehicles both Saab and Volvo manufacture aeroplanes and aeroplane engines for both civil and military use. Most of the production is located in Linköping. Trains are mainly manufactured in Västerås, where ABB Traction is the dominant producer.

Founded in 1742 by the county governors Ko(skull) and Sta(ël von Holstein), Kosta glassworks in eastern Småland is Sweden's oldest producer of crystal glass, famous for its studio glass.

Other Industries

THE CHEMICAL INDUSTRY

As well as the production of chemicals, fertiliser, paint, pharmaceuticals and the like, the chemical industry comprises chemical-based products such as plastics and rubber products. Oil refining and the production of lubricants and asphalt are also usually considered to be part of the chemical industry.

The Swedish chemical industry is a classical industrial branch in which products like matches and explosives are connected with well-known Swedish inventors and industrialists in the late 19th century. The modern chemical industry is also one of those that have developed most rapidly since the Second World War. An important factor in this growth has been the development of new chemical processes and materials with wide applications.

The need of chemical products for paper and pulp manufacture meant that the chemical industry became integrated with the forestry industry at an early stage. The manufacture of chemicals by the Swedish forest companies is less important today, partly as a result of changes in production technology.

Much of the chemical sector is very capital intensive and operates large-scale production. As the industry has been transformed over the past few decades, new groups of companies have been formed. Among them mention should be made of Akzo-Nobel, now Dutch-owned, Norwegian-owned Hydro-Supra AB which manufactures fertilisers at Köping and AGA, which mainly produces industrial gases. The paint industry is dominated by companies like Beckers and Casco Nobel, and the rubber industry by Gislaved and AB Trelleborg.

Many of the chemical industries are research and development intensive, not least the pharmaceutical industry, which has been very successful over the past few years. Companies like Astra and Pharmacia & Upjohn devote some 20 per cent of their turnover to R&D. Their dependence on skilled research staff means that they need to be located close to a university. Pharmacia is in Uppsala and apart from its factory at Södertälje Astra has important R&D centres in Göteborg (Hässle) and Lund (Draco).

With these exceptions the chemical industry has a fairly scattered locational pattern. This is because the chemical sector is a heterogeneous business, whose various subsectors often have very different locational factors.

THE MINERAL INDUSTRY

A typical feature of the mineral industry is its strong concentration on the home market. The raw materials for the mineral industry are relatively cheap—earth, clay, stone and sand—and the finished products are often heavy and bulky. That is why transport costs make up a large part of the price, and it is also the reason why sales have traditionally been restricted to national, regional and in certain cases local markets. The mineral industry is above all dependent on the domestic construction market, so the deep decline in house-building in the 1990s struck it a hard blow. In the long term, too, it is possible to see a low increase in employment in the mineral industry. The most important products are cement, concrete, stoneware, bricks, mineral wool, glass, porcelain and pottery.

As in most industries, the long-term restructuring of the mineral industry has meant fewer but larger companies and production plants. In the light concrete industry, for example, all production is by two companies: Yxhult at Kvarntorp (Närke) and Siporex at Dalby (Skåne). A similar concentration is found in the brick industry, where Stråbruken and Sydtegel are among the few remaining manufacturers today. Mineral wool is also produced by only two large companies, Gullfiber and Rockwool. The most obvious example of this trend, however, is Cementa, which for many years has had practically a monopoly of the Swedish cement market. Of the seven factories that were in operation in the mid–1970s, only three remain today: Slite on Gotland, Degerhamn on Öland and Skövde in Västergötland, which is threatened with closure.

In the ceramic industry, which produces domestic porcelain and sanitary ware, two companies are dominant, Gustavsberg near Stockholm and Ifö Sanitär at Bromölla in Skåne. Finally, the glass industry comprises bottle and flat-glass manufacturers, as well as the companies in Småland producing their classic decorative ware. PLM Plåtmanufaktur is the wholly dominant manufacturer of bottles and jars, and production is now concentrated in the plant at Limmared in Småland. Window glass and glass for the car industry is mainly produced by a British company, Pilkington Brothers, at Halmstad and the French-owned company, Emmaboda Glasverk.

THE TEXTILE AND CLOTHING INDUSTRY

The whole post-war period has seen production in the Swedish textile and clothing industry decline. Between 1950 and 1990 the number of people employed in the industry fell by almost 100,000. This decline can mainly be explained by increased international trade since the Second World War, which resulted in increasing competition from low-wage countries, initially in Europe (e.g. Portugal) and later in Asia (e.g. India and China). The response from the Swedish textile industry to this situation was at first to move a good deal of Swedish production to Finland and then to Portugal. Since the early 1990s several textile companies have also opened factories in the Baltic states. Today the industry aims mainly at specialised niches (e.g. work and protective clothing, exclusive leisure wear and fashion clothing) with the emphasis on technical know-how and advanced design. Most work-intensive production now takes place outside Sweden and imports of clothing are spread over a wide range of countries. However, Swedish membership of the EU is partly changing the situation for the Swedish textile industry, since certain tariffs and import quotas have been reintroduced against countries outside Europe.

The industry is dominated by small firms, particularly ready-made clothing, which is characterised by relatively low capital intensity. Another feature of the industry is the large proportion of women workers, more than 50 per cent in the early 1990s. The textile industry was established in the Sjuhärad district at an early date and even today the Borås district and west Sweden are central in the location pattern. Other early centres were Göteborg and Norrköping, as well as several other medium-sized towns. For the shoe industry Örebro and Kumla were important centres.

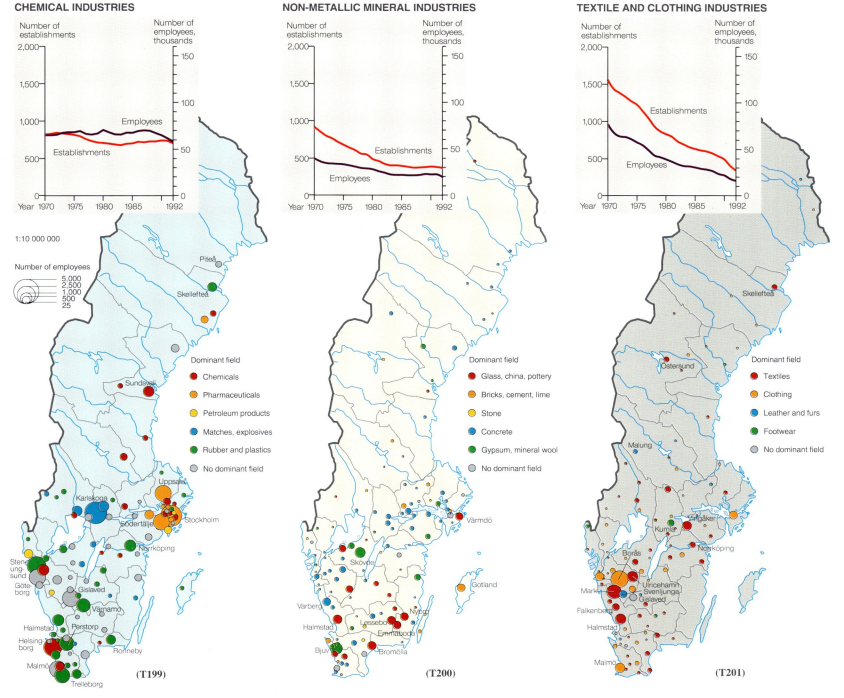

Service Industries

The service sector is the part of Swedish industry that has shown the most rapid rate of growth since the Second World War, measured in employment and share of the GNP. As early as the 1940s this sector accounted for as much employment and production value as the manufacturing industries. Today service industries account for 60 per cent of Sweden's total employment. The percentage of employees producing services is not decreasing at the same rate as in manufacturing, where rationalisation and automation can be introduced on a larger scale.

A considerable part of the production of services is directly related to changes in the production of goods, in commerce and communications, for example, which have developed into important industries as the division and specialisation of work has spread. Similarly the increasing need for information processing has led to new occupations. It is important to remember that manufacturing companies produce services for themselves in fields such as transport, stock-keeping, administration and the like. In other words, the production of services and goods is an integrated business, often difficult to distinguish in practice.

The service sector is dominated today by various kinds of public services, above all within health care, the care of young children and the elderly, and education. Of course such traditional state responsibilities as defence, customs and excise and taxation also fall within the public sector. The expansion of the public sector has come to an end at present; instead the political agenda proposes great changes in the form of cuts and privatisation. What follows describes the service industries in terms of the distinction between private and public services.

THE PRIVATE SERVICE SECTOR

The private service sector comprises such widely differing activities as retailing, hotels and catering, transport, post and telecommunications, tourism and banking, insurance and consultancy services. This part of business life employed almost 700,000 people in 1993 (18% of all employment). Some of the firms are small in, for example, hotels and catering, tourism and parts of retailing. In these cases the location patterns generally speaking follow the geographical distribution of the population, but Stockholm in particular has a level of activity that exceeds the population level. Where large firms are dominant, as in banking and insurance or large chains of food stores, their activities are often organised regionally in the form of local branches or stores covering the whole country. Here, too, the geographical pattern reflects the distribution of the population.

The private service sector covers a wide range of skills and educational standards among its personnel. It includes everything from simple cashiers' jobs to highly demanding computer-system work. An example of a field which is dominated by knowledge-based companies and highly-educated staff is consultancy. This comprises computer consultants, technical consultants, advertising agents, accountants, architects, management consultants and so on. What these companies have in common is that they sell their services to other companies or organisations in the first place, and only occasionally deal with ordinary consumers. The term "business or producer services" is therefore often used to describe these types of services.

Consultancy work is the part of the private service sector that grew most rapidly in the 1980s. Between 1985 and 1990, for example, the number of consultancy firms increased by 15 per cent a year, and employment by almost 8 per cent a year. A not insignificant reason for the growth of this type of services was the extensive externalisation of functions like information and data processing by large companies and organisations, in the form of separate companies. One rea-

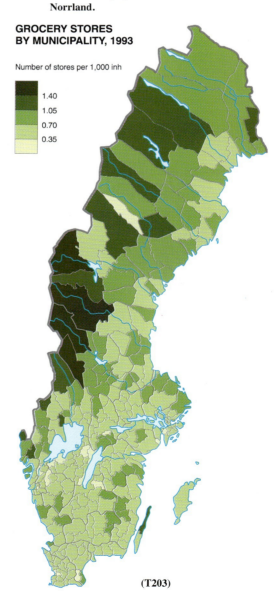

The location of the private service sector generally speaking follows the distribution of population, but the metropolitan regions are over-represented.

SHARE OF EMPLOYMENT IN PRIVATE SERVICES SECTOR BY LABOUR–MARKET REGION, 1990

1:10 000 000

Share of total employment, %
- 35
- 30
- 25
- 20

Labour–market region boundary

Mixed
- Companies
- Households

(T202)

The largest number of food stores in relation to the size of the population is in the interior of Norrland.

GROCERY STORES BY MUNICIPALITY, 1993

Number of stores per 1,000 inh
- 1.40
- 1.05
- 0.70
- 0.35

(T203)

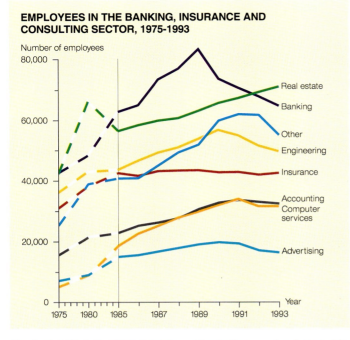

Employment in the banking, insurance and consultancy sectors increased in most cases up until the late 1980s. However, the crisis in the early years of the 1990s hit these sectors as well.

son for this trend is that many companies do not have the capacity to develop the knowledge and expertise they need by themselves, another that a specialised service company can benefit from being allowed to sell its services on the open market.

Proximity to the market (in the form of clients) is usually given as the factor that primarily influences the location of service companies. Particularly in the case of sophisticated services, personal contact is important for creating confidence between buyer and seller, as is a good understanding of the client's business. If the services are simple and can be performed as routines, however, the need for the client to be close to the producer is reduced. Often personal meetings in such cases can be replaced by modern telecommunications.

In most companies in the consultancy sector human resources are by far the most important. Knowledge, experience and personal client relations are normally the most significant means of competition. That is why access to well-educated and well-qualified staff is also a very important location factor for this type of company. The big-city regions and university towns obviously have an advantage regarding the supply of well-educated staff. The location pattern of the consultancy sector is not surprisingly characterised by being considerably over-represented in the Stockholm region in particular. However, the present trend in many consultancy fields is for employment to grow faster in medium-sized towns.

Computer services companies are above all over-represented in the Mälardalen region. The computer sector is also well represented in regions which have a university. (T204)

Building consultants and architects are most numerous in the metropolitan areas. (T205)

Technical consultants are often over-represented in local labour markets dominated by industrial companies. (T206)

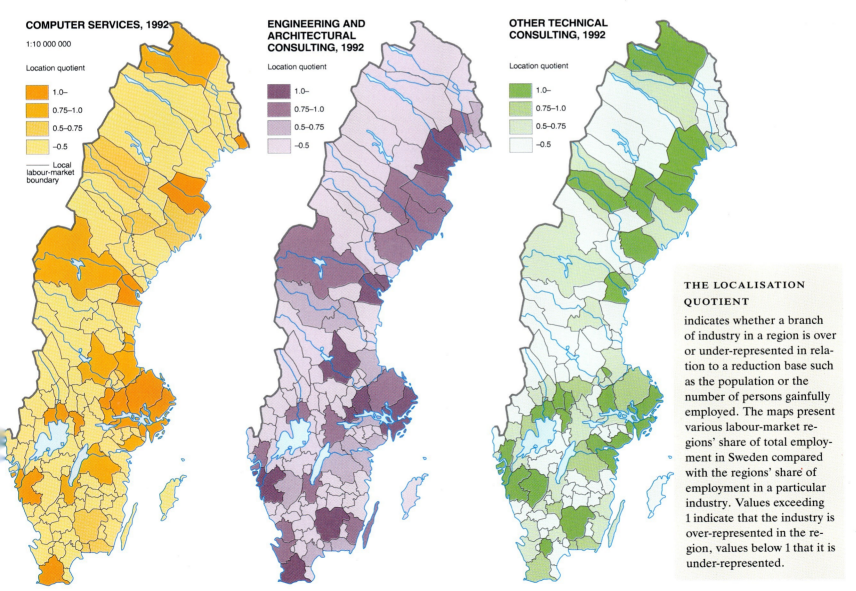

THE LOCALISATION QUOTIENT

indicates whether a branch of industry in a region is over or under-represented in relation to a reduction base such as the population or the number of persons gainfully employed. The maps present various labour-market regions' share of total employment in Sweden compared with the regions' share of employment in a particular industry. Values exceeding 1 indicate that the industry is over-represented in the region, values below 1 that it is under-represented.

PUBLIC SERVICES

The public sector has a unique position in Swedish industry in that its activities are under political control. Another special feature is its financing, since most of its income comes from various kinds of taxes. As public services have increased, public expenditure expressed as a percentage of the GNP has increased, above all in the 1960s and 1970s. The expenditure that has increased most dramatically in the past few decades is transfer payments, including pensions, family allowances, housing allowances and unemployment benefit. Despite extensive efforts to restrict transfer payments, this type of expenditure continued to grow in the early 1990s, mainly because of greatly increased unemployment. As a result the gap between government revenue and expenditure grew dramatically in the early 1990s; in 1994 the Swedish national debt amounted to 1,287 billion SEK.

The expansion of the public sector resulted in the first place in increased employment for women. Sweden's high rate of employment for women in an international perspective is directly connected with the rapid growth of the public sector. At the beginning of the 1990s the proportion of women employed in the public sector was about 75 per cent. The public sector is by far the most important labour market for women, not least because it offers the possibility of part-time work. The number of part-time employees is particularly large in county councils and municipalities, where they work in the social services.

The public sector is often defined as the work carried out by the state, municipalities and county councils. This distinction is based on the authority responsible for the work, but the services and occupations for which various authorities are responsible are not absolutely defined. Examples of changes in responsibility in recent years are the transfer of almost 70,000 employees working in geriatric care from the county councils to the municipalities in 1992, and the transfer of teachers from state to municipal employment in the late 1980s. Such changes have contributed greatly to the municipal sector's increased share of employment in the public sector.

Sweden's public services are, as in most countries, organised territorially. We see three main geographical levels: national, regional (normally the 24 counties) and local (the 288 municipalities). In the first place the state looks after matters of national importance, but is also represented at the other geographical levels. An example of a state body which operates at all three levels is the Labour Market Agency, with the Labour Market Board at its centre, the county labour boards at the regional level and the local employment offices at the base of the hierarchy. The various county council offices operate primarily at the regional level but also have certain responsibilities at the local level. Most services at the local level are provided by the municipalities.

Generally speaking the location of the public sector follows the geographical distribution of the population. This is only natural, since most public services are aimed at meeting the public's needs for welfare, care and education within a particular district. The demand for these kinds of services is not, however, equally distributed but varies according to the population's age structure and state of health in different parts of the country. Far-reaching decentralisation of services is also restricted by financial, technical and transport limitations. In addition differences in political majorities and practical politics in municipalities, for example, can also lead to

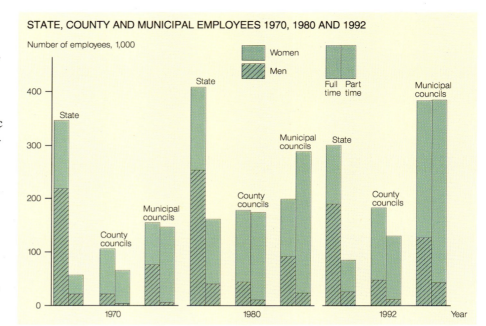

State, county council and municipal employees by sex and working hours. Women predominate above all in the county councils and municipalities; women are also the employees that to a greater extent work part-time.

During the post-war period there has been a steady increase in the county councils' and municipalities' share of public employment.

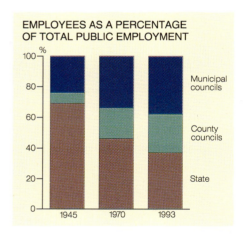

Public expenditure's share of the GNP has generally speaking increased throughout the whole of the 20th century.

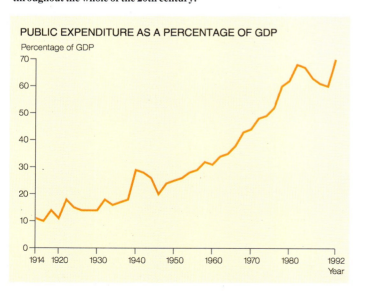

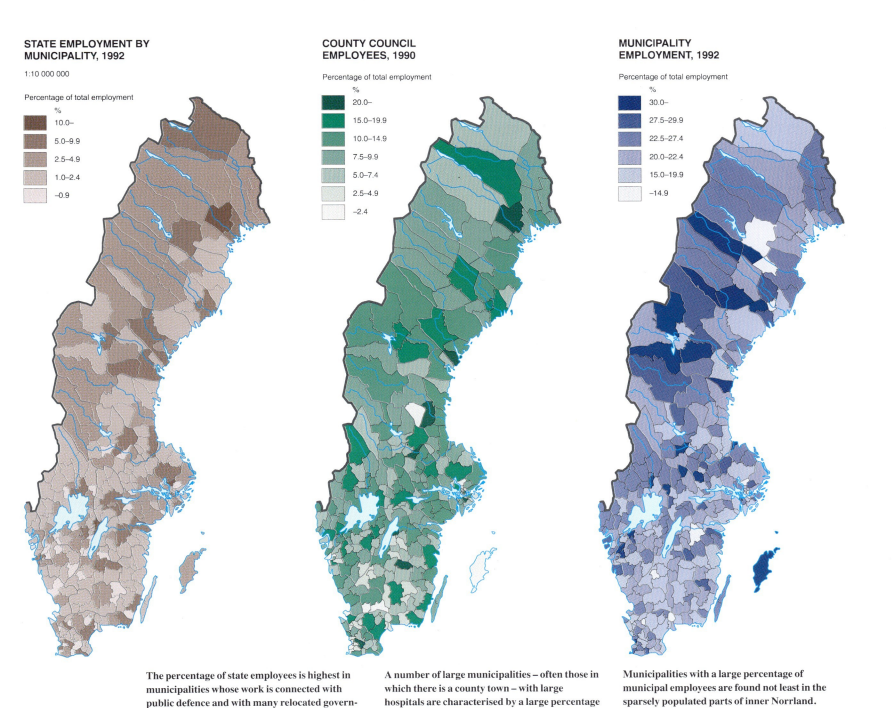

STATE EMPLOYMENT BY MUNICIPALITY, 1992

1:10 000 000

Percentage of total employment
%
- 10.0–
- 5.0–9.9
- 2.5–4.9
- 1.0–2.4
- –0.9

COUNTY COUNCIL EMPLOYEES, 1990

Percentage of total employment
%
- 20.0–
- 15.0–19.9
- 10.0–14.9
- 7.5–9.9
- 5.0–7.4
- 2.5–4.9
- –2.4

MUNICIPALITY EMPLOYMENT, 1992

Percentage of total employment
%
- 30.0–
- 27.5–29.9
- 22.5–27.4
- 20.0–22.4
- 15.0–19.9
- –14.9

The percentage of state employees is highest in municipalities whose work is connected with public defence and with many relocated government agencies. (T207)

A number of large municipalities – often those in which there is a county town – with large hospitals are characterised by a large percentage of county council employees. (T208)

Municipalities with a large percentage of municipal employees are found not least in the sparsely populated parts of inner Norrland. (T209)

geographical differences in the range of public services. In general it may be said that the more specific and exclusive a service, the more centralised it will be. A clear example of this is the localisation of higher education in a small number of towns in Sweden. Another example is specialist hospital care.

The future size, direction and organisation of the public sector is the subject of lively debate today. A central issue is financing, another the possibility of privatising parts of the public sector. Many people also claim that the public sector will become increasingly internationalised in the future.

Avesta Hospital on the river Dalälven, a part of the public sector, is run by the county council.

Transport Flows and Gateways to the World

Traffic in the Swedish infrastructure reflects the geographical distribution of the population and industry as well as a lack of geographical correspondence between production and consumption sites for various kinds of goods. Traffic flows between Stockholm–Göteborg–Malmö and within these metropolitan regions are particularly intense.

For goods transportation there is competition among different means of transport for distances above 200 km. Transportation which is subject to competition accounts for three quarters of long-distance transports.

Within Sweden lorries dominate the market, with just over 50 per cent of the traffic. Compared with the patterns for railways and shipping long-distance lorry traffic is also more equally distributed in Sweden, partly because of the level of costs but also because of the greater flexibility and accessibility of road transport.

If we divide the amount of goods carried by lorries according to industry, we see that forestry, commerce and foodstuffs are dominant. Forestry transports account for almost 20 per cent of long-distance traffic, heavily concentrated to Norrland, with deliveries from north to south and from inland to coast. More than 75 per cent of the flows of foodstuffs, wooden goods, engineering products, other manufactured goods and commerce are by lorry, and they are heavily concentrated to southern Sweden. Short-distance goods transports are mainly of sand and gravel, concentrated round the metropolitan regions.

Railway traffic is particularly extensive on the main lines of the national network, including the northern lines. Deliveries of iron ore from Kiruna to Narvik also leave their mark on the map.

The networks of the four dominant main means of transport differ; shipping and aviation follow routes which in principle have no physical links. Investments here are in coordinating systems and in the handling of goods at nodes: ports, terminals and the like. Railways require investments in both nodes and links and are the physically most fixed of the four types of transport. In aviation, shipping and railways it is only possible to enter the networks at their stations. The road network requires investments primarily in the links between the nodes, while the nodes themselves are more flexible and adaptable to individual needs.

Since 1970 the total volume of goods transported has decreased by 10 per cent, but the total amount of traffic has risen by 37 per cent. The reason is that the average distance for goods transports has increased from 88 km to 122 km. Increases in distance and decreases in loads affect the competitiveness of the various types of transport.

The heavy costs of the infrastructure for the state lead to constant political debates about imbalances in the level of subsidies between different means of transportation and the bal-

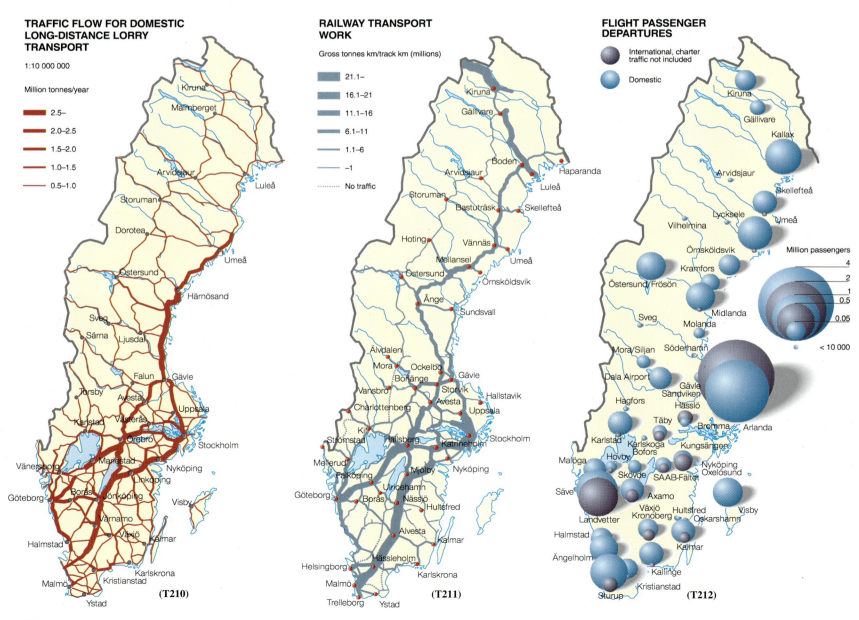

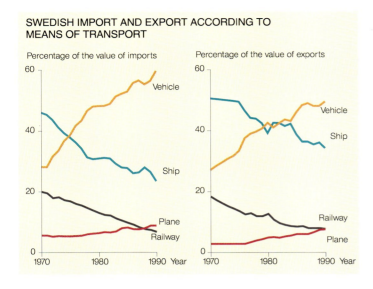

ance between economic and ecological factors when reaching decisions.

Domestic and international aviation have grown very rapidly in the field of passenger traffic, and heavy investments have been made throughout the country to provide industry, even in small and relatively remote municipalities, with good access to major cities both in Sweden and abroad. The role of aviation for freight traffic, particularly international freight, has also grown for products with a high value per kilo and for fresh goods. Geographically the aviation network is characterised by a considerable degree of centralisation and a strongly hierarchical system between nodes. Large countries are able to have several hubs, but the Swedish air network has at present only one hub — Arlanda Airport. Aviation's share of long-distance (over 100 km) domestic passenger traffic has grown from 10 per cent to 33 per cent since the mid-1960s. The number of passengers has risen more than tenfold to 8 million per year.

Swedish international trade passes mainly through gateways along the west and south coasts, but exports from industries in Norrland are also significant. Historically shipping has been totally dominant in the export trade. In the 1970s, however, the value of imported goods carried by road traffic was greater and in the following decade a corresponding change took place for exports. There has also been a recent shift in the battle for third place between different types of transportation. Today aviation accounts for a larger share of exports in terms of value than the railways.

Freight traffic is fourteen times greater today than in 1900; passenger traffic is almost 100 times greater. This development would not have been possible without the explosive growth of communications by mail and telephone. Trade depends on the exchange of information; face-to-face meetings often need preparatory contacts. The infrastructure for the communication of information is now the focus of attention at least as much as the traditional means of transport. Geographical and social questions concerning access to the new digital information highways are at the top of the 1990s political agenda.

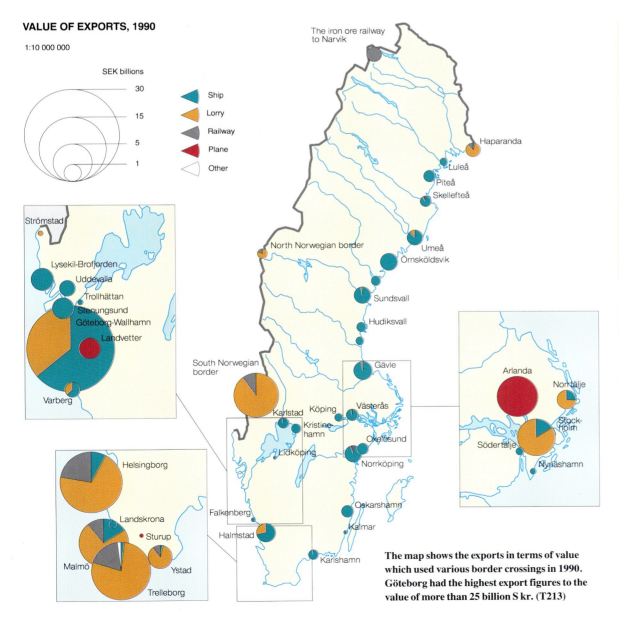

The map shows the exports in terms of value which used various border crossings in 1990. Göteborg had the highest export figures to the value of more than 25 billion S kr. (T213)

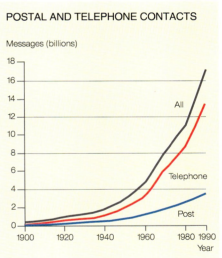

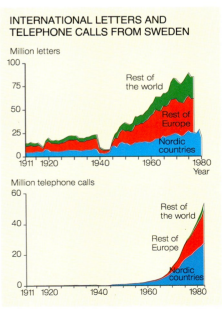

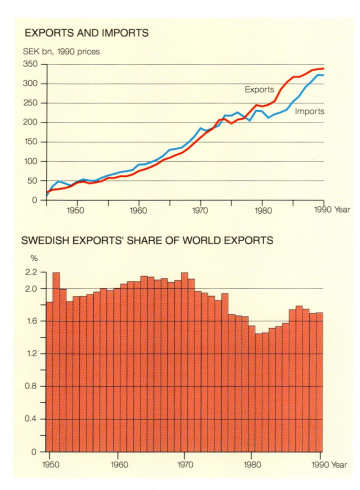

The percentage of exports rose steadily after the Second World War up until 1970. After a decline in the early 1970s, the percentage rose again after the devaluation of the krona in 1982, though not to the same level as before. There was a new downturn in the 1990s, but after the krona declined in value in 1992 there was another rise in exports.

The diagram shows the ratio between export values and import values. The groups of goods that have shown a trade deficit throughout the whole of the post-war period are chemical products, fuels, foodstuffs and textiles. In all these cases the balance of trade has relatively speaking improved.

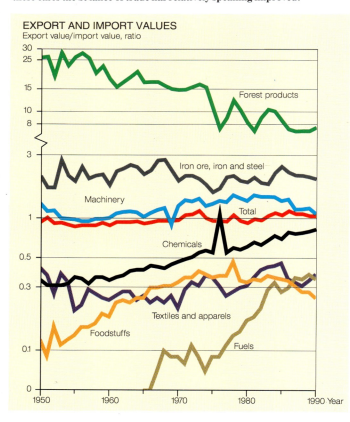

Foreign Trade

International trade in goods has increased rapidly since the Second World War. In contrast to the period 1918–1939, between the world wars, when foreign trade decreased, the period since the late 1940s has been characterised by almost continuous growth. Brief fluctuations in this trend have been caused by the trade in oil. Both technological and political changes have encouraged the rapid expansion of trade.

The share that Swedish exports have in world trade rose steadily until 1970, when it was more than 2 per cent, after which it followed the trend by falling a few tenths. For most countries it is true to say that the concentration of goods is greatest in the

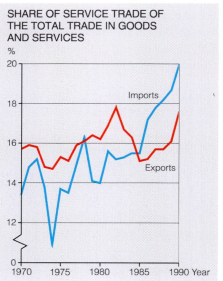

The trade in services is becoming more important for the overall export trade. Previously it had its highest percentage among exports, but now it is most important among imports.

export trade, since foreign trade is based on specialisation of each country's production. That is why the trend towards more highly processed goods in foreign trade has been more rapid among exports. A decline is particularly noticeable in forestry goods and minerals such as iron ore, sawn wood and paper pulp. This group accounted for almost half of Sweden's total export value in the early 1950s, but forty years later the figure was less than 10 per cent.

Some groups of goods have traditionally made a net contribution to foreign trade inasmuch as they have always provided the major export surpluses, while other groups have always shown a negative trade balance. The group of goods that has had the largest relative surplus is forest products, whose export/import ratio has usually been about 15–25 to 1. The group that has the largest absolute surplus is, however, engineering products, where the ratio is now about 1.5 to 1.

The groups of goods that have had a trade deficit ever since the Second World War are chemical products, fuel, foodstuffs and textiles. In each of these cases the balance of trade has improved relatively.

Sweden's most important trading partners have for many years been other developed industrial countries,

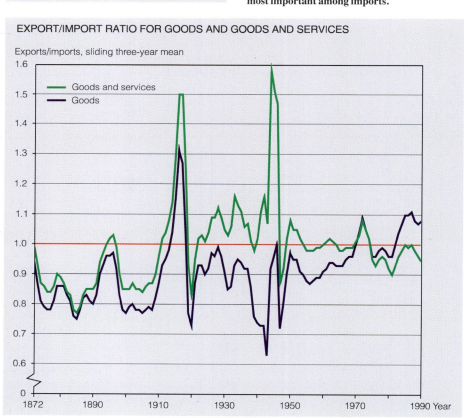

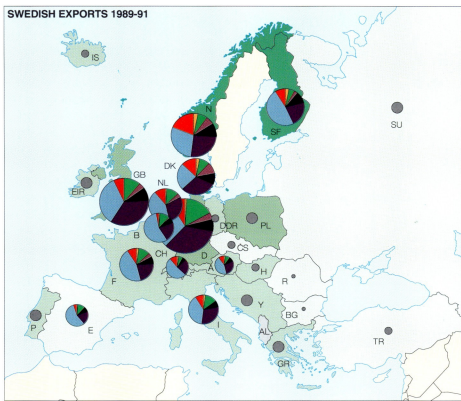

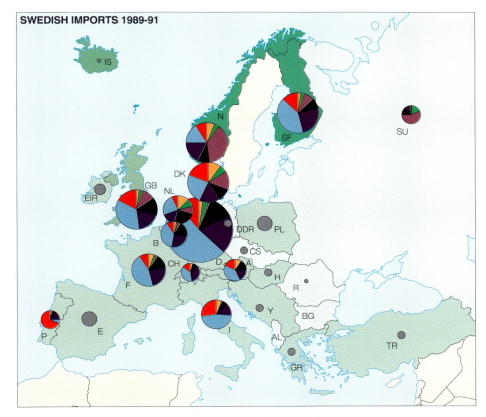

During the past decade the focus of Swedish exports has shifted south, mainly to Italy, Spain and France. West German's dominance as the leading supplier of goods to Sweden has been further strengthened, while Britain's role has declined. (T214, T215)

mainly the OECD countries in Europe and the US-Canada. But the fastest relative growth has been in East and Southeast Asia. More than 90 per cent of both exports and imports are accounted for by the above-mentioned groups of countries.

Swedish membership of the European Union since 1st January, 1995 will affect Swedish foreign trade, but limited to specific product areas and the short term. The EU is a unified customs area and the duties on most imports are low for third-party countries, though somewhat higher than those previously imposed by Sweden. The greatest problems have been expected to concern Swedish banana imports from Central America, textile imports from India, China and other such countries and imports of electronic equipment from the US and Southeast Asia. The EU imposes trade quotas with low rates of duty for many types of goods, but imports exceeding the quotas may in many cases face heavy penalties. Those goods whose production within the Union the EU is particularly anxious to protect, above all foodstuffs, may face higher rates of duty on imports from outside countries than Sweden previously applied.

Membership of the European Union — in practice the now outdated EES agreement — opens up new opportunities for Swedish exports to the EU, as a result of trade restrictions being lifted for several product areas, for example for services and public tenders. The new GATT agreement will in the long term both reduce EU tariff rates and open up completely new markets for world trade. For the first time in history the new GATT agreement will also regulate and deregulate the expanding trade in services.

GEOGRAPHICAL DISTRIBUTION OF SWEDISH EXPORTS, % OF TOTAL VALUE OF EXPORTS, MEAN OF YEARS REPORTED

	1949/51	1959/61	1969/71	1979/81	1993/94
OECD countries in Europe	65.8	73.1	74.9	71.1	70.1
Eastern Europe-Soviet Union	7.5	4.3	4.6	4.0	3.1
Middle East	1.2	1.3	1.6	4.9	2.5
South Asia	1.3	1.3	0.5	0.6	0.5
East Asia-Southeast Asia	1.9	1.8	2.3	4.1	9.1
Oceania	2.9	1.6	1.2	1.3	1.5
Africa	3.6	3.8	3.5	3.8	1.4
USA-Canada	6.1	7.2	7.9	7.0	9.3
Latin America	9.7	5.6	3.5	3.2	2.1
Total	100.0	100.0	100.0	100.0	100.0

GEOGRAPHICAL DISTRIBUTION OF SWEDISH IMPORTS, % OF TOTAL VALUE OF IMPORTS, MEAN OF YEARS REPORTED

	1949/51	1959/61	1969/71	1979/81	1993/94
OECD countries in Europe	59.2	68.3	73.2	67.4	71.3
Eastern Europe-Soviet Union	7.4	4.3	4.7	5.2	3.9
Middle East	3.1	2.8	2.0	6.2	1.5
South Asia	1.3	0.5	0.4	0.3	0.5
East Asia-Southeast Asia	2.9	3.0	3.4	5.8	11.0
Oceania	1.8	0.4	0.3	0.4	0.3
Africa	3.9	2.0	2.3	2.7	0.5
USA-Canada	9.7	12.1	9.2	8.4	9.3
Latin America	10.7	6.6	4.5	3.6	1.7
Total	100.0	100.0	100.0	100.0	100.0

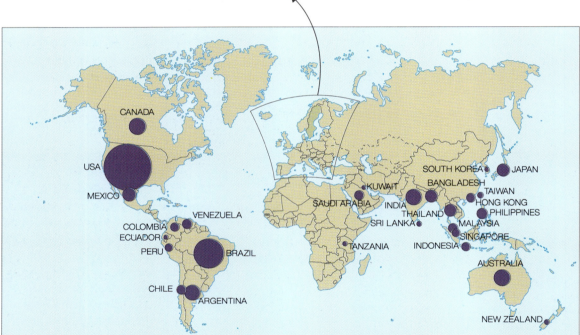

Those employed by Swedish companies outside Sweden are to be found in 121 countries (1990). There is a strong concentration, however, of 50 per cent within the European Union. (T216)

Internationalisation

The industrial picture changed significantly after 1960. In the wake of this transformation followed restructuring and change-over problems on the labour markets. The advanced industrial countries suffered a decrease in the number of employees in manufacturing industries. At the same time service industries and information processing expanded. Foreign trade in goods also revealed new trends in production. Product groups like electronics, telecommunications products, other sophisticated engineering products, chemicals and pharmaceuticals increased their share of trade in these countries, measured in terms of value. The continuing rise in the standard of living was in other words more and more dependent on various kinds of goods and services whose value was mainly created by research and advanced development work — products whose technological content was high.

At the same time industry became more global and more mobile than before. Industry after industry tended to move their most routine production from the old centres of the industrialised world to more remote areas like the Philippines, Taiwan, South Korea, Nigeria and Brazil. What was left in the centres in Europe, North America and Japan was primarily research, development and management. It should, however, be emphasised that there were in fact several examples of different localisation trends. Nevertheless, in general it seems that global industrial integration grew, which meant greater geographical dependence. It became less easy for the territorial states to control and direct developments. For many of them the very rapid expansion of the multi-national companies symbolised the spatial and social distancing of power that many people have experienced during the past 25 years.

Considering its small home market Sweden has a large number of big companies. There are several reasons for this: firstly, the big Swedish companies were internationalised at a very early date, in several cases even before the First World War; secondly, government industrial policy and the fact that a large part of industrial production has been controlled by a few large financial groups such as the Wallenberg sphere have favoured the development of big companies. Structural rationalisation in the form of ac-

SWEDISH COMPANIES' SHARE OF TOTAL WORLD DIRECT INVESTMENTS, 1981–89, AND FOREIGN COMPANIES' SHARE IN SWEDEN, PERCENTAGE

Year	Swedish	Foreign
1981	1.6	0.3
1982	4.2	0.3
1983	2.7	0.1
1984	2.1	0.3
1985	2.3	0.5
1986	3.4	1.1
1987	2.3	0.3
1988	3.3	0.7
1989	3.8	0.5

SWEDISH COMPANIES WITH THE LARGEST NO. OF EMPLOYEES ABROAD

		1990		1980
Ranking	Company	Employees abroad	% of total no. of empl.	% of total no. of empl.
1	Asea Brown Boveri	182,200	85	25
2	Electrolux	123,300	82	60
3	STORA	47,600	68	12
4	SKF	44,300	90	81
5	Ericsson	39,400	56	58
6	Volvo	22,800	32	28
7	SCA	19,500	65	32
8	Atlas Copco	17,200	80	68
9	Sandvik	15,900	60	57
10	Alfa Laval	15,600	75	59

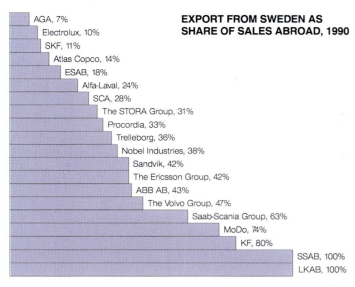

EXPORT FROM SWEDEN AS SHARE OF SALES ABROAD, 1990

The percentage of exports of a few large companies' total sales abroad. High percentage: a large part of the export sales is exports from Sweden. Small percentage: production units abroad account for a large part of the sales.

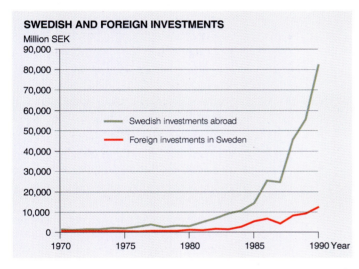

Swedish direct investments (gross) abroad and foreign investments (gross) in Sweden in current prices. Reinvested profits are not included.

Business trips by Swedish companies to Europe are characterised by Sweden's trade relations. Most of the journeys are to London, Frankfurt, the Scandinavian capitals, Brussels, Düsseldorf and Paris. (T217)

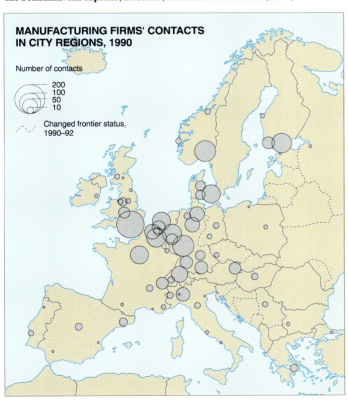

quisitions and amalgamations has been encouraged. There has been no attempt to block dominance of the home market and until quite recently it has been difficult for foreign interests to buy Swedish companies. A third important reason is that the Swedish state has not tried to prevent the establishment of companies abroad by restricting the export of capital.

Some twenty Swedish groups account for half of all Swedish exports. However, the rapid increase in overseas production during the 1980s meant that an increasingly small share of these group's trading affected Sweden. There is an evident trend for some subsidiaries abroad to form production, product-development or marketing centres within their group, thus achieving a strong position in relation to the parent company.

The internationalisation of the economy is in both directions; at the end of 1990 there were 2,600 foreign companies in Sweden, which accounted for 9 per cent of all employment. About two thirds of the foreign-owned subsidiaries are to be found in manufacturing, while less than 20 per cent are in the wholesale trade. Employment in these companies is mainly in the southern and central parts of Sweden, especially the metropolitan areas of Stockholm, Göteborg and Malmö. The increase in recent years of foreign-owned business in Sweden has, however, reduced the metropolitan regions' share from 60 per cent in 1980 to just over 43 per cent in 1990.

Since the deregulation of the currency and financial markets in the 1980s indirect foreign influence on Swedish industry has also increased dramatically. More and more Swedish companies are now listed on foreign stock exchanges, and major investors from other countries now buy shares on the Stockholm stock exchange. Especially after the battle to defend the Swedish krona was lost in the turbulent currency conditions in Europe in the summer and autumn of 1992, foreign capital has acquired large blocks of Swedish shares in the major Swedish export companies. The weak Swedish krona since autumn 1992 has made it relatively cheaper to buy Swedish resources than previously. Nowadays it has become more and more difficult to decide what is Swedish and what is not, and the need to make such distinctions is also debatable.

Against the background of Sweden's industrial internationalisation and geographical position, Swedish membership of the European Union is from industry's viewpoint only natural. Before the referendum on Swedish membership on 13 November 1994, the advocates of membership also took up the question of weakened national economic control which has characterised developments over the past decade. Membership of the European Union was seen as a strong argument for trying to regain political power, though at a supra-national level. The opponents, who emphasised particularly the general democratic problems arising from Swedish membership, did not see it as a way of tackling the increasing geographical scattering and, in many people's opinion, the less secure geographical position of Swedish companies.

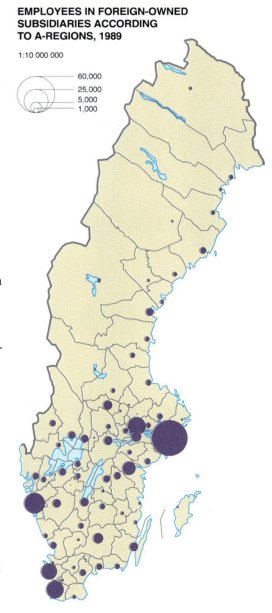

EMPLOYEES IN FOREIGN-OWNED SUBSIDIARIES ACCORDING TO A-REGIONS, 1989

During the 1980s the number of employees in foreign-owned subsidiaries increased throughout Sweden. The largest increase was in the Västerås labour region. (T218)

GEOGRAPHY OF OWNERSHIP, WHOLE INDUSTRY, 1993

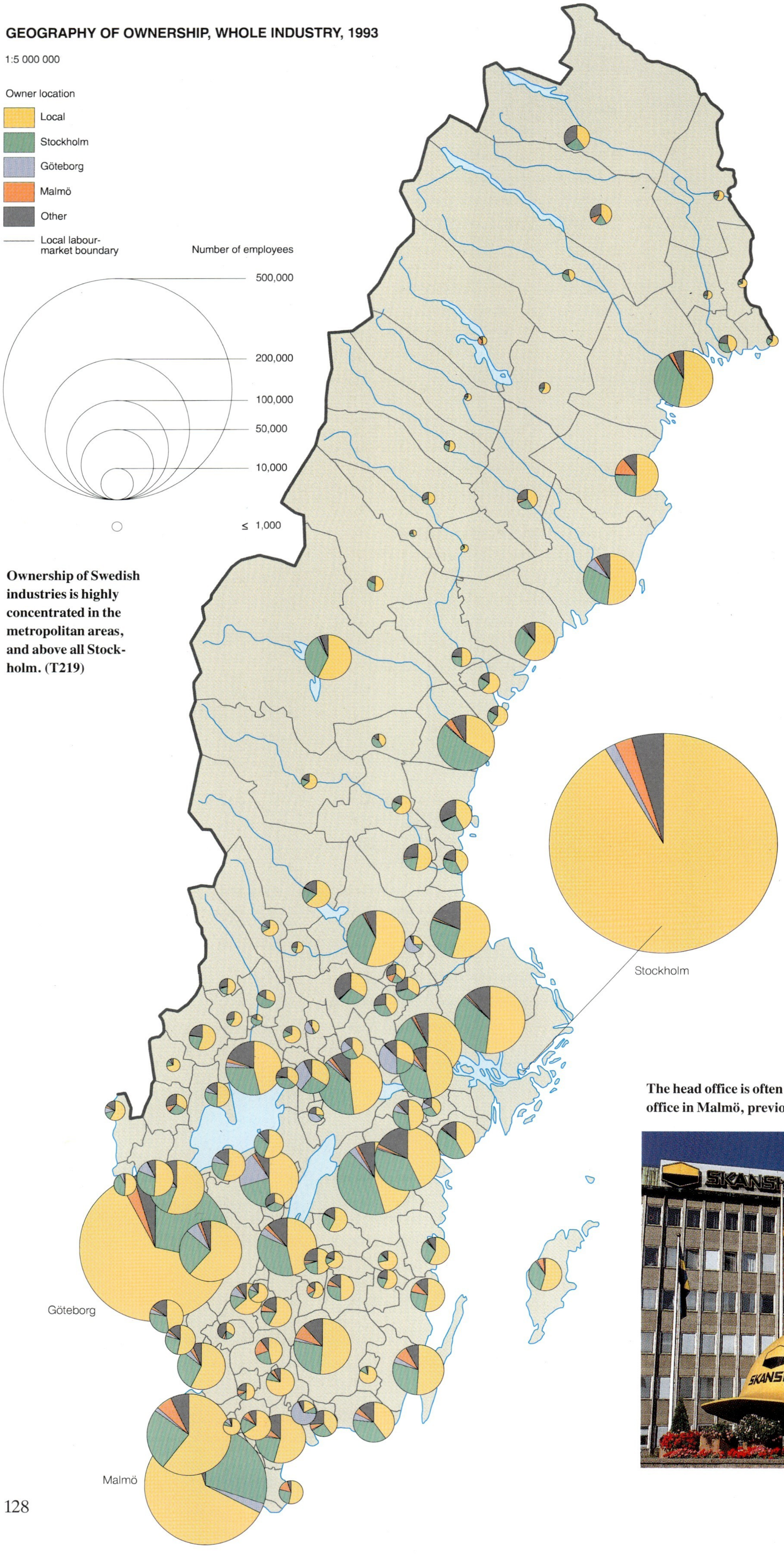

1:5 000 000

Owner location
- Local
- Stockholm
- Göteborg
- Malmö
- Other

Local labour-market boundary

Number of employees: 500,000; 200,000; 100,000; 50,000; 10,000; ≤ 1,000

Ownership of Swedish industries is highly concentrated in the metropolitan areas, and above all Stockholm. (T219)

Stockholm

Göteborg

Malmö

Regional Division of Labour

Since the Second World War a geographical division of labour on new principles has become more and more evident. Regions specialise in various parts of the production chain rather than in the production of different goods. This spatial division of labour is in part a consequence of the hierarchical structure and geographically scattered localisation patterns of large, growing companies.

Head offices and similar strategic functions are gathered in metropolitan regions, together with research and development units, while traditional industrial regions, like Bergslagen, for example, are still dominated by activities that demand experienced and skilled labour. On the other hand the production of standardised goods and services is often placed in remote and weakly industrialised regions, not least in the interior of Norrland.

A typical feature of Swedish industry is its high degree of concentrated ownership. This is also reflected in the geography of ownership, since management power is to a large extent concentrated in the metropolitan regions, in particular Stockholm. A consequence of this geographical concentration of ownership is that local industrial ownership is often poorly developed. In most regions outside the metropolitan regions more than 40 per cent of privately-employed personnel work in companies that have their head office outside the region.

The head office is often the most evident symbol of a large company. Skanska's office in Malmö, previously the head office of Skånska Cement AB.

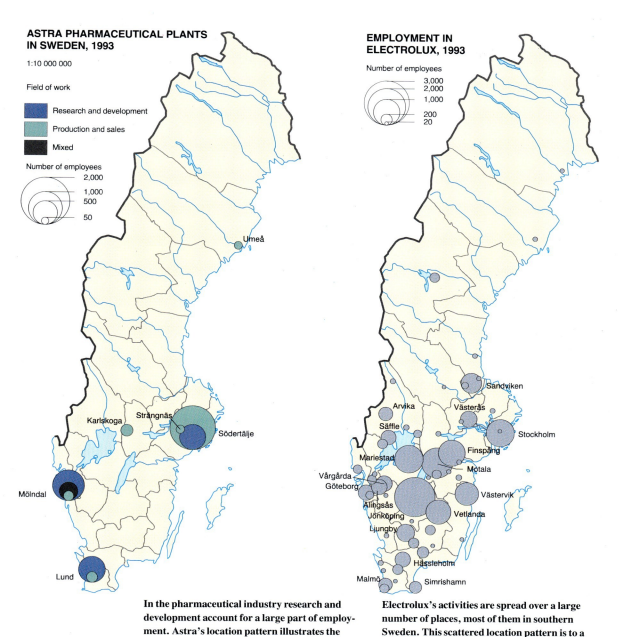

ASTRA PHARMACEUTICAL PLANTS IN SWEDEN, 1993
1:10 000 000
Field of work
- Research and development
- Production and sales
- Mixed

Number of employees
2,000
1,000
500
50

EMPLOYMENT IN ELECTROLUX, 1993
Number of employees
3,000
2,000
1,000
200
20

In the pharmaceutical industry research and development account for a large part of employment. Astra's location pattern illustrates the importance of proximity to university and research environments. (T220)

Electrolux's activities are spread over a large number of places, most of them in southern Sweden. This scattered location pattern is to a large extent the result of extensive take-overs. The head office is in Stockholm. (T221)

The integration of several companies and plants into large groups is motivated by the possibilities to utilise resources jointly, to coordinate administrative routines and sales organisations, and to benefit from large-scale research and development work. If a geographically scattered company is to be controlled effectively, there usually have to be highly standardised branch offices. The uniformity of the personnel, a narrow product range and a lack of research and development resources means that there are often fewer innovations in remote-controlled branches than in locally run offices and plants.

R&D work in Swedish companies is also concentrated in metropolitan areas. One reason for this is the need to locate R&D at the same place as the head office, but the good supply of skilled labour in the largest towns is also a significant factor, as well as the opportunities to utilise the advantages that university environments offer. R&D is most evident in industries like pharmaceutics, electronics and telecommunications and parts of the vehicle industry. Investments in R&D are also mainly made in a few large industrial groups. There has been a tendency in recent years to internationalise R&D work in the largest Swedish companies.

All in all this geographical division of labour results in increasing regional polarisation. Well-paid jobs that demand higher education are mostly found in certain central regions, whereas poorly-paid and routine jobs are found in more peripheral regions.

The Olofström factory in Blekinge presses and assembles chassis components for the Volvo 800 and 900 series.

PERCENTAGE OF EMPLOYEES IN REMOTE CONTROLLED COMPANIES NOT PUBLICLY OWNED, 1993
1:20 000 000

%
- 40–100
- 20–39
- 0–19

Local labour–market boundary

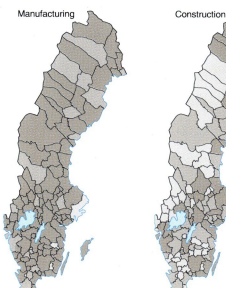

Manufacturing   Construction

In the manufacturing industry the number of employees in centrally controlled units is large in most parts of Sweden, but the construction industry is to a greater extent run by locally owned companies. (T222, T223)

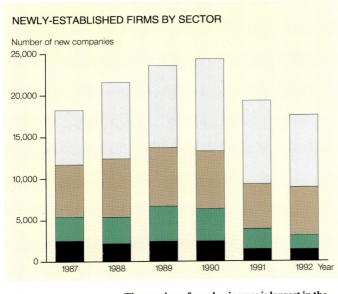

The number of new businesses is largest in the service sector, in the retail trade, hotels and catering and business consultancy, for example. In contrast new industrial companies account for a modest share of new businesses.

Regional Change

The range and structure of industry in any region will change as a result of various processes. New companies and new jobs will arise all the time, while some of the old work disappears. Among the companies that survive, some will expand and others will shrink. Business activities will also move into or out of a region, though this is not very common.

Great attention has been paid in recent years to the importance of new industries for economic and regional development. One reason is the marked increase in new businesses that occurred from the mid-1980s onwards. It is also often claimed that the establishment of new firms is strategically important for employment, renewal and variety in industrial life. The majority of new firms are small, and many of them continue as one-man operations or businesses on the side, in which independence and the opportunity to be self-sufficient are the main motives. Most new businesses are in the service industries, above all in retailing, hotels and catering. During the late 1980s there was also a rapid increase in the number of new consultancies, but the number of new industrial companies is relatively small.

Sweden has comparatively large regional differences in the establishment of new businesses. There is a high level in the metropolitan regions, and parts of southern Norrland, northern Värmland, the Siljan district and western Småland also have a larger number of newly-established businesses than the national average.

Blekinge, eastern Småland and northern Skåne are three of the regions that have a low level of newly-established businesses. Bergslagen, parts of Svealand and northern Norrland also contain areas where there are few new businesses. The ability to create a new company has proved to be most limited in traditional mill towns.

These regional differences in new businesses are determined by factors like the structure of the population, the size and density of the regional market, local and regional access to investment capital and inherited busi-

A large number of new businesses is a characteristic feature of all three metropolitan regions, as well as some of the more sparsely populated parts of Sweden. (T224)

Apart from the metropolitan regions, the west coast, parts of Östergötland and Bergslagen as well as parts of upper Norrland were hardest hit by the wave of bankruptcies that swept over Sweden in the early 1990s. (T225)

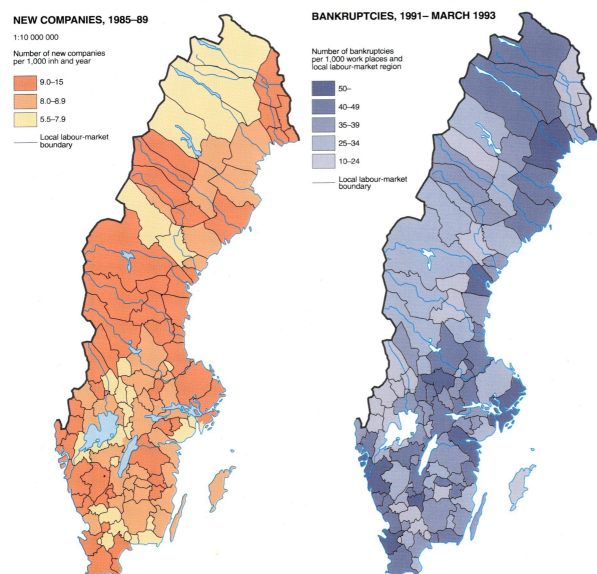

In the hotel and catering industry both bankruptcies and new businesses are frequent. The figures are for the period January 1987 to June 1993.

A picture from a regional development area in rural Norrland. The school at Sjöbotten was closed in 1969 and its buildings were used for a lampshade factory, which did not last long. It was followed by several companies, which had limited success. The school building has now been demolished and replaced by a house.

ness structure. Investigations have shown, for example, that regions with many small companies also have a high level of newly-established businesses. Regional differences in business traditions and attitudes to private enterprise may also be significant factors.

In the early 1990s Swedish industry suffered the deepest depression since the 1930s. The large increase in the number of bankruptcies during these years show the depth of this economic crisis. More than 21,000 companies went bankrupt in 1992, which for the first time in many years exceeded the number of new companies. As with newly-established companies, the majority of companies that went bankrupt were small ones, but as the crisis worsened, larger companies with many employees were also hit.

The metropolitan regions and a number of other large towns were among those worst hit, but the regional distribution of bankruptcies is not restricted to big towns. In the early 1990s there was a higher than average rate of bankruptcies in three areas in particular: along the west coast, in a belt running from Östergötland through Bergslagen and in the far north of Norrland. This regional pattern is probably explained to a large extent by differences in industrial structure. Thus bankruptcies were particularly frequent in retailing and hotels and catering, which are typical big-city occupations. It is also conceivable that the number of bankruptcies is related to regional economic activity. Regions with a high level of new businesses are often those that have a large number of bankruptcies.

Regional variations in new businesses, closures and rate of growth, for example, lead to regional redistribution of companies and employment. In Sweden throughout practically the whole of the post-war period manufacturing industries have moved from the largest towns and traditional industrial regions to smaller towns and poorly industrialised regions in both the north and the south of the country.

The metropolitan regions, for example, have lost a quarter of their employment in manufacturing in the 1980s alone. Similarly the most heavily industrialised regions have lost industrial jobs at a rapid rate, while industrial employment in previously poorly industrialised regions has in some cases increased by 20 per cent. Some of the general factors underlying this process are differences in labour costs, land prices and balanced transport costs. Government regional development policies have of course also played a part.

Employment in other sectors has developed in the opposite direction, however. The big cities in particular have very successfully managed to compensate for their weak industrial development by expansion in both the public and the private service sector. This is also a basic factor in the growth of the population in the metropolitan regions, above all in the Stockholm region.

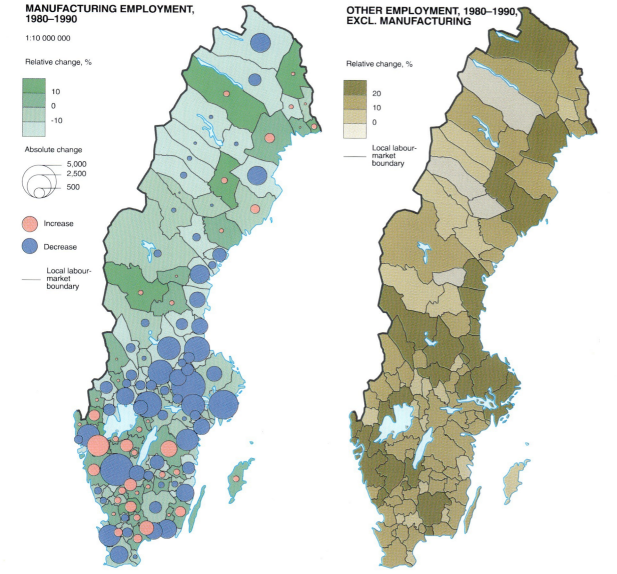

Industrial employment decreased in most local labour markets during the 1980s, and at a particularly rapid rate in the big cities and large industrial towns, for example in Bergslagen. (T226)

In virtually all local labour market regions other employment (excluding industry) increased during the 1980s. The increase was greatest in the metropolitan regions, western Sweden and southern Norrland. (T227)

Regional Development Policies

Government regional policies are one of the most important instruments for counteracting the uncontrolled expansion of the population and employment in the metropolitan regions, and a corresponding impoverishment of job opportunities and services in the rural areas of Sweden.

Even though "the regional problem" has occupied a dominant position in Swedish economic and social policies for a very long time, the starting point of modern regional policies was the mid–1960s, with the introduction of "active" relocation policies. A fundamental aim was to help increase production in general by utilising the labour force and other resources throughout the country more effectively. Another aim was to take over wherever measures to stimulate the mobility of the labour force had failed. There was also a need to try to slow down by more active measures migration to the metropolitan regions, which was a characteristic of the 1950s and 1960s.

The area that could receive grants was restricted to the four most northerly counties and parts of Gävleborg, Kopparberg and Värmland. This assisted area has been continually revised since the introduction of the new regional policy. Up to the 1980s the area was gradually extended and the level of grants raised. After that there were some limitations and simplification of the geographical divisions. Some regions have been entitled to grants temporarily, for example much of Bergslagen and many ship-building towns in west Sweden, which was included in the regional development area during the structural crisis that affected the ship-building and steel industries in the late 1970s.

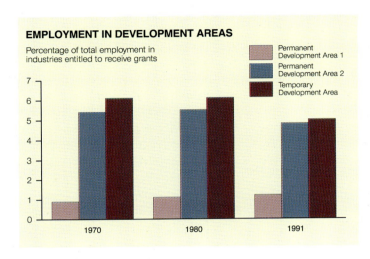

It is extremely difficult to measure the effects of regional development policies on employment. But the diagram shows that the assisted areas' share of total employment in those sectors entitled to grants has increased noticeably.

The regional development area covers much of Norrland. The area which has been given the highest priority comprises inner Norrland and Tornedalen. (T228)

Since 1995 Swedish regions are entitled to grants from EU's regional development fund: *Objective Area 2* – industrial regions in transition, *Objective Area 5b* – rural development, *Objective Area 6* – sparsely populated regions. (T229)

General regional development aid has largely been given to the towns along the coast of Norrland, which reflects in particular the larger number of companies in this part of the development area. (T230)

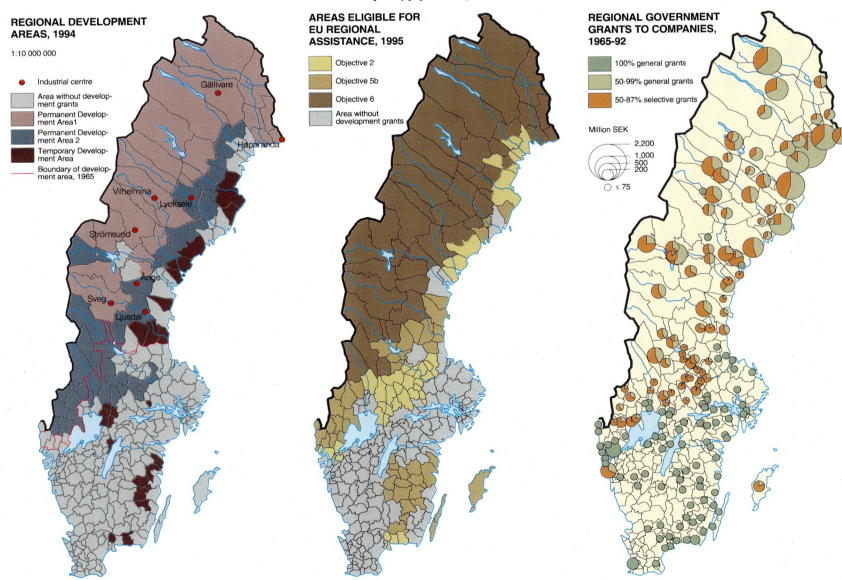

The Central Office of the National Land Survey was relocated to Gävle in 1974, where, like other relocated government offices, it moved into newly-built premises.

Initially, regional development policies were based on location grants to industrial companies in the form of subsidies and investment loans. Gradually, however, the number of types of grants increased substantially. General support, that is, reduced employers' contributions, employment grants and transport subsidies, was mainly given to the more densely populated parts of the assisted area. This allocation mainly reflects the absolute number of companies in various parts of the development area. Selective support, however, is more equally divided between coastal districts and inland.

During the 1980s considerable efforts were also made to build up the infrastructure and competence of these regions. The expansion of the regional university colleges, for example, has helped to strengthen the supply of skilled labour in the regions.

In the same way regional development policies have changed from being strictly directed towards manufacturing companies to embrace a wide range of activities today. The decreasing number of jobs in industry and the great growth of jobs in the private service sector are significant factors behind increased efforts to persuade metropolitan-based service companies to relocate some of their work to smaller towns in the assisted area. In the early 1970s and in a second round in the 1980s there was also extensive relocation of government offices, mainly to a number of large regional centres.

Nevertheless, most jobs created by regional development policies are in manufacturing, particularly in the forest industry and the metal goods and machine industries. Because of the dominant position of the manufacturing industries only one third of the jobs were for women.

What effects have regional development policies had? Apart from the problem of measurement, it is evident that employment has developed more slowly in the development area than in the country as a whole. Nor have the policies been very successful in holding back growth in Stockholm and the other metropolitan regions.

The development of employment and the level of services in different parts of Sweden are also greatly affected by other types of government transfer payments such as tax equalisation, which redistributes large sums of money among the municipalities. The transfers of resources via the national budget are far greater than the regional development grants.

The structure of Swedish regional development will be greatly influenced in the future by decisions made outside Sweden, as a consequence of its being a member of the EU. The negotiations for membership, for example, resulted in much of Norrland being placed in the Objective 6 area, a structural fund newly established for the Nordic countries, which aims at "developing and restructuring regions with a very low population density". An important future question concerns what level of support of a general nature, and to individual companies, will be permitted without competitiveness between companies in the European Union being distorted.

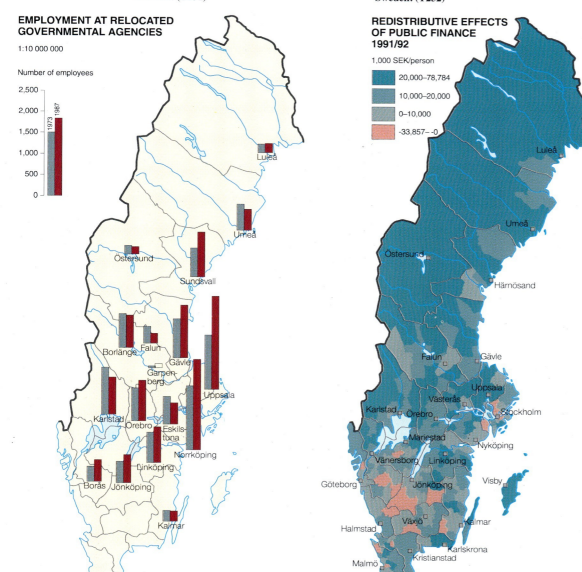

The government offices that were relocated from Stockholm during the 1980s and 1990s were placed mainly in large regional centres in central Sweden. (T231)

Large sums of money are transferred via the national budget from certain municipalities to others, mainly from the south to the north of Sweden. (T232)

Living Conditions and Life Patterns

Population Development and Settlement Patterns

During the past 250 years the population of Sweden has increased almost five times over. The large diagram showing population development reflects the great transformation — "modernisation" — of Sweden which began to accelerate in the first half of the 19th century.

War, crop failure, famine and plague led to large variations in the birth and death rates in poverty-stricken agrarian Sweden. The *demographic transition* began with a decrease in the death rate thanks to improved hygiene and better food supplies. The growth of the population accelerated until family planning was introduced and the birth rate fell within a few generations, but there was for many years serious overpopulation and widespread proletarianisation of the landless rural population. More than a million Swedes emigrated between 1860 and 1930 to find a new life, mainly in North America.

Land reforms and other types of rationalisation reduced the demand for labour in agriculture and forestry, and the expansion of industry and later

POPULATION 1737-1990
- Fertility
- Mortality
- Immigration
- Emigration

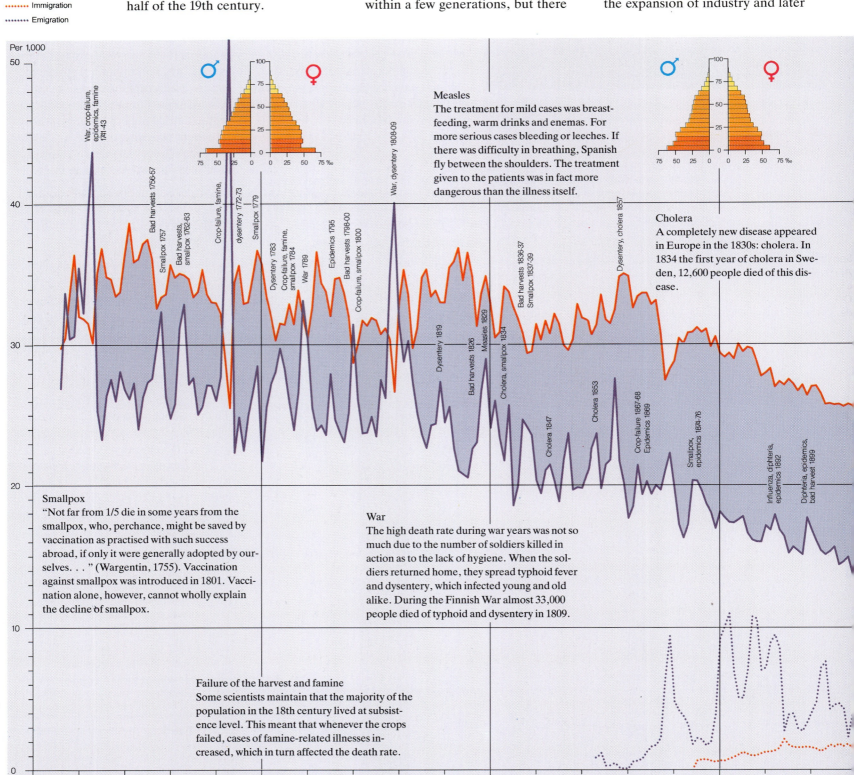

Measles
The treatment for mild cases was breastfeeding, warm drinks and enemas. For more serious cases bleeding or leeches. If there was difficulty in breathing, Spanish fly between the shoulders. The treatment given to the patients was in fact more dangerous than the illness itself.

Cholera
A completely new disease appeared in Europe in the 1830s: cholera. In 1834 the first year of cholera in Sweden, 12,600 people died of this disease.

Smallpox
"Not far from 1/5 die in some years from the smallpox, who, perchance, might be saved by vaccination as practised with such success abroad, if only it were generally adopted by ourselves..." (Wargentin, 1755). Vaccination against smallpox was introduced in 1801. Vaccination alone, however, cannot wholly explain the decline of smallpox.

War
The high death rate during war years was not so much due to the number of soldiers killed in action as to the lack of hygiene. When the soldiers returned home, they spread typhoid fever and dysentery, which infected young and old alike. During the Finnish War almost 33,000 people died of typhoid and dysentery in 1809.

Failure of the harvest and famine
Some scientists maintain that the majority of the population in the 18th century lived at subsistence level. This meant that whenever the crops failed, cases of famine-related illnesses increased, which in turn affected the death rate.

the service sector restructured Swedish working life so completely that these sectors now provide work for more than 95 per cent of the working population. Since the 1950s Sweden has also been a country of immigrants — at first through immigrant labour and in recent decades through refugees.

A development that ran parallel with and was at the same time dependent on the transformation of industrial life as a result of the expansion of urban industry was urbanisation — the massive redistribution of the population from the countryside to towns. In 1880 only one Swede out of five lived in a town, in 1930 it was every other Swede and today more than four out of five live in a town.

The contrast between the population picture 200 years ago and today is striking. In 1800 the birth and death rates were high and population growth was to a great extent determined by variations in the death rate. Today we have low birth and death rates and it is principally the birth rate that varies — because of generation changes and attitudes to childbearing. The age structure has changed radically. In 1800 the population pyramid was a fairly regular triangle, with a broad base of children and fewer and fewer adults towards the top. Today the population pyramid is more like a rectangle consisting of very much more similar age groups. As a nation we have become older on average — the average length of life for new-born females is 81 years today, and 75 years for males.

WE LIVE FAR APART — AND YET CLOSE TOGETHER

Sweden is sparsely populated — 21 inhabitants per square kilometre of land — but the population is so unevenly distributed that this figure does not say much. In fact many people live close together; half the population live in the 3 per cent of the country that is most densely populated, in urban areas.

The map that shows the local population base — a kind of population density map — reveals a pattern that in general was created at an early date. It is the old agricultural districts, the trade routes along the coasts and to some extent the mining districts that still form the basic structure of the

The map shows the number of inhabitants that can be reached from a point in a circle with a radius of 30 km. (T233)

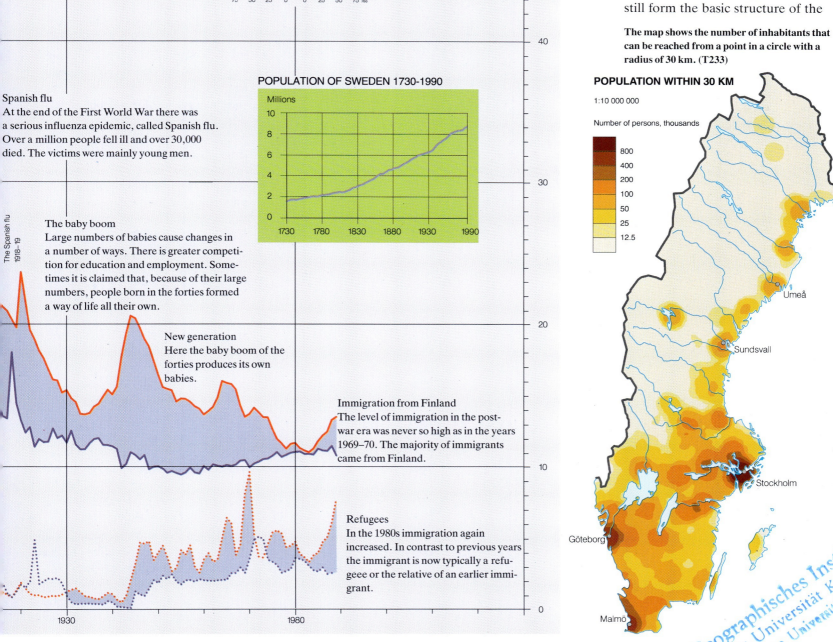

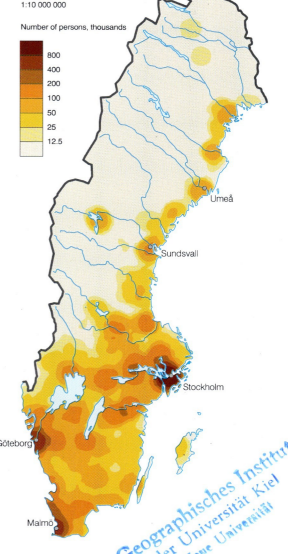

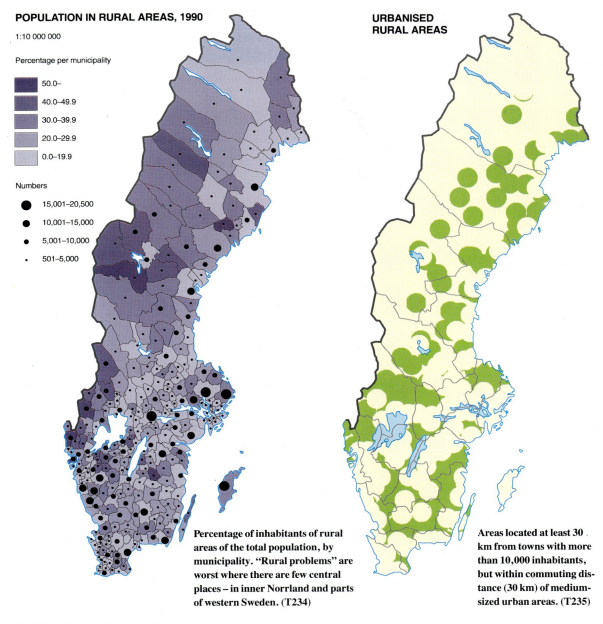

POPULATION IN RURAL AREAS, 1990

Percentage of inhabitants of rural areas of the total population, by municipality. "Rural problems" are worst where there are few central places – in inner Norrland and parts of western Sweden. (T234)

URBANISED RURAL AREAS

Areas located at least 30 km from towns with more than 10,000 inhabitants, but within commuting distance (30 km) of medium-sized urban areas. (T235)

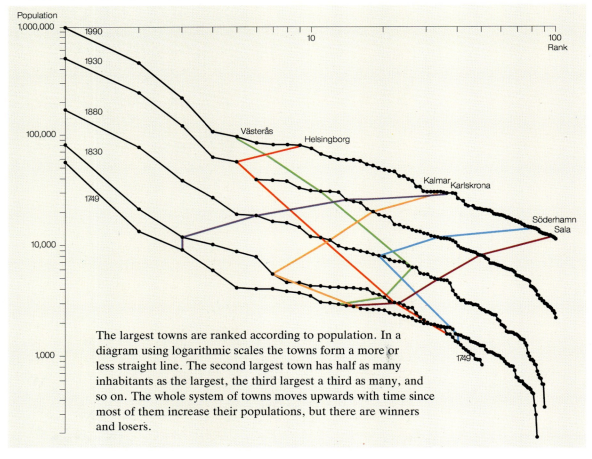

POPULATION IN TOWNS, 1749–1990

The largest towns are ranked according to population. In a diagram using logarithmic scales the towns form a more or less straight line. The second largest town has half as many inhabitants as the largest, the third largest a third as many, and so on. The whole system of towns moves upwards with time since most of them increase their populations, but there are winners and losers.

population pattern. The growth in population and process of urbanisation during the past century have accentuated this pattern, but the distribution of the population among the three major regions—Götaland, Svealand and Norrland—has not shown any radical change since 1900. Urbanisation has to a great extent taken place in the form of an *intraregional* redistribution of the population from rural to urban areas. Stockholm County accounts for the highest *interregional* redistribution figure, by increasing its share of Sweden's population from 7 to 19 per cent within about 100 years.

URBAN AREAS AND RURAL AREAS

Swedish population statistics distinguish between urban areas and rural areas. An *urban area* must have at least 200 inhabitants living fairly close together (not more than 200 m between houses). Even such a small place as this can act as a local service centre in a rural area, but is, of course, not by any means a town. A common lower limit for urban areas in Western Europe is 2,000 inhabitants; with this definition Sweden would have about 450 urban areas and 73 per cent of the population would be urban.

The term "town" (Sw. *stad*) is no longer used today as an administrative concept—there are only municipalities—but the word is used in everyday speech to refer to large urban areas. If we decide on an arbitrary minimum of 10,000 inhabitants, there were 110 "towns" in Sweden in 1990, where two thirds of the total urban population lived. Almost a third of the urban population live in the three largest metropolitan areas, Stockholm, Göteborg and Malmö. Here, and round a few large towns mostly in southern and central Sweden, we can speak of areas of continuous urban settlement.

Today 16–17 per cent of the population live in *rural areas*, but the statistical term "rural area" comprises a very wide range of population densities. In central Norrland and parts of western Sweden there are a number of municipalities where more than half the population live in rural areas. Along the mountain chain, in a few areas in inner Norrland and in northern Dalarna, there are large areas which are virtually uninhabited. But rural populations also live close to large towns and medium-sized urban areas, and in

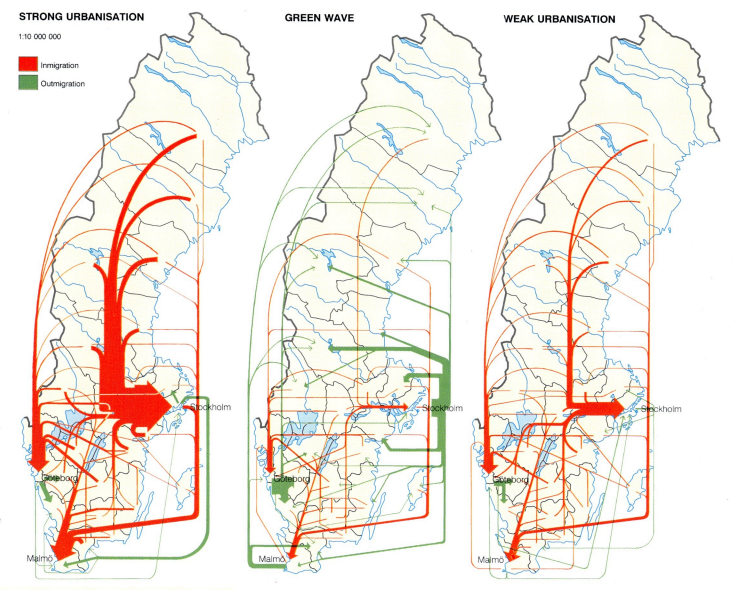

STRONG URBANISATION

1:10 000 000

- Inmigration (red)
- Outmigration (green)

During the 1960s there was a great inflow of people to the big cities. (T236)

GREEN WAVE

The "Green Wave" of the 1970s, which meant net outflows from the large towns. (T237)

WEAK URBANISATION

The 1980s were characterised by slight inflows of people to the big cities. (T238)

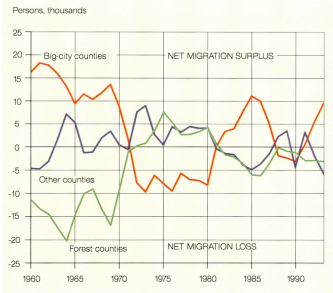

Domestic net migration between the big-city counties, the forest counties and other counties, 1960–1993. The diagram summarises the process that is shown in the maps above and illustrates the waves of metropolitan expansion.

many parts of Sweden these populations are growing. People live in the countryside but work in town. About one million people live in these *urbanised rural areas*, if the small towns are included. Most of them work in the industrial and service sectors and share most of the urban life style with the urban population. The same is mostly true of the 100,000 or so inhabitants of the true *rural areas*, where changes in traditional livelihoods have been slower and the real rural-area problems exist.

MIGRATION

On average we move house ten times in our lives. Most of these moves are over short distances — to a house within a town or local labour market. Young people leave home, households are formed and dissolved.

When a family grows, it looks for a larger home, and when the children move out, a smaller one. Altered financial conditions and the desire for better living conditions are other reasons for moving house.

Moves over long distances are made on average only once or twice in our lifetime, but it is regional migration that can change the distribution of the population in the long term. Nowadays the number of people that move out from a place is usually about the same as of those that move in, but at earlier stages of urbanisation there was a prolonged period of net emigration from rural areas to towns, as well as regional redistribution.

The net migration between various regions may also vary over short periods. The urbanisation process culminated in the 1960s with a strong net inflow to the big-city counties, mainly from the "forest counties" — the five Norrland counties plus Kopparberg and Värmland. This was followed in

TOWNS IN SWEDEN 1990

	Big cities	Medium-sized towns	Small towns	Towns	Urban villages
Number of settlements	3	16	91	344	1,389
Population, thousands	1,730	1,143	1,860	1,513	916
Percentage of total urban population	24	16	26	21	13
Inhabitants		>50,000	10,000-50,000	2,000-10,000	200-2,000

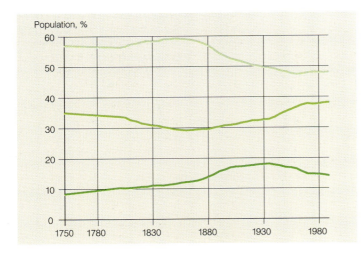

All three parts of Sweden have increased their populations during the past 200 years, but Götaland has increased more slowly than the other two. The colonisation and later the industrialisation of Norrland led to a major increase in population up to 1930. Since then eastern Svealand and above all Stockholm have had the most expansive population growth.

the 1970s by the "green wave", a net outflow from the large towns that was connected with slower economic growth and above all a new sense of values about living environments. During the 1980s there was again a net inflow to the big cities, but on a moderate scale, and mainly because the previous outflow of families with children decreased.

DEMOGRAPHIC CONSEQUENCES OF MIGRATION

The population in an area develops as a result of natural changes — a surplus or deficit of births — and migration. There is a relationship between these two factors, since migration often sharpens differences in the age structure of inflow and outflow areas; young people of child-bearing age move out, leaving the elderly population behind.

In 1992 there were just over 800,000 foreign-born people in Sweden, rather more than half of whom were Swedish citizens. The metropolitan regions, particularly Stockholm, have attracted many immigrants. In the border districts, like Tornedalen, the percentage of immigrants from the neighbouring countries is especially large. (T240)

In a longer, 200-year perspective we can identify clear but comparatively moderate shifts in percentage between the three major regions. In a shorter perspective, over two generations or so, we can see in greater detail some of the effects of urbanisation, for example on the map showing the percentage of the population that continue to live in the county where they were born. Much of inner Norrland, western Svealand and south-east Sweden show high figures; migration from other counties has been small and to other counties large. In contrast Stockholm and its neighbouring counties show low figures, since the inflow has been large.

The tendency to move (or not to move) is affected by many factors which often interact in complex ways. It is often pointed out that people more often stay put in areas that are a long way from large towns and in large towns with a broad labour market, or when they have a short, unspecialised education. Now that the urbanisation process has slowed down it is likely that regional differences in the percentage of those who do not move will be levelled out. Today's large local labour markets make it easier to change jobs and houses within one's home region. About 90 per cent of those who are born in Stockholm live there as adults. When both adults in a household work for a living, which is the usual state of affairs, it becomes more difficult to find jobs for both of them at another place, which also deters people from moving.

The effects of migration on the age structure are illustrated in the map showing the percentage of old-age pensioners. The greatest number of old people are in areas from which few people move. In inner Norrland, western Svealand and south-east Götaland there are areas where more than one inhabitant in four is over 65. In these rural areas the distribution of the sexes is also uneven, sometimes with a considerable surplus of men aged 20–40 who would like to start a family.

Immigration has also left its mark on the distribution of the population. There is an evident concentration of immigrants in the big-city and industrial areas in central Sweden, where there have been jobs in industry and low-paid service occupations. Immigrants from the Nordic countries have led to denser populations in the bor-

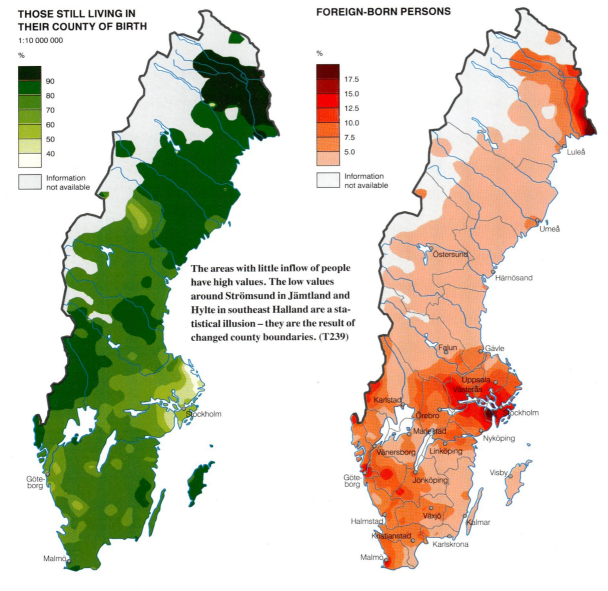

THOSE STILL LIVING IN THEIR COUNTY OF BIRTH

The areas with little inflow of people have high values. The low values around Strömsund in Jämtland and Hylte in southeast Halland are a statistical illusion – they are the result of changed county boundaries. (T239)

FOREIGN-BORN PERSONS

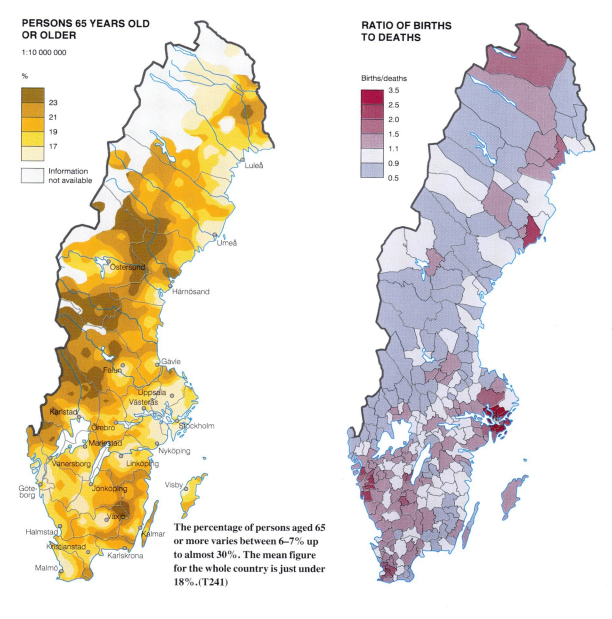

PERSONS 65 YEARS OLD OR OLDER

The percentage of persons aged 65 or more varies between 6–7% up to almost 30%. The mean figure for the whole country is just under 18%. (T241)

RATIO OF BIRTHS TO DEATHS

The ratio between births and deaths for the years 1983–1993. The average figure for all municipalities is just over 1. A large percentage of families of child-bearing age gives high values in the suburbs of the big cities. An ageing population in rural areas gives low values. (T242)

der districts, particularly with Finns in Tornedalen but also Norwegians in the west and Danes in the southern counties.

A VARIETY OF LOCAL PROBLEMS

Trends and the pace of population change create various problems for municipalities. Whatever the cause of the growth or decrease in population, natural changes (the birth/death ratio) and migration affect the age structure, which in turn affects the tax base and the ability to meet demands for child care, education and geriatric care. The information box below illustrates these problems with two examples. Pajala, a rural municipality in Norrbotten with a declining population and a large percentage of old-age pensioners, represents one extreme, and Håbo in Uppsala County, an expansive suburb of Stockholm with a relatively young population, the other.

A simple but effective way of describing the population situation in an area is to calculate the ratio between births and deaths. If in the long run this figure is close to or less than 1, there will be zero growth or a continual reduction of the population, a situation that can only be changed by an inflow or higher fertility.

During the period 1983–1993 the birth/death ratio varied between 0.51 and 3.43 in the municipalities of Sweden. The geographical pattern is obvious and, as one might expect, tallies with the maps showing the rural populations and the percentage of old-age pensioners.

The highest figures are in the suburbs of the big cities and in some expanding county centres like Umeå and Luleå. The municipalities in much of Götaland, eastern Svealand and along the coast of Norrland have figures around the national average, which is just above 1.

Low figures are found in many parts of the seven northernmost forest counties and in south-east Sweden. The population situation here may well be called serious. If these districts are to be revitalised, people of child-bearing age will have to move in, which in turn presumes the creation of new jobs in these mainly very sparsely-populated areas.

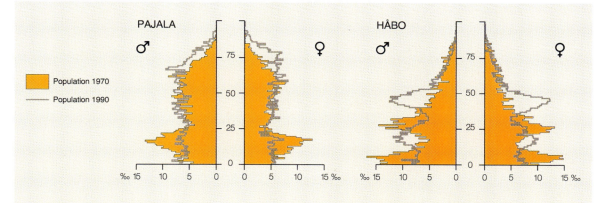

	Pajala	Håbo
Population, 1993	8,400	16,200
Changes in population, 1973–93	−19 %	+111 %
Birth/death ratio, 1983–93	0.71	3.36
Inhabitants/km²	1	114
Average income, kr	108,100	157,400
Tax base (% of national average)	78 %	111 %
% of population over 65	23 %	6 %
Municipal expenditure/inh.	39,400	23,800
Tax equalisation grant (% of municipal income)	25 %	0 %

The population pyramids for Pajala (left) and Håbo (right) show the municipalities' populations in 1970 and 1990. In comparison with Pajala Håbo has a young population with a high level of income providing a good tax base. The municipality's expenditure on social services is lower than in Pajala with its older population. The diminishing tax base in Pajala has to be compensated by means of state equalisation grants. When Håbo was expanding rapidly families with young children were in the majority, but the population pyramid changes quickly as the cohorts climb the scale.

Health

Health is perhaps the most important of our resources. But the old Swedish saying "Health holds its tongue" is true enough; it is mainly information about illness that is collected by various government agencies: data about sick leave, number of days of hospitalisation, causes of death and the like.

The distinction between health and illness is also a vague one; it is easier to identify illness than to agree on what constitutes good health. In the recurrent investigations into people's living conditions, three quarters of those interviewed between the ages of 16 and 84 usually say that they judge themselves to be in good health and for most people it is not until they are in their 70s that serious ill health is a reality. Thanks to modern medical treatment more people can live in spite of an acute or chronic illness; the death rate is falling, but the sickness rate is to some extent rising.

HEALTH RISKS

Figures for the death rate and the relative frequency of various causes of death may be related to a wide range of factors: age, sex, life style, eating habits, occupation and working environment. The most common causes of death are of course related to natural ageing. Diseases of the circulatory system and tumours are the cause of three quarters of all deaths in both sexes, even though men suffer from circulatory diseases at an earlier age than women. The number of deaths caused by accidents varies with both age and sex; road accidents affect men more often than women, especially in younger years. Injuries caused by falling are a somewhat more common cause of death among women, but compared with men the number is small up to the age of 70, after which it increases greatly, because more women than men live to a very high age when falling is a large risk factor.

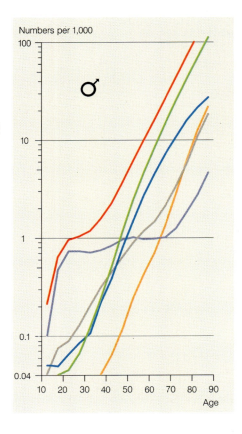

In general the maps of the death rates for women and men agree with each other – high rates mainly in parts of northern and central Sweden, lower rates in southern Sweden. There is a clear difference, however, in the central districts of the metropolitan areas, with a considerably higher death rate among men. (T243, T244)

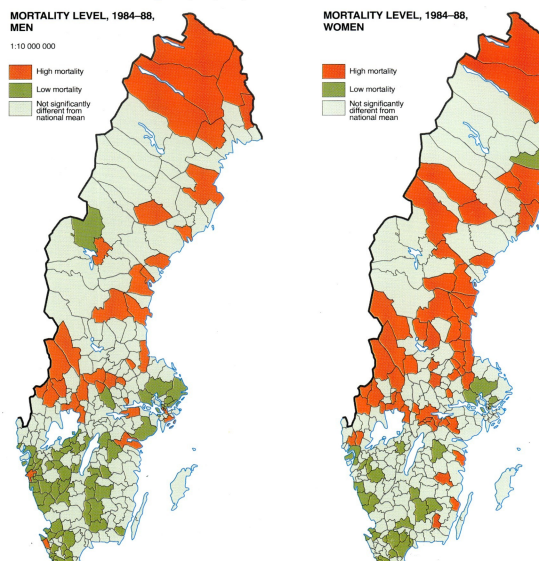

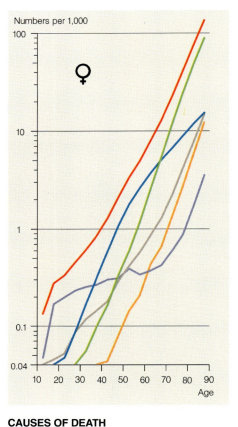

CAUSES OF DEATH

- Respiratory system
- Circulatory system
- Cancer
- Injury and poisoning
- Other causes
- All causes

Injuries dominate the causes of death for boys and young men. In old age it is above all diseases of the circulatory system and cancer that lead to death. Cancer is a more common cause of death among middle-aged women than among men. Death caused by injuries is very uncommon among girls and young women.

DEATHS FROM CIRCULATORY SYSTEM DISEASES 1982–86, MEN

1:20 000 000

Age-standardized mortality ratio
- 115–
- 105–114
- 95–104
- 85–94
- –84

DEATHS CAUSED BY CANCER 1982–86, WOMEN

ALCOHOL MORTALITY 1969–78, MEN

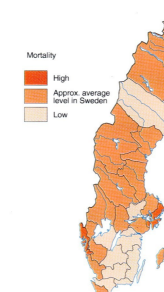

Mortality
- High
- Approx. average level in Sweden
- Low

Death from diseases varies regionally, but the underlying causes are often complex. Differences due to sex and age can be identified, but the influence of different life-styles, eating habits, work and environment are more difficult to measure. (T245, T246)

Death from alcohol-related diseases is particularly common in Stockholm and Göteborg. (T247)

The numbers of elderly people who have home help and who live in special apartments for old people have been amalgamated and related to the number of inhabitants over 65 years of age. Each municipality is then compared with the national average. A large percentage of old people over 75 gives specially high values. (T248)

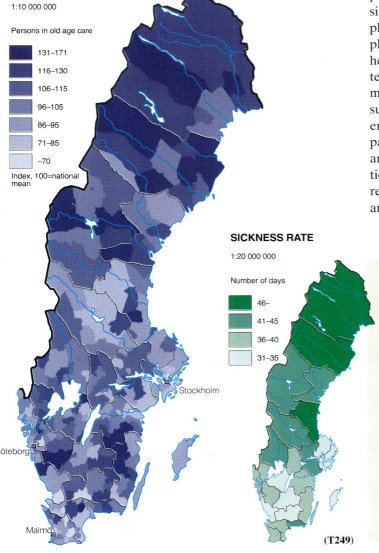

GERIATRIC CARE

1:10 000 000

Persons in old age care
- 131–171
- 116–130
- 106–115
- 96–105
- 86–95
- 71–85
- –70

Index, 100=national mean

SICKNESS RATE

1:20 000 000

Number of days
- 46–
- 41–45
- 36–40
- 31–35

THE "SICKNESS RATE" is the sum of the days with sickness benefit (from the 15th day of sickness) or sickness pension per insured person and year. This gives a picture of long or permanent sickness leave. The national average for 1993 was 39 days, two thirds of which was accounted for by sickness pension/benefit. There are great differences between municipalities behind the county figures – the highest value is more than four times larger than the lowest. Age distribution is one explanation of these regional variations, heavy work another.

(T249)

Health, and illness, are to a large extent a question of individual life styles, which in turn are connected with people's social situations. Life styles, eating habits, family life and many other factors interact in complex ways. Nor can one reject the possibility that there are factors in the physical and social environment that play a part in determining a person's health, though it is difficult to attempt to present this information in maps. Stress and environmental pressure in big-city environments, differences in eating habits in different parts of the country, unemployment and the social structure of the population may be factors that contribute to regional variations in the death rate and alcoholism, for example.

ILLNESS AND HEALTH CARE

Health care is not a reliable way of measuring ill health. Whether or not a person goes to a doctor or is taken in for an operation may depend on the availability of health care, the waiting time for certain kinds of treatment and so on. By far the greatest part of health care in Sweden is provided by the public sector, above all the county councils. The public sector accounts for 80 per cent of some 25 million visits to doctors.

Some important reforms were carried out in the health care sector in the early 1990s. In 1992 the municipalities took over responsibility for geriatric care and two thirds of the beds in geriatric wards were transferred from the county councils to the municipalities. In the same year the rules for the sickness benefit system were changed. Nowadays employers pay sickness pay for the first 14 days of a period of sickness, and only after that is sickness benefit paid. These reforms have meant that the statistics for health care and absence due to sickness are no longer completely comparable over time.

Need for health care is of course very unequally distributed among the age groups. People over the age of 75 constituted 8 per cent of the population in 1991, but they accounted for 60 per cent of hospital bed days. The growing number of old people puts increasing demands on municipal geriatric care, from home helps and home treatment to various kinds of sheltered living like service flats and convalescent homes.

Absence from work due to illness varies in several respects. In 1991, when the statistics still reported the first 14 days of sickness, the "sickness rate" for women was about 26 days and for men about 18 days, and three times higher at the age of 60 than in the age range 20–29. Just over a third of those insured were, however, never on the sick list and another 25 per cent for a maximum of 5 days.

Sickness and the amount of health care used varies a good deal both from one part of the country to another and within counties. Age structure and the distribution of the sexes are part of the explanation, access to health care another, and the distribution of occupations is probably yet another contributory factor — the number of disablement pensions is very high, for example, in rural and industrial municipalities.

Education

"Knowledge gives power" and education is a central issue for both the individual and society in general, more than ever before. Labour-market demands for specialised education are increasing, and higher education and research are generally considered to play a decisive role in Sweden's competitive power.

All the talk about an explosion in education in the past few decades is no exaggeration. All young people attend the nine-year compulsory school established in the 1950s, 90 per cent of each age group continue in one of the upper secondary school programmes and just over a quarter go on to higher education. Education is becoming more and more a life-long activity if one includes municipal adult education, retraining courses, in-service training in companies, for example.

Education is calculated within the ordinary educational system, from elementary school to post-graduate training. County towns and university towns have the largest percentages of well-educated people. (T250)

A CHANGING PICTURE

This rapid expansion of education facilities means that the average level of education varies a good deal between young and old people. Just over half the adult population only have pre-high school education, but the percentage of school leavers with a longer education is increasing every year.

The previously large differences in educational levels between regions and between rural and urban areas have been evened out but not eliminated. The expansion of high-school education in the 1960s and 1970s reduced the differences between places with and without a upper secondary school, but they are still apparent in the higher frequency of employees in rural areas with a short education.

There are also evident discrepancies, from district to district, in the transition from high school to university. Geographical proximity plays a certain part; the percentage going on

The percentage of employed people with only compulsory education is largest in rural areas with a traditional industrial structure and upper secondary schools that were formed at a late date. (T251)

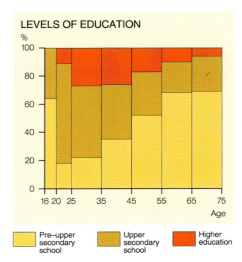

The "education explosion" has successively lengthened the time spent on education by each new generation.

to university is higher closer to university towns. The localisation of higher education has been given high priority in regional policies, and the establishment of a number of university colleges after 1970, alongside the universities and institutes of technology, has broadened entry to university education.

The map showing how employees' length of education varies in Sweden reveals a clear pattern. The highest values are found in the major cities and round the county towns; this is where the majority of universities are located, where many students remain after taking their degree and where the social structure plays a role since the children of university graduates more often choose a long education. The supply of skilled labour is an important location factor in the information society, so university towns offer great potential as high-growth centres thanks to their large populations of highly-educated people.

POPULAR EDUCATION

There are two forms of studies outside the normal educational system which deserve special mention: the Folk High School and the Study Circle. Both are closely connected with popular national movements.

Folk High Schools are a special form of education, originally Danish, for adult students. The first Swedish folk high schools were founded in the late 1860s to provide education for young people in farming districts. To begin with most of them were boarding schools in the countryside, but later more and more of the now 130-odd grant-aided folk high schools were established in towns, recruiting students

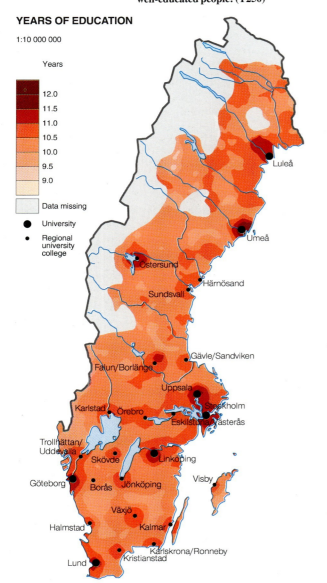

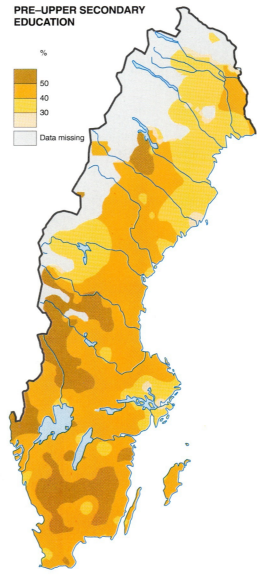

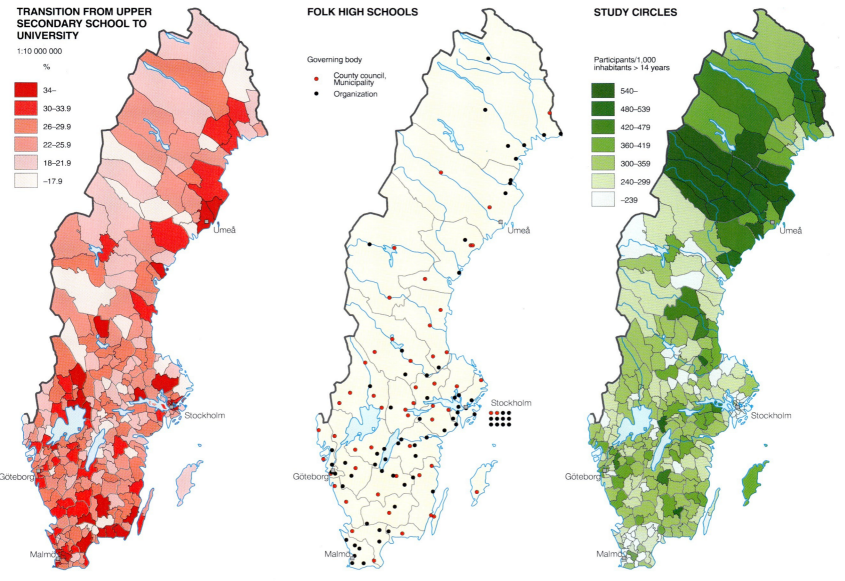

The highest figures are often, but not always, found close to university towns. (T252)

Places with folk high schools entitled to receive state grants, 1991. The fairly evenly spread picture still reflects the fact that many folk high schools were originally established in rural areas. (T253)

The local variations in participation in study circles are large. High values occur in rural municipalities with a strong tradition of popular education. Low values in some metropolitan areas may reflect the competition from the many other cultural activities there. (T254)

Choice of education is very traditional. In the 1990s the upper secondary school offers 14 vocational and two academic national programmes (social sciences and natural sciences). More than 90 per cent of the pupils that take technical programmes are usually boys, while girls are in the majority in the social service programme.

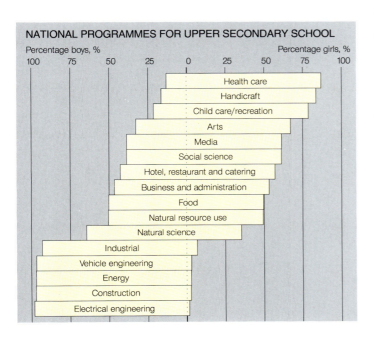

from a wide variety of backgrounds.

The educational programmes at folk high schools can take many forms. The humanities and social studies are traditional subjects, but many schools have a special profile as well — music, Third-World studies, the training of youth-club staff and so on.

Taking part in a *study circle* must be considered typically Swedish. The eleven study organisations are linked to political and union organisations, various religious groups and other popular national movements. During recent years the numbers attending study circles have varied between 2.6 and 2.9 million; more than a quarter of the population between 16 and 84 took part in one or sometimes more than one of the 340,000 or so study circles in 1990/91, with women in a slight majority. The geographical variations in enrolment figures are considerable — low in the metropolitan areas, especially high in parts of upper Norrland. Competition from other leisure activities may be the explanation in the former case and strong popular movement traditions in the latter case.

The "aesthetic subjects" category accounts for 40 per cent of all study circles, and social studies and languages together for 30 per cent. Apart from the thirst for knowledge and opportunities to develop a hobby, social contact is certainly a major factor for many students.

The folk high school is part of the educational system and therefore has more in common with the state school system than study circles have. Both forms of education, with their roots in *the popular education movement*, have proved to be viable in the era of expanding compulsory education.

Households — Housing and Economy

Families and households are concepts connected with the way we live together. Both are defined by the way people live, but the term family takes into account the relationships between children and parents. Even though it has become more and more common in recent years for people to live together without being married, 80 per cent of all families are still based on marriage.

The household is in many respects a social phenomenon of central importance. The composition of households affects the demand for accommodation, income and consumption patterns, and one of the great "social projects" — child-rearing — is one of the main functions of the family.

MANY SMALL HOUSEHOLDS

Sweden today is a nation of small households; households of one or two persons constituted about 70 per cent of all households in 1990. In particular it is the percentage of one-person households that has increased noticeably in the past few decades. The extensive housing programmes of the 1960s and 1970s made it possible for many more households to be formed, especially through adult children leaving their parental home. Another reason is that the number of elderly people has increased. The number of households consisting of people above the age of 65 increased by more than 70 per cent between 1970 and 1990, and many of them consist of single persons, 80 per cent of them women, who to a large extent live longer than their husbands.

In 1990 the number of households with children was practically the same as the number consisting only of people aged 65 or more. On average there were 1.7 children per household in the 900,000 or so households with children aged 0–15. The great majority of children live in traditional nuclear families with both their parents and at least one brother or sister; the percentage of families with a single parent has been gradually increasing, but is not more than about 14 per cent of all families with children.

HOME CONDITIONS

Of the housing units in the Swedish housing stock, 46 per cent are one-family houses and 54 per cent in apartment blocks. Swedish households are almost evenly divided between these two types of home: 49

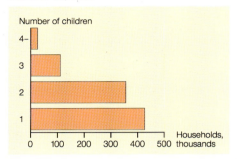

HOUSEHOLDS WITH CHILDREN AGED 0–15, 1990

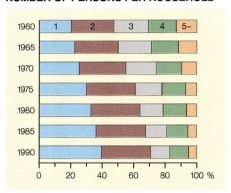

NUMBER OF PERSONS PER HOUSEHOLD

The percentage of small households is increasing all the time.

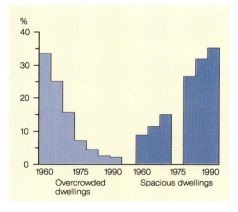

LIVING SPACE, 1960–1990

The amount of living space has increased greatly in the past few decades. The norm for overcrowding is more than two persons per room, and for a high standard more than one room per person (kitchen and one room excluded). There is no data available for the high standard for 1975.

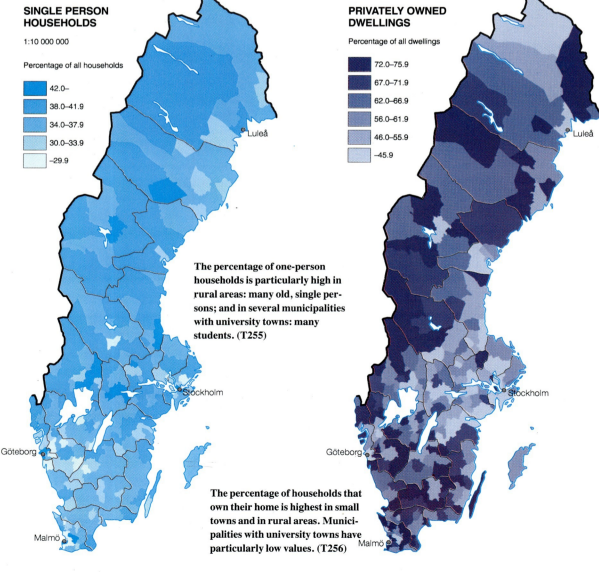

SINGLE PERSON HOUSEHOLDS
1:10 000 000
Percentage of all households
- 42.0–
- 38.0–41.9
- 34.0–37.9
- 30.0–33.9
- –29.9

The percentage of one-person households is particularly high in rural areas: many old, single persons; and in several municipalities with university towns: many students. (T255)

PRIVATELY OWNED DWELLINGS
Percentage of all dwellings
- 72.0–75.9
- 67.0–71.9
- 62.0–66.9
- 56.0–61.9
- 46.0–55.9
- –45.9

The percentage of households that own their home is highest in small towns and in rural areas. Municipalities with university towns have particularly low values. (T256)

According to the population statistics a *family* consists of at least two persons, a cohabiting couple with or without children under 18 at home, or of a single person with a child or children at home. A family is also a *household unit*, which may, however, be only one person.

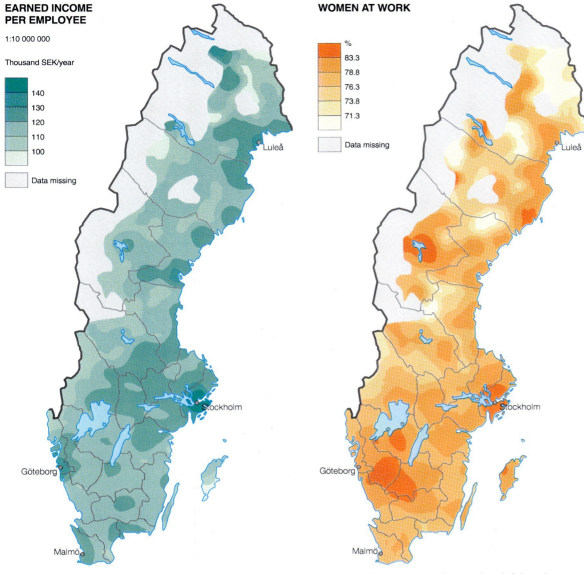

EARNED INCOME PER EMPLOYEE

1:10 000 000

Thousand SEK/year
- 140
- 130
- 120
- 110
- 100
- Data missing

Earned income for those gainfully employed reflects variations in industrial structure and pay levels. It is highest in regions with large towns, particularly the metropolitan areas, and lowest in rural areas. Data from 1989. (T257)

WOMEN AT WORK

%
- 83.3
- 78.8
- 76.3
- 73.8
- 71.3
- Data missing

The percentage of women in gainful employment is generally highest in large towns and regional centres with a large service sector, but the traditional textile and small business areas in the southwest of Sweden also have high values. (T258)

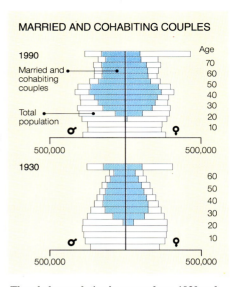

MARRIED AND COHABITING COUPLES

The whole population by age and sex, 1930 and 1990. In 1990 just over 80 per cent of those living together were married.

Part-time work and low wages in many typically female occupations are the main reasons for the differences in annual income between women and men.

EARNED ANNUAL INCOME, MEN AND WOMEN

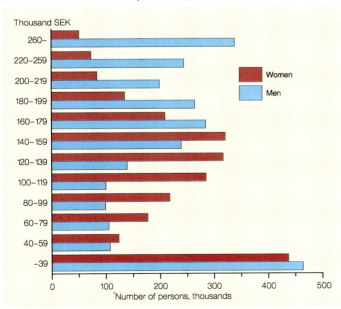

REGIONAL AND LOCAL VARIATIONS

There is a close connection between household structure and housing conditions, but the geographical patterns of these phenomena are in turn determined, for example, by differences in the age structure of the population, by migration and by the quality of and changes in the housing stock.

The central districts of the big cities and municipalities with large population inflows, for example those with higher education institutions, but also areas where there are many old people, have the largest proportion of small households. The suburbs of the big cities present a fragmented picture, depending very much on the inhabitants' financial status; in some districts there are many families with small children, few old people, few single-person households and a large proportion of people living in apartment blocks. In other districts there is a similar pattern of households, but one-family houses dominate. Generally speaking it is least common for people to own their home in the big cities and other large towns, while in small towns and in rural districts people live to a much greater extent in houses of their own.

HOUSEHOLD FINANCES

The great majority of households base their economies on earned income, and except for one-person households it is most common nowadays for a household to have two incomes. One of the great changes in the Swedish labour market during the past few decades is the increased number of women working outside the home. Since women work part-time much

and 51 per cent respectively. The percentage of households living in one-family houses has grown in the past few decades, though not greatly. The trend has been towards increasing owner-occupancy, as indicated, for instance, by an increase in the share of tenant-owner apartments at the expense of rented accommodation.

Generally speaking, and particularly in an international perspective, it may be said that Swedish housing is of a high standard. Living space relative to household size — admittedly not an absolute measure of quality — has been increasing steadily over the past decades; in 1990 only two per cent of all households were living in overcrowded conditions. The largest number was among immigrant families and families with children, whereas small households consisting of middle-aged and elderly people usually had the largest amount of living space per person.

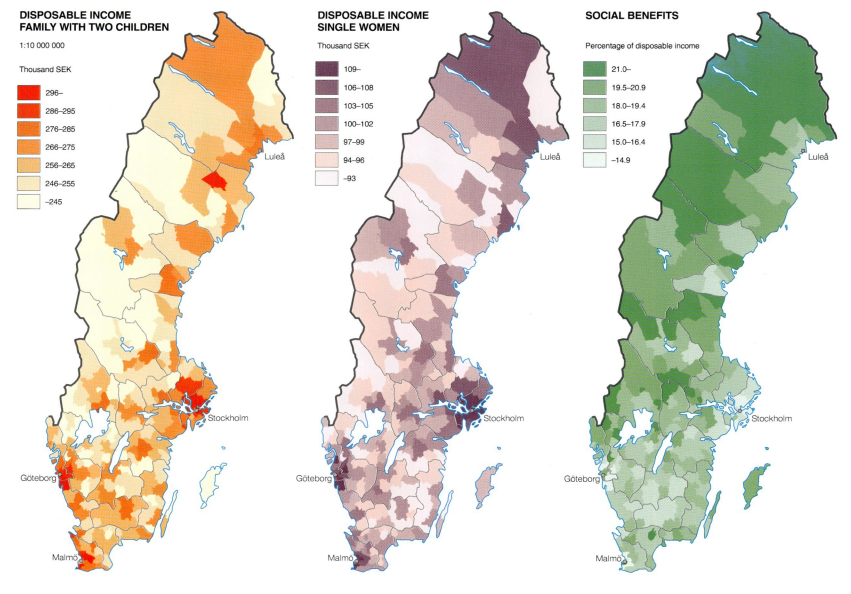

Average disposable income, 1991, for households consisting of two married or cohabiting adults with two children. Big cities and other large towns have the highest incomes. (T259)

The average disposable income for single working women is lower that that of a family with children, but the regional pattern is similar. (T260)

The share of transfer payments of total disposable income gives a reversed image of the income maps to the left. Both taxable and tax-free payments are included. (T261)

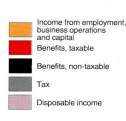
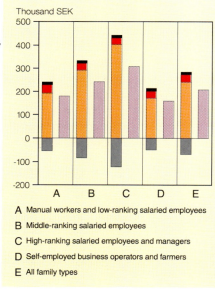

DISPOSABLE INCOME HOUSEHOLD TYPES

- Income from employment, business operations and capital
- Benefits, taxable
- Benefits, non-taxable
- Tax
- Disposable income

A Manual workers and low-ranking salaried employees
B Middle-ranking salaried employees
C High-ranking salaried employees and managers
D Self-employed business operators and farmers
E All family types

Even after the redistribution of financial resources by taxation and transfer payments, average disposable income clearly varies from one type of household to another.

more than men do, and many of them have poorly paid jobs, the working income of a woman is on average about 70 per cent of that of a man.

Disposable income is considered to be the best measure of a household's paying capacity. It is calculated by adding positive transfer payments (children's allowance, supplementary benefit and unemployment benefit, for example) to income and deducting tax. Disposable income gives some idea of a household's ability to pay for the "well-being" that can be bought for money in the formal economy. The well-being that is created in the informal economy, by household work, for example, lies outside these calculations, and it should be remembered that work in the home is to some extent an alternative to buying goods and services on the market.

In an international perspective income is equally distributed in Sweden. There are, however differences between incomes: between men and women, between different occupations, between people with good and poor educations and between age groups.

Behind this comparatively far-reaching equalisation of disposable household income lie several factors, apart from pay development on the Swedish labour market. One of them is the redistribution of income through taxation and transfer payments in the form of social benefits and allowances.

REGIONAL VARIATIONS AND LOCAL CONTRASTS

When the mean values for disposable household income are worked out for municipalities, many of the differences in income in the population are concealed. Since income varies greatly from one type of household to another, and since household structure is not uniform all over the country, regional variations in disposable in-

SOCIO-ECONOMIC DIFFERENTIATION IN UPPSALA

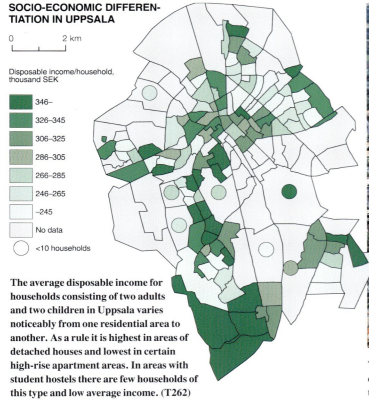

0   2 km

Disposable income/household, thousand SEK

- 346–
- 326–345
- 306–325
- 286–305
- 266–285
- 246–265
- –245
- No data
- ○ <10 households

The average disposable income for households consisting of two adults and two children in Uppsala varies noticeably from one residential area to another. As a rule it is highest in areas of detached houses and lowest in certain high-rise apartment areas. In areas with student hostels there are few households of this type and low average income. (T262)

This photograph of Uppsala is taken facing north. Comparing the photograph and the map shows quite clearly how differences in types of housing are reflected in income levels. The light-coloured buildings to the right are student hostels.

In 1992 the mean value for municipalities varied from 200,000 S kr. to 1.4 million S kr. The variation at the household level is far greater – 4% of households account for 25% of the total capital assets in Sweden. Areas with detached houses have the highest values. In some rural areas agricultural and forest property accounts for a great deal of the capital assets. (T263)

ASSESSED CAPITAL ASSETS

1:10 000 000

Average per household, thousand SEK

- 350–
- 325–349
- 300–324
- 275–299
- 250–274
- 225–249
- –224

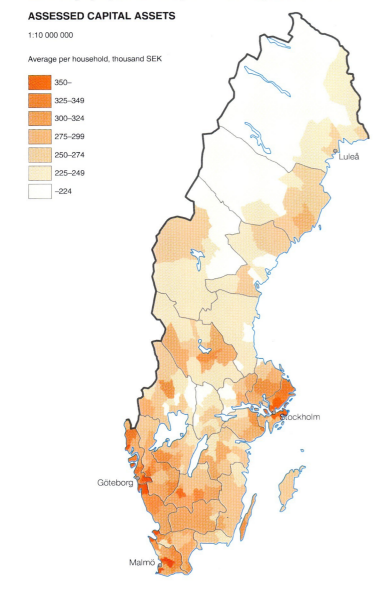

come for two types of household are presented here.

"Families with children" consisting of two parents and two children have a comparatively high income. Half of all municipalities fall within a relatively narrow band (250–270,000 S kr.) lying round the mean value for 1991, which was just under 260,000 S kr. — indicating fairly equal distribution. High incomes are found, with a few exceptions, in the metropolitan areas, especially in certain suburbs which have a large proportion of families with children living in their own houses, and in other large towns. The other end of the scale comprises the rural municipalities of inner Norrland, western Svealand and south-east Götaland.

Apart from the fact that the disposable income for households consisting of "single women" is lower than for families with children, the regional picture is remarkably similar.

It should be added that a lower disposable income in rural areas does not necessarily mean a lower material standard of living; this can be compensated by lower housing costs and more informal, unpaid work.

The share of transfer payments in disposable household income varied among municipalities in the early 1990s from just under 8 per cent up to 29 per cent. The regional pattern, as would be expected, reflects the income maps, with the lowest figures in some of Stockholm's suburbs and the highest in Tornedalen.

Behind the fairly uniform picture of regional variations provided by the maps based on data for municipalities, there are often *great local contrasts*, above all in the big cities. Household paying capacity on the housing market plays a decisive role in the settlement pattern. Where areas of apartment blocks or detached houses are more or less clearly separated, there may be sharp contrasts in the social composition of the population, and hence large differences in income, between districts that lie close together. This segregation is often reinforced by the fact that poor households, immigrant families, for example, are placed in areas where the public housing associations have their apartment blocks.

CAPITAL ASSETS

The statistics for private capital must be studied with caution. Quite a few assets are not declared at all in tax returns — one large type being pension assets — or are not declared at their full market value, for example real estate and shares. Undeclared "black money" is another source of error, how large is unknown.

The home is the largest single item in private capital. The municipalities with many detached houses in the metropolitan regions have the highest values on the map showing private capital. The relatively high values in parts of southern Sweden, Värmland and Dalarna probably reflect the ownership of farms and forests.

Politics, Popular Movements and Associations

A large survey of associations in Sweden in 1992 revealed that 92 per cent of the population between 16 and 84 were members of at least one organisation or club, and most people were members of a couple of associations of some kind. The total number of memberships was almost 20 million, to which can be added about 1.2 million children aged 7–15 who are members of some organisation.

We organise ourselves in associations and clubs for various reasons. The classic popular national movements, with their roots in the 19th century — labour, free church and teetotaller movements — were a way of gaining political and religious freedom and of fighting against social injustice. Trade unions, tenants' associations and consumer cooperatives are examples of organisations with many members because work, the home and consumption of goods and services are fundamental functions of society. A wide range of organisations and clubs have gradually grown up round our leisure activities, to look after the interests of special groups — immigrants, women, parents — or to lobby for special issues.

A NATION OF ACTIVE CLUB MEMBERS

More than half the adult population, 3.5 million people, were actively engaged in at last one club in 1992, and of these almost 2 million had one or more posts of responsibility on committees. A rough estimate is that the unpaid work done in a total of 2.8 million committee posts corresponds to 145,000 full-time jobs — an impressive figure!

There are, however, variations among different kinds of organisations with regard to the active participation of their members. This is shown by the diagram of organisations and clubs with more than 500,000 members. In most of the big organisations there is a small percentage of active members — most people are in the union, cooperative society, or tenants' association for other reasons than playing an active part in the organisation. Some organisations, for example those concerned with environmental issues and humanitarian aid, seem to have a large number of supporting members, but few active ones. It is in the leisure sector that one finds the most active members; in sports, cultural and hobby associations between 55 and 65 per cent of the members are active. Similar figures are found in small organisations like church societies, volunteer defence organisations and local action groups.

THE MAP OF NATIONAL POLITICS

We exercise our political power as citizens mainly at parliamentary, municipal and county council elections. Comparatively few people are members of a political party, only 11 per cent of the adult population, but compared with other countries our turnout at elections is high. In the past few decades it has varied between 86 and 92 per cent.

Since the 1920s the most important dividing line in Swedish politics has

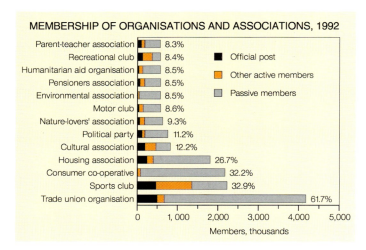

The percentages indicate the share of members of the population aged 16–84.

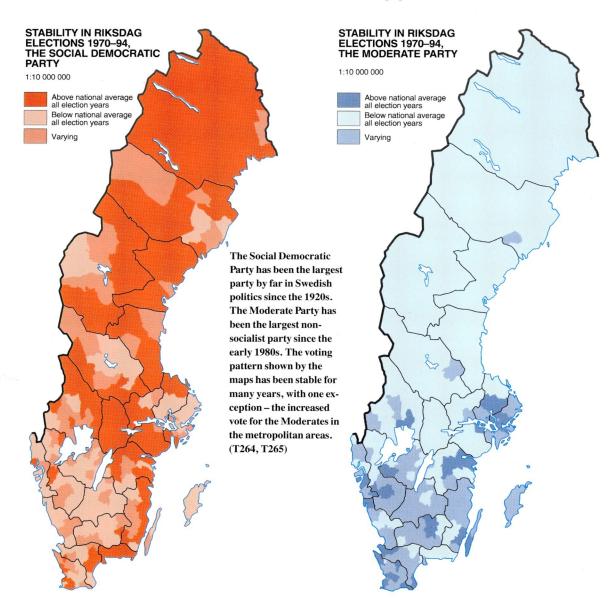

The Social Democratic Party has been the largest party by far in Swedish politics since the 1920s. The Moderate Party has been the largest non-socialist party since the early 1980s. The voting pattern shown by the maps has been stable for many years, with one exception – the increased vote for the Moderates in the metropolitan areas. (T264, T265)

The right to vote has gradually been extended to an increasingly large part of the population. Women got the right to vote in 1921. In an international comparison the election turnout is high; it was 86% in the 1994 election.

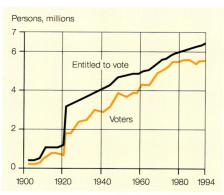

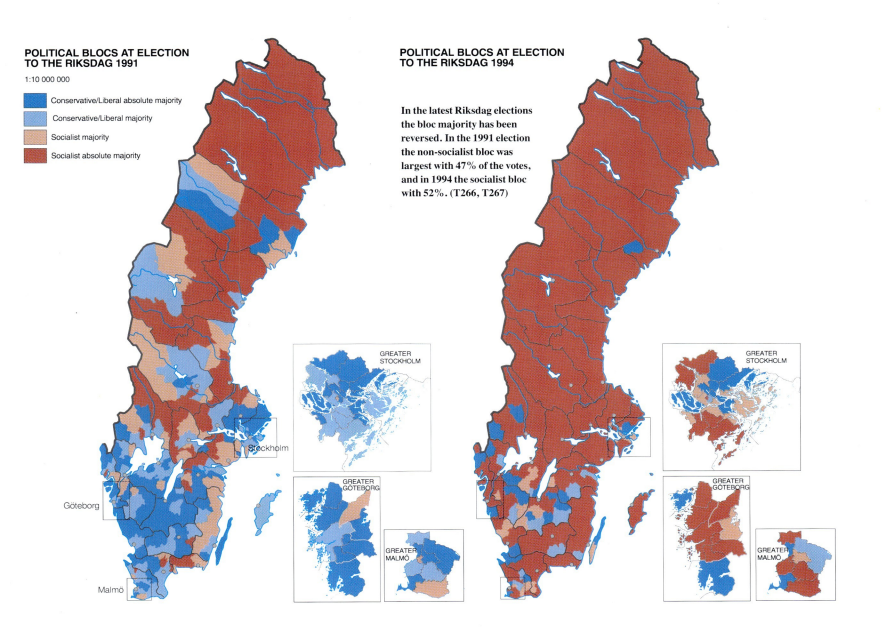

POLITICAL BLOCS AT ELECTION TO THE RIKSDAG 1991

1:10 000 000

- Conservative/Liberal absolute majority
- Conservative/Liberal majority
- Socialist majority
- Socialist absolute majority

POLITICAL BLOCS AT ELECTION TO THE RIKSDAG 1994

In the latest Riksdag elections the bloc majority has been reversed. In the 1991 election the non-socialist bloc was largest with 47% of the votes, and in 1994 the socialist bloc with 52%. (T266, T267)

PERCENTAGES OF PARTY VOTES IN RIKSDAG ELECTIONS, 1973–1994

	1973	1976	1979	1982	1985	1988	1991	1994
M	14.3	15.6	20.3	23.6	21.3	18.3	21.9	22.2
Fp	9.4	11.1	10.6	5.9	14.2	12.2	9.1	7.2
C	25.1	24.1	18.1	15.5	12.4	11.3	8.5	7.7
kd	1.8	1.4	1.4	1.9		2.9	7.1	4.1
S	43.6	42.7	43.2	45.6	44.7	43.2	37.7	45.4
V	5.3	4.8	5.6	5.6	5.4	5.8	4.5	6.2
Mp				1.7	1.5	5.5	3.4	5
NyD							6.7	1.2

Note: In 1985 The Centry Party and the Christian Democrat Party had a joint election campaign.

M = The Moderate Party (Moderata samlingspartiet)
Fp = The Liberal Party (Folkpartiet Liberalerna)
C = The Centre Party (Centerpartiet)
kd = The Christian Democrat Party (Kristdemokraterna)
S = The Social Democratic Party (Socialdemokratiska arbetarpartiet)
V = The Left Party (Vänsterpartiet)
Mp = The Green Party (Miljöpartiet de Gröna)
NyD = New Democracy (Ny Demokrati)

been between the socialist and the non-socialist blocs. During practically the whole of the post-war period the balance of power between these two blocs has been strikingly stable, but with long periods of a slight majority for the socialist bloc and with mainly Social Democrat governments.

The political map has been stable for many years, seen from a bloc-political point of view. The main changes have been *within* the non-socialist bloc: during the last 20 years, for example, the Centre Party's share of the votes has varied between 8 and 25 per cent, and that of the Moderate (Conservative) Party between 14 and 24 per cent. Since the two blocs have long hovered around the 50-per-cent mark, however, quite small changes between the blocs can alter the majority position in many constituencies, leading to a significant shift in the political map. This is clearly illustrated when comparing the election result in 1991, when the non-socialist parties won, with the 1994 election, when the socialist parties were victorious.

Broadly speaking, it may be said that the non-socialist bloc has traditionally been strong in western Götaland and has also gradually improved its position in the large towns, whereas the socialist bloc has for many years been dominant in Norrland, in the central-Swedish industrial belt and in a wedge running down into south-east Sweden. The explanation of this pattern must be sought in the first place in the varied and changing socio-economic composition of the electorate, even though political traditions in various districts may be persistent, slowing down changes in party line-ups.

LOCAL POLITICS

The municipality has been called "the local state". Municipal independence and its right to impose taxes has a long tradition in Sweden, and the municipalities have considerable freedom to act independently within political spheres like social services, physical planning and public transport. At the same time the municipalities are in

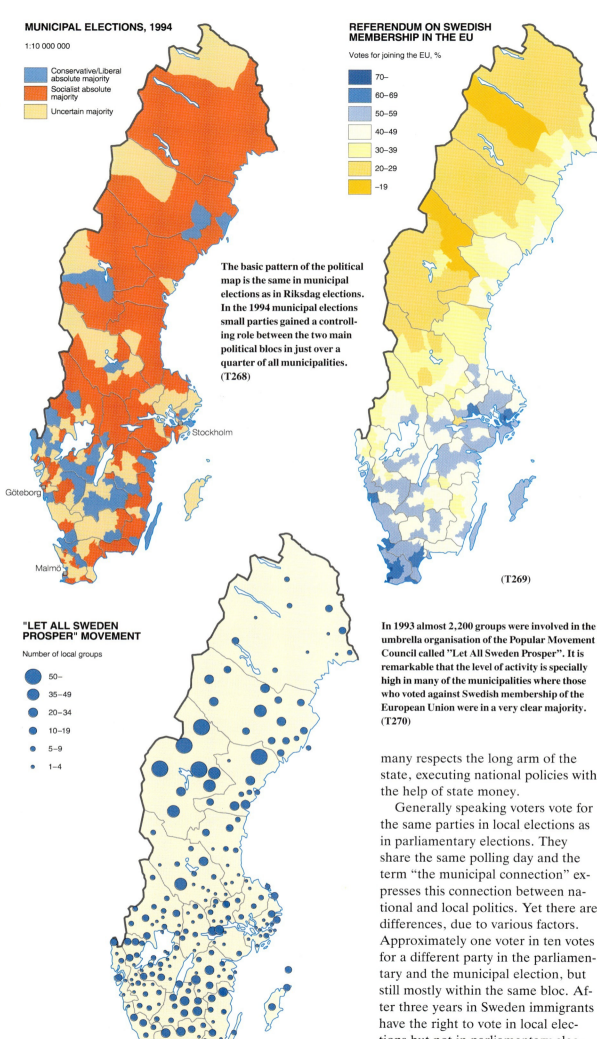

MUNICIPAL ELECTIONS, 1994

1:10 000 000

- Conservative/Liberal absolute majority
- Socialist absolute majority
- Uncertain majority

The basic pattern of the political map is the same in municipal elections as in Riksdag elections. In the 1994 municipal elections small parties gained a controlling role between the two main political blocs in just over a quarter of all municipalities. (T268)

REFERENDUM ON SWEDISH MEMBERSHIP IN THE EU

Votes for joining the EU, %
- 70–
- 60–69
- 50–59
- 40–49
- 30–39
- 20–29
- –19

(T269)

In the referendum in November 1994 52.7 % voted for and 47.3 % against Sweden joining the European Union (disregarding the 0.9 % who returned a blank ballot paper). The geographical pattern is a striking one. The yes voters had their strongholds in the towns in the south; the opposition was compact in the northern rural districts, and in all municipalities within the limits of EU's regional development areas (based on extremely sparse population) a large majority voted against the proposal.

It is remarkable how strongly the geographical results in the EU referendum reflect the picture obtained when mapping urbanisation, migration and non-migration, age distribution, household structure, level of education, industrial structure and occupational distribution, income and political elections. It may be claimed with some certainty that this represents a basic demographic, social and economic pattern in modern Sweden that occurs in many contexts, and which has two geographical and opposing fields of force: between town and country and between north and south.

"LET ALL SWEDEN PROSPER" MOVEMENT

Number of local groups
- 50–
- 35–49
- 20–34
- 10–19
- 5–9
- 1–4

In 1993 almost 2,200 groups were involved in the umbrella organisation of the Popular Movement Council called "Let All Sweden Prosper". It is remarkable that the level of activity is specially high in many of the municipalities where those who voted against Swedish membership of the European Union were in a very clear majority. (T270)

many respects the long arm of the state, executing national policies with the help of state money.

Generally speaking voters vote for the same parties in local elections as in parliamentary elections. They share the same polling day and the term "the municipal connection" expresses this connection between national and local politics. Yet there are differences, due to various factors. Approximately one voter in ten votes for a different party in the parliamentary and the municipal election, but still mostly within the same bloc. After three years in Sweden immigrants have the right to vote in local elections but not in parliamentary elections. In particular, special local circumstances may mean that small parties attract voters, which sometimes gives them a controlling role, allowing them to form coalitions with one of the two blocs. These may be parties that exist at the national level, but also local groups that have revolted against the established parties or have a special issue on their programme; names like "Lindesberg's Independent Democrats", "The Hospital Party" and "Stop the E4 West" indicate the wide range of such parties.

DAY-TO-DAY POLITICS AT THE GRASS-ROOTS LEVEL

It is at the local level that the great majority of active members take part in organisation and club activities, whether it is a local branch of a large, hierarchical national organisation or a parents' cooperative in a residential area. Many people feel it is particularly important to involve themselves in activities concerning their everyday life and their own home district. About half a million people were members of cooperative associations and societies — school, consumer, road and neighbourhood associations,

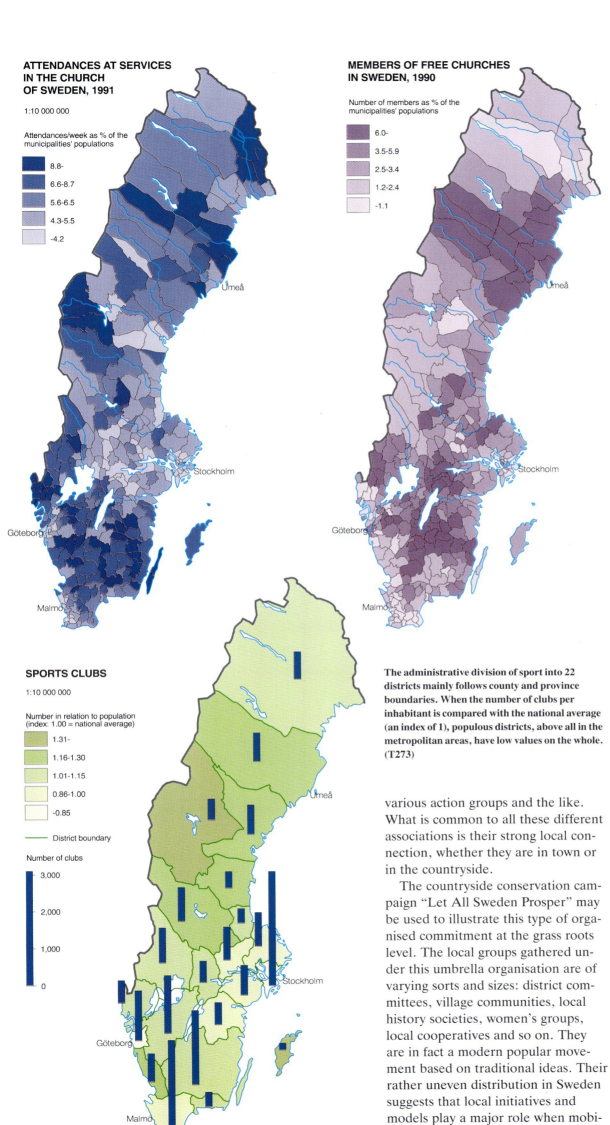

ATTENDANCES AT SERVICES IN THE CHURCH OF SWEDEN, 1991

1:10 000 000

Attendances/week as % of the municipalities' populations
- 8.8-
- 6.6-8.7
- 5.6-6.5
- 4.3-5.5
- -4.2

MEMBERS OF FREE CHURCHES IN SWEDEN, 1990

Number of members as % of the municipalities' populations
- 6.0-
- 3.5-5.9
- 2.5-3.4
- 1.2-2.4
- -1.1

SPORTS CLUBS

1:10 000 000

Number in relation to population (index: 1.00 = national average)
- 1.31-
- 1.16-1.30
- 1.01-1.15
- 0.86-1.00
- -0.85

— District boundary

Number of clubs
- 3,000
- 2,000
- 1,000
- 0

The administrative division of sport into 22 districts mainly follows county and province boundaries. When the number of clubs per inhabitant is compared with the national average (an index of 1), populous districts, above all in the metropolitan areas, have low values on the whole. (T273)

The pattern of church-going is generally speaking determined by history. High values are found in the areas where the 19th-century Revivalist movements sprang up and the free church movement has its strongholds. (T271, T272)

SUNDAY OBSERVANCE OR SUNDAY SPORTS?

Sweden is seen as a secularised country, although more than nine out of ten people are members of the established Church of Sweden. The Protestant free churches have about 300,000 members and other churches, which have grown rapidly thanks to immigration, have even more. The members of free churches are very active. Church attendance in the Church of Sweden is in contrast low, even though 60 per cent of all weddings and more than 90 per cent of all funerals take place there.

The church as a popular movement rests on centuries of tradition but has lost its former role as one of the pillars of society. The modern sports movement is considerably younger — it is only about 100 years old — but it is today perhaps our largest popular movement. Only the trade union movement has more organised members, and with regard to the number of active members in relation to the whole population sports associations hold a special position among the big organisations.

The geographical pattern of church attendance is to a great extent historical, and still characterised by the heritage of the 19th-century revivalist movement, which was particularly strong in Småland and Västerbotten. The fact that the geography of the sports movement partly resembles that of religion is mainly a result of the relationship between town and country. In the early days of sports the big towns were the centres. It was here that new sports were introduced, to spread later throughout the country. Today most of the major sports are played all over the country, but in relation to the population, the number of clubs (22,000) and members (2.2 million) is greater in the countryside than in the metropolitan regions.

If the headline "Sunday Observance or Sunday Sports?" is somewhat provocative, it serves to make one think about the diversity of organised activities that are connected with life style, sex and age, for example. The members of church organisations are elderly, those of sports clubs younger; in the former, the majority are women, in the latter they are men.

various action groups and the like. What is common to all these different associations is their strong local connection, whether they are in town or in the countryside.

The countryside conservation campaign "Let All Sweden Prosper" may be used to illustrate this type of organised commitment at the grass roots level. The local groups gathered under this umbrella organisation are of varying sorts and sizes: district committees, village communities, local history societies, women's groups, local cooperatives and so on. They are in fact a modern popular movement based on traditional ideas. Their rather uneven distribution in Sweden suggests that local initiatives and models play a major role when mobilising interest in this kind of activity.

How We Use Our Time

Everything we do takes time. And everything we do takes place somewhere. For most of us everyday life is filled with activities that require us to move from one place to another, and it is not always easy to get the bits of the puzzle to fit together: activities, places and journeys. There just is not enough time, also because space — the geographical distribution of places for different activities and the distances between them — limits what we can manage to do.

When we speak of the geographical distribution of the population, we usually mean the "night population", that is, where we live. If we consider the length of time we spend at different places, the home is indeed the most important place. People of working age spend on average two thirds of their time at home — sleeping, eating, doing the housework or looking after their personal hygiene — while about a quarter of their time is spent at places outside the home, above all at work but also in shops, sports centres and so on. Thus during a large part of the daytime there is a different distribution of the population, which is determined by the location of various types of activities.

Yet another population pattern is created by our travelling. Journeys account for between five and six per cent of our time, on average one hour twenty minutes per day. This might not sound very much, but travelling is a lubricant without which our daily programmes would seize up. The reason why we manage to move about so much today — on average 40 km a day — is the dramatic increase in the speed of travel rather than an increase in travelling time.

TIME SCALES

In a lifetime — from the cradle to the grave — we spend most of our time asleep! Sleeping, eating and personal hygiene are necessary for mankind's primary project — survival. Other major projects are education, mainly from the age of 7 up to the 20s, and work, which covers the period between the 20s and 65.

The use of time within one day can be described in greater detail, as in the diagram showing the way men and women use their time. On average men work longer hours than women, but women still devote more time to housework and for that reason in particular the ranking of various activities varies between the sexes. In addition there are the systematic variations connected with weekdays, weekends and holidays.

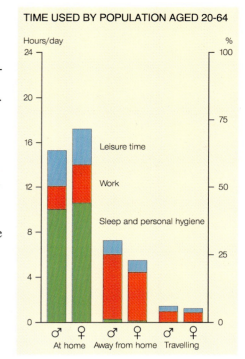

We spend most of our time at home, and not just to sleep.

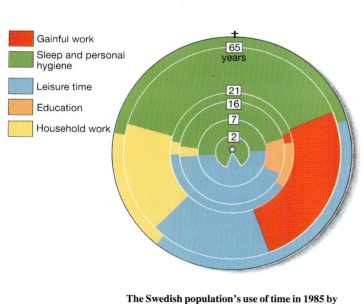

The Swedish population's use of time in 1985 by age group (shown by age rings) and activities (coloured sectors).

The diagram shows both similarities and dissimilarities between the lives of men and women. The similarities have increased with the years because women's gainful employment outside the home has increased. But women still spend more time than men doing various household tasks.

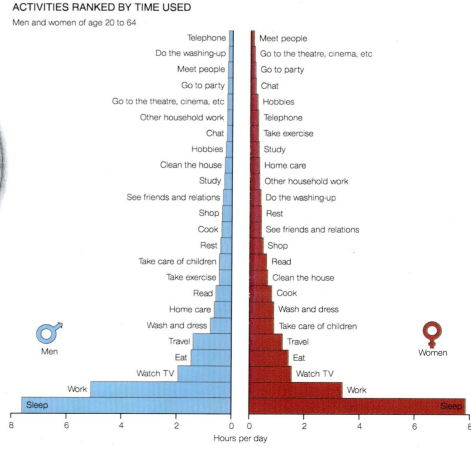

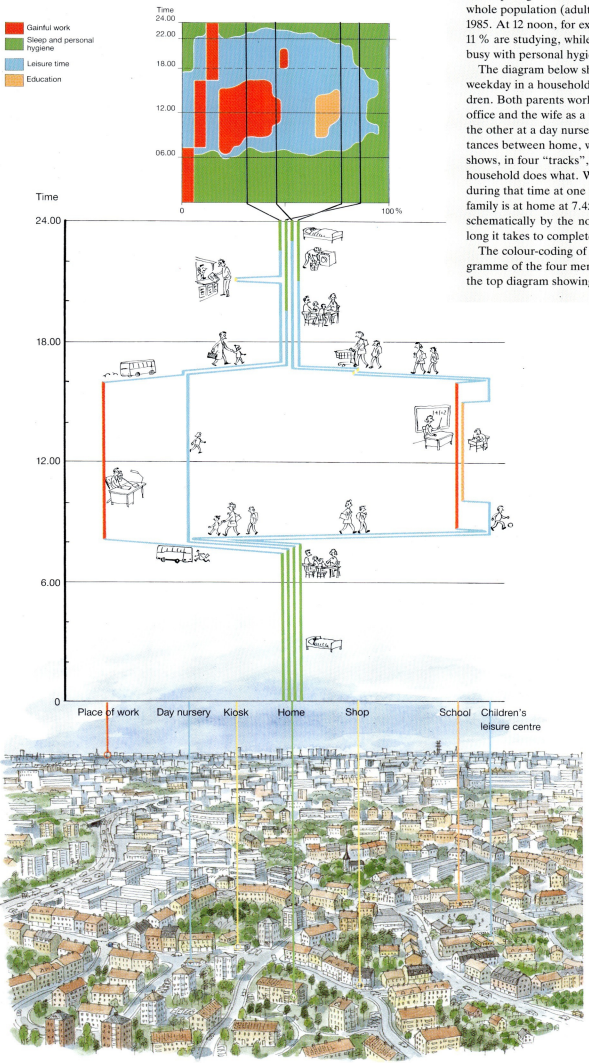

The top diagram shows the distribution of the activities of the whole population (adults and children) during a weekday in 1985. At 12 noon, for example, 31 % are gainfully employed and 11 % are studying, while 48 % are free and 10 % are asleep or busy with personal hygiene.

The diagram below shows the use of time on an ordinary weekday in a household consisting of two adults and two children. Both parents work during the daytime, the husband at an office and the wife as a teacher. One of the children is at school, the other at a day nursery. The family lives in a big town, so distances between home, work and school are long. The diagram shows, in four "tracks", where and when each member of the household does what. When a track is vertical that person is during that time at one place, as, for example, when the whole family is at home at 7.45 in the morning. Movement is marked schematically by the not quite horizontal lines – they show how long it takes to complete it.

The colour-coding of the tracks shows how the daily programme of the four members of this household can be placed in the top diagram showing the use of time of the whole population.

SCHEDULING EVERYDAY ACTIVITIES IN TIME AND SPACE

The problem of organising activities in time and space for a day, a week or a longer period is not only a question of what we *want* to do but is decided to a large extent by various obstacles or constraints in our surroundings. Working hours, school timetables, opening hours of shops, banks and post offices, bus and train timetables, how long the day centre is open and when your son's ice-hockey practice begins — the examples of such constraints could be endless.

Another type of constraint is connected with the fact that we have to coordinate our daily programmes with other people's. We have to attend meetings at work or visit friends and relations, and not least within the family we have to divide up the housework, satisfy the parents' and the children's interests and plan how each and every one of us is going to spend the day.

The overall constraints are the physical needs of sleep, food and the like. There are limits here that can be stretched, but not exceeded in the long run.

Examples of these types of restrictions in everyday life are shown in the diagram of a family's typical day. Daily programmes like this have a basic pattern that is generally speaking repeated every day — they are routine. If you think for a moment about your own daily life, you will probably realise that accessibility to places and whether or not you can travel play a very important role.

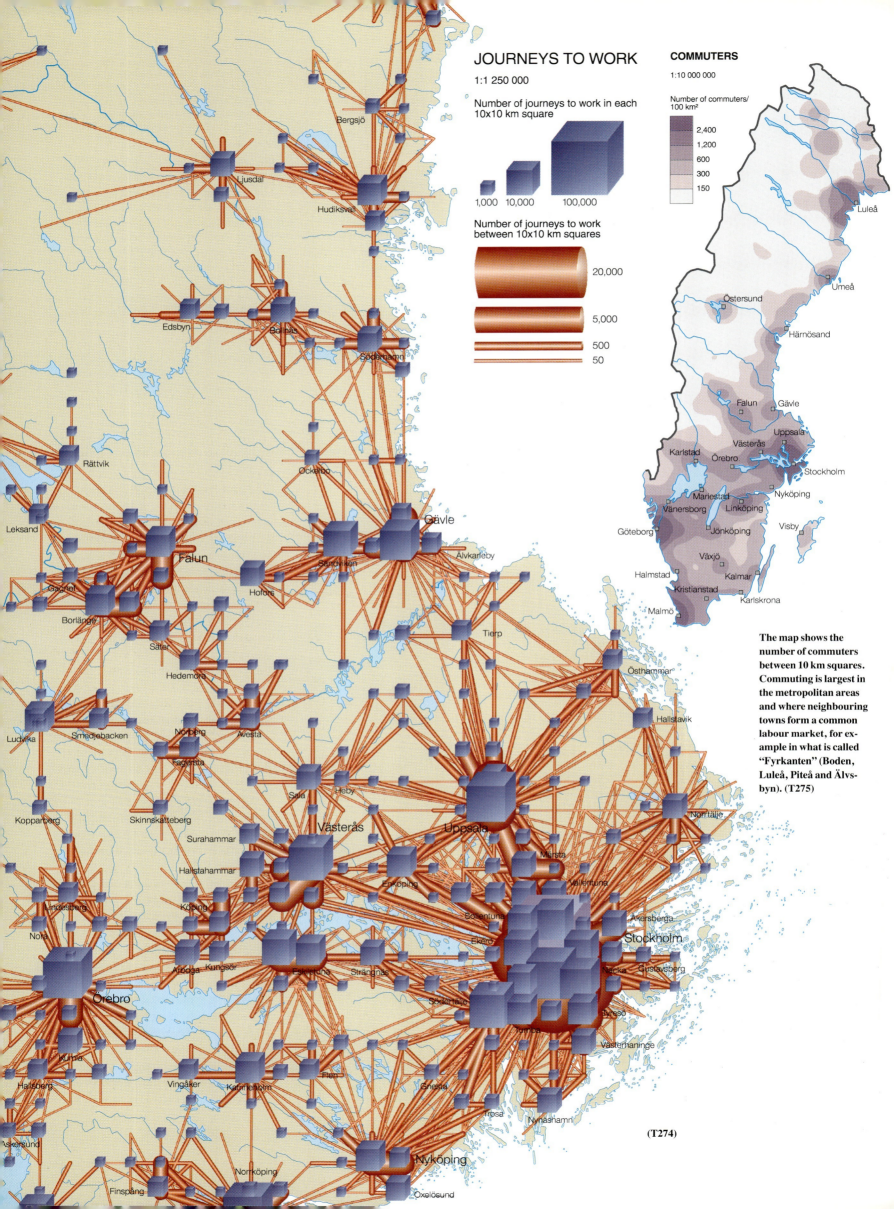

The car is our most popular means of transport, not last for household tasks.

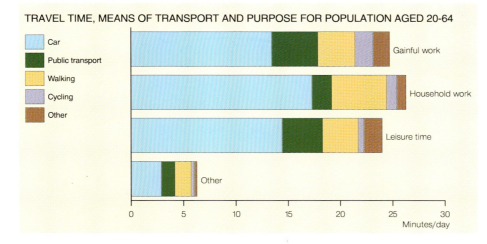

JOURNEYS TO WORK...

In pre-industrial towns home and work place were close together. Today residential areas and places of work are usually separate, and many people have to travel a long way to get to work. Improved transport systems, and private car ownership in particular, which has expanded enormously since the 1950s, made it possible to travel long distances to and from work. Commuting to work may be a necessity, but also a choice because you want to live in a certain way or because it is the alternative to moving house when you change jobs. Weekly commuting, with very long journeys to and from work, is, however, comparatively uncommon. A 45–60 minute journey is usually considered a maximum that most people do not want to exceed.

Commuting has increased greatly in the past few decades. The number of people in work increased by 30 per cent between 1970 and 1989, but the number of commuters across municipal boundaries by 118 per cent. In the early 1990s one employee in four, just over one million, commuted to work in another municipality than their home municipality. In larger regional labour markets like the metropolitan regions the pattern of daily commuting today is very complex. Waves of journeys flow not only into and out of the city centres with their many work places but also cross-country between residential estates and fringe areas where many work-places are located.

BUSINESS TRAVEL, 1989

The large map on the left is based on data for grid squares covering 100 km². The cubes symbolize journeys to work *within* each grid square. The volume of the cubes is proportional to the number of commuters (min. 100 journeys).

The "pipes" represent commuting to work *between* grid squares. The pipes' cross-section or "thickness" is proportional to the number of commuters (min. 25 commuters). Two such pipes between the same grid squares means commuting in both directions.

It is easy to see the local commuting areas round medium-sized towns, but the map of the Stockholm region is very complicated and many thick "pipes", commuting flows between suburbs and the city centre, are obscured by the cubes.

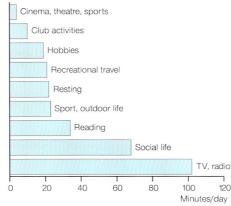

Our free time is just under 20% of a normal weekday.

... AND FOR RECREATION

We spend most of our leisure time enjoying activities in and round our homes which do not require travelling—television, social meetings, reading and the like. The time needed for recreational travelling is not very long, yet about the same as commuting and journeys for household business. Weekends and long holidays account for a large part of travelling time.

Nevertheless, for many households journeys are essential for weekday leisure activities, and owning a car is for many people undoubtedly a vital factor in their leisure plans. Not least families with children have to reckon on making plenty of journeys to organised activities such as training sessions, competitions and displays of various kinds.

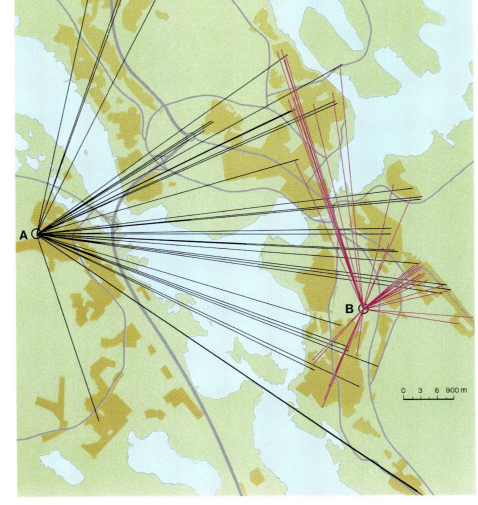

The map shows the central parts of the municipality of Piteå in Norrbotten. The lines link homes and training grounds for the children who regularly take part in the skiing club of Strömnäs Sports Club. The youngest children train on one of the illuminated tracks (B), while the older ones practice skating at A. (T276)

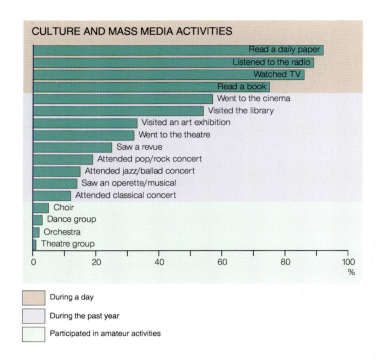

Cultural Life

The term "culture" in its widest sense comprises the whole network of social and economic factors, material things, life style and thought patterns that mould people's places in society. Here we shall focus on a few of those activities that many people in everyday conversation connect with culture in a narrower sense: music, theatre, museums, literature and so on. The range of cultural activities is enormous, and it is possible to give only a few examples of geographical patterns in cultural life and the way Swedes take part in it.

The diagram to the left gives a general picture of the cultural and media behaviour of the adult (16–74) population, but behind these figures lie a large number of variations connected with sex, age, social background and education as well as where people live, since opportunities for cultural activities vary from town to town and region to region. There are also interesting differences between children and adults. While 17 per cent aged 16–74 play an instrument of some kind, half the girls and a third of the boys aged 7–15 do so.

THEATRE AND MUSIC

Organised theatre and music life, whether it is professional or amateur, is the backbone of Swedish theatre and music. The geographical distribution of these activities is of course largely determined by the distribution of the population and the size of towns. In particular the large permanent theatres and music organisations, which need a large public, are found in the large towns. Amateur performances are more scattered across the country, but here too the

Audiences in 1992/93 at the state, local and regional theatres which receive grants. Stockholm has a dominant position with the Royal Dramatic Theatre, the Opera House, the National Touring Theatre and the Stockholm City Theatre. (T277)

Performances by the institutional theatres and free drama groups, 1992/93. Touring groups play an important part in theatre life outside the large towns with their own permanent theatres. (T278)

The map shows the number of performances per inhabitant that the National Touring Theatre gave in various counties in 1990, and the performance plan for one of the productions. It also shows member associations in the National Federation of Amateur Theatres at the beginning of the 1990s. (T279)

Cinema visits by municipality in 1991. Most visits to the cinema are made in Stockholm, more than five a year. Large towns, especially university towns, have high figures, while rural areas have low ones. (T280)

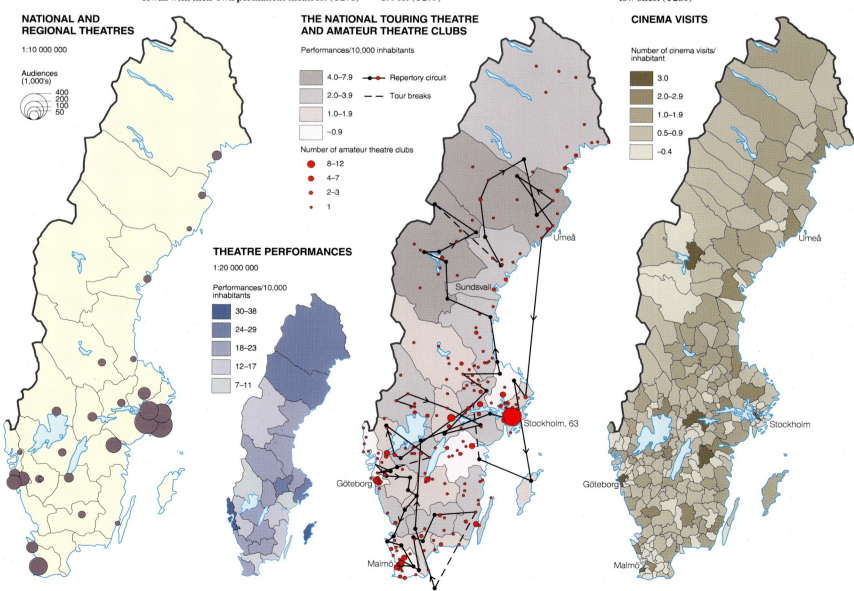

size of the population plays a significant role. It is not so easy in a small town to recruit musicians for an amateur symphony orchestra as it is to form a choir or an accordion club.

Even though the range of professional music and theatre is largest in densely-populated areas, this picture needs to be modified. The map of the national theatres (The Royal Dramatic Theatre, The Opera and The National Touring Theatre), the city theatres and the county theatres suggests that they are highly concentrated in the big cities, especially Stockholm. But even though The National Touring Theatre, the largest producer of theatre in Sweden, is based there, it tours the whole country. The same is true of many of the professional "free" theatre groups, which produce a great many plays for children. Many of the county theatres tour their own county. This evens out the geographical variations in the amount of theatre available, and when the number of performances is related to the population, quite a few remote and sparsely-populated counties show high figures, although the range of theatre is far smaller in inner Norrland than in Stockholm.

Many institutions and organisations contribute to the total range of programmes in a field of culture such as music, for example. Professional symphony and chamber orchestras had a total audience of about 700,000 in 1992. The 20 county music institutions, with their own professional musicians and freelancers, give many concerts all over their districts and had a total audience of just over a million. There are orchestral societies with large amateur orchestras in some 70 towns, and other ensembles in many more. The music and song programmes of the study organisations attracted more than 4 million, the municipal music schools arrange ambitious programmes in many places, church music plays an important role in local culture and the "free" groups which work professionally within jazz, rock and folk music are examples of touring ensembles.

There is an impressive range of organisations in the cultural sector. Many of them work primarily as organisers, for example the theatre societies that are members of The National Touring Theatre. Others are associations for active artists, like the choir and folk musicians' federations. These are often organised as national federations, divided regionally into districts or counties with a base of local associations. But especially in the field of music there is of course plenty of activity at the grass-roots level, alongside the more organised music programmes; this does not appear in statistical reports but we take part in or listen to it in various contexts — the office choir, music and singing at home, and the youngest popbands playing in garages and basements.

THE CINEMA — UNDER PRESSURE FROM TELEVISION

Technological innovations like the gramophone, radio, television and video have revolutionised our enjoyment of culture, but have also increased the competition for viewers and listeners. This is particularly true in fields where amusement and light entertainment are dominant.

The arrival of television in Sweden led to a 50-percent decline in cinema audiences between 1956 and 1963. The continuous expansion of domestic, satellite and cable television and a growing videofilm market was followed by another 50-percent decline from 40 to just over 20 million cinema tickets sold at the beginning of the 1980s. This decline has since continued, but at a slower pace.

Going to the cinema is very much a young people's activity. Cinema visits also have a clear geographical pattern. The large towns are dominant, where the population is large enough to allow the cinemas to survive through modernisation.

The orchestras of the music institutions are professional. Other orchestras consist mainly of amateurs and are usually members of the Swedish Federation of Orchestra Societies or of the National Federation of Amateur Orchestras. Only one symbol per place is given; a place with a professional orchestra may also have an orchestra association or some other ensemble. (T281)

The members of the National Federation of Amateur Orchestras are shown by municipality. Many of them are brass bands. (T282)

Members of the Federation of Swedish Folk Musicians, 1990. The traditional "Polska Belt" in central Sweden also includes Uppland with its rich folk music traditions, but these figures are reduced by the large population of Stockholm. (T283)

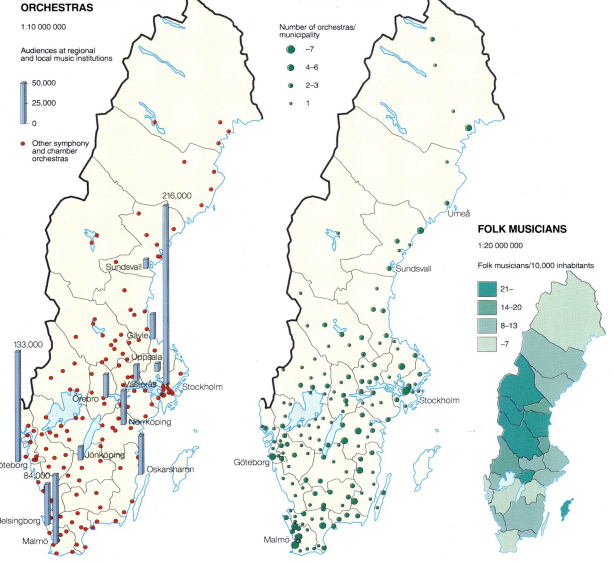

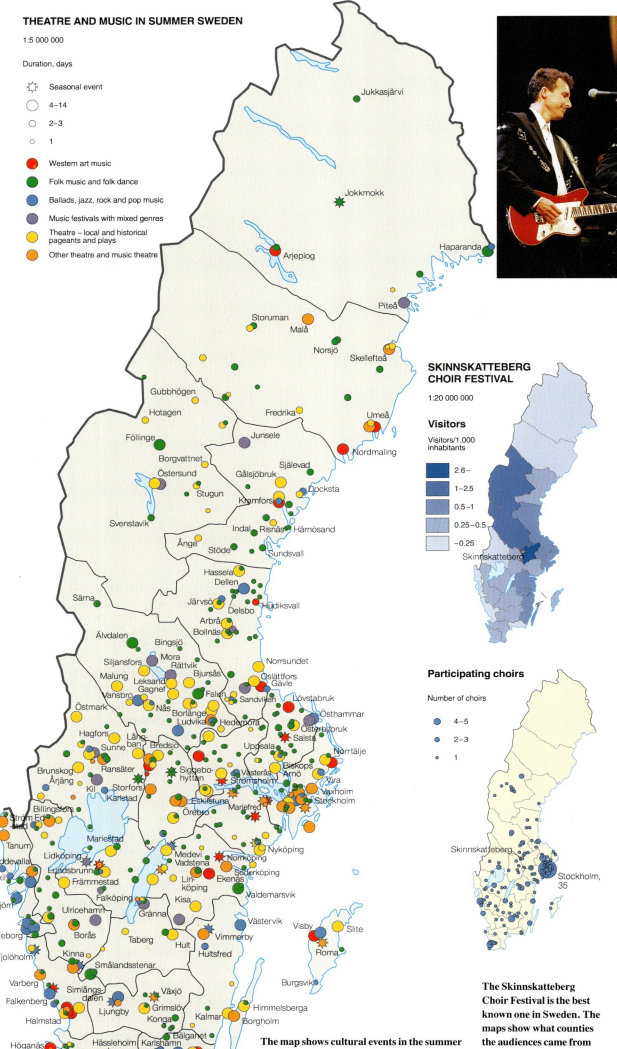

THEATRE AND MUSIC IN SUMMER SWEDEN
1:5 000 000

Duration, days
- ☆ Seasonal event
- ○ 4–14
- ○ 2–3
- ○ 1

- ● Western art music
- ● Folk music and folk dance
- ● Ballads, jazz, rock and pop music
- ● Music festivals with mixed genres
- ● Theatre – local and historical pageants and plays
- ● Other theatre and music theatre

SKINNSKATTEBERG CHOIR FESTIVAL
1:20 000 000

Visitors
Visitors/1,000 inhabitants
- 2.6–
- 1–2.5
- 0.5–1
- 0.25–0.5
- –0.25

Participating choirs
Number of choirs
- 4–5
- 2–3
- 1

The map shows cultural events in the summer of 1991. It does not pretend to be complete, but it gives a fair picture of the great variety of cultural activities available in the summer.

The Skinnskatteberg Choir Festival is the best known one in Sweden. The maps show what counties the audiences came from and the home towns of the choirs that took part in the early 1990s. (T285, T286)

"Dance-band Culture" is a very Swedish phenomenon, loved by many, looked down upon by others. These bands play at dance halls, People's Parks and restaurants. The basic pattern is a few guitars, a double-bass, drums, a synthesiser, a few musicians who can play various wind instruments, mostly hit songs – and a good PA system. A quarter of the people aged 16–24 go to a dance hall or a disco at least once a week.

IN THE GOOD OLD SUMMER TIME...

Summer music and theatre programmes have increased enormously in the past few decades; there is now a very mixed bag of music festivals, folk music meets, summer operas, pageants, open-air theatres and a great deal more. Many of these events are small, getting both performers and audiences from the local population; many folk music meets and pageants fall into this category. The big events, music weeks with hundreds of performances covering several kinds of music, the most popular folk music meets, rock and song festivals and a few well-known theatre productions, attract audiences of tens of thousands from all over Sweden.

A famous and popular summer event can be economically valuable for the host municipality, helping to put the place on people's mental map. This applies mainly to the big events, but even the small ones play an important role by rallying many local interests in projects that stimulate and vitalise local culture.

MUSEUMS AND EXHIBITIONS

There are some 16–17 million visitors annually to the museums that are "museum institutions", that is, they meet certain requirements concerning opening hours, trained staff and the like. There were 201 museum institutions in Sweden in 1992. But there are many more museums than that in

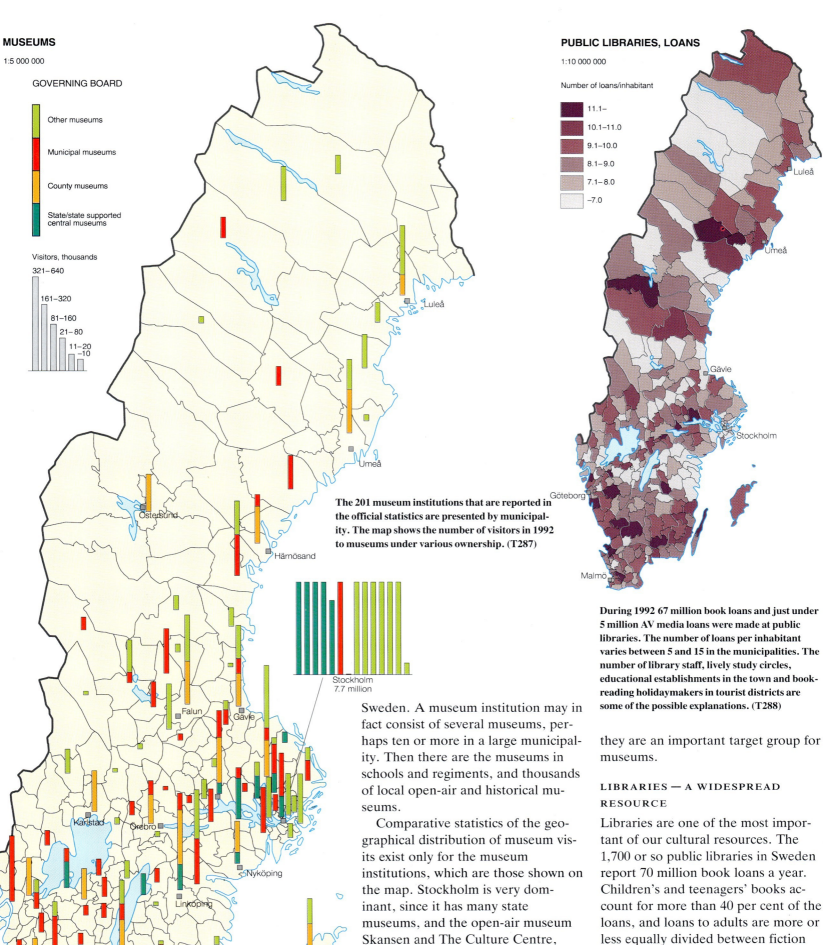

MUSEUMS

1:5 000 000

GOVERNING BOARD
- Other museums
- Municipal museums
- County museums
- State/state supported central museums

Visitors, thousands
321–640
161–320
81–160
21–80
11–20
–10

The 201 museum institutions that are reported in the official statistics are presented by municipality. The map shows the number of visitors in 1992 to museums under various ownership. (T287)

PUBLIC LIBRARIES, LOANS

1:10 000 000

Number of loans/inhabitant
- 11.1–
- 10.1–11.0
- 9.1–10.0
- 8.1–9.0
- 7.1–8.0
- –7.0

During 1992 67 million book loans and just under 5 million AV media loans were made at public libraries. The number of loans per inhabitant varies between 5 and 15 in the municipalities. The number of library staff, lively study circles, educational establishments in the town and book-reading holidaymakers in tourist districts are some of the possible explanations. (T288)

Sweden. A museum institution may in fact consist of several museums, perhaps ten or more in a large municipality. Then there are the museums in schools and regiments, and thousands of local open-air and historical museums.

Comparative statistics of the geographical distribution of museum visits exist only for the museum institutions, which are those shown on the map. Stockholm is very dominant, since it has many state museums, and the open-air museum Skansen and The Culture Centre, with more than three million visitors, are also included among the museum institutions.

Approximately one third of the adult population visit a museum or exhibition at some time during the year, women more often than men and well-educated people more than other groups. Two out of three school children visit a museum in a year; they are an important target group for museums.

LIBRARIES — A WIDESPREAD RESOURCE

Libraries are one of the most important of our cultural resources. The 1,700 or so public libraries in Sweden report 70 million book loans a year. Children's and teenagers' books account for more than 40 per cent of the loans, and loans to adults are more or less equally divided between fiction and non-fiction books. Even if book loans are their primary function, libraries are also a cultural and educational resource in other respects. Loans of cassette books and phonograms, information services and reference books, newspapers and magazines are areas that have grown in importance, broadening the libraries' scope.

Sports and Keep-fit Activities

The Sunday excursion on skis; sweaty laps on the illuminated ski track; taking part in "Open Track", the non-competitive version of the Vasa Ski Race; skiing contests against the clock and with lists of results — all these are based on the same activity, but with a growing level of intensity, performance and competition. The dividing lines between open-air recreation, exercise, recreational sport and competitive sport are elastic. This section will emphasise the last two categories, which are practised in more organised and regulated forms, at agreed times and places and within the framework of club activities.

This is of course a wide definition, embracing the company club's training session and a premier league match, a mass of joggers taking part in an organised run and the county championship in cross-country running. There may be an element of competition in many types of recreational sport, but it is active physical recreation that most of the participants are looking for. In contrast competitive sports focus on results, are characterised by the competitive spirit and have developed into "sport as entertainment".

The interest in physical exercise and sports among the population aged 16–74 is shown by a few figures for the number of people that took part in some sort of sports activity at least once a month in 1991. Three quarters went for long walks, cycle rides or ski runs, half went in for other more specialised activities, 13 per cent had taken part in competitions and a quarter had been spectators at sports contests and matches. Women were somewhat more active in taking recreational exercise than men, while men, especially young men, were the majority of those who took part in or watched competitive sport.

GEOGRAPHICAL PATTERNS

The distribution and relative importance of various sports in different parts of Sweden depend on many factors — where a sport was first intro-

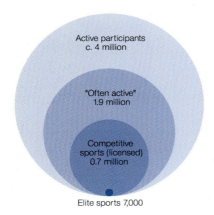

Number of participators in sports and recreational exercise at various levels in Sweden.

Number of seasons played by teams in the National League, 1924–1993. Large towns and western Sweden have maintained their dominant position over the years. (T289)

Number of seasons played in the top division, 1930–1993/94. Climatic conditions and tradition lie behind the spread of the "Bandy Belt", in which many small towns have had successful teams. (T290)

Number of seasons played in the top division, 1922–1993/94. Ice-hockey first found a foothold in the Stockholm area and then spread north. Indoor ice rinks and good public support have led to a rapid growth of ice-hockey in southern Sweden. (T291)

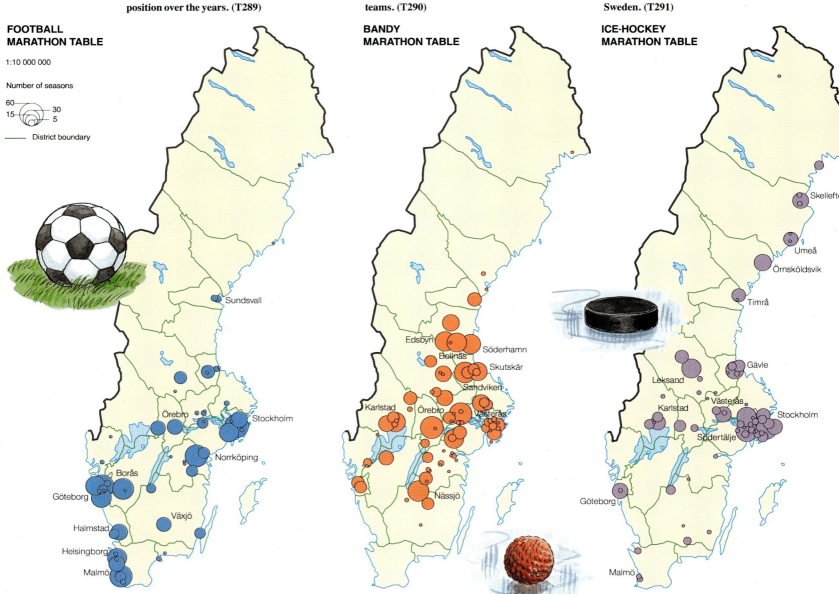

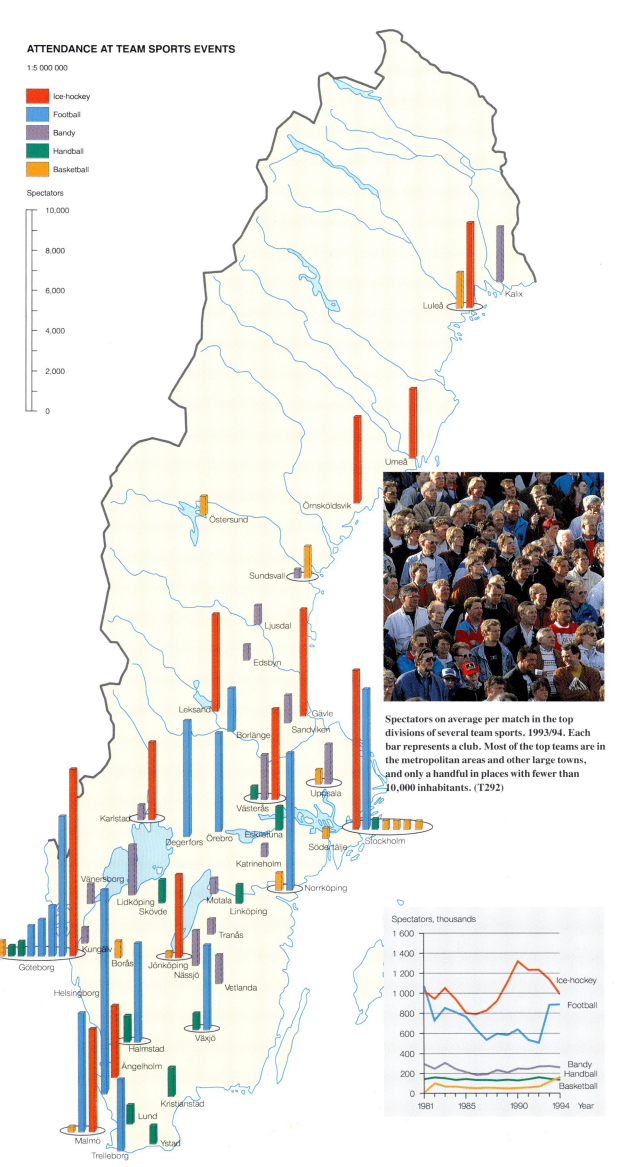

ATTENDANCE AT TEAM SPORTS EVENTS
1:5 000 000

- Ice-hockey
- Football
- Bandy
- Handball
- Basketball

Spectators: 10,000 / 8,000 / 6,000 / 4,000 / 2,000 / 0

Spectators on average per match in the top divisions of several team sports. 1993/94. Each bar represents a club. Most of the top teams are in the metropolitan areas and other large towns, and only a handful in places with fewer than 10,000 inhabitants. (T292)

duced; the size of the population—which affects the recruitment of both players and spectators; financial resources and access to sports stadiums; and the climatic conditions allowing certain sports to be pursued. This last factor has been important in Sweden since there are considerable regional differences in the winter climate in particular.

The three major team sports, football, ice-hockey and bandy, are examples of the way different factors have governed developments.

Football, the number one sport in Sweden as in so many other countries, is played everywhere, but elite football was strong at an early stage in industrial and large towns in particular. The original heart of football was in western and southern Sweden; football was introduced to Sweden from Britain via Göteborg ("the capital of Swedish football") and the mild climate and the relatively dense population there provided favourable conditions.

Bandy is played more or less in the same parts of Sweden as football—football players usually played bandy in the winter—but the "bandy belt" stretches further north and its southernmost limit is the highlands of Småland. Further south the climate was not suitable for sports on natural ice, so instead the indoor sport of handball took over along the west coast and in Skåne.

Ice-hockey first found a foothold in the large towns of central Sweden and along the coast of Norrland, where there was natural ice and a relatively large population. The map of the premiere hockey league teams still reflects this pattern, but today the sport is played all over Sweden. A decisive factor was the development of ice-rink technology. Outdoor rinks with artificial ice and above all indoor ice stadiums (more than 250 of them at present) have made it possible for ice-hockey to spread to the south, where new elite teams have established themselves thanks to good public support and strong financial resources. Malmö IF have been the Swedish champions several times.

The variations in the climate have

The diagram shows the number of spectators at matches in each sport's top divisions. Apart from changes in the sports' popularity the figures may also be affected by the fact that the number of teams in the divisions has changed and that particularly popular teams have been promoted or demoted.

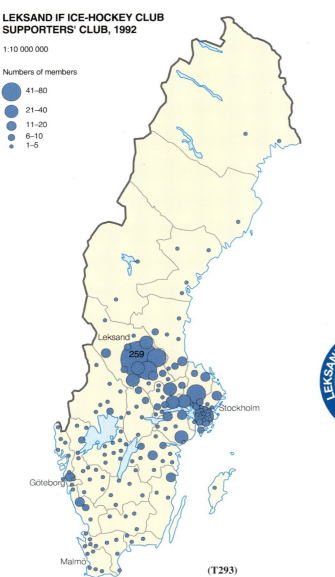

LEKSAND IF ICE-HOCKEY CLUB SUPPORTERS' CLUB, 1992
1:10 000 000
Numbers of members
- 41–80
- 21–40
- 11–20
- 6–10
- 1–5

(T293)

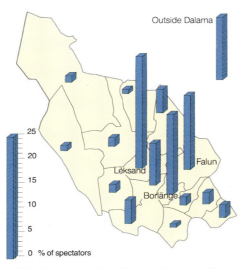

The map shows where the spectators came from at a match between Leksand and Djurgården in the autumn of 1992. (T294)

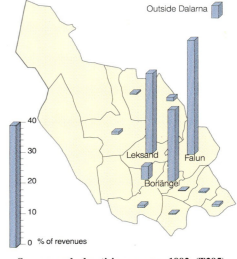

Sponsor and advertising revenue, 1992. (T295)

Leksands IF Ice-hockey Club has a longer unbroken series of seasons in the top league of ice-hockey than any other club in Sweden. Leksand has only 15,000 inhabitants but its team has about 120,000 spectators at its home matches. The club's annual turnover places it among the 20 largest "companies" in Leksand, but its ice hockey is not just a local matter. Spectator and sponsor revenue flows in from a larger region in central Dalarna, and some 60 per cent of the supporter's club's members live outside Dalarna. The PR value the club brings to the district and to sponsors is indisputable, though difficult to measure, and ice hockey is a dominant feature of life in Leksand for a long season lasting from September to April.

generally speaking become less important; today snow canons lengthen the season for downhill skiers, even providing snow in "green" winters. In contrast, sports stadiums of various kinds keep out the cold so that it is now possible to do sports at more places and for longer seasons than ever before.

"GOING TO THE MATCH?"

Sports often play an important role in local life, both socially and for local identity, especially in small places. Sports become events and can, with the help of the media, help to put a town or district on our mental map.

One characteristic of the Swedish sports movement is that elite sports are based on a broad foundation. On a normal Sunday in the football season, it is estimated that 300,000 Swedes play or watch football in the lower divisions (3 and below); the best total public gate for one match day in the top Swedish division in 1993 was not much more than 50,000. At local derbies in one of the "village" divisions you can feel the local patriotism and the tradition of a popular movement, whereas top-level professional sport has become a part of the entertainment industry, highly influenced by strong financial interests and intensive efforts to bring in advertising and gate money.

The major team and motor sports attract the big crowds. Football is played by many more men and women than ice-hockey, but as a spectator sport it was dethroned in the early 1980s by ice-hockey, whose top three divisions attract annual gates of 2 millions.

MASS COMPETITIONS AS RECREATIONAL SPORT

Recreational sport is represented by all those who jog, ski, do gymnastics or swim on their own in order to keep fit. Among the more spectacular forms of organised recreational sport are the mass competitions which became very popular in the 1980s, even though several of the better-known events go back further in time.

These mass events — especially in running, cross-country skiing, cycling and orienteering — attract not only large numbers of participants but also vast crowds of spectators, especially those that combine elite and mass races like the Vasa Ski Race, the Lidingö Race or the Stockholm Marathon. Behind the elite runners come the top amateurs, perhaps chasing a Swedish Classic Sportsman diploma which they can win if in one and the same year they complete the Vasa Ski Race (90 km), the Vättern Bicycle Tour (300 km), the Vansbro Swimming Race (3 km) and the Lidingö Race (30 km cross-country). And further back in the field are the great mass of "keep-fitters" for whom taking part is both a confirmation that physical exercise pays off and a stimulating social event.

MASS-PARTICIPATION SPORTS EVENTS

1:20 000 000

(T296)

1. **The Vindelälv Race** is a road relay race over 350 km, divided into 24 stretches. Entries, 1993: 314 teams, c. 6,300 competitors.

2. **The Vasa Race** is a 90 km ski race between Sälen and Mora. The Women's Vasa Race is 30 km. Entries, 1994: 15,826 + 7,325 on Open Tracks; Women's Race 5,652. A Classic Sportsman event.

3. **The Sola Relay Race** is an event for students and teachers at universities and university colleges. The distance is 270 km, with 31 stretches in six stages. Entries, 1994: 85 teams, c. 2,600 competitors.

4. **The Göta Canal Race** is a canoe race over 42 km, 18 km and for juniors 7 km. Entries, 1994: 790.

5. **The Vättern Bicycle Tour** covers 300 km round Lake Vättern. Entries, 1994: 15,500. A Classic Sportsman event. **The Women's Race** is a 90 km keep-fit event. Entries, 1994: 5,700.

6. **The Ringsjö Race** is a cycle race over 125 km and 65 km. Entries, 1994: 7,327

Riding is one of the great youth sports, with girls in a clear majority. The number of riding-school members is certainly large in the well-populated regions, but relatively speaking riding is more popular in other parts of southern and central Sweden. (T297)

7. **The Round Glan Race** is a cycle race over 70 km. Entries, 1993: 3,393.

8. **The Vansbro Swimming Race** is 3 km for men and 1 km for women. Entries, 1994: c. 2,000 men and 1,000 women. A Classic Sportsman event.

9. **The Göta Jog** is over 15 km. Entries, 1994: 6,600 (plus 1,200 children who ran 1–3 km).

10. **The Engelbrekt Race** is a cross-country skiing race over 60 km. Entries, 1994: 1,626. A Classic Sportsman event.

11. **The Mill Race** is a canoe race over 47, 25 and 12 km. Entries, 1994: 628.

12. **The Caroline Race** is a skiing race over 30 km. Entries, 1994: 750.

13. **The Göteborg Lap** is a long-distance running event over 21 km. Entries, 1993: 34,500.

14. **The Field Relay** includes running, rowing, cycling, shooting, steeplechase and grenade throwing. Entries, 1993: 12,000 (1,500 teams).

15. **The Maja Gräddnos Race** is a running race for women over 11 and 5 km. Entries, 1994: 20,200.

16. **The 25-man Team Orienteering Race** is a relay race of between 2 and 9 km. Entries, 1993: 9,218.

17. **The Bellman Relay** is 5 x 4 km. Entries, 1993: 1,891 teams, 9,455 competitors.

18. **The Lidingö Race** has several different classes: 30 km, 15 km for women, the Little Lidingö Race for juniors and the team relay. Entries, 1993: 10,869 for 30 km, 31,457 in all. A Classic Sportsman event.

19. **The Stockholm Marathon** is the classic Marathon distance of 42 km. Entries, 1994: 11,400.

20. **The Women's Ten-Kilometre Run** has become a model for women-only keep-fit events. The distance is 10.3 km. Entries, 1994: 35,000.

21. **The Women's Bike Race**, 42 km, is the world's biggest women's cycle race. Entries, 1994: c. 9,500.

22. **The O-Ring** arranges every year a five-day orienteering event for elite runners and amateurs. It is held in a different part of Sweden each year and at its peak attracted more than 20,000 competitors. They are divided into many classes according to age, sex and athletic ambitions. Entries, 1994 (at Örnsköldsvik): c. 14,850.

RIDING-SCHOOL MEMBERS

1:10 000 000

Number in relation to population (Index: 1.00 = national average)
- 1.20–
- 1.10–1.19
- 1.00–1.09
- 0.90–0.99
- –0.89
- District boundary

WOMEN'S FOOTBALL, 1995

- National league
- Division 1
  - North
  - Central
  - South
- District boundary

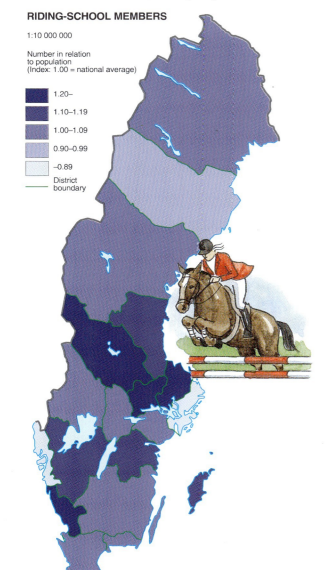

Football is one of the most important women's sports. In many cases the top teams have grown up in small towns and in clubs that have no tradition of playing in the men's top division. Öxabäck in Västergötland, Mallbacken in Värmland, Sunnanå (Skellefteå) and Gideonsberg (Västerås) are a few examples. (T298)

WOMEN'S SPORTS

Women comprise some 43 per cent of active sports club members, but the percentage of women is considerably smaller in club committees and among coaches; in many people's opinion men's and boys' sports have traditionally been given higher priority than women's sports when allocating financial resources.

The number of active women members is particularly large where keep-fit activities play a major role. KORPEN, the inter-company sports organisation, gymnastics, athletics, swimming and golf are typical examples. Several team sports also have a large proportion of active women members: basketball, football, handball and volleyball. Two of the major sports associations, riding and gymnastics, are dominated by women, where they account for 80–85 per cent of the members. Major sports associations with very few women members are, for example, ice-hockey (2%), shooting, car-racing and weight-lifting.

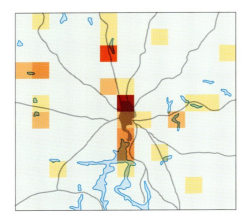
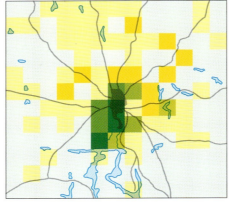

Outdoor Recreation, Second Homes and Tourism

Outdoor recreation and tourism are concepts that partly overlap. Most definitions of the word *tourist* include spending at least one night away from home. A week hiking in the mountains or sailing is then a tourist trip with the emphasis on outdoor recreation, while a day excursion by bike close to home is not. But tourism is much more than just outdoor recreation. Tourism may be for nature-lovers, but it is also very much more — for culture, entertainment and the like.

Day excursions round Uppsala. The deeper the colour, the more visits. The fragmented picture for swimming trips (left) is determined quite simply by the location of suitable lakes. Walking in the forests and countryside (right) has a more homogenous pattern; there are large areas for recreation near the city and close to the main roads. (T299, T300)

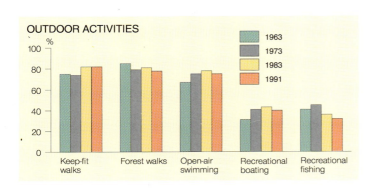

Percentage of the population that has outdoor recreation at least once a year. On the whole the levels are stable over time. Small variations between the years may be due to changing weather conditions, for example.

OUTDOOR RECREATION

Sweden is fortunate in the opportunities it can offer for outdoor recreation. It is sparsely populated, it has a long coastline, and it has many lakes and rivers. Most Swedes have easily accessible countryside close at hand, and Sweden's archipelagos and mountains are unique natural resources of national importance. *The general right of access to private land (allemansrätten)* enables us to make use of land and water for outdoor recreation to an extent that is unique in Europe.

The most common activities are also the "simplest" ones, those that can be enjoyed almost everywhere and do not require special facilities: walking in the countryside, swimming in the summer, skiing in the winter. The day-excursion area round one's home is where we usually go for our outdoor recreation.

But the opportunities to pursue certain activities vary from one part of Sweden to the other, depending on the climate and terrain, or cultural traditions. Three quarters of all the pistes for downhill skiing are in the seven northernmost counties, where only one fifth of the population lives. Fishing is one of the most popular activities, but most fishing waters are in the forest districts, which is reflected in the geographical distribution of organised recreational fishing. Hunting, like fishing, used to be an important source of income for people in rural districts, but today it is mostly a leisure activity. The percentage of hunters is still largest in the forest districts, but in particular in the autumn many "urban" hunters return to take part in the moose hunting in their native country districts.

There is a high percentage of hunters in rural areas, and at the great hunting event of the year, the moose hunt, many "urban hunters" return to their hunting team in their home district. Men form the majority of both hunters and amateur fishermen. (T301)

Amateur fishermen who are members of the national organisation for amateur anglers via local fishing societies. The forest districts with their many lakes have most amateur fishermen. (T302)

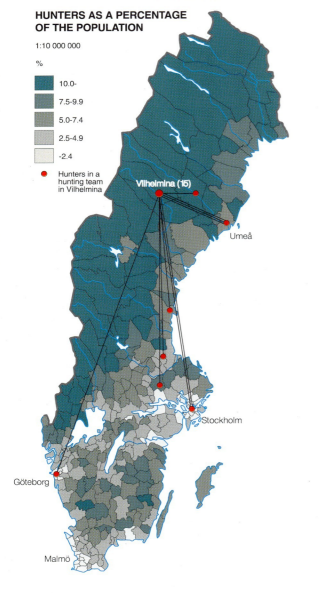
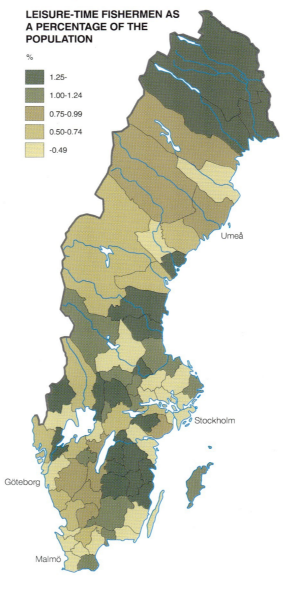

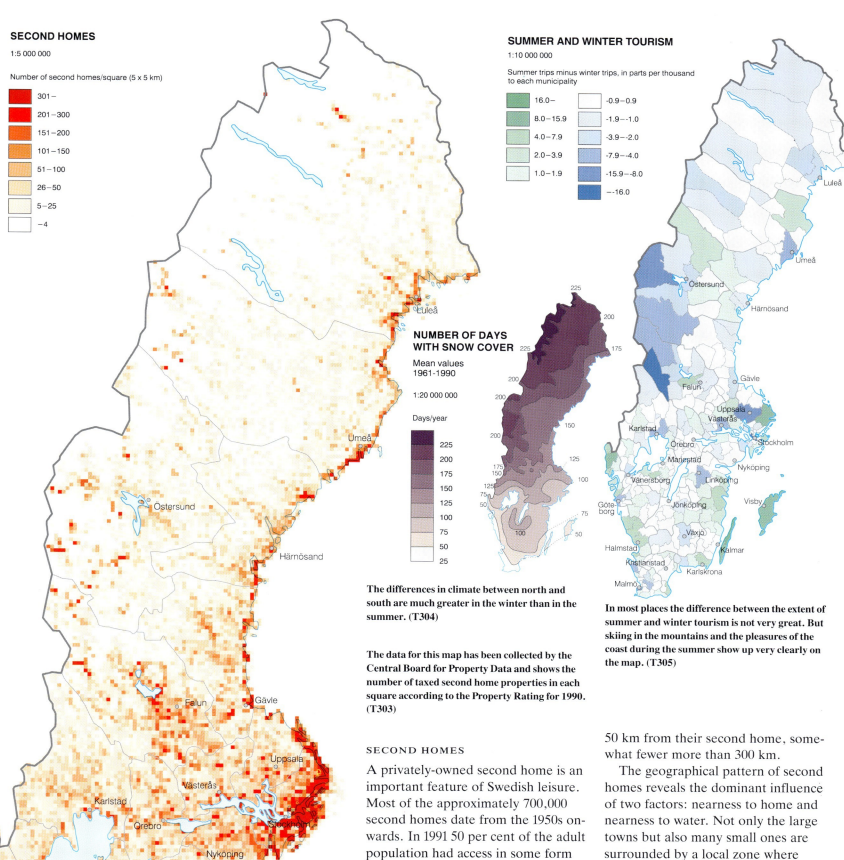

SECOND HOMES
1:5 000 000

Number of second homes/square (5 × 5 km)
- 301–
- 201–300
- 151–200
- 101–150
- 51–100
- 26–50
- 5–25
- –4

SUMMER AND WINTER TOURISM
1:10 000 000

Summer trips minus winter trips, in parts per thousand to each municipality
- 16.0–
- 8.0–15.9
- 4.0–7.9
- 2.0–3.9
- 1.0–1.9
- -0.9–0.9
- -1.9–-1.0
- -3.9–-2.0
- -7.9–-4.0
- -15.9–-8.0
- –-16.0

NUMBER OF DAYS WITH SNOW COVER
Mean values 1961-1990
1:20 000 000

Days/year: 225, 200, 175, 150, 125, 100, 75, 50, 25

The differences in climate between north and south are much greater in the winter than in the summer. (T304)

The data for this map has been collected by the Central Board for Property Data and shows the number of taxed second home properties in each square according to the Property Rating for 1990. (T303)

In most places the difference between the extent of summer and winter tourism is not very great. But skiing in the mountains and the pleasures of the coast during the summer show up very clearly on the map. (T305)

SECOND HOMES

A privately-owned second home is an important feature of Swedish leisure. Most of the approximately 700,000 second homes date from the 1950s onwards. In 1991 50 per cent of the adult population had access in some form or other to a second home, and 40 per cent of them had their own second home. An increased standard of living, longer holidays, access to land or buildings that were no longer in use in agriculture and forestry, and perhaps, too, the tradition of having "a cottage in the country", are some of the explanations of this expansion. Better communications, above all by car, have made it easier for people to make use of a second home a long way from their home town. But many people still have their country cottage near to home — a third live less than 50 km from their second home, somewhat fewer more than 300 km.

The geographical pattern of second homes reveals the dominant influence of two factors: nearness to home and nearness to water. Not only the large towns but also many small ones are surrounded by a local zone where many of the inhabitants have their second homes. The map of second homes clearly shows their great concentration near the coast, the big lakes and rivers, but many isolated squares with high figures also contain an attractive lake, too small to be shown on the map.

TOURISM IN SWEDEN

As already mentioned, tourism is a very broad term. There are many reasons, often interconnected, for going on a holiday trip. Long holiday journeys with overnight stays away from

DESTINATION OF SWEDISH TOURISTS

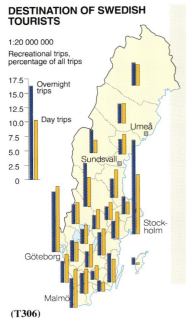

1:20 000 000
Recreational trips, percentage of all trips

(T306)

Almost one recreational trip in three involving an overnight stay is to a big-city county, but the main stream of travel is from the more densely populated parts of Sweden to the more sparsely populated areas. Recreational day trips have a more even regional distribution than trips involving overnight stays. Typical tourist areas like Gotland, Dalarna and Jämtland attract a far larger share of trips with overnight stays than of day trips. Distances are greater in northern Sweden, so the number of long day trips (more than 100 km one way) is relatively greater there than anywhere else.

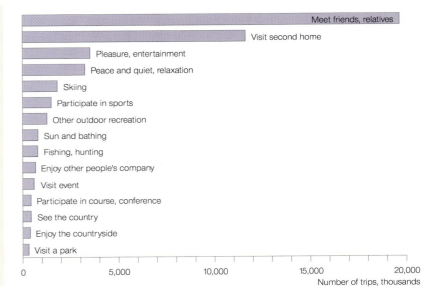

The fifteen most frequent reasons for holiday trips with overnight stays in Sweden, 1993. Many trips are, of course, made for several reasons. Meeting friends and relations is the main reasons for almost half of all trips with overnight stays.

PURPOSE AND DESTINATION OF RECREATIONAL TRIPS

1:20 000 000

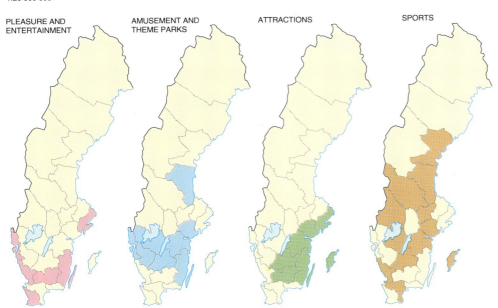

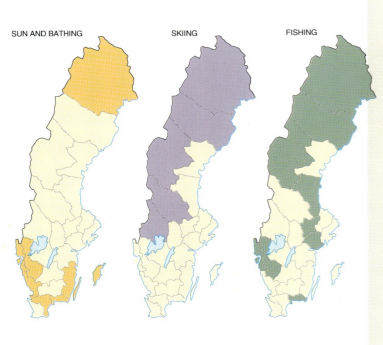

(T307–313)

Camping is the most common form of commercial accommodation. In 1993 there were more than 11 million overnight stays at Sweden's 700 or so authorised camping sites. Swedish tourists are in the majority (80%). Summer is the great camping season.

CAMPING

1:10 000 000

Overnight stays, thousands

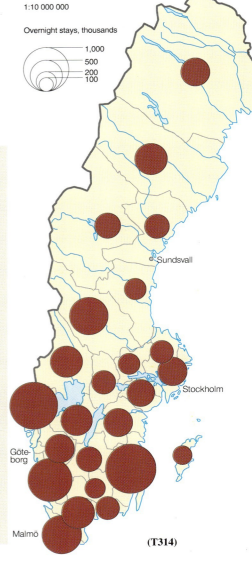

(T314)

Visiting friends and relatives or going to one's second home or just getting away to find a bit of peace and quiet are the most usual reasons for recreational trips with overnight stays. As for other kinds of trips, the travel pattern reveals which counties are more attractive for the stated purpose of the trip than the average. The big cities top the list for entertainment, and large entertainment and theme parks create a special pattern. Where people travel for beach holidays in the sun, skiing or fishing is, of course, to a large extent determined by the location of the best geographical conditions. Trips for "sports" are quite frequent and fairly well distributed throughout the country. In contrast "visiting a tourist attraction" is quite an unusual reason for trips, probably because this is something one combines with other activities.

FOREIGN TOURISTS, NUMBER OF GUEST NIGHTS 1990

1:20 000 000

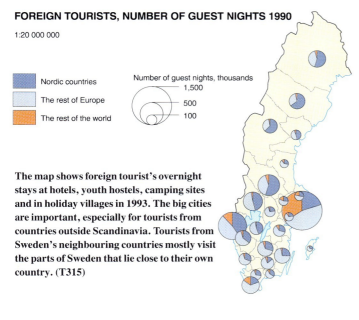

The map shows foreign tourist's overnight stays at hotels, youth hostels, camping sites and in holiday villages in 1993. The big cities are important, especially for tourists from countries outside Scandinavia. Tourists from Sweden's neighbouring countries mostly visit the parts of Sweden that lie close to their own country. (T315)

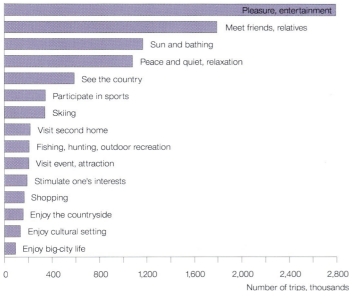

The fifteen most frequent reasons for holiday trips abroad with overnight stays, 1993. Recreation and entertainment in the company of family and friends, preferably in sunny lands, is what most people look for.

RECREATIONAL TRIPS ABROAD

1:40 000 000

Trips to countries outside Europa

North America 12.9%
West Indies 0.8%
Central and South America 2%
East Africa 0.9%
The Arab countries 0.7%
India 1.1%
The rest of Asia 2.2%
Australia/
The South Sea Islands 2%

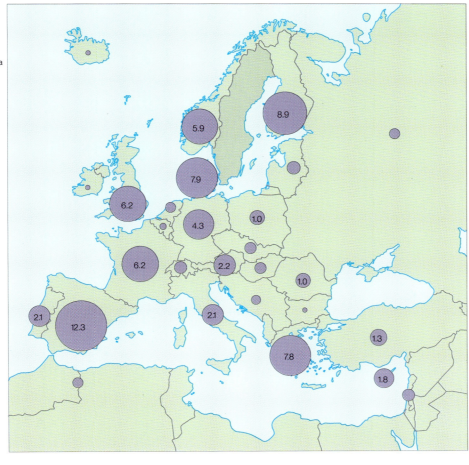

Number of overnight stays by country as a percentage of all overnight stays on holiday trips abroad, 1993. Scandinavia, the Mediterranean and areas outside Europe each accounted for 25–30% of all overnight stays. (T316)

home are for many people "proper tourism", but in Sweden day excursions are also counted as tourism if the journey is more than 200 km return. This limitation is quite arbitrary, but it includes quite a lot of travelling which is similar to trips with overnight stays, as far as reasons and activities are concerned.

In an international comparison Swedes travel a lot in their free time, and this has increased continuously during the past few decades. The frequency of travelling is fairly high in all age groups, increasing with rising income and educational levels; it is high in the metropolitan regions and considerably lower in rural areas. This is true of journeys both within and outside Sweden. But not everyone has the same opportunities to travel in their free time; money, the situation at home and ill health can create obstacles. A quarter of the adult population stated in a survey made in 1991 that they neither had access to a second home nor had gone on a holiday trip during the year.

Between 40 and 50 per cent of all long holiday trips within Sweden are primarily to visit friends and relatives. A quarter are to second homes. Both these types of journeys may also involve sight-seeing, bathing, visiting museums, entertainment parks or music festivals and many other activities that we associate with tourists, but it is the remaining third of the long trips which might be called "proper tourism". Regardless of what type of journey it is, the most usual pattern seems to be the direct journey to and from a destination: tours involving overnight stays at many different places are less common.

SWEDISH TOURISM ABROAD

In relation to its population, Sweden has a high level of tourism abroad. Foreign travel has both increased greatly and expanded geographically since the Second World War. During the 1950s, which saw an upsurge of coach tours, travelling outside the Nordic countries increased threefold, and the air package tours of the 1960s doubled the number of trips abroad. Since then the rate of growth has been less striking and even at time stagnated owing to recessions and changes in currency rates. The falling rate of the Swedish krona in the early 1990s has led to more tourism in Sweden, while foreign travel has become more expensive and declined.

Holiday trips within Sweden are six times more frequent than trips abroad, but the latter are financially significant, accounting for half of all travel expenditure. Measured in *the number of journeys* the Nordic countries are by far the most important travel area for holiday trips abroad which involve overnight stays, and the same applies of course to day trips abroad: shopping and leisure trips.

If one looks at *the number of overnight stays* abroad, the picture is quite different. The Mediterranean and the Spanish and Portuguese islands in the Atlantic account for 30 per cent of all overnight stays, the Nordic countries for 25 per cent and destinations outside Europe for almost the same share. Sun and beach tourism is predominant; since the 1970s Spain (including the Canary Islands) has been the leading tourist country for Swedish holiday makers, but competition from Greece, for example, and new, exotic destinations has gradually increased. During the first few years of the 1990s holiday trips to the US have increased most rapidly.

Sources and Methods

The aim of geography, to describe and explain the various phenomena of the earth's surface, demands data relating to specific locations. Our sources must help us to specify location or the distribution of various phenomena such as climate, density of population or land use. But they must also provide knowledge of distribution and interdependence between places, through transportation, trade and other types of contact, for example. By using a number of different sources geography also builds up our knowledge of the interdependence between natural conditions and human activities, as well as their effects on geographical conditions. This makes it possible to interpret the factors underlying the varying character of the landscape and the earth's surface.

Maps are the natural and indispensable aids in all geographical work. They provide a general picture of both large and small districts; they quickly show variations in the earth's surface and make it possible to analyse different types of interaction, for example between climate, agriculture and land use. Maps from different eras help us to reflect the current landscape seen in relation to the processes of change that have created the present situation. Other sources are aerial photographs and satellite images. Satellite images showing the way in which the earth's surface reflects visible and invisible solar radiation help us to identify resource and environmental problems such as air and water pollution, damage to plant life and desert formation. Up-to-date maps, like aerial photographs and satellite images, may also be used as the starting point for forecasts and scenarios.

In its analyses geography often needs to use other sources as well, such as first-hand reports collected by field observations or interviews. There is a long tradition of field stud-

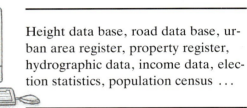

Height data base, road data base, urban area register, property register, hydrographic data, income data, election statistics, population census …

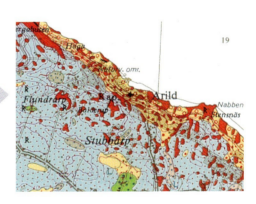

Air photos, maps and data banks containing positioned data are important sources of geographical information today. GIS, the Geographical Information System, helps us deal with the vast amounts of data.

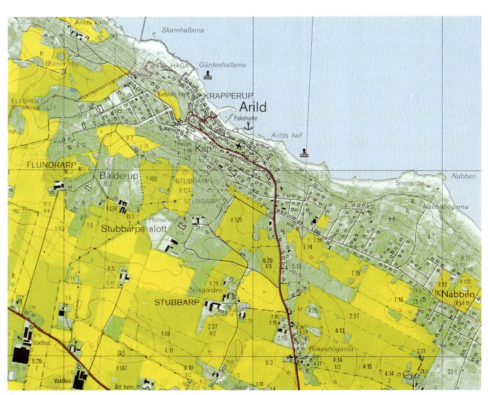

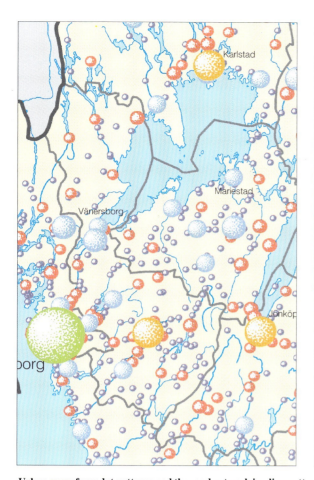

Urban areas form dot patterns and the road network is a line pattern. Geographical reality may be analysed as dot patterns, line patterns or surface patterns. (T317, T318)

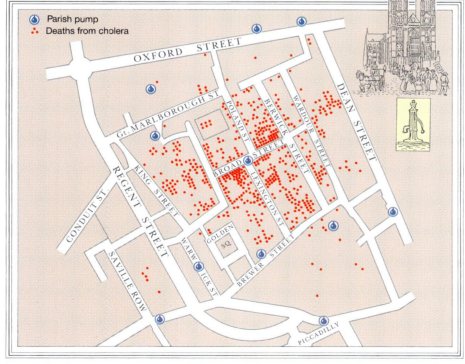

A compilation of positioned data can reveal cause-effect relationships. Here, from a cholera epidemic in London in the 1840s. The polluted wells in the centre caused deaths from cholera. (T319)

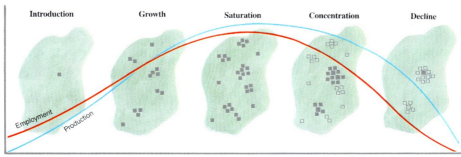

It is possible to trace the spread of a phenomenon by means of historical source material. Here, an example of the development of a settlement pattern over time.

ies in geography as a means of collecting primary geographical data. Other examples of important sources are scientific reports, statistical data stored in data banks, archives or various kinds of publications. The analysis of photographs is an important teaching complement to other sources and methods. Photographs of landscapes and environments are used here as the basis for analysing real-life geography.

Data-based geographical information systems (GIS) have been developed to store, process and present large amounts of geographical data in digital form. GIS systems can be used to retrieve such data from various data banks and combine it to create maps of various kinds: vegetation, population, roads, buildings and so on.

The analytical methods of geography must be able to help us describe and explain the various phenomena of the landscape and the earth's surface. The aim is to identify and explain both unique and general features in the landscape, such as contact points and interdependence between places. We also try to understand the relationship between human activity and landscape conditions in the form of natural resources, for example.

Specific data can be described and analysed in the form of geographical patterns; buildings, for example, make a pattern of dots while roads create a pattern of lines. Chronological (statistical) methods may be used to describe and analyse the character of different types of dot patterns. Flow analysis can be used in the same way for linear patterns such as fluctuations in the transportation of silt in rivers or the density of traffic in a road network.

The aim and character of geography involves a holistic approach. It implies a desire to explain and understand the unity and diversity represented by phenomena on the earth's surface. In this connection functional explanation is one of the ways to understanding, when phenomena and activities on the earth's surface can be seen to interact functionally and the total picture is often more than the sum of the parts. An example of this is the central-place theory, by which the location and size of any place may be seen as the result of a functional cause-and-effect relationship between the places within a certain area.

Geology

Sea and Coast

Geography of Plants and Animals
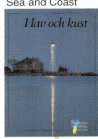

The Forests

Agriculture

Manufacturing and Service
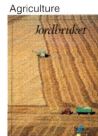

Climate, Lakes and Rivers

Sweden in the World
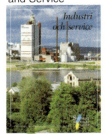

The Land
Physical geography

The Economy
Economic geography

The Environment
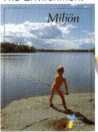

The Population

The Geography of Sweden

Maps and Mapping

Work and Leisure

Landscape and Settlements

Culture Life, Recreation and Tourism

The Cultural Landscape
Human geography

Living Conditions and Life Patterns
Human geography

Cultural Heritage and Preservation

The Infrastructure

NATIONAL ATLAS OF SWEDEN

THE NATIONAL ATLAS OF SWEDEN — THE WAY TO GREATER KNOWLEDGE OF SWEDEN

The Geography of Sweden gives a general picture of the country's geography. To find more detailed information, please refer to the thematic volumes whose contents are listed on the following page. All in all these 16 volumes comprise about 2,800 pages, 2,300 maps, and a large number of diagrams, drawings and photographs.

The thematic volumes fall into four main groups related to different branches of geography: The Land, The Economy, The Cultural Landscape and Living Conditions and Life Patterns. Together they provide an exhaustive picture of the geographical diversity of Sweden.

Contents of the National Atlas of Sweden's 16 Thematic Volumes

Agriculture
Agriculture in a historical perspective
Soil types and climate
Food supply
Agricultural policy
How the land is used
Arable land and meadow
The agricultural labour force
Mechanization
Farm buildings
Crop production, horticulture
Livestock, reindeer husbandry
Farm properties
The farmer's economy
Agriculture in the national economy
Research, training and extension
National authorities and organisations

Climate, Lakes and Rivers
A global perspective
From the Ice Age to our age
Solar radiation
Air temperature, air pressure and wind
Humidity and evaporation
Clouds and fog
Precipitation and thunderstorms
Snow cover
Local climate
Runoff, the movement of water
Water systems in Sweden
River discharge
Lakes
Water temperature and ice
Air and water transport material
Plants and animals in rivers and lakes
Lake drainage, canals and log floating
Water power and lake regulation
Conflicting water claims
Climate and water in the future

Cultural Heritage and Preservation
The history of the settlement of Sweden
Early hunting cultures
Stone Age peasants
Bronze Age settlement
Rock art
Graves and Iron Age settlement
Agriculture during the Iron Age and the Middle Ages
Strongholds and power
Runic inscriptions
Routes and fairways
The cultural landscape of iron
Traps and trapping
The Saami cultural environment
Places of sacrifice and popular belief
Our churches
Buildings and farms in rural areas
Castles, palaces and manor houses
Public buildings
Towns
The cultural environment of township
Industrial monuments
Place names
Historic areas of national interest

Cultural Life, Recreation and Tourism
Music, theatre and film
Museums and exhibitions
Libraries and public records
Cultural life based on the popular movement
Mass media
Public expenditure on culture
Sports – its organisations and facilities
Competitive sports
Recreational landscapes and outdoor recreation
Second homes
Tourism in Sweden
Places of tourist interest in Sweden
Some tourist regions
Swedish tourism abroad
Tourism in the Swedish economy

The Environment
Geographical regions
Pollution knows no limits
The forests
The mountains
Wetlands
Lakes and rivers
The coastal landscape
Endangered species
Acidification and liming
Metals in soil and groundwater
Spreading and leaching of nutrients
Toxic substances
Disturbed and undisturbed waters
The quality of air, noise
Waste management, transportation and storage of hazardous substances
Environmental policy in Sweden
Environmental protection: national parks, nature reserves etc.
Outdoor recreation

The Forests
The forests of the Earth
Changes in the forest – three selected examples
Land use, land classes
Geology and climate
Forest ecology
Tree species, growing stock, age classes, growth potential
Forest industry
Firewood
The forests as a resource for outdoor activities
One hundred years in the life of a forest
Forests are not only trees
Damage to the forests
Forestry transport
Forest work
Who owns the forests?
The economic importance of forestry
Forestry organisations
Research and training
The national forest inventory
Forest mapping

Geography of Plants and Animals
Sweden's natural history
From the Ice Age to present day
Geographical classifications of plants and animals
Various types of distribution
Ecosystems
Species diversity
Patterns in genetic variation
Places of biological interest
Changes in flora and fauna
Red-listed species
Migration, movements and dispersal
Hunting and fishing
Domestic animals and cultivated plants
Wild plants as food and medicine
Research

Geology
Geology – understanding time
Structure of the earth
The bedrock
The Swedish Precambrian
The Caledonides
Fossiliferous bedrock outside the Swedish mountain chain
Bedrock of the Swedish continental shelf
Morphology of the bedrock surface
Ores and mineral deposits
Industrial minerals
Geophysics
Magnetic field of the Earth crust
Quaternary deposits
Glacials and interglacials
The glaciation
Vegetational history
Development of the Baltic Sea and the Skagerrak/Kattegat
Regions of Quaternary deposits
Quaternary deposits on the sea floor
Groundwater
Geochemistry
Changes to the landscape

The Infrastructure
Transportation in a historical perspective
Accessibility of towns
Shipping
Railways, road traffic, air traffic
Postal services, telecommunications
Radio and TV
Energy: supplies, uses, environmental effects
Administrative divisions: counties, municipalities, county councils, courts, the police service, customs department, the sea-traffic areas, defence, the church, schools, universities
Water and sewage

Landscape and Settlements
Mankind and the landscape
Patterns in the landscape
Ten thousand years in Sweden
Landscape research
The landscape and the transformation of society
Sweden's cultural landscape
The cultural landscape – 35 selected examples from Skåne in the south to Malmberget in the north
Planning for future landscapes

Manufacturing and Services
Swedish industry in a historical perspective
The transformation of industry
Industrial employment
Industrialisation by regional development policies
Industries: food, forest, mining, metal, and others
The geography of ownership
Private services: commerce, transport, banking, insurance, building, and others
Public services
The future of Swedish industry

Maps and Mapping
The character of Sweden – short facts
The map – an image of reality
Maps and the past
Five centuries of Sweden on maps
National map authorities, map publishers
Geodesy
Official map series
Place-names on maps
Nautical charts
General maps
Geological maps
Municipal maps
Maps for orienteering
Aerial photographs
Geographical data banks
Map production
Remote sensing for thematic mapping
Satellites for peace and global environmental monitoring
Map collections in Sweden
SNA Map of Sweden 1:700 000

The Population
Sweden and its people, the population pyramid
Territorial divisions: counties, provinces
Geographic distribution, the Swedish kommuns
Urban areas
Old population statistics
Fertility, mortality, causes of death
Today's towns and urban areas
Mobility
Health, education
Money, transfer payments
Homes
Power and influence, political elections
Ways of living together
A cultural mix
The future

Sea and Coast
The oceans
Bottom topography in the Baltic Sea and the Skagerrak/Kattegat
Bottoms and sediments
Coast and shore
Weather and climate
Elements in the water
Water turnover and salinity
Temperature and ice
Wind waves, water level, currents
Life in the sea
Marine resources
Boundaries of the sea
Fisheries and aquaculture
Shipping and navigation
Energy resources
Emissions
Mineral resources
The changing sea

Sweden in the World
The map as a mirror of time
Sweden's relations with the world
Culture and the media
Internationalisation of firms
Foreign trade
Investments and employment
Swedish regions in international competition
Information flows and contact routes
Universities and the outside world
Europe in transition
World map: countries and capitals

Work and Leisure
Introduction to the time perspective
Time and space in a historical perspective
Use of time in everyday life
Transformation of everyday life
Education
Full-time and part-time employment
Employment, labour markets
Journeys to work
Unemployment
Absence due to illness
Organisation of work
Regional policies
Leisure time activities, holiday trips
Recreational areas
Future time use

Literature and references

Aldskogius, G., 1992. *Svensk regionalpolitik. Utveckling och framtid*. Allmänna förlaget. Stockholm.

Allhems förlags landskapsböcker. Malmö.

Atlas över Sverige. SSAG. Stockholm 1953–71.

Bergström, S., 1993. *Sveriges hydrologi – grundläggande hydrologiska förhållanden*. SMHI. Norrköping.

Brusewitz, G. & Emmelin, L., 1985. *Det föränderliga landskapet*. LTs förlag. Stockholm.

Det moderna Sverige, chief editor Magnus Lundquist, vol. 1–6, 1969–70. Bonniers. Stockholm.

Ekman, S. 1922. *Djurvärldens utbredningshistoria på Skandinaviska halvön*. Bonniers. Stockholm.

Ehrensvärd, U., 1991. *Kartor – fem seklers svensk kartografi*. Stockholm. ISBN 91-970255-7-7.

Hoppe., 1983. *Fjällens terrängformer*. Naturvårdsverket. Solna.

Hultén, E. 1971. *Atlas över växternas utbredning i Norden*. Generalstaben. Stockholm.

Hyenstrand, Å., 1984. *Fasta fornlämningar och arkeologiska regioner*. RAÄ. Stockholm.

Kulturmiljö. Historien i landskapet, 1990. Chief editor Nils Blomkvist. Utbildningsradion. Stockholm.

Lindström, M., Lundquist, J. & Lundquist, Th., 1991. *Sveriges geologi från urtid till nutid*. Studentlitteratur. Lund.

Lundmark, J.-E., 1986–89. *Skogsmarkens ekologi del 1 och 2*. Jönköping.

Länkar till vår forntid – en introduktion i Sveriges arkeologi (red. G. Burenhult, E. Baudou and M. P. Malmer). 1988. Höganäs.

Molén, M. & Bergsjö, A., 1989. *Lantbrukets bebyggelsemiljö Landskap-Gård-Byggnad*. Sveriges Lantbruksuniversitet. Lund.

Myhrman, J., 1994. *Hur Sverige blev rikt*. SNS. Stockholm.

National Atlas of Sweden, 17 vol., 1990–1996. SNA Publishing, Stockholm.

Riksintressanta kulturmiljöer i Sverige. 1990. Riksantikvarieämbetet. Stockholm.

Rosenberg, R., 1982. *Havets liv och miljö*. Liber. Stockholm.

Sporrong, U., Ekstam U. & Samuelsson, K. 1995. *Svenska Landskap*. Naturvårdsverket. Solna.

Stephansson, O., 1983. *Sveriges vandring på jorden*. Liber. Stockholm.

Year-books of Svenska Turistföreningen, especially the provice-books 1915–1940, 1961–1985 and 1996-

Sverige, Land och Folk, chief editor Hans Wson Ahlman, vol. 1–3, 1966. Natur och Kultur. Stockholm.

Värt att se i Sverige. A travellers guide, 1992. Bonniers. Stockholm.

Authors

Aldskogius, Hans, 1933, Reader, Dep. of Social and Economic Geography, Uppsala
Andersson, Roger, 1952, Reader, Dep. of Social and Economic Geography, Uppsala
Helmfrid, Staffan, 1927, Professor Emeritus of Human Geography, Stockholm
Hogdal, Jon, 1940, BA, Dep. of Social and Economic Geography, Uppsala
Jonasson, Christer, 1954, Senior Lecturer, Dep. of Physical Geography, Stockholm
Lundmark, Mats, 1957, Senior Lecturer, Dep. of Social and Economic Geography, Uppsala
Östman, Peter, 1941, Senior Lecturer, Dep. of Human Geography, Stockholm

Acknowledgements for Illustrations

Permission for distribution of maps approved by Security Officer, the National Land Survey of Sweden 1996–06–20.
Photographs from METRIA approved for distribution 1996–05–02.

A Maps and Mapping
B The Forests
C The Population
D The Environment
E Agriculture
F The Infrastructure
G Sea and Coast
H Cultural Life, Recreation and Tourism
I Sweden in the World
K Work and Leisure
L Cultural Heritage and Preservation
M Geology
N Landscape and Settlements
P Climate, Lakes and Rivers
R Manufacturing and Services
S Geography of Plants and Animals

CFD = The Central Board for Real Estate Data
FoB = Population and Housing Censuses
G = Department of Human and Economic Geography, School of Economics and Commercial Law, Gothenburg
IF = Statistics on Income
IVL = Environmental Research Institute
KB = Royal Library
L = Department of Social and Economic Geography, Lund University
LB = Vital Population Statistics
LMV = National Land Survey/METRIA
N = Agency of Nature Photographers/Sweden
RAÄ = Central Board of National Antiquities
RT = National Forest Survey
SCB = Statistics Sweden
SGU = Geological Survey of Sweden
SMHI = Swedish Meteorological and Hydrological Institute
SNA = National Atlas of Sweden
SNV = National Environmental Protection Agency
STR = Swedish Tourist Board
TDB = Tourist and Travelling Data Base
Tio = Tiofoto AB
ULF = Investigations of Living Conditions

M: Map
D: Diagram
P: Photo
Dg: Drawing

Page
2 P: Lars Bygdemark
6 P: Staffan Brundell/GreatShots
Dg: Nils Forshed/*M*, *N*
7 M: top left SNA/*M*, data SGU et al.
M: top right SNA/*E*, data SCB, SGU
M: mid SNA/*C*, data LB, SCB
M: bottom SNA/*S*, data Enemar, Källander, Svensson
8 M: top Hans Sjögren, from Geografi, A&W, 1994
M: bottom left SNA/*C*, data SCB
M: mid SNA/*C*, data SCB
M: bottom right SNA/*H*, data Sotenäs kommun
9 Dg: top Nils Forshed/*K* from Ellegård
Dg: bottom Karin Feltzin/*C*, data Demografiska databasen in Umeå
10 M: left SNA/*P*, data SMHI
10, 12 M: SNA/*D*, *G*, data Nordiska ministerrådet, SMHI
11, 13 M: SNA, data SCB
12 M: SNA/*P*, data SMHI
14 M: top left SNA/*N*, data Utrikesdepartementet
M: bottom left SNA/*N*
M: right SNA
15 M: top and bottom SNA/*C*, data SCB
M: left SNA/*I*, data Utvandrarnas hus, Växjö
M: mid SNA/*I*, data SCB
M: right SNA, data SCB
D: right SNA/*C*, data SCB
D: left Hans Sjögren/*N*, *K*, *C*
16 M: SNA/*M*, data Karna Lidmar-Bergström
P: Lennart Mathiasson/*N*
17 M: SNA/*M*, data LMV
P: top Peter Lindberg/*N*
P: bottom Jan Töve J:son/*N*
18 Hans Sjögren, from Karl-Erik Perhans
19 P: Jan Rietz/Tio
Dg: Hans Sjögren/*M*, from Torsvik et al.
20 M: and Dg: Hans Sjögren, from Maurits Lindström
P: Tore Hagman/*N*
21 M: top SNA/*M*, data SGU
M: bottom SNA/*M*, data SGU
P: top P Roland Johansson/*N*
P: bottom Jan Töve J:son/*N*
22 M: SNA/*M*, from Denton & Hughes
23 M: SNA/*M*, data SGU
Dg: Hans Sjögren/*M*, from J Lundqvist, A-M Robertsson
24 M: SNA/*M*
Dg: Hans Sjögren/*M*, from A-M Robertsson
25 M and D: right SNA/*M*, data Ekman et al.
D: left SNA/*P*, from Dansgaard, Karlén
26 M: right SNA, from Karl-Erik Perhans
M: top and bottom SNA/*M*, data SGU
27 M: SNA, from Karl-Erik Perhans
28–29 Nils Forshed/*M*, from C Fredén
30 SNA/*M*, data SGU et al.
31 M: SNA/*M*, *P*, data SGU et al.
P: top Göran Hansson/*N*
P: bottom Arne Philip
32 P: from above Jan Töve J:son/*N*, Tore Hagman/*N*, Björn Uhr/*N*, Tore Hagman/*N*, Lennart Mathiasson/*N*
Dg: Hans Sjögren/*E*, from Karin Feltzin, data SGU
33 M: SNA, data T Troedsson, from Nationalencyklopedin, Typoform/Marie Peterson
P: Mats Olsson
34 M: SNA/*P*, data SMHI
35 M: top SNA/*P*, data SMHI
M: bottom SNA/*G*, data SMHI
36 M: SNA/*P*, data SMHI
37 SNA/*P*, data SMHI
38 SNA/*P*, data SMHI
39 M: left SNA/*P*, data SMHI
M: right SNA/*D*, data SNV
40 M: SNA/*S*, data Nordiska ministerrådet
P: top left Tore Hagman/*N*
P: top right Janos Jurka/*N*
P: bottom left Axel Ljungquist/*N*
P: bottom right Klas Rune/*N*
41 M: top SNA/*S*, data Fabricius, Tyrberg
M: mid left SNA/*S*, data Svenska Jägarförbundet
M: mid right SNA/*D*, data SNV
M: bottom SNA/*S*, data Tyrberg, Naturhistoriska Riksmuseet
42–45 SSC Satellitbild
46–55 M: SNA/*B*, data LMV; *C*, data LB, SCB, CFD; *M*, data SGU et al.; *K*, data SCB; *P*, data SMHI; *F*, data LMV, SCB; *D*, data SNV, LMV; *N*, data Sporrong
56 M: SNA, from Gerd Enequist
D: Hans Sjögren, data SCB
Gröna kartan 8G SV, 1:50 000
Gröna kartan 8G NO, 1:50 000
Gröna kartan 2D SO, 1:50 000
57 M: SNA/*N*, data Sporrong, Helmfrid
P: LMV
58 M: left SNA/*P*, data SMHI
M: right Hans Sjögren, from Häggström
Dg: Nils Forshed, from Cabouret
Ekonomisk karta 9F 5g 1948 and 1981, 1:20 000
59 P: Lars Jarnemo/*N*
Dg: top Nils Forshed/*N*
Dg: bottom Hans Sjögren
60 M: SNA, from Vegetationskarta 20G NO
Dg: Nils Forshed/*B*
61 M: top SNA/*B*, data Riksskogstaxeringen
M: bottom left SNA/*D*, data Sveriges Lantbruksuniv.
M: bottom mid SNA/*B*
M: bottom right SNA/*D*, data IVL
62 M: SNA/*M*, data SGU
P: LMV
63 M: SNA/*M*, data Torvproducentföreningen
P: top Göran Hansson/*N*
P: bottom LMV
64 M: SNA/*N*, data Elert
P: top Torleif Svensson/Tio
P: bottom Nordiska Museet/A Blomberg
65 Ekonomisk karta 22K 8j 1958 and 1984, 1:20 000
SNA/*F*, data Vägverket
66 M: top William-Olsson,

Ekonomisk-geografisk karta över Sverige, 1960
M: bottom SNA/P, data Kanalrådet
68 M: left SNA/D, data Räddningsverket
M: mid SNA/P, data Svenska Kraftverksföreningen
M: right SNA/D, data SNV
M: bottom SNA/D, data Kustbevakningen
69 M: left SNA/G, data Cato; P, data SNV
M: mid SNA/M, data SGU
M: right SNA/D, data IVL
D: SNA/F, data Statens energiverk
70 SNA/L, data Medeltidsstaden
71 M: SNA/L, from old town plans
P: top Krigsarkivet
P: bottom LMV
72 Gula kartan 8B:48, 1:20 000
P: bottom KB
73 Mjölby kommun, Turist- och informationskarta
P: bottom LMV
74 Gula kartan 11G:17, 1:20 000
P: bottom KB
75 M: top William-Olsson
Dg: Hans Sjögren, from a model at Kungl Tekniska Högskolan in Stockholm
P: Torleif Svensson/Tio
M: bottom KartCentrum
76 SNA/L, data RAÄ, länsmuseerna
77 SNA/L, data RAÄ, Brink, Kulturhist. lexikon et al.
78 SNA/L, data RAÄ, Nordiska museets register, Edenheim
79 SNA/L, data Bergskollegii register, Industriminnen i Västernorrland 1–2
80 M: SNA/H, data Svenska kommunförbundet, Sv hockeyförbundet
D: SNA/H, data Svenska Golfförbundet
P: Hasse Schröder/Naturbild
81 M: SNA/H, data SNV et al.
P: Lars Bygdemark
Gula kartan 10J:42, 1:20 000
82 M: left SNA/N
M: right SNA, data SCB
83 M: top SNV
M: bottom Vallentuna kommun
84 Regionplane- och trafikkontoret
85 Vallentuna kommun
86 M: SNA, data SCB
D: SNA/E, data Myrdal, Söderberg, SCB
Dg: Nils Forshed
87 M: SNA/N, data SCB
D: SNA, data SCB

88 M: right SNA/L, data Lundin
M: right SNA/F, data Transportrådet
89 M: top SNA/F, data Sveriges järnvägsmuseum
M: bottom Hans Sjögren
90–91 M and D: SNA, data SCB, Andersson, R., 1987: Den svenska urbaniseringen. Geografiska regionstudier nr 18. Kulturgeogr. inst., Uppsala univ.
P: LMV
92 William-Olsson, Ekonomisk-geografisk karta över Sverige, 1946
93 SNA, data SCB
94–95 SNA, data SCB
96 M: SNA/R, data SCB, et al.
97 M: top SNA/R, data SCB, Industristatistik
M: bottom SNA, data SCB
D: SNA/I, data SCB
98 SNA, data SCB
99 M: top SNA, data SCB
M: bottom SNA, Tjänstemännens centralorganisation, Arbetsmarknadsstyrelsen
D: SNA/K, data SCB
100 M: top SNA/E, P, data SMHI
M: bottom SNA/E, data Jordbruksverket
101 M and D: SNA/E, data SCB
102 M: SNA/G, data SCB
Dg: Hans Sjögren, data Uhlin, Hoffman
103 M and D: SNA/R, data SCB et al.
104 M: SNA/B, D, data RT, Sveriges Lantbruksuniversitet
D: SNA/B, data RT
105 M: SNA/B, data RT
D: Hans Sjögren, data Skogsindustrierna
Dg: Hans Sjögren, data SCB, Skogsstatistisk årsbok
106 M: SNA/B, data Skogsindustrierna
107 M: SNA/B, data Skogsindustrierna
P: LMV
108 M: left SNA/P, data SMHI
M: right SNA, data SCB
D: SNA/F, data SCB et al.
109 M: SNA/F, data Svenska Gasföreningen, Vattenfall
P: LMV
110 Dg: Hans Sjögren, data NUTEK, SCB, Skogsstyrelsen
D: SNA, SMHI et al.
111 M: top SNA/F, data Vattenfall
M: bottom left SNA/F, data SMHI
M: bottom right SNA, data Vattenfall, Vindkompaniet

112 M: top SNA/R, data SCB
M: mid Hans Sjögren, data LKAB
M: bottom SNA/M, data SGU
D: SNA/R, data SCB
113 SNA/R, data SCB
114–115 SNA, data SCB
116 LMV
117 SNA, data SCB
118 SNA, data SCB
119 SNA, data SCB
120 SNA, data SCB
121 M: SNA/R, data SCB
P: LMV
122 M: left SNA/F, data Transportrådet
M: mid SNA/F, data Tåg- och vagnrörelsen
M: right SNA/F, data Luftfartsverket
123 M and D: top SNA/I, data G, L
D: bottom SNA/F, I data Posten, Televerket
124 D: SNA/I, data G, SCB
125 SNA/I, data G
126 SNA/I, data L
127 M: left SNA/I, data Cederlund et al.
M: right SNA/I, data L
D: top SNA/I, data L
D: bottom SNA/I, data L, Sveriges Riksbank
128 M: SNA/R, data SCB
P: Jan Rietz/Tio
129 M: SNA/R, data Astra, Electrolux, SCB
P: Lennart Larsson Bildbyrå
130 SNA/R, data SCB
131 M: SNA, data SCB
P: Pål-Nils Nilsson/Tio
132 M: SNA, data Arbetsmarknadsdep., NUTEK Analys
133 M: SNA, data SCB
P: LMV
134–135 D: SNA/C, data SCB et al.
135 M: SNA/H, data SCB
136 M: left SNA/E, data SCB
M: right SNA/C, data SCB
D: SNA/C, data SCB et al.
137 SNA/C, data SCB, LB, FoB 1990
138 M: SNA/C, data SCB
M: right SNA/I, data SCB
D: SNA/C, data SCB
139 M: left SNA/C, data SCB, LB
M: right SNA, data SCB, LB
D: SNA/C, data SCB, LB
140 M: SNA/C, data SCB, LB
D: SNA/C, data SCB et al.
141 M: top SNA/C, data SCB et al.
M: bottom left SNA, data SCB, Socialtjänst- och sjukförsäkringsstatistik
M: bottom right SNA, data Riksförsäkringsverket

142 M: left SNA/K, data SCB
M: right SNA/C, data SCB
D: SNA/C, data SCB
143 M: left SNA/C, data Skolverket
M: mid SNA/F, data Folkhögskolornas informationstjänst
M: right SNA/H, data Statistiska meddelanden Ku 10
D: SNA, data SCB, Utbildningsstatistik
144 SNA, data SCB, FoB 1990
145 M and D: top SNA/K, data SCB
D: bottom SNA, data SCB
146 M: SNA, data SCB, IF
D: SNA, data SCB, Skatter, inkomster och bidrag, 1994
147 M: SNA, data SCB, IF
P: LMV
148 M: SNA/C, data SCB
D: top SNA, data ULF, rapport 86
D: bottom SNA/C, data SCB
149 SNA/C, data SCB, Valstatistik
150 M: top left SNA/C, data SCB, Valstatistik
M: top right SNA, data SCB, Valstatistik
M: bottom SNA, data Folkrörelserådet Hela Sverige ska leva
151 M: top SNA/K, Svenska kyrkans forskningsråd
M: bottom SNA/H, data Sveriges Riksidrottsförbund
152 D: left Hans Sjögren/K, from Ellegård
D: right SNA/K, data SCB
153 Nils Forshed and Hans Sjögren/K, from Ellegård
154 SNA/K, data SCB
155 M: SNA, data SCB
Dg: Hans Sjögren/K, from B. Jansson
156 M: left SNA/H, data Statens kulturråd, Teaterårsboken
M: right SNA/K, data Svenska filminstitutet
D: SNA, data SCB, Kulturstatistik, 1985–92
157 SNA/H, data Statens kulturråd, Sveriges Orkesterföreningars Riksförbund, Riksförbundet Sveriges Amatörorkestrar, Sveriges Spelmäns Riksförbund
158 M: left SNA/H, data STR et al.
M: top right SNA, data Bohlin, Hanefors, Körstämman i Skinnskatteberg 1992
M: bottom right SNA/H, data Körstämman i Skinnskatteberg, programkatalog

P: Weine Lexius/Pressens Bild
159 SNA/H, data SCB, Statistiska meddelanden
160 M: SNA/H, data Svenska Fotbollförbundet, Bandyförbundet, Ishockeyförbundet
D: SNA/H, data SCB
161 SNA/H, data from the sporting clubs
P: Bengt-Göran Carlsson/Tio
162 SNA, data Aldskogius, H., 1993: Leksand, Leksand, Leksand! En studie av ishockeyns betydelse för en bygd. Gidlunds. Hedemora.
163 M: top SNA/H, data från resp arrangörsförening
M: bottom left SNA/H, data Svenska Ridsportens Centralförbund
M: bottom right SNA/H, data Svenska Fotbollförbundet
164 M: top SNA/H, data Aldskogius
M: bottom left SNA/K, data Svenska jägarförbundet
M: bottom right SNA/K, data Fritidsfiskarna
D: SNA/H, data Friluftslivet i Sverige 1964, Fritid-friluftsliv 1974, SCB, ULF 56
165 M: left SNA/H, LMV
M: mid SNA/P, data SMHI
M: right SNA/H, data STR
166 M: top and bottom left SNA/H, data TDB, Swedline
M: bottom right SNA, data SCB, Inkvarteringsstatistik
D: SNA/H, data TDB, Swedline
167 M: top SNA/H, data SCB, Inkvarteringsstatistik
M: bottom and diagram SNA/H, TDB, Swedline
168 Jordartskartan Höganäs NO/Helsingborg NV, 1:50 000
Topografisk karta 3B NO/3C NV, 1:50 000
Gula kartan 3B:88, 1:20 000
P: LMV
169 M: top left SNA/C, data SCB
M: top right SNA/F, data Vägverket
Dg: mid Hans Sjögren, from Dudley-Stamp, 1964: Some aspects of medical geography. Oxford Univ. Press. London.
Dg: bottom Nils Forshed/N
170 P: National Atlas of Sweden, covers
Dg: Bertil Hjerpe/Typoform

Thematic maps

MAP	SCALE	THEME	PAGE
T1	1:1,25M	Quaternary deposits, detail	7
T2	1:1,25M	Arable land and meadow, detail	7
T3–T4		Fertility, Stockholm and Göteborg	7
T5–7	1:20M	Grasshopper warbler, 1957, 1968 and 1990	7
T8		Densely populated areas, the world	8
T9	1:10M	Densely populated areas	8
T10	1:700 000	Population per km² in Sundsvall municipality	8
T11		Dwellings in Smögen	8
T12	1:2,5M	Physical regions	10, 12

MAP	SCALE	THEME	PAGE
T13	1:2,5M	Population, distribution and density	11, 13
T14	1:20M	Number of days with snowcover	10
T15	1:20M	Length of growing season	12
T16	1:10M	Age of permanent settlements and Swedens borders	14
T17–19		Municipalities in western Sweden	14
T20–23		Swedens frontiers	14
T24–T25		Population density, 1880 and 1980	15
T26	1:20M	Emigrants, 1881–1890	15

MAP	SCALE	THEME	PAGE
T27	1:20M	Foreign-born persons, 1990	15
T28	1:20M	Population in urban areas >10,000, 1990	15
T29	1:5M	Types of terrain	16
T30	1:5M	Relief	17
T31		Nappes in the Swedish mountain chain	20
T32		Platform sediments, Lower Palaeozoic	21
T33		Sedimentary deposits, Upper Cretaceous	21
T34		The Elster, Saale and Weichsel glaciation	22
T35	1:5M	Deglaciation	23
T36–39		Development of the Baltic Sea and the Skagerrak/Kattegat	24
T40	1:20M	Shoreline displacement and recent land uplift	25
T41	1:5M	Bedrock	26
T42	1:20M	Bedrock provinces	26
T43	1:20M	Limestone bedrock and calcareous deposits	26
T44	1:20M	Mines, 1995	27
T45	1:10M	Industrial minerals and rocks, 1995	27
T46	1:5M	Quaternary deposits	30
T47	1:10M	Glaciofluvial sediments	31
T48	1:10M	Soils	33
T49-T52	1:10M	Mean temperatures, January, April, July, October	34
T53	1:10M	Annual mean temperatures	34
T54	1:20M	Length of growing season	35
T55	1:20M	Frost frequency	35
T56	1:20M	Continental and maritime areas	35
T57	1:10M	Ice freeze-up	35
T58	1:10M	Ice break-up	35
T59	1:5M	Annual precipitation	36
T60	1:10M	Number of days with snow cover	37
T61	1:10M	Wind, annual mean	37
T62	1:5M	Lakes	38
T63	1:5M	Discharge	39
T64	1:10M	Hydro-electric power regulation	39
T65	1:10M	Vegetation zones	40
T66	1:20M	Canada goose	41
T67	1:20M	Roe deer	41
T68–T69	1:20M	Lynx, 19th century and 1990	41
T70–72	1:20M	White-tailed eagle, 1850, 1970 and 1990	41
T73	1:2,5M	The cultural landscape	42–43
T74	1:1,25M	Land classes and land use, 9 areas	46–55
T75	1:1,25M	Population distribution, 9 areas	46–55
T76	1:1,25M	Quaternary deposits, 9 areas	46–55
T77	1:1,25M	Journeys to work, 9 areas	46–55
T78	1:1,25M	Water systems in Sweden, 9 areas	46–55
T79	1:1,25M	Administrative divisions, 9 areas	46–55
T80	1:1,25M	Protected areas 1990, 9 areas	46–55
T81	1:1,25M	Cultural landscapes, 9 areas	46–55
T82	1:10M	Distribution of cultivation	56
T83	1:10M	"Enskifte" or "Laga skifte"	57
T84	1:10M	Lowered and reclaimed lakes	58
T85		Flood meadows in Lycksele	58
T86	1:200 000	Clear-felled areas in Jämtland and Västernorrland	60
T87–91	1:20M	Pine, spruce, birch, oak and beech	61
T92	1:20M	Distribution of mature forest	61
T93–T94	1:20M	Defoliation, pine and spruce	61
T95–T96	1:20M	Total deposition in spruce forest	61
T97	1:5M	Industrial minerals and rocks	62
T98	1:10M	Ongoing production and abandoned quarries	62
T99	1:10M	Energy peat	63
T100	1:10M	Industrial areas, 1960	64
T101–T102	1:2,5M	The road network, 1990, two areas	66
T103–T104		Economic map of Sweden, 1960	67
T105		Canals	67
T106	1:10M	Railway transports of hazardous substances	68
T107	1:10M	Energy in lakes and watercourses	68
T108	1:10M	Mercury	68
T109	1:10M	Oil transports and oil spills	68
T110	1:20M	Acidification, chlorine in sediment	69
T111	1:20M	Cadmium in stream plants	69
T112–T113	1:20M	Fallout of lead 1975 and 1990	69
T114	1:10M	Towns founded during the middle ages, before 1500	70
T115	1:10M	Towns founded during the period 1500–1800	70
T116	1:10M	Towns founded during the industrial revolution, after 1800	70
T117	1:5M	Ancient monument sites	76
T118	1:20M	Remains of old routes	76
T119	1:10M	Rune stones	77
T120	1:10M	Trapping pits	77
T121	1:10M	Place-name elements	77
T122	1:10M	Dioceses and cathedrals	77
T123	1:5M	Monasteries and abbeys	77
T124	1:5M	Selected urban areas	78
T125	1:20M	Shealing system around 1900 and today	78
T126	1:5M	Castles and manor-houses	78
T127	1:5M	Blast furnaces and tilt hammers	79
T128		Industrial area of Sundsvall	79
T129	1:10M	Marinas	80
T130	1:10M	Indoor ice-hockey arenas	80
T131	1:10M	Downhill skiing facilities	80
T132	1:5M	Hiking trails and cycle tourist routes	81
T133	1:5M	Landscapes protected by law	82
T134	1:10M	Population connected to waste-water treatment plant	82
T135–T136		Hornborgasjön, 1965 and 2000	83
T137		Vallentuna – plans and regulations	83
T138		Regional plan for Stockholm county, 1990–2020	84
T139		Vallentuna – cultural heritage preservation programme	85
T140		Detailed plan, Vallentuna	85
T141	1:10M	Population 1910, by industry	86
T142	1:10M	Employment by industry, 1990	87
T143	1:5M	18th-century road network	88
T144	1:5M	Main road network 1990	88
T145–T146	1:10M	The railway network, 1916 and 1956/1996	89
T147		Steamboats, railways and aviation in Sweden	89
T148		Regions in northern Västerbotten	90
T149		Population in northern Västerbotten, 1860–1990	91
T150		Economic map of Sweden, 1946	92
T151	1:2,5M	Industrial structure of urban areas, 1990	94–95
T152–154	1:20M	Dominant industries, 1891, 1951 and 1991	96
T155–157	1:20M	Employment in manufacturing, 1891, 1951 and 1991	96
T158	1:10M	Municipalities with large and small companies	97
T159	1:10M	Employment in manufacturing in main sectors	97
T160	1:10M	Gross regional product	99
T161–163	1:20M	Unemployment, unionised salaried employees	99
T164	1:10M	Length of growing season	100
T165	1:10M	Humidity, beginning of the growing season	100
T166	1:10M	Temperature sum	100
T167	1:10M	Fertility of arable land	100
T168	1:10M	Tenancy of arable land, 1995	101
T169	1:10M	Farms with forest, 1995	101
T170	1:10M	Area of different crops, 1995	101
T171	1:10M	Cattle per 100 ha of arable land, 1995	101
T172		The development of some Swedish fisheries	102
T173	1:20M	Professional fishermen, 1990	102
T174–T175	1:10M	Employment in food industry	103
T176	1:10M	Growing stock, all species	104
T177	1:10M	Annual growth	104
T178	1:10M	Average distance to roads	104
T179	1:10M	Species distribution of growing stock	105
T180	1:10M	Sawmills	106
T181	1:5M	Pulp industry, 1995	106
T182	1:5M	Paper industry, 1995	107
T183	1:10M	Number of heating degree days	108
T184	1:10M	Total energy consumption, 1994	108
T185	1:5M	Hydro-electric plants, nuclear power plants and district heating	109
T186		The Nordel main grid, 1995	111
T187	1:20M	Annual mean winds	111
T188		Wind power plants on southern Gotland, 1995	111
T189–191	1:20M	Employment in mining and quarrying	112
T192		Shipment of iron ore from LKAB	112
T193		Ore deposits and mineralisations in the Skellefte field	112
T194	1:5M	Basic metal industries, employment by location	113
T195	1:10M	Metal manufacturing	114
T196	1:10M	Machine industries	114
T197	1:10M	Electric and instrument industries	114
T198	1:10M	Vehicle industries	115
T199	1:10M	Chemical industries	117
T200	1:10M	Non-metallic mineral industries	117
T201	1:10M	Textile and clothing industries	117
T202	1:10M	Share of employment in private services sector	118
T203	1:10M	Grocery stores, 1993	118
T204	1:10M	Computer services, 1992	119
T205	1:10M	Engineering and architectural consulting, 1992	119
T206	1:10M	Other technical consulting, 1992	119
T207	1:10M	State employment, 1992	121
T208	1:10M	County council employees, 1990	121
T209	1:10M	Municipality employment, 1992	121
T210	1:10M	Traffic flow for domestic long-distance lorry transport	122
T211	1:10M	Railway transport work	122
T212	1:10M	Flight passenger departures	122
T213	1:10M	Value of exports, 1990	123
T214–T215		Swedish exports and imports, 1989–91	125
T216		Swedish companies employment in other countries	126
T217		Manufacturing firms contacts, 1990	127
T218	1:10M	Employees in foreign-owned subsidiaries	127

MAP	SCALE	THEME	PAGE
T219	1:5M	Geography of ownership, whole industry, 1993	128
T220	1:10M	Astra pharmaceutical plants in Sweden, 1993	129
T221	1:10M	Employment in Elektrolux, 1993	129
T222–T223	1:20M	Percentage of employees in remote controlled companies, 1993, manufacturing and construction	129
T224	1:10M	New companies, 1985–89	130
T225	1:10M	Bankruptcies, 1991-March 1993	130
T226	1:10M	Manufacturing employment, 1980–1990	131
T227	1:10M	Other employment, 1980–1990	131
T228	1:10M	Regional development areas, 1994	132
T229	1:10M	Areas eligible for EU regional assistance, 1995	132
T230	1:10M	Regional government grants to companies	132
T231	1:10M	Employment at relocated governmental agencies	133
T232	1:10M	Redistributive effects of public finance, 1992	133
T233	1:10M	Population within 30 km	135
T234	1:10M	Population in rural areas, 1990	136
T235	1:10M	Urbanised rural areas	136
T236	1:10M	Strong urbanisation	137
T237	1:10M	Green wave	137
T238	1:10M	Weak urbanisation	137
T239	1:10M	Those still living in their county of birth	138
T240	1:10M	Foreign-born persons	138
T241	1:10M	Persons 65 years old or older	139
T242	1:10M	Ratio of births to deaths	139
T243–T244	1:10M	Mortality level, 1984–88, men and women	140
T245	1:20M	Deaths from circulatory system diseases, men	141
T246	1:20M	Deaths caused by cancer, 1982–86, women	141
T247	1:20M	Alcohol mortality, 1969–78, men	141
T248	1:10M	Geriatric care	141
T249	1:20M	Sickness rate	141
T250	1:10M	Years of education	142
T251	1:10M	Pre-upper secondary education	142
T252		Transition from upper secondary school to university	143
T253	1:10M	Folk high schools	143
T254	1:10M	Study circles	143
T255	1:10M	Single person household	144
T256	1:10M	Privately owned dwellings	144
T257	1:10M	Earned income per employee	145
T258	1:10M	Women at work	145
T259	1:10M	Disposable income, family with two children	146
T260	1:10M	Disposable income, single women	146
T261	1:10M	Social benefits	146
T262		Socio-economic differentiation in Uppsala	147
T263	1:10M	Assessed capital assets	147
T264–T265	1:10M	Stability in Riksdag elections 1970–94	148
T266–T267	1:10M	Political blocs at election to the Riksdag	149
T268	1:10M	Municipal elections, 1994	150
T269	1:10M	Referendum on Swedish membership in the EU	150
T270	1:10M	"Let all Sweden prosper" movement	150
T271	1:10M	Attendances at services in the church of Sweden	151
T272	1:10M	Members of free churches in Sweden, 1990	151
T273	1:10M	Sports clubs	151
T274	1:1,25M	Journeys to work	154
T275	1:10M	Commuters	154
T276		Skiing activities in Piteå	155
T277	1:10M	National and regional theatres	156
T278	1:20M	Theatre performances	156
T279	1:10M	The National Touring Theatre and amateur theatre clubs	156
T280	1:10M	Cinema visits	156
T281	1:10M	Symfony and chamber orchestras	157
T282	1:10M	Amateur orchestras	157
T283	1:20M	Folk musicians	157
T284	1:5M	Theatre and music in summer Sweden	158
T285–T286	1:20M	Skinnskatteberg choir festival	158
T287	1:5M	Museums	159
T288	1:10M	Public libraries, loans	159
T289	1:10M	Football marathon table	160
T290	1:10M	Bandy marathon table	160
T291	1:10M	Ice-hockey marathon table	160
T292	1:5M	Attendance at team sports events	161
T293	1:10M	Leksand IF Ice-hockey Club supporters club, 1992	162
T294–T295		Leksand IF Ice-hockey Club, revenue	162
T296	1:20M	Mass-participation sports events	163
T297	1:10M	Riding-school members	163
T298	1:10M	Womens football, 1995	163
T299–T300		Recreational trips round Uppsala	164
T301	1:10M	Hunters	164
T302	1:10M	Leisure-time fishermen	164
T303	1:5M	Second homes	165
T304	1:20M	Number of days with snow cover	165
T305	1:10M	Summer and winter tourism	165
T306	1:20M	Destination of Swedish tourists	166
T307–313	1:20M	Purpose and destination of recreational trips	166
T314	1:10M	Camping	166
T315	1:20M	Foreign tourists, number of guest nights, 1990	167
T316	1:40M	Recreational trips abroad	167
T317	1:2,5M	Urban areas, detail	169
T318	1:2,5M	The road network, 1990, detail	169
T319		Deaths from cholera in London	169

Index

ABB 115
abbeys 77 (**T123**)
acidification 69 (**T110**)
administrative divisions 14, **46–55 (T79**)
AGA 116
agriculture 100, 102
airport 67
alcohol mortality 141 (**T247**)
Alfa-Laval 115
alpine zone 40
aluminium 113
ammonia 68 (**T106**)
ancient monuments 76 (**T117**)
animals 40
Anrick, C-J 56
arable land 7 (**T2**), 100 (**T167**), 101, **101 (T168**)
architectural consulting 119 (**T205**)
associations 148
Astra 116, **129 (T220**)
aviation 89 (**T147**)

Baltic Sea development 24 (**T36– 39**)
Baltic Shield 26
bandy 160 (**T290**)161
bankruptcies 130, **130 (T225**)
bedrock 26, **26 (T41**), 26 (**T42**)
beech 61 (**T91**)
bioenergy 110
birch 61 (**T89**)
births/deaths 139 (**T242**)
blast furnaces 79 (**T127**)

Boda 21
borders 14 (**T16**)
boreal zone 40
boreonemoral zone 40
Borlänge 52
business travel 155

cadmium 69 (**T111**)
calcareous deposits 26 (**T43**)
Caledonides 16, 21, 26
cambisols 33
camping 166 (**T314**)
Canada goose 41 (**T66**)
canals 67 (**T105**)
cancer 141 (**T246**)
capital assets 147, **147 (T263**)
carbon dioxide 69
cardboard 105
cartography 7
castles 78 (**T126**), 79
cathedrals 77 (**T122**)
cattle 101 (**T171**)
causes of death 140
chemical industry 116, **117 (T199**)
children per women 7 (**T3–4**)
chlorine 68 (**T106**), 69 (**T110**)
choir festival 158 (**T285–286**)
cholera in London 169 (**T319**)
Church of Sweden 151, **151 (T271**)
churches 76, 151, **151 (T272**)
cinema 156 (**T280**), 157
circulatory system diseases 141 (**T245**)
clear-felled area 60 (**T86**)
climate 22, 34
clothing industry 116, **117 (T201**)

cohabiting 145
combine harvesters 86
combined power 108, 109
commuting 154, **154 (T275**)
companies, new 130 (**T224**)
computer services 119 (**T204**)
coniferous forest 42–43 (**T73**)
construction 129 (**T222–223**)
consulting 119 (**T206**)
continental area 35 (**T56**)
continental drift 19
copper 27, 63, 112, 113
country houses 79
county council employees 120
crops **101 (T170**)
cultivated landscape 56
cultivation 56 (**T82**)
cultural landscape 14, **46–55 (T81**)
cultural life 156
cycle routes 81 (**T132**)

Dannemora 63
deaths 141 (**T245–247**)
deciduous forest 42–43 (**T73**)
defoliation, 61 (**T93–94**)
deglaciation 22, **23 (T35**), 24 (**T36–39**),28, 29
demographic transition 15, 134
detailed plan 85 (**T140**)
development area 132, **132 (T228**)
dioceses 77 (**T122**)
discharge 39 (**T63**)
district heating 109 (**T185**)
downhill skiing facilities 80 (**T131**)
drainage **46–55 (T78**), 58

drainage basins **46–55 (T78**)
dune 28
dwellings, privately owned **144 T256**)

Economic Map of Sweden 67 **T103–104**), 92 (**T150**)
economy 86
education 142, **142 (T250, T251**)
election, municipality **150 (T268**)
election, Riksdag 148 (**T264–265**)
electric industry **114 (T197**), 115
electricity consumption 110
Electrolux **129 (T221**)
Elster 22, **22 (T34**)
emigrants 15 (**T26**)
employees 119, 126, **127 (T218**), employment **126 (T216**), 86, **87 T142**), 93, 96
employment, county council 121 **T208**)
employment, industry 96 (**T155–157**), 97 (**T158**)
employment, manufacturing 131 (**T226**)
employment, municipality 121 (**T209**)
employment, other 131 (**T227**)
employment, state 121 (**T207**)
energy 102, 108, **108 (T184**), 110
engineering 119 (**T205**)
engineering industry 114
enskifte 57 (**T83**)
environmental problems 68
environmental protection 82
eon 19

epoch 22
era 19
Ericsson 115
esker 31
EU referendum 150, **150 (T269**)
excursions round Uppsala 164 (**T299–300**)
exhibitions 158
exports 98, 105, 123, **123 (T213**), 124, 125, **125 (T214–215**), 127

Falun 52
faults 16 (**T29**)
Fennoscandia 19
firms' contacts 127 (**T217**)
fishermen 102 (**T173**)
fishermen, leisure-time 164 (**T302**)
fishing industry 102, **102 (T172**)
fishing zone **10, 12 (T12**)
flight passenger 122 (**T212**)
flooding system 58 (**T85**)
Folk High School 142, **143 (T253**)
folk musicians 157 (**T283**)
food industry 100, 103, **103 (T174–175**)
football 160 (**T289**), 161
football, women's 163 (**T298**)
foreign trade 124
foreign-born persons 15 (**T27**), 138 (**T240**)
forest **10, 12 (T12**), 101 (**T169**)
forest companies 105
forest industry 104
forest landscape 60
forest, annual growth **104 (T177**)

175

forest, mature **61 (T92)**
freight traffic 123
frontiers **14 (T20–23)**
frost frequency **35 (T55)**

geography 6, 168
geomorphology 25, 28, 29
geriatric care **141 (T248)**
GIS 169
glacial deposits 31
glaciation 22, **22 (T34)**
glaciofluvial deposits **31 (T47)**
glaciofluvial sediment 29
glassworks 116
GNP 98, 120
gold 112
golf 80
Gotland **111 (T188)**
government agencies, relocated **133 (T231)**
grain harvest 86
Grasshopper warber **7 (T5–7)**
green wave **137 (T237)**
grocery stores **118 (T203)**
gross regional product **99 (T160)**
growing season **12 (T15)**, **35 (T54)**, **100 (T164)**
growing stock **104 (T176)**, **105 (T179)**
Gällivare 55
Göteborg 44

Halmstad 47
health 140, 141
heating degree days **108 (T183)**
heating plant 108
Helsingborg 47
highest shoreline **10, 12 (T12)**, 24, 28, 29, **31 (T47)**
hiking trails **81 (T132)**
hilly terrain 17
holiday trip 166, 167
Holmhällar 19
Hornborgasjön 83, **83 (T135–136)**
horses 86
household 144, **144 (T255)**
household finances 145
housing 110
humidity **100 (T165)**
hunters **164 (T301)**
hydro-electric plants 108, **109 (T185)**
hydro-electric power regulation **39 (T64)**
hydropower plant **68 (T107)**
Hylte papermill 107
Håbo 139
Håverud 2
Härnösand 54
Höga Kusten 17

ice break-up **35 (T58)**
ice freeze-up **35 (T57)**
ice-hockey **80 (T130)**, **160 (T291)**, 161
illness 141
immigration 138
imports 123, 124, 125, **125 (T214–215)**
income 145, **145 (T257)**, 146
income, family with two children **146 (T259)**
income, farmers 101
income, single women **146 (T260)**
Indalsälven 57
industrial area **64 (T100)**, **79 (T128)**
industrial character 93, 96
industrial landscape 64
industrial life 86
industrial minerals **62 (T97, T98)**
industrial rocks **62 (T97, T98)**
industrial sectors 97
industrial structure 92, **94–95 (T151)**
industry **86 (T141)**, **87 (T142)**, **96 (T152–154)**, 98, 110, 116

industry, main sectors **97 (T159)**
industry, ownership **128 (T219)**
infrastructure 88, 122
instrument industry **114 (T197)**, 115
internationalisation 126
investments 126, 127
iron 27, 63, 112, **112 (T192)**
iron industry 113
irrigation 58

journeys to work **46–55 (T77)**, **154 (T274)**
Jutholmen 81
Järpen 53

Kalmar 49, 71
Karlskrona 49
Kiruna 55
Kista 64
Kosta 116
Kramfors 54

laga skifte **57 (T83)**
Lagastigen **76 (T118)**
lakes 38, **38 (T62)**
lakes, lowered **58 (T84)**
lakes, reclaimed **58 (T84)**
land classes **46–55 (T74)**
land reform 57
land uplift 19, **25 (T40)**
land use 44, **46–55 (T74)**, 56
land value 75
Landsat 42
landscape development 18
lead **69 (T112–113)**, 112, 113
Leksand IF ice-hockey club **162 (T293–295)**
Let All Sweden Prosper movement **150 (T270)**, 151
libraries 159, **159 (T288)**
Lids-Örsta 57
life pattern 134
lime works 21
limes norrlandicus 40
limestone 21
limestone bedrock **26 (T43)**
Linköping 50
living condition 134
Ljunggren, Gustaf 72
LKAB 112, **112 (T192)**
localisation quotient 119
lorry transport **122 (T210)**
Lycksele 58, **58 (T85)**
Lynx **41 (T68–69)**

machine industry **114 (T196)**, 115
mail 123
Malmö 44
manor-houses **78 (T126)**
manufacturing **129 (T222–223)**
map scale 8
marinas **80 (T129)**
maritime area **35 (T56)**
married 145
meadow **7 (T2)**
media 156
mercury **68 (T108)**
metal industry 113, **113 (T194)**
metal manufacturing 114, **114 (T195)**
migration 137, **138 (T239)**
mineral industry 116
mineralisation 27, **112 (T193)**
minerals 27, **27 (T45)**, **62 (T97, T98)**
mines **27 (T44)**, 62
mining 112, **112 (T189–191)**
Mjölby 73
Moderate Party **148 (T264–265)**
monasteries 76, **77 (T123)**
monuments 78
Mora 52
mortality **140 (T243–244)**
Moskosel 17
mountain 16
mountain chain **20 (T31)**
municipal employees 120
municipalities **14 (T17–19)**

museum 158, **159 (T287)**
music 156, **158 (T284)**
Mälardalen 51

nappes **20 (T31)**
National Atlas of Sweden 170
National Land Survey 133
Natural Resources Act 82
nature conservation 82
nemoral zone 41
Nissastigen **76 (T118)**
nitrogen 59, **61 (T96)**
nitrogen oxides 69
non-metallic mineral industries **117 (T200)**
Nordel **111 (T186)**
Norrköping 50
Norrland terrain 16
nuclear power 108, **109 (T185)**
Nyköping 50

oak **61 (T90)**
objective area **132 (T229)**
occupation 98, 99
oil spills **68 (T109)**
oil transports **68 (T109)**
Omberg 16
open area **42–43 (T73)**
open landscape **10, 12 (T12)**
orchestra 157 **(T281, T282)**
ore deposit **112 (T193)**
ores 27
organisation 148

Pajala 139
palaces 79
paper 105
paper industry **107 (T182)**
papermill 107
passenger traffic 123
peat 28, 31, 63, **63 (T99)**
peat cutting 62
period 19, 22
persons, older **139 (T241)**
Pharmacia & Upjohn 116
physical planning 84
physical region **10, 12 (T12)**
physical training 160
pilgrim route **76 (T118)**
pine **61 (T87, T93)**
Piteå **155 (T276)**
place name 76, **77 (T121)**
Planning and Building Act 82, 84
plants 40
podzols 33
political blocs **149 (T266–267)**
politics 148
pollen 24
popular movements 148
population **8 (T8, T9, T10)**, 11, **13 (T13)**, **46–55 (T75)**, **86 (T141)**, **90 (T148)**, 139, 145
population development **15 (T24–25)**, 90, **91 (T149)**, 134
population within 30 km **135 (T233)**
population, urban area **15 (T28)**
ports 67
post-glacial landscape 24
post-glacial sediments 31
precipitation 36, **36 (T59)**
protected area **46–55 (T80)**
protected landscapes **82 (T133)**
public expenditure 120
public finance, redistribution **133 (T232)**
pulp industry 105, **106 (T181)**

quarries 62
Quaternary deposits **7 (T1)**, 18, 28, **30 (T46)**, 30, 31, 32, **46–55 (T76)**
Quaternary glaciation 22

railway network 66, **89 (T145–147)**
railway transport **68 (T106)**, **122 (T211)**
Rapaselet 20

recreation 80, 155, 164
recreational sport 162
recreational trips **166 (T307–313)**, **167 (T316)**
referendum, Swedish membership in the EU **150 (T269)**
regional change 130
regional division of labour 128
regional government grants **132 (T230)**
regional plan **84 (T138)**
regional policies 132
regional specialisation 96
regulation reservoirs **68 (T107)**
relief 16, **17 (T30)**
restrictions 9, 153
riding-school members **163 (T297)**
Riksdag election 149
road network 66, **66 (T101–102)**, **88 (T143, T144)**, 89, 122, **169 (T318)**
roads, average distance to **104 (T178)**
rocks 27, **27 (T45)**, **62 (T97, T98)**
Roe deer **41 (T67)**
royal tour **76 (T118)**
rune stones **77 (T119)**
rural area, population 136, **136 (T234)**
rural area, urbanised **136 (T235)**

Saab 115
Saale 22, **22 (T34)**
sawmill 106, **106 (T180)**
school, upper secondary 143
second home 164, 165, **165 (T303)**
sectors 130
sediment **21 (T32, T33)**
sedimentary rocks 19
service industry 118
service, private 118, **118 (T202)**
service, public 120
settlement **14 (T16)**, 134
shealing system **78 (T125)**, 79
shoreline displacement **25 (T40)**
sickness rate **141 (T249)**
Siljan 52
silver 27, 63, 112
Skagerrak/Kattegat development **24 (T36–39)**
Skanska 128
Skellefte field 112, **112 (T193)**
Skellefteå 65, 90
SKF 115
skiing club **155 (T276)**
Skinnskatteberg **158 (T285–286)**
Smögen **8 (T11)**
snow cover **10 (T14)**, **37 (T60)**, **165 (T304)**
snow depth 37
social benefits **146 (T261)**
Social Democratic Party **148 (T264–265)**
socio-economic differentiation **147 (T262)**
soil 32, **33 (T48)**
solar energy 111
sports 151, 160
sports clubs **151 (T273)**
sports events **161 (T292)**, **163 (T296)**
SPOT 42
spruce **61 (T88, T94–96)**
state employees 120
Stavsnäs 81
steamboat **89 (T147)**
steel industry 113
Stockholm 45, 75, 84
stone quarry 63
Storsjön 53
striae **23 (T35)**
study circle 143, **143 (T254)**
sulphide ore 112
sulphur dioxide **68 (T106)**, 69
sulphur, deposition **61 (T95)**

Sundsvall **8 (T10)**, 54, **79 (T128)**
Swedish Touring Club 80

table hill 21
telephone 123
temperature 25, 35
temperature sum **100 (T166)**
temperature, annual mean **34 (T53)**
temperature, monthly mean **34 (T49–52)**
terrain, types of **16 (T29)**
textile industry 116, **117 (T201)**
theatre 156, **156 (T277, T279)**
theatre **158 (T284)**
theatre performances **156 (T278)**
till 31
tilt hammers **79 (T127)**
timber supplies 104
time geography 9, 152, 153
time use 152
tourism 164, 165, **165 (T305)**, **166 (T306)**, **167 (T315)**
towns 70, **70 (T114–116)**, 71, 137
towns, population 136
tractor 86
traffic flow **122 (T210)**
transport 86, 87, 110, 122, 123
transport flows 122
transport landscape 66
trapping pit **77 (T120)**
travel time 155
Trollhättan 64

Uddevalla 48
Ullångerfjärden 17
Umeå 45, 71
unemployment **99 (T161–163)**
university, transition from upper secondary school **143 (T252)**
Uppsala 71, 147, **147 (T262)**, **164 (T299–300)**
urban area, population 136
urban area 92, 93, **169 (T317)**
urban area, older **78 (T124)**
urban landscape 70
urbanisation 15, 90, **90 (T148)**, **137 (T236, T238)**

Vallentuna 83, **83 (T137)**, 85, **85 (T139, T140)**
vegetation zone 40, **40 (T65)**
vegetation, colonisation 25
vehicle industry 115, **115 (T198)**
vinyl chloride **68 (T106)**
Volvo 115, 129
vote 148
Vänersborg 48, 72
Västerbotten 90, **90 (T148)**, **91 (T149)**
Västerås 51, 74

waste-water treatment plant **82 (T134)**
water power 111
water systems **46–55 (T78)**
watercourses 38, 39
waterways 67
wave erosion 24
Wegener, Alfred 19
Weichsel 22, **22 (T34)**, 23
White-tailed eagle **41 (T70–72)**
William-Olsson, William 64, 67, 75, 92
wind 37, **37 (T61)**, **111 (T187)**
wind power 111, **111 (T188)**
women's sports 163
women at work **145 (T258)**
work 98

Ystad 71

zinc 112, 113
zoogeographical province 41

Ålleberg 21
Åre 53

Örebro 51
Österlen 57
Östersund 53